KEY TO COVER PAINTING BY PETER EDWARDS

1. Emily Brontë. 2. Toru Dutt. 3. Charlotte Brontë. 4. Phillis Wheatley.
5. Mary Wroth. 6. Christina Rossetti. 7. Amy Levy. 8. Ann Yearsley.
9. Aphra Behn. 10. Emily Dickinson. 11. Isabella Valancy Crawford.
12. Anne Brontë. 13. Elizabeth Barrett Browning.

ELIZA'S BABES

four centuries of women's poetry
in English, *c.* 1500-1900

EDITED BY
ROBYN BOLAM

BLOODAXE BOOKS

ISBN: 1 85224 521 2

First published 2005 by
Bloodaxe Books Ltd,
Highgreen,
Tarset,
Northumberland NE48 1RP.

www.bloodaxebooks.com
For further information about Bloodaxe
please visit our website or write to
the above address for a catalogue.

Bloodaxe Books Ltd acknowledge
the financial assistance of
Arts Council England, North East.

For all poets and readers of poetry today

Cover printing by J. Thomson Colour Printers Ltd, Glasgow.

Printed in Great Britain by
Bell & Bain Limited, Glasgow, Scotland.

CONTENTS

INTRODUCTION

Many of the women poets, whose work is represented here, tried to write their way out of poverty: others were highly privileged. Some belong to an oral tradition and were unable to write at all; some were self-taught; others had a formal education. The poems in this book are by dairywomen, domestic servants, a spy, a mill girl, queens of the realm, titled court women, an artist's model, musicians, schoolteachers, post-mistresses, a scientist, a librarian, social workers, journalists, critics, dramatists, novelists, translators, essayists, song writers, travel writers, children's writers, hymnists, parodists, essay and short-story writers, biographers and collaborative writers. At least a fifth of these women poets died aged 40 or younger, through childbirth complications, heart failure, cancer, smallpox, tuberculosis, various overdoses, appendicitis or measles. Nine of these died in their 20s, making their achievements all the more remarkable.

Some of their poetry is very closely interlinked with the works of male poets in their times. Mary Sidney completed and revised her brother, Philip's translations of the Psalms. As a literary patron, she encouraged many younger writers, such as Edmund Spenser and Samuel Daniel, as well as being an inspiration to such inventive women writers as her niece, Mary Wroth, and Aemilia Lanyer. In her turn, and in different ways, Mary Wroth was an inspiration to George Herbert and Ben Jonson.

In the next century, according to Isobel Grundy's biography (OUP, 1999), Lady Mary Wortley Montagu had, apparently, already turned to writing satire before her literary rival and one-time friend, Alexander Pope, chose to move in that direction. William Wordsworth acknowledged a debt to his sister, Dorothy, and while his relationship with the poetry of Isabella Lickbarrow is harder to fathom, he knew her work and subscribed to her volume. Isabella's poems about her native Lake District are contemporary with his own and have some striking similarities. Mary Tighe's possible influence on Keats' poetry has long been debated and Jonathan Wordsworth makes a strong case for it in his book, *Visionary Gleam: Forty books from the Romantic Period* (Woodstock, 1996), where he also draws attention to the impact Joanna Baillie's writings had on Coleridge and Wordsworth, albeit mostly in relation to her plays. Coleridge's literary reputation was certainly indebted to the efforts of his daughter, Sara Coleridge, who appears to have sacrificed the opportunity to develop her own poetic talent because of the need she felt to edit and annotate his works.

Although, as time went on, women poets increasingly built on their female poetic heritage (many celebrated the achievements of Aphra Behn and the 'matchless Orinda', Katherine Philips, while later, Emily Dickinson looked back as far as Anne Bradstreet), their first inspiration came, of necessity, from male poets. Initially, some seemed unable to do more than try to emulate their heroes, yet the way Katherine Philips reworks John Donne's conceits, Mary Collier responds to Stephen Duck's poem in 'The Woman's Labour', and Lucy Larcom revisits 'The Lady of Shalot', demonstrates that many of these women did not only revere male poets who had long dominated the literary tradition – they also dared to challenge them.

In the same year, 1830, but on different sides of the Atlantic, two of the most unconventional and experimental of all these women poets were born. Emily Dickinson (whose poetry reaches back to the 17th-century metaphysical poets and forward to anticipate the 20th-century Imagists) and the incomparable Christina Rossetti, whose influence extended to Philip Larkin and beyond, have been given as much space as possible. Yet, there is also a place for the more conventional. Some of these poets were far more famous in their own day than they are now because they appealed to a large popular readership: this should not be forgotten. Both Elizabeth Barrett Browning (in 1850) and Alice Meynell (in 1895 and 1913) were nominated for Poet Laureate, though neither was appointed.

Their biographies often reveal amazing narratives of courage and perseverance. Even in the 16th century, there is evidence that poetry was not the sole preserve of the wealthy or the highly educated. Isabella Whitney, probably the first English woman to publish a volume of poetry, may not have had a formal education and, although a 'gentlewoman', appears also to have been a servant. In the later 1500s, a Suffolk dairywoman's advice was handed down in a guide to dairying in the form of a brief, but memorable lyric. Religion provided acceptable subject matter for early women writers and some also wrote out of a family literary tradition (like Mary Sidney), but many women defied convention and took their inspiration from their own experiences, the world around them, their imaginations, and their, often limited, reading.

It is sometimes hard for us to appreciate, in the 21st century, how groundbreaking some of these women were. Anne Askew was a religious martyr, prompted to write by courageous defiance. Addressed first to God, by the time her poetry reached its human readership, the enemies of whom she writes, had killed her. Aemilia Lanyer was a feminist writer before the term was invented and her 'Description of Cookeham' was probably the first of a new genre of country house poetry as it existed before Ben Jonson's 'To Penshurst'. Mary Wroth, the first Englishwoman to publish a complete sonnet sequence, revived and revised the Petrarchan tradition in the process. (She was also the first woman to publish a full-length work of fiction.) Elizabeth Cary was the first English woman to publish a full-length original play and an extract from her *The Tragedy of Mariam, the Fair Queen of Jewry* has been included because it can also be read as a self-contained poem.

Rachel Speght reworks a medieval form in 'The Dream' and Margaret Cavendish's quirky philosophy makes her an eccentric but original poet. Aphra Behn shows humour and wit when she adopts the persona of a tree, felled to make the stays in women's corsets, but she also takes unconventional perspectives on love and religion in the other poems selected here. Anne Killigrew writes positively on death. Mary Wortley Montagu's pioneering travel writing is reflected in her 'Verses...overlooking Constantinople' and Anne Wilson has been claimed as an early eco-poet. Lanyer, Speght, Chudleigh, Collier, and others could be described as early protest writers. Anna Seward published one of the first poems about the French Revolution. Phillis Wheatley, the first black woman to publish a book of poetry in North America, did so while still enslaved.

These poets also broke new ground in their writing practices and the way they reached out to new audiences. Adah Isaacs Menken was an early practioner of free verse and Augusta Webster led the way in rejecting capitalisation at the beginning of every line of her blank verse. Kathleen Bradley and Edith Cooper (aunt and niece respectively) became a successful collaborative team, writing under one name – Michael Field. Toru Dutt experimented with free verse, traditional forms, and the mythological heritage of her own country, India. Emily Pauline Johnson revived her Native American heritage and became a successful performance poet.

It would have needed many more pages to set these women poets where they belong – cheek by jowl with their male counterparts. The works of male poets are already widely available, but women poets have always been less visible – and more of them wrote poetry during this period than can be included here. This volume brings together as wide a variety of female voices as possible to give readers a better understanding of the range and diversity of poetry in English through these centuries, in the hope that they will be inspired to read more of it – by both women and men.

Covering a variety of poetic movements, styles, and subjects, the anthology crosses several continents, travelling from the United Kingdom and Ireland to the United States, Canada, India, Australia and New Zealand. Poems are sometimes written in different forms of English, but translations have been avoided, except in rare cases where they particularly demonstrate the originality of the writer (e.g. Mary Sidney's translations of the Psalms, Anne Wharton's treatment of Ovid's *Epistles*, and Michael Field's development of Sappho's fragments). The span *c.* 1500-1900 is, inevitably, an approximation. All these poets were born after 1500 and before 1900, and all wrote poetry before 1900, though in a few cases texts selected may have been published slightly later.

Wherever possible, poems have been taken from early printed versions or manuscripts. For ease of reading, spellings have been modernised where this does not change the poetic effect of the poem (rhyme, assonance, etc.) – otherwise the original spelling has been retained with a note. Punctuation has been preserved as closely as possible, but capitalisation and the use of italics have been regularised in some early poems where the significance of this was unclear. Whenever the use of capitals or italics appears to be a deliberate poetic choice rather than a printer's convention, they have been retained. Where the omission of syllables is necessary for scansion, contractions have been retained, but where there is now no difference in the pronunciation of the words, with or without the apostrophes, the full forms are given (e.g. 'shou'd' becomes 'should' in line 14 of Behn's 'To the Fair Clarinda...'). Due to lack of space, some long poems have, reluctantly, been extracted. In these cases the original line numbers have been used to indicate where cuts have been made.

There was no representative woman poet during these centuries, though several belonged to poetic movements or côteries at particular times. From the 16th century, women were writing from all social backgrounds right across the globe – on familiar and unfamiliar subjects and in a variety of forms and styles. Had space allowed a full range of work in translation this would have been even more apparent. It has also to be remembered that many women poets, from Britain and elsewhere, wrote in Latin, and more than we may ever know set their poetry down anonymously, or recited and sang it, but had no means of leaving a written record. All the women whose words are represented here were passionate in their thoughts, whether or not these resembled what Eliza called, the 'soul's sweet babes', that may translate themselves into poems to immortalise God or the poet. In 'To a Lady that Bragged of her Children', she wrote:

> Thine at their birth did pain thee bring,
> When mine are born, I sit and sing.

These poets sang through terrors and trials as well as at times of celebration, and it is appropriate that one of their poems (Emma Lazarus's 'The New Colossus') is inscribed on the Statue of Liberty. Nor was the beginning of the 16th century the beginning of their story. What we know of Sappho and her contemporaries, the Japanese women poets of the Heian period (794-1185), the tenth-century women poets in religious orders (Hildegard of Bingen, Hrotswith von Gandersheim), and the medieval female troubadours of Provence (1100-1300), or individuals such as Marie de France (*fl.* 1181), makes it possible for us to begin to sketch a fragmented map of women poets, known and unknown, who are forerunners of the women in this book. Looking forward, the poets in the following pages, although only part of a larger global history, left a significant legacy that helped to pave the way to the most productive period in the history of poetry by women so far – and, for this, we should value them.

ROBYN BOLAM

ACKNOWLEDGEMENTS

This anthology has taken many years to complete and would not be here now if it were not for the unfailing, efficient assistance and patience of the staff at the British Library, for which I thank them – particularly staff in the Rare Books Reading Room and the Manuscript Collections. I am also grateful to librarians and curators of manuscripts at the Bodleian Library, University of Oxford (particularly the staff of Duke Humfrey's Library), Princeton University Library (particularly Margaret Sherry Rich of Rare Books & Special Collections), and the New York Public Library, for making material in their care available to me. Lizzie MacGregor, of the Scottish Poetry Library, generously answered my queries and provided useful biographical information, and I am grateful to the National Library of Wales for advice. Tess Nowell of the Learning Resources Centre and Ruth Mellor and the staff of Reprographics have been a wonderful St Mary's support team and deserve grateful thanks for their many efforts.

I would like to acknowledge the help I have had from all over the world: Dr Vivian Smith (University of Sydney), Dr Sue Roe (University of Sussex), and Dr Susan Doran (University of Oxford) generously read and commented on particular sections; Professor Rob Pope (Oxford Brookes University) helped with Latin translation; Professor Bill Manhire (Victoria University of Wellington, NZ) and Professor Judith Fetterley (University of Albany, US) assisted in the copyright trail; Professor Shakuntala Bharvani (Department of English, Government Law College, Mumbai) and Dr Rose Atfield (Brunel University) helped me to explore Indian and Irish women's poetry, respectively. I am also grateful for conversations with Gill Gregory, Gary Disher, Janet Clare, and Sue Wiseman over the years.

Without the generous hospitality and friendship of Bill and Eileen Bassler, I would not have been able to explore the libraries of New York and New Jersey so productively: they both played a significant part in helping me to extend the range of this book. Nigel Burt and Jane Shillaker sent poems from New Zealand and provided years of valued support at home, as did Marianne Barber, who also helped in numerous ways. To all, thanks are due.

I am grateful to all those who have previously researched, edited, anthologised, and written about the women poets of these years, particularly Isobel Armstrong, Paula Bennett, Joseph Bristow, Peter Davidson, Germaine Greer, Elaine Hobby, Angela Leighton,

Roger Lonsdale, Bill Manhire, Erlene Stetson, Jane Stevenson, Janet Todd and Betty S. Travitsky. Poems in manuscript by Mary Tudor (Add. ms 36452. fo.218), Elizabeth Tudor (Stowe ms 962, fo.231^v), Mary Sidney (Sloane ms. 1303), Eleanora Finch (Add. ms 62135 fo.337^r and fos. 334^r-336^v) and Arabella (Pen.) Moreton (Add. ms 28, 101. fo.49) are published with permission from the British Library. I am grateful to the Bodleian Library, University of Oxford for permission to publish poems in manuscript by Elizabeth Tudor (MS. Rawl. poet. 108, fol. 44^v) and Hester Wyat (MS. Rawl. D.360, fol. 53^r). 'An Extempore Ode in a Sleepless Night...' by Annis Boudinot Stockton, located in the Stimson Collection of Elias Boudinot, Manuscripts Division, Department of Rare Books and Special Collections, Princeton University Library, is published with permission of the Princeton University Library. Dorothy Wordsworth's 'Thoughts on my Sick Bed' is published by permission of the Wordsworth Trust, Dove Cottage, Grasmere.

The selection of poems by Emily Dickinson is reprinted by permission of the publishers and the Trustees of Amherst College from *The Poems of Emily Dickinson: Reading Edition*, Ralph W. Franklin, ed., Cambridge, Mass.: The Belknap Press of Harvard University Press, Copyright © 1998 by the President and Fellows of Harvard College. Copyright © 1951, 1955, 1979, 1983 by the President and Fellows of Harvard College. Poems by Jane Austen are reprinted from Jane Austen: Collected Poems and Verse of the Austen Family (Jane Austen Society in association with Carcanet, 1996), by kind permission of the editor, David Selwyn, the Jane Austen Society, and Carcanet Press.

Every reasonable effort has been made to obtain the necessary permissions to include the poems in this anthology. If any omissions have been made, copyright owners are invited to contact the editor and publisher.

ABBREVIATIONS

BL   British Library
CERLC   *A Companion to English Renaissance Literature and Culture*, ed. Michael Hattaway (Blackwell, 2000).
EMWP   *Early Modern Women Poets (1520-1700): an anthology*, ed. Jane Stevenson and Peter Davidson (OUP, 2001)
EWP   *Eighteenth-century Women Poets*, ed. Roger Lonsdale (OUP, 1990)
fl   flourished
ms   manuscript
PBEW   *Poetry by English Women: English Women's Poetry, Elizabethan to Victorian*, ed. R.E. Pritchard (Carcanet, 1990)
RWF   *The Poems of Emily Dickinson: reading edition*, ed. R.W. Franklin (The Belknap Press of Harvard University Press, 1999)
Urania   Mary Wroth, *The Countess of Montgomeries Urania* (1621)
WWIE   *Women's Writing in English*, ed. Lorna Sage (CUP, 1999)

MARY TUDOR (Mary I)

1516–58

Mary Tudor, the daughter of Henry VIII and Catherine of Aragon, became Queen of England in 1553, after a disputed succession on the death of her brother, Edward VI. In 1557, the Venetian ambassador wrote that the Queen was fluent in Latin, French and Spanish, could understand Italian, and was an accomplished player of the clavichord and the lute. She married the 28-year-old Philip II of Spain at Winchester in 1554, but died childless. Known as 'Bloody Mary' because of the persecution of Protestants during her reign, she was more famous for her fervent religious beliefs than for her poetry, of which this is a rare example. The following is taken from a manuscript collected in the Aston Papers vol. IX: 'Private Correspondence 1613-1703' (BL Add. 36452 fo.218). Underneath the poem is written: 'Queen Mary when she was princess not yet come to the crown, gave the book in which these words were writ with her own hand to the Duchess of Suffolk.' The recipient was probably Frances Brandon (just over a year older than Mary). Frances was the daughter of Henry VIII's sister and Charles Brandon, the Duke of Suffolk: she married Henry Grey, Marquis of Dorset, in 1533. He became Duke of Suffolk in 1551. The warning note the poem strikes becomes more significant when it is remembered that Frances was also the mother of Lady Jane Grey. Mary knew what the Suffolks and John Dudley, Duke of Northumberland (who was father to Jane's husband), were plotting. Under their influence, Edward VI tried to exclude both Mary and her half-sister, Elizabeth, from the throne in order to leave the succession to Jane, the Protestant granddaughter of Henry VIII's sister, Mary. Jane did, for nine days, become queen in July 1553. After Jane's father joined forces with Sir Thomas Wyatt in an unsuccessful rebellion in early 1554, Mary signed death warrants for Jane and her husband.

Get you such riches as when the ship is broken may
swim away with the master. For divers chances
take away the goods of fortune. But the goods of the soul
which only be the true goods, neither fire nor water
can take away.

If you take labour and pain to do a virtuous thing
the labour goeth away but the virtue remaineth.
If through pleasure you do a vicious thing
the pleasure goeth away
but the vice remaineth.

Good madam, for my sake remember this:
Your loving mistress, Mary princess.

7-8 *remaineth./If:* this ed. remaineth if through/pleasure BL ms. 8-9 *thing/ the pleasure:* this ed. thing…away/but BL ms. 12 *princess:* Mary lost this title when she was declared illegitimate on her father's marriage to Anne Boleyn and became the Lady Mary. In using it here, she is reminding the Duchess that she considers herself to be the rightful heir.

ANNE ASKEW (*later* KYME)

c. 1521–46

Originally from Lincolnshire, Anne Askew had an arranged, unhappy marriage and two children. Cast out by her husband for her theological practices, she came to London in 1545 and, unsuccessfully, sought a divorce. She was accused of heresy because she denied the Catholic doctrine of transubstantiation and the ritual of the Mass. Imprisoned, interrogated, and tortured, she was finally burnt at the stake for refusing to recant her Protestant faith. Her interrogators appear to have tried to use her to implicate women close to her childhood friend, Henry VIII's last queen, Katherine Parr, but their attempts failed. After her death, accounts of her examinations and execution, which are attributed to her, were smuggled out of England and published, in Germany, by John Bale, Bishop of Ossory. The following is taken from this text, dated 1546. John Foxe detailed her suffering in his *Acts and Monuments* (1563).

The Ballad which Anne Askew made and sang when she was in Newgate

Like as the armed knight
Appointed to the field
With this world will I fight
And faith shall be my shield.
    Faith is that weapon strong
Which will not fail at need
My foes therefore among
Therewith will I proceed.
    As it is had in strength
And force of Christes way   10
It will prevail at length
Though all the devils say nay.
    Faith in the fathers old
Obtained righteousness
Which make me very bold.
To fear no world's distress.
    I now rejoice in heart
And hope bid me do so
For Christ will take my part
And ease me of my woe.   20
    Thu sayst Lord, who so knock
To them wilt thu attend
Undo therefore the lock
And thy strong power send.
    More enemies now I have

26

Than heeres upon my heed
Let them not me deprave
But fight thu in my steed.
On thee my care I cast
For all their cruel spite   30
I set not by their hast
For thu art my delight.
I am not she that list
My anchor to let fall
For every drizzling mist
My ship substantial.
Not oft use I to write
In prose nor yet in rhyme
Yet will I show one sight
That I saw in my time.   40
I saw a royal throne
Where Justice should have sit
But in her stead was one
Of modye cruel wit.
Absorbed was righteousness
As of the raging flood
Satan in his excess
Sucked up the guiltless blood.
Then thought I, Jesus lord
When thu shalt judge us all   50
Hard is it to record
On these men what will fall.
Yet lord I thee desire
For that they do to me
Let them not taste the hyre
Of their iniquity.

10 *Christes:* Christ's. 15 *make:* makes. 21 *Thu:* a form of 'Thou', preserved here for the internal rhyme. 21-2 see *Matthew* 7:7. 26 *heeres:* hairs; *heed:* head. 28 *steed:* stead. 31 *set* i.e. as the sun sets; *hast:* command. 44 *modye:* arrogant, wrathful. 55 *hyre:* reward.

ELIZABETH TUDOR (Elizabeth I)
1533–1603

The daughter of Anne Boleyn and Henry VIII, Elizabeth's movements were severely restricted during the reign of her half-sister, Mary Tudor, as the first three poems show. On the death of Mary, in November 1588, Elizabeth became queen. Her right to the throne was challenged by her Catholic cousin, Mary

Queen of Scots, who, during her time as a prisoner in England was involved in plots against Elizabeth (*see* 'The Doubt of Future Foes' below). Elizabeth translated works from several languages, as well as writing some poetry and her own speeches. She never married, perpetuating a cult of the Virgin Queen. 'On Monsieur's Departure' may refer to the departure of the Duke of Anjou in 1582, after an unsuccessful wooing campaign, or it could refer to her relationship with the Earl of Essex as it was found with papers relating to him. 'Written with a diamond...' is printed in John Foxe's *Acts & Monuments* (1563) and in Holinshed's *Chronicles* vol. 3 (1587). The text for 'Written on a wall...' appears in Paul Hentzner's *Itinerarium* (Nuremberg, 1612), and was collected during a visit to Woodstock in 1597. 'Written in her French psalter' was found undated, with Elizabeth's signature, on the last page of her book of psalms. This is now in the possession of Queen Elizabeth II, who loaned it to the 1958 Stratford Poetry Festival exhibition. The text here is taken from the *Poetry Book Society Bulletin*, 19 (August 1958), in which the verse was reprinted. 'The Doubt of Future Foes' (based here primarily on Bodleian Library Rawlinson poetical ms 108, fo. 44^V) was attributed to Elizabeth by her godson, Sir John Harington, and exists in six manuscripts and two early printed forms. There are three manuscripts of 'On Monsieur's Departure' (based here on BL, Stowe 962 ms, fo.231^V). Where versions do not concur, major variants are noted. Leicester Bradner edited *The Poems of Queen Elizabeth I* for Brown University Press in 1964.

Written with a diamond on her window at Woodstock

Much suspected by me,
Nothing proved can be,
Quoth Elizabeth prisoner.

Title *Woodstock:* Elizabeth was under house-arrest in the Royal Lodge at Woodstock, Oxfordshire (1554-55). 1 *by:* concerning

Written on a wall at Woodstock

Oh Fortune, thy wresting wavering state
Hath fraught with cares my troubled wit,
Whose witness this present prison late
Could bear, where once was joy's loan quit.
Thou caused'st the guilty to be loosed
From bands where innocents were inclosed,
And caused the guiltless to be reserved,
And freed those that death had well deserved.
But all herein can be nothing wrought,
So God send to my foes all they have thought.

Written in her French Psalter

No crooked leg, no bleared eye,
    no part deformed out of kind,
Nor yet so ugly half can be
    as is the inward suspicious mind.

The Doubt of Future Foes

The doubt of future foes exiles my present joy,
And wit me warns to shun such snares as threaten mine annoy;
For falsehood now doth flow, and subjects' faith doth ebb,
Which should not be if reason ruled or wisdom weaved the web.
But clouds of joys untried do cloak aspiring minds,
Which turn to rain of late repent by changed course of winds.
The top of hope supposed the root upreared shall be,
And fruitless all their grafted guile, as shortly ye shall see.
The dazzled eyes with pride, which great ambition blinds,
Shall be unsealed by worthy wights whose foresight falsehood finds.
The daughter of debate that discord aye doth sow
Shall reap no gain where former rule still peace hath taught to know.
No foreign banished wight shall anchor in this port;
Our realm brooks not seditious sects, let them elsewhere resort.
My rusty sword through rest shall first his edge employ
To poll their tops that seek such change or gape for future joy.

6 *rain:* Puttenham's *Arte of English Poesie* (1589), *raige:* Bodleian ms. 7 *upreared:* Bodleian ms. Other versions give 'of Rue' and 'of ruth'. 10 *wights:* people. 11 *doth:* 'do ye', Bodleian ms. 14 *seditious sects:* Bodleian ms 'strangers force', Puttenham's *Arte of English Poesie* (1589). 16 *poll:* cut off; *gape for:* long for.

On Monsieur's Departure

I grieve and dare not show my discontent,
I love and yet am forced to seem to hate,
I do, and dare not say I ever meant,
I seem stark mute but inwardly do prate.
I am and am not, freeze and yet am burned,
Since from myself another self I turned.

My care is like my shadow in the sun,
Follows me flying, flies when I pursue it,

29

Stands, and lies by me, doth what I have done.
This too familiar care doth make me rue it.   10
No means I find to rid him from my breast,
Till by the end of living it be supprest.

Some greater passions slide into my mind,
For I am soft and made of melting snow;
Or be more cruel, love, and so be kind.
Let me or float, or sink, be high or low.
Or let me live with some sweet content,
Or die, and so forget what love ere meant.

5 *am not:* not Bodleian ms. *freeze:* I freeze Bodleian ms. 10 *This:* His Bodleian ms. 12:
living: things Bodleian ms. 13 *greater passions:* gentler passion Bodleian ms. 17 *some sweet:*
some more sweet Bodleian ms.

ISABELLA WHITNEY
c. 1540 – *after* 1580

Isabella Whitney was probably the first Englishwoman to be a professional
woman poet. She published two collections: *Copy of a Letter...in Meter by a
Young Gentlewoman to her Unconstant Lover* in 1567, and *A Sweet Nosegay* in
1573 – possibly to try to raise money. Isabella and some of her siblings worked
as servants in London, where their parents lived (see lines 217-18). She was
aware of the literary conventions of her time, but may not have had a formal
education. When she wrote the following (apparently autobiographical) poem,
Isabella appears to have lost her position and does not even have the money to
pay for her own burial (lines 261-62). She left London, perhaps to escape her
creditors. Evidence in her brother's will suggests that she may have married
a man called Eldershae and had two children. Her brother, Geoffrey Whitney,
is known as a writer of emblem books. *The Manner of Her Will...* is an un-
usual poem for an early woman writer, being a lively guide to the city and an
imaginative form of autobiography.

from The Manner of Her Will, & What She Left
to London: and to all those in it: at her departing

I whole in body and in mind,
    but very weak in purse,
Do make and write my testament
    for fear it will be worse;
And first I wholly do commend
    my soul and body eke
To God, the Father and the Son,

so long as I can speak.
And after speech, my soul to him,
  and body to the grave: 10
Till time that all shall rise again
  their Judgement for to have;
And then I hope they both shall meet
  to dwell for aye in joy,
Whereas I trust to see my friends
  released from all annoy.
Thus have you heard touching my soul
  and body what I mean:
I trust you all will witness bear
  I have a steadfast brain;   20
And now let me dispose such things
  as I shall leave behind,
That those which shall receive the same
  may know my willing mind.
I first of all to London leave,
  because I there was bred,
Brave buildings rare, of churches store,
  and Paul's to the head.
Between the same, fair streets there be,
  and people goodly store;   30
Because their keeping craveth cost,
  I yet will leave him more...

[...]

To all the bookbinders by Paul's,
  Because I like their art,
They every week shall money have,
  When they from books depart.
Amongst them all my printer must
  Have somewhat to his share;
I will my friends these books to buy
  Of him, with other ware.   200
For maidens poor, I widowers rich
  Do leave, that oft shall dote:
And by that means shall marry them
  To set the girls afloat.
And wealthy widows will I leave
  To help young gentlemen:
Which when you have, in any case,
  Be courteous to them then,
And see their plate and jewels eke

31

May not be marred with rust, 210
Nor let their bags too long be full,
For fear that they do burst.
To ev'ry gate under the walls
That compass thee about,
I fruit-wives leave to entertain
Such as come in and out.
To Smithfield I must something leave,
My parents there did dwell:
So careless for to be of it,
None would accompt it well. 220
Wherefore it thrice a week shall have
Of horse and neat good store,
And in his spital, blind and lame
To dwell for evermore.
And Bedlam must not be forgot,
For that was oft my walk:
I people there too many leave,
That out of tune do talk.
At Bridewell there shall beadles be,
And matrons that shall still 230
See chalk well chopped, and spinning plied,
And turning of the mill.
For such as cannot quiet be,
But strive for house or land,
At th'Inns of Court I lawyers leave
To take their cause in hand.
And also leave I at each Inn
Of Court, or Chancery,
Of gentlemen, a youthful roote,
Full of activity: 240
For whom I store of books have left
At each bookbinder's stall,
And part of all that London hath
To furnish them withal.
And when they are with study cloyed,
To recreate their mind,
Of tennis courts, of dancing schools
And fence, they store shall find.
And every Sunday at the least,
I leave, to make them sport, 250
In divers places players, that
Of wonders shall report.

Now London have I (for thy sake)
    Within thee, and without,
As comes into my memory,
    Dispersed round about
Such needful things as they should have
    Here left now unto thee:
When I am gone, with conscience
    Let them dispersed be.   260
And though I nothing named have
    To bury me withal,
Consider that above the ground,
    Annoyance be I shall.
And let me have a shrouding sheet
    To cover me from shame:
And in oblivion bury me
    And never more me name.
Ringings nor other ceremonies
    Use you not for cost: 270
Nor at my burial make no feast,
    Your money were but lost.
Rejoice in God that I am gone
    Out of this vale so vile,
And that of each thing, left such store,
    As may your wants exile.
I make thee sole executor because
    I loved thee best,
And thee I put in trust to give
    The goods unto the rest.   280
Because thou shalt a helper need
    In this so great a charge,
I wish good Fortune be thy guide, lest
    Thou shouldst run at large.
The happy days and quiet times,
    They both her servants be,
Which well will serve to fetch and bring
    Such things as need to thee.
Wherefore (good London) not refuse
    For helper her to take: 290
Thus being weak and weary both
    An end here will I make.
To all that ask what end I made,
    And how I went away,
Thou answer may'st like those which here

No longer tarry may.
And unto all that wish me well,
　Or rue that I am gone:
Do me commend, and bid them cease
　My absence for to moan.　　　　　　　　300
And tell them further, if they would
　My presence still have had:
They should have sought to mend my luck
　Which ever was too bad.
So fare thou well a thousand times,
　God shield thee from thy foe:
And still make thee victorious
　Of those that seek thy woe.
And though I am persuade that I
　Shall never more thee see:　　　　　　　310
Yet to the last I shall not cease
　To wish much good to thee.
This 20 of October, I,
　In Anno Domini
A thousand five hundred seventy three,
　(As almanacs descry),
Did write this will with mine own hand
　And it to London gave
In witness of the standers-by,
　Whose names (if you will have)　　　　　320
Paper, Pen, and Standish were
　At that same present by,
With Time who promised to reveal,
　So fast as she could hie
The same, lest of my nearer kin
　From anything should vary.
So finally I make an end:
　No longer can I tarry.

6 *eke:* also. 27 *store:* abundance. 28 *Paul's:* St Paul's Cathedral. 32 *him:* London. 193 St Paul's Churchyard was the address of many printers and booksellers. 197 *my printer:* Richard Jones, who published other female authors. 209 *plate:* silver- or gold-plated ware. 217 *Smithfield:* a horse and general livestock market but, formerly, a holy place. 210 *accompt:* account. 222 *neat:* oxen, cattle. 223 *spital:* hospital (St Bartholomew's). 225 *Bedlam:* St Mary of Bethlem, the Bethlehem Hospital for the insane, sometimes visited for entertainment in C16 and C17. 229 *Bridewell:* a house of correction; *beadles:* church officers. 239 *a roote:* a noisy crowd (with overtones of sexual activity). 245 *cloyed:* wearied to excess. 248 *fence:* fencing. 251 *players:* actors. 261 *nothing named have:* have nothing to my name. 269 *Ringings:* i.e. of church bells. 286 & 290 *her:* Fortune. 316 *descry:* reveal. 321 *Standish:* an inkpot. 324 *hie:* hurry. 325-26 *lest…vary:* lest my close relatives contest my will.

34

KATHERINE DOWE

fl. before 1588

Katherine Dowe was a Suffolk dairywoman in charge of 140 cows and seven dairy maids. Her son, Bartholomew, included her poem at the end of his *A dairie Booke for good huswives* (1588) which was 'annexed' to Torquato Tasso's *The Householders Philosophie...* (first written in Italian and later translated into English by the dramatist, Thomas Kyd). A dialogue in the text reveals that, as eight or nine cows was the usual allocation for one milkmaid, these women, who needed to milk twenty cows each, must have risen very early – hence the subject of the poem. The copy text here is Antiq. e. E. 1588.5, sig. C2^r, reproduced by permission of the Bodleian Library. University of Oxford.

Arise Early

Arise early.
Serve God devoutly.
Then to thy work busily,
To thy meat joyfully,
To thy bed merrily.
And though thou fare poorly,
And thy lodging homely
Yet thank God highly.

7 *homely:* simple, primitive.

MARY SIDNEY (*later* Herbert), Countess of Pembroke

1561-1621

Mary Sidney was the younger sister of Sir Philip Sidney, the niece of Elizabeth I's favourite, Robert Dudley, and the aunt of the poet Mary Wroth (*née* Sidney). She grew up in Wales (Ludlow Castle), Dublin, and at the Sidney family home, Penshurst, in Kent. At 15, she became the third wife of Henry Herbert, Earl of Pembroke: they had three children. A rich woman from a politically powerful family, she was highly educated and translated works from several languages. When her brother, Philip, was killed in 1585, Mary completed and revised his translations of the Psalms in an imaginative manner, receiving praise from Ben Jonson, John Donne and George Herbert. Her innovative verse forms and meditative explorations influenced the development of the devotional lyric. At her country estate, Wilton, near Salisbury, and elsewhere, Mary was a celebrated literary patron, encouraging writers such as Edmund Spenser and

Samuel Daniel. Aemilia Lanyer dedicated *Salve Deus Rex Judaeorum* to her in 1611. After her husband's death in 1601, she lived in Bedfordshire and died of smallpox, in London, aged 59. Mary Sidney is best remembered for her patronage and her versions of the Psalms, which are more like original poems than literal translations. A manuscript copy of them (transcribed by John Davies 'in the reign of James I') remains at Penshurst Place. The first printing of this occurred in 1823. 'Our Saviour's Passion' is from Sloane ms no.1303 in the British Library.

from Our Saviour's Passion

6

Put all the woes of all the world together,
Sorrow and death set down in all their pride,
Let misery bring all her muses hither,
With all the sorrows that the heart may hide;
    Then read the fate but of my rueful story,
    And say my grief hath gotten sorrow's glory.

7

For nature's sickness sometime may have ease,
Fortune (though fickle) some time is a friend,
The mind's affliction, patience may appease,
And death is cause that many torments end;
    But ever sick, crazed, grieved, and living dying,
    Think on the subject in the sorrow lying...

[...]

18

There is a lack that tells me of a life,
There is a loss that tells me of a love,
Betwixt them both, a state of such a strife,
As makes my spirit such a passion prove,
    That lack of one, and th'other's loss alas
    Makes me the woeful'st wretch that ever was.

19

My dearest love, that dearest bought my love,
My only life, by whom I only live,
Was never faith did such affection prove,
Or ever grace did such an honour give.
    But such a lack, and such a loss (aye me)
    Must needs the sorrows of all sorrows be.

20

My love is fair, yea fairer than the sun,
Which hath his light but from his fairest love.
O fairest love, whose light is never done,
And fairest light doth such a love approve,
  But such love lost, and such a light obscured,
  Can there a greater sorrow be endured?

21

He came from high to live with me below,
He gave me life and showed me greatest love.
Unworthy I so high a worth to know,
Left my chief bliss, a baser choice to prove.
  I saw his wounds, yet did I not believe him,
  And for his goodness with my sins did grieve him.

22

I saw him faultless, yet I did offend him,
I saw him wronged and yet did not excuse him,
I saw his foes, yet fought not to defend him,
I had his blessings, yet I did abuse him.
  But was it mine, or my forefathers' deed?
  Whose'er it was, it makes my heart to bleed.

23

To see the feet, that travailed for our good,
To see the hands, that brake that lively bread,
To see the head, whereon our honour stood,
To see the fruit, whereon our spirit fed;
  Feet pierced, hands bored, and his head all bleeding,
  Who doth not die with such a sorrow reading?

24

He placed all rest, and had no resting place,
He healed each pain, yet lived in sore distress,
Deserved all good, yet lived in great disgrace,
Gave all hearts joy, himself in heaviness;
  Suffered them live, by whom himself was slain.
  Lord, who can live to see such love again?

25

A virgin's child by virtue's power conceived,
A harmless man that lived for all men's good,

A faithful friend that never faith deceived,
An heavenly fruit for heart's especial good,
    A spirit all of excellence divine,
    Such is the essence of this love of mine.

26

Whose mansion Heaven, yet lay within a manger,
Who gave all food, yet sucked a virgin's breast,
Who could have killed yet fled a threatening danger,
Who sought all quiet by his own unrest,
    Who died for them that highly did offend him,
    And lives for them that cannot comprehend him.

27

Who came no further than his father sent him,
And did fulfil but what he did command him,
Who prayed for them that proudly did torment him,
For telling truly of what they did demand him,
    Who did all good that humbly did entreat him,
    And bare their blows, that did unkindly beat him.

7.5 *crazed:* broken, crushed, bruised. 20.2 *love.:* this ed. love Sloane ms. 22.3 *fought:* the
first letter is unclear and could, perhaps, be 's'.

Psalm CXIII
Laudate, pueri

O you that serve the Lord,
To praise his name accord:
Jehova now and ever
Commending, ending never,
Whom all this earth resounds,
From east to western bounds.

He monarch reigns on high;
His glory treads the sky.
Like him, who can be counted
That dwells so highly mounted?
Yet stooping low beholds
What heaven and earth enfolds.

From dust the needy soul,
The wretch from miry hole

He lifts: yea kings he makes them,
Yea kings his people takes them.
He gives the barren wife
A fruitful mother's life.

Title *Laudate, pueri:* Praise the Lord, you servants. 3 *Jehovah:* principal name of God.

AEMILIA LANYER (*née* Bassani)

1569–1645

Aemilia Lanyer's father died when she was a child, and her mother when she was 18. She became the mistress of Henry Cary, the Lord Chamberlain, who 'maintained' her 'in great pomp' (her words to the astrologer, Simon Foreman). In 1592, when she was pregnant, a marriage was arranged for her with Alfonso Lanyer, one of Queen Elizabeth I's musicians. Her son, Henry, lived until 1633, but a daughter, Odillya, born in 1598, survived less than a year. Despite her father's initial prosperity and her relationship with Cary, Lanyer succumbed to debt after her marriage. The situation improved in 1604 when her husband received a patent from James I, but he died in 1613. Aemilia founded a school at St Giles in the Field in 1617; however, this venture foundered in 1619. She was involved in law-suits with her husband's relatives, concerning the patent, for many years.

Salve Deus Rex Judaeorum was the title-poem of a volume published in 1611. Lanyer adopts the persona of Pilate's wife in the lines below and, in her attempt to dissuade her husband from his persecution of Christ, she rewrites Eve's story from a feminist perspective. A spirited defence of womankind, the poem also pays tribute to a number of living women in its prefaces. 'The Description of Cookeham' may be the first country house poem in English Literature, pre-dating Ben Jonson's 'To Penshurst'. It celebrates Lanyer's patron, Lady Margaret Clifford, and her daughter, Anne. During her time at Cookham (leased to her brother in 1603) Margaret Clifford was fighting a legal battle with her estranged husband and his brother for her own and her daughter's rights to the Clifford estates.

from Salve Deus Rex Judaeorum

Now Pontius Pilate is to judge the cause
Of faultless Jesus, who before him stands;
Who neither hath offended Prince, nor Laws,
Although he now be brought in woeful bands.
O noble Governor, make thou yet a pause;
Do not in innocent blood imbrue thy hands,   750
    But hear the words of thy most worthy wife
    Who sends to thee to beg her Saviour's life.

Let barb'rous cruelty far depart from thee,
And in true justice take affliction's part.
Open thine eyes, that thou the truth may'st see;
Do not the thing that goes against thy heart,
Condemn not him that must thy Saviour be,
But view his holy life, his good desert.
    Let not us women glory in men's fall,
    Who had power given to over-rule us all.   760

Till now your indiscretion sets us free,
And makes our former fault much less appear.
Our Mother Eve, who tasted of the tree,   *Eve's Apology*
Giving to Adam what she held most dear,
Was simply good, and had no power to see;
The after-coming harm did not appear:
    The subtle serpent that our sex betrayed,
    Before our fall so sure a plot had laid.

That undiscerning ignorance perceived
No guile, or craft that was by him intended;   770
For, had she known of what we were bereaved,
To his request she had not condescended.
But she (poor soul) by cunning was deceived,
No hurt therein her harmless heart intended:
    For she alleged God's word, which he denies,
    That they should die, but even as gods, be wise.

But surely Adam cannot be excused,
Her fault, though great, yet he was most to blame;
What weakness offered, strength might have refused,
Being Lord of all, the greater was his shame: 780
Although the Serpent's craft had her abused,
God's holy word ought all his actions frame:
    For he was Lord and King of all the earth,
    Before poor Eve had either life or breath.

Who being framed by God's eternal hand,
The perfect'st man that ever breathed on earth,
And from God's mouth received that strait command,
The breach whereof he knew was present death:
Yea having power to rule both sea and land,
Yet with one Apple won, to lose that breath   790
    Which God hath breathèd in his beauteous face,
    Bringing us all in danger and disgrace.

And then to lay the fault on Patience' back,
That we (poor women) must endure it all;
We know right well he did discretion lack,
Being not persuaded thereunto at all.
If Eve did err, it was for knowledge sake;
The fruit being fair persuaded him to fall.
    No subtle serpent's falsehood did betray him;
    If he would eat it, who had power to stay him?   800

Not Eve, whose fault was only too much love,
Which made her give this present to her dear,
That what she tasted, he likewise might prove,
Whereby his knowledge might become more clear.
He never sought her weakness to reprove
With those sharp words, which he of God did hear:
    Yet men will boast of knowledge, which he took
    From Eve's fair hand, as from a learned book.

If any evil did in her remain,
Being made of him, he was the ground of all.   810
If one of many worlds could lay a stain
Upon our sex, and work so great a fall
To wretched man, by Satan's subtle train;
What will so foul a fault amongst you all?
    Her weakness did the serpent's words obey;
    But you in malice God's dear Son betray.

Whom, if unjustly you condemn to die,
Her sin was small, to what you do commit;
All mortal sins that do for vengeance cry,
Are not to be compared unto it.   820
If many worlds would altogether try,
By all their sins the wrath of God to get;
    This sin of yours surmounts them all as far
    As doth the sun, another little star.

Then let us have our liberty again,
And challenge to your selves no sovereignty;
You came not in the world without our pain,
Make that a bar against your cruelty.
Your fault being greater, why should you disdain
Our being your equals, free from tyranny?   830
    If one weak woman simply did offend,
    This sin of yours hath no excuse, nor end.

41

Title: *Salve...Judaeorum:* Hail God, King of the Jews. 748 *bands:* restraints. 758 *good desert:* worthiness, character that deserves good. 763 *apology:* vindication. 765 *simply:* artlessly, naturally (also at line 831); *after-coming:* following. 771 *bereaved:* robbed, dispossessed. 775-76 *see* Genesis 3:3; 3:6. 783-44 *see* Genesis 2:7-22. 787 *strait:* strict. 800 *stay:* restrain, check. 803 *prove:* experience. 810 *see* Genesis 2:21-23; *ground:* foundation. 813 *train:* treachery, long body (like the serpent's). 826 *challenge:* claim.

from The Description of Cookeham

...And you sweet Cookeham, whom these ladies leave,
I now must tell the grief you did conceive
At their departure, when they went away,
How every thing retained a sad dismay;   130
Nay, long before, when once an inkling came,
Me thought each thing did unto sorrow frame:
The trees that were so glorious in our view,
Forsook both flowers and fruit, when once they knew
Of your depart; their very leaves did wither,
Changing their colours as they grew together.
But when they saw this had no power to stay you,
They often wept, though speechless, could not pray you,
Letting their tears in your fair bosoms fall,
As if they said, 'Why will ye leave us all?'   140
This being vain, they cast their leaves away,
Hoping that pity would have made you stay;
Their frozen tops, like Age's hoary hairs,
Shows their disasters, languishing in fears:
A swarthy rivelled rine all over spread
Their dying bodies, half alive, half dead.
But your occasions called you so away,
That nothing there had power to make you stay.
Yet did I see a noble grateful mind,
Requiting each according to their kind;   150
Forgetting not to turn and take your leave
Of these sad creatures, powerless to receive
Your favour, when with grief you did depart,
Placing their former pleasures in your heart;
Giving great charge to noble Memory,
There to preserve their love continually;
But specially the love of that fair tree,
That first and last you did vouchsafe to see,
In which it pleased you oft to take the air,
With noble Dorset, then a virgin fair,   160
Where many a learned book was read and scanned;
To this fair tree, taking me by the hand,

42

You did repeat the pleasures which had past,
Seeming to grieve they could no longer last.
And with a chaste, yet loving kiss took leave,
Of which sweet kiss I did it soon bereave,
Scorning a senseless creature should possess
So rare a favour, so great happiness.
No other kiss it could receive from me,
For fear to give back what it took of thee: 170
So I ungrateful creature did deceive it,
Of that which you vouchsafed in love to leave it.
And though it oft had given me much content,
Yet this great wrong I never could repent:
But of the happiest made it most forlorn,
To show that nothing's free from Fortune's scorn,
While all the rest with this most beauteous tree,
Made their sad consort Sorrow's harmony.
The flowers that on the banks and walks did grow,
Crept in the ground; the grass did weep for woe.   180
The winds and waters seemed to chide together,
Because you went away they knew not whither:
And those sweet brooks that ran so fair and clear,
With grief and trouble, wrinkled did appear.
Those pretty birds that wonted were to sing,
Now neither sing, nor chirp, nor use their wing;
But with their tender feet on some bare spray,
Warble forth sorrow, and their own dismay.
Fair *Philomela* leaves her mournful ditty,
Drowned in dead sleep, yet can procure no pity.   190
Each arbour, bank, each seat, each stately tree,
Looks bare and desolate now for want of thee;
Turning green tresses into frosty grey,
While in cold grief they wither all away.
The sun grew weak, his beams no comfort gave,
While all green things did make the earth their grave:
Each brier, each bramble, when you went away,
Caught fast your clothes, thinking to make you stay.
Delightful Echo wonted to reply
To our last words, did now for sorrow die;   200
The house cast off each garment that might grace it,
Putting on dust and cobwebs to deface it.
All desolation then there did appear,
When you were going whom they held so dear.
This last farewell to Cookeham here I give,

43

When I am dead thy name in this may live,
Wherein I have performed her noble hest,
Whose virtues lodge in my unworthy breast,
And ever shall, so long as life remains,
Tying my heart to her by those rich chains.   210

Title: *Cookeham:* Cooke-ham manor near Maidenhead, Berkshire. 127 *these ladies:* Lady
Margaret Clifford, Countess of Cumberland and her daughter, Lady Anne Clifford,
Countess of Dorset. 138 *pray:* beg. 143 *hoary:* grey, white. 145 *rivelled:* furrowed; *rine:*
rind (as bark). 160 *Dorset:* Lady Anne. 166 *bereave:* rob. 172 *vouchsafed:* condescended to
grant. 178 *consort:* concert. 185 *wonted:* accustomed. 199 *Philomela...ditty:* In classical
mythology, Philomela, closely attached to, but separated from her sister, Procne, after
the latter's marriage, was raped by her brother-in-law when he came to return her to her
sister. Afterwards, he cut out her tongue. Philomela was later changed into a nightingale,
and Procne into a swallow; they died through excess of grief. Both birds have plaintive
songs. 199 *Echo:* Echo, deprived of speech by Juno and rejected by Narcissus, whom
she loved, pined away and was transformed into a stone that echoed others' words. 207
hest: behest, command (i.e. from her patron to write the poem).

ELIZABETH CARY (*née* Tanfield), Viscountess Falkland
1585-1639

Elizabeth Cary, the first Englishwoman to publish a full-length original play,
was born in Burford, Oxfordshire. She educated herself to read French, Spanish,
Italian, Latin, and Hebrew, reading against her parents' wishes with candles
she paid the servants to bring her. During her difficult life she translated a
variety of texts, wrote poetry and dramatic verse, and the lives of several women
saints (in verse), as well as a life of Edward II. She married Henry Cary in
1602. He later became a viscount and Lord Chief Deputy of Ireland; whilst
there she learned Gaelic. Brought up a Protestant, Elizabeth converted to
Catholicism (*c.* 1626). As a result, her husband took away her eleven children
and refused to maintain her. In poverty, she appealed to the court and, in 1627,
the Privy Council ordered her husband to support her, but he did not do so.
Elizabeth smuggled two of her sons to Europe to be educated as Catholics,
with financial help from Queen Henrietta Maria. Several of her daughters
became nuns and one, Dame Lucy Magdalen Cary, wrote a biography of her
mother. The Queen assisted a partial reconciliation and Elizabeth helped to
nurse her husband just before his death in 1633. She died, still impoverished,
and was buried in the Queen's chapel. *Mariam, the Faire Queen of Jewry* was
written *c.* 1603 and published in 1613.

from The Tragedy of Mariam, the Fair Queen of Jewry
CHORUS ACT 4, SCENE 8

The fairest action of our human life
Is scorning to revenge an injury:

For who forgives without a further strife,
His adversary's heart to him doth tie.
And tis a firmer conquest truly said,
To win the heart, than overthrow the head.

If we a worthy enemy do find,
To yield to worth, it must be nobly done:
But if of baser metal be his mind,
In base revenge there is no honour won.
  Who would a worthy courage overthrow,
  And who would wrestle with a worthless foe?

We say our hearts are great and cannot yield,
Because they cannot yield it proves them poor:
Great hearts are tasked beyond their power, but felled,
The weakest lion will the loudest roar.
  Truth's school for certain doth this same allow,
  High heartedness doth sometimes teach to bow.

A noble heart doth teach a virtuous scorn,
To scorn to owe a duty over-long:
To scorn to be for benefits forborne,
  To scorn to bear an injury in mind,
  To scorn a free-born heart slave-like to bind.

But if for wrongs we needs revenge must have,
Then be our vengeance of the noblest kind:
Do we his body from our fury save,
And let our hate prevail against our mind?
  What can 'gainst him a greater vengeance be,
  Than make his foe more worthy far than he?

1 *human:* humane 1613 ed.

MARY WROTH (*née* Sidney)
1587 – *c*.1653

Lady Mary Wroth, the first Englishwoman to publish a full-length work of
fiction and a complete sonnet sequence, was brought up at Penshurst in Kent,
and in the Netherlands. Her aunt (Mary Sidney), uncle (Philip Sidney), and
father (Robert) were all poets. She married Sir Robert Wroth, who preferred
hunting and fishing to literary pursuits, in 1604. He died in 1614, leaving her
£23,000 in debt, with a son, James. She had two more (illegitimate) children
by her cousin, William Herbert (son of Mary Sidney), who features as the

faithless lover, Amphilanthus, in her sonnet sequence below. When she fell from Queen Anne's favour in 1612, Mary left the court for Penshurst and wrote a long prose romance (including songs, poems, and the appended sonnet sequence, *Pamphilia to Amphilanthus*), which was published in 1621 as *The Countess of Montgomeries Urania*. Wroth claimed this was done without her permission when she was accused, by Lord Denny, of personal satire. He demanded the books be recalled from sale but there is no evidence that this occurred. The following poems are taken from a copy in the British Library (86.h.9). Mary Wroth danced in Ben Jonson's *The Masque of Blackness*. Jonson dedicated his play *The Alchemist* to her and wrote that he had become 'a better lover and much better Poet' after reading her sonnets. She also wrote an unpublished pastoral tragi-comedy, *Love's Victorie*. Josephine A. Roberts edited a thorough edition of the poems for Louisiana State University Press in 1992; this contains details of all surviving manuscripts. For an essay on *Pamphilia to Amphilanthus* by Robyn Bolam and a list of further reading, see *CERLC*, 257-66.

from Pamphilia to Amphilanthus
FIRST SEQUENCE

23

When every one to pleasing pastime hies,
Some hunt, some hawk, some play, while some delight
In sweet discourse, and music shows joy's might:
Yet I my thoughts do far above these prize.

The joy which I take, is that free from eyes
I sit, and wonder at this day-like night,
So to dispose themselves as void of right,
And leave true pleasure for poor vanities.

When others hunt, my thoughts I have in chase;
If hawk, my mind at wishèd end doth fly:
Discourse, I with my spirit talk, and cry
While others music choose as greatest grace.

O God, say I, can these fond pleasures move?
Or music be but in sweet thoughts of love?

1 *hies:* hurries. 5 *eyes:* scrutiny. 7 *void of:* not graced or ennobled by.

40

It is not love which you poor fools do deem,
That doth appear by fond and outward shows
Of kissing, toying, or by swearing's gloze:
O no, these are far off from love's esteem.

46

Alas, they are not such that can redeem
Love lost, or winning keep those chosen blows:
Though oft with face and looks love overthrows;
Yet so slight conquest doth not him beseem.

'Tis not a show of sighs or tears can prove
Who loves indeed, which blasts of feigned love
Increase, or die as favours from them slide;

But in the soul true love in safety lies
Guarded by faith, which to desert still hies:
And yet kind looks do many blessings hide.

3 *swearing's gloze:* exaggerated fair words. 8 *beseem:* suit, become. 13 *desert:* deserving, worthiness of recompense.

42

If ever love had force in human breast,
If ever he could move in pensive heart,
Or if that he such pow'r could but impart
To breed those flames whose heat brings joy's unrest,

Then look on me; I am to these addressed.
I am the soul that feels the greatest smart;
I am that heartless trunk of heart's depart
And I, that one, by love, and grief oppressed;

None ever felt the truth of love's great miss
Of eyes, till I deprivèd was of bliss;
For had he seen, he must have pity showed;

I should not have been made this stage of woe
Where sad disasters have their open show:
O no, more pity he had sure bestowed.

1 *human:* humaine 1621 ed. and Folger ms. 7 *heartless...depart:* an image of a body, the heart having been removed (i.e. stolen by the loved one, martyred, etc.). 12 *this...woe:* Pamphilia sees her body as a stage which displays her personal tragedy, by look and gesture, for all to see. For a possible link with John Ford's play, *'Tis Pity She's a Whore,* see *CERLC,* 276-83.

48

How like a fire doth love increase in me,
The longer that it lasts, the stronger still,
The greater, purer, brighter, and doth fill
No eye with wonder more; then hopes still be

Bred in my breast, when fires of love are free
To use that part to their best pleasing will,
And now impossible it is to kill
The heat so great, where Love his strength doth see.

Mine eyes can scarce sustain the flames, my heart
Doth trust in them my passions to impart,
And languishingly strive to show my love;

My breath not able is to breath least part
Of that increasing fuel of my smart;
Yet love I will, till I but ashes prove.

Pamphilia.

14 *Yet...will:* a possible allusion to Wroth's lover, William Herbert. Wroth signed the name 'Pamphilia' below this poem to signify the end of the first sequence of songs and sonnets.

THIRD SEQUENCE

from A Crown of Sonnets Dedicated to Love

1

In this strange labyrinth how shall I turn?
Ways are on all sides, while the way I miss:
If to the right hand, there, in love I burn;
Let me go forward, therein danger is.

If to the left, suspicion hinders bliss;
Let me turn back, shame cries I ought return,
Nor faint, though crosses with my fortunes kiss;
Stand still is harder, although sure to mourn.

Thus let me take the right, or left hand way;
Go forward, or stand still, or back retire:
I must these doubts endure without allay
Or help, but travail find for my best hire.

Yet that which most my troubled sense doth move
Is to leave all, and take the thread of Love.

Title *A Crown of Sonnets:* in the Italian poetic form of the corona or crown, the last line of a stanza or sonnet became the first line of the next. 1 *labyrinth:* Wroth's spelling, 'labourinth', in manuscript and 1621 ed., inspired feminist critics to see this as a reflection of the arduous nature of love for a female version of Theseus in a reworking of the Minotaur myth. The image of love as a labyrinth or maze occurs in Petrarch and in other Renaissance verse, including that of Wroth's father, Robert Sidney. 7 *crosses:* trials; also the crossed paths she contemplates. 11 *allay:* alleviation, diminishment. 12 *travail:* laborious effort; *hire:* reward. 14 *take...thread:* as Theseus used the thread given to him by Ariadne to find his way out of the labyrinth, Pamphilia takes the thread offered by Cupid, god of Love.

48

2

Is to leave all, and take the thread of Love,
Which line straight leads unto the soul's content,
Where choice delights with pleasure's wings do move,
And idle fant'sy never room had lent.

When chaste thoughts guide us, then our minds are bent
To take that good which ills from us remove:
Light of true love brings fruit which none repent,
But constant lovers seek, and wish to prove.

Love is the shining star of blessing's light,
The fervent fire of zeal, the root of peace,
The lasting lamp, fed with the oil of right,
Image of faith, and womb for joy's increase.

Love is true virtue, and his end's delight;
His flames are joys, his bands true lovers' might.

8-12 *constant...lovers:* faithful, unchanging love is the 'womb' at the heart of the labyrinth
that gives birth to joy. 13 *virtue:* vertu Folger ms and 1621 ed. incorporates a love of
fine arts with love of virtue.

3

His flames are joys, his bands true lovers' might,
No stain is there, but pure, as purest white,
Where no cloud can appear to dim his light,
Nor spot defile, but shame will soon requite.

Here are affections, tried by Love's just might
As gold by fire, and black discerned by white,
Error by truth, and darkness known by light,
Where faith is valued for Love to requite.

Please him, and serve him, glory in his might
And firm he'll be, as innocency white,
Clear as th'air, warm as sun beams, as day light,
Just as truth, constant as fate, joyed to requite.

Then Love obey, strive to observe his might
And be in his brave court a glorious light.

4, 8, 12 *requite:* repay. 13-14 *Love...court:* in this crown of sonnets, Cupid is transformed
from mischievous winged boy (the Anacreontic Cupid) to mighty god and great monarch.

4

And be in his brave court a glorious light,
Shine in the eyes of Faith, and Constancy,

Maintain the fires of Love, still burning bright,
Not slightly sparkling, but light flaming be.

Never to slack till earth no stars can see,
Till sun and moon do leave to us dark night,
And second chaos once again do free
Us, and the world from all division's spite.

Till then, affections which his followers are,
Govern our hearts, and prove his power's gain.
To taste this pleasing sting, seek with all care,
For happy smarting is it with small pain.

Such as although it pierce your tender heart,
And burn, yet burning you will love the smart.

5-8 *Never...spite:* endure until the end of the world.

5

And burn, yet burning you will love the smart,
When you shall feel the weight of true desire,
So pleasing, as you would not wish your part
Of burden should be missing from that fire;

But faithful and unfeignèd heat aspire,
Which sin abolisheth, and doth impart
Salves to all fear, with virtues which inspire
Souls with divine love, which shows his chaste art,

And guide he is to joyings; open eyes
He hath to happiness, and best can learn
Us means how to deserve, this he descries,
Who, blind, yet doth our hidden'st thoughts discern.

Thus we may gain, since living in blest love,
He may our profit and our tutor prove.

8 *chaste:* pure; faithful. 9-14 *he:* Cupid. 14 *profit:* profitt, Folger ms; Prophet 1621 ed.
Both 'gain' and 'revealer or interpreter of God's will' are implied.

13

Free from all fogs, but shining fair and clear,
Wise in all good, and innocent in ill,
Where holy friendship is esteemed dear,
With truth in love, and justice in our will.

In Love these titles only have their fill
Of happy life maintainer, and the mere
Defence of right, the punisher of skill
And fraud, from whence directions doth appear.

To thee then, Lord commander of all hearts,
Ruler of our affections kind, and just
Great King of Love, my soul from feignèd smarts
Or thought of change, I offer to your trust

This crown, my self, and all that I have more,
Except my heart, which you bestowed before.

4 *will:* a possible pun on William Herbert. 5 *fill/ Of:* fulfilment in. 7 *skill...fraud:* deceitful devisings. 13 *This crown:* the crown of sonnets. 14 *bestowed:* provided with lodging.

14

Except my heart, which you bestowed before,
And for a sign of conquest gave away
As worthless to be kept in your choice store,
Yet one more spotless with you doth not stay.

The tribute which my heart doth truly pay,
Is faith untouched, pure thoughts discharge the score
Of debts for me, where Constancy bears sway,
And rules as Lord, unharmed by envy's sore,

Yet other mischiefs fail not to attend,
As enemies to you, my foes must be;
Curst Jealousy doth all her forces bend
To my undoing, thus my harms I see.

So though in love I fervently do burn,
In this strange labyrinth how shall I turn?

3 *worthless:* another pun on Wroth. 14 *In...turn:* a return to the first line of the first sonnet, completing the crown, and implying either that Pamphilia is still lost and confused in the labyrinth of love, or that the way she turned in the first sonnet was inwards, to a personal exploration of the nature of love itself, which has brought her an even greater awareness of its complexities, but has not provided a solution.

FOURTH SEQUENCE

2

Late in the forest I did Cupid see
Cold, wet, and crying, he had lost his way,

And being blind was farther like to stray;
Which sight, a kind compassion bred in me.

I kindly took, and dried him, while that he,
Poor child, complained he starved was with stay,
And pined for want of his accustomed prey,
For none in that wild place his host would be.

I glad was of his finding, thinking sure
This service should my freedom still procure,
And in my arms I took him then unharmed,

Carrying him safe unto a myrtle bower,
But in the way he made me feel his pow'r,
Burning my heart, who had him kindly warmed.

2-8 *Cold...be:* Cupid as a homeless beggar was a common motif in Renaissance poetry, but Pamphilia's response is particularly maternal. 6 *stay:* tarrying, lingering. 12 *myrtle:* an evergreen, white-flowered, scented shrub, sacred to Venus.

9

My muse, now happy, lay thyself to rest,
Sleep in the quiet of a faithful love,
Write you no more, but let these fant'sies move
Some other hearts; wake not to new unrest,

But if you study, be those thoughts addressed
To truth, which shall eternal goodness prove;
Enjoying of true joy, the most and best,
The endless gain which never will remove.

Leave the discourse of Venus and her son
To young beginners, and their brains inspire
With stories of great love, and from that fire
Get heat to write the fortunes they have won,

And thus leave off; what's past shows you can love,
Now let your constancy your honour prove,
                                                    Pamphilia.

1 *My muse:* the last poem in the final sequence addresses Pamphilia's poetic inspiration, now laid to rest. 9 *son:* sunn 1621 ed. 13 *leave off:* in the sense of 'pass the baton on to younger runners'; *what's past:* both her past experience of love and the poems she has written. 14 *constancy:* in *Urania* Pamphilia accepts the keys to the Throne of Love from Constancy, who then: 'vanished, as metamorphosing her self into her breast' (I.i.141).

ELEANORA FINCH (*née* Wyatt)

after 1591 – 1623

A great-granddaughter of the poet, Sir Thomas Wyatt (1503?-42), Eleanora was probably born at Allington Castle, Boxley, Kent. Her grand-father (also Sir Thomas Wyatt) rebelled against Mary I's marriage to Philip II of Spain and was executed in 1554. Her father was his only son, Sir George Wyatt, and her mother was Jane Finch. Eleanora was the third daughter of at least six children. She married Sir John Finch in 1612 (Wyatt Papers, BL Add. ms 62135, fo. 454^r), appears to have had an unhappy marriage (they parted for a time in 1619, BL Add. ms 62135, fo. 485^r), and may have died after the child she was expecting perished in the womb (see 'An Epitaph on the Death of Mrs E.F.', BL Add. ms 62135, fo. 334). She was buried at Boxley church in December 1623. The following poems, by a woman signing herself, 'E', and identified as 'Eleanora Finch' (*EMWP*, 208), are taken from a pamphlet of poems by several authors collected in BL Add. ms 62135 (fo.337^r, fos. 334^r – 336^v), apparently by her eldest brother, Sir Francis Wyatt, Governor of Virginia, 1621-41.

'Tis true I weep, I sigh, I wring my hands,
But thou, o love, hast yet no cause to laugh.
For whilst I wring my hands, I thence shake off
What once I kept for ornaments, thy bands.
And those deep sighs to fan the fire that served,
To blow away the storms are now reserved.

1 *ornaments,:* this ed. ornaments BL ms. 5 *that:* this ed. y^t BL ms, possibly, but less likely transcribed as 'it'.

When I first was brought to light

1

When I first was brought to light,
Rather into darkness thrown,
Midst of such a stormy night
As i'th' dark could not be known
But unseen have past untold,
Not among the rest enrolled.

2

Not a beam of light was seen,
Not a star peeped through the skies,
Fled from heaven the night's pale Queen,
Nor my birth would patronize.
Blue the trembling tapers burned,
All fair eyes in blackness mourned.

3

The first light to greet mine eyes,
Was the blaze of lightning flashes
   Which a proud tower raised to skies
In an instant struck to ashes.
   In such darkness have I seen
   By such light still blinded been.

4

Me my sad forsaken mother
(Then her love eclipsed remaining)
   Bred me not at first of other,
After from her breast sustaining
   Me, who from her woes did borrow
   But the pure extract of sorrow.

5

I was still brought up in woe,
Music pleased me not so well,
   As of those that felt the blow
Weeping for to hear them tell
   Of that storm, which threatening all
   Only on our house did fall.

6

Other stories oft supplied,
Though our own might well content,
   Being born on either side
To much woe by our descent
   And I would our race's fate
   In my harms might terminate.

7

Mourning black best pleased mine eyes,
And methought became me best.
   Sad and direful tragedies
Still I liked above the rest.
   And those best I ever loved
   Who most spite of fortune proved.

8

Saddest looks had sweetest grace,
Grieved with grief content yet showing.

Nought so well became the face
As the cheeks with tears o'erflowing.
Wreathed arms, neglected hair
Best methought adorned the fair.

9

From my wailing hour of birth
To this present weeping hour
Never had I joy on earth,
But what served to make me more
Feel my harms and brought with it
Greater ills, than that could quit.

10

My desires were ne'er effected
But where I mine ill desired.
Else they came so long protracted
That the tide was back retired
When they came and let me see
Such as these thy wishes be.

11

Any gift had fortune lent me,
Not that I can boast of many.
Any grace had nature sent me,
Yet I say not I had any.
Not so little can be thought
As were great the harms they brought.

12

Yet would mine accursed star
Had in me his beams confined,
Whose infection spreading far
Struck at those to me were joined
In acquaintance, love, or blood
More or less as near they stood.

13

Some in their estates were wracked,
Some proved luckless in their love,
Some with false defame were blacked,
Some their friends' unkindness prove.
Those the least of ills have tried
Who (alas) untimely died.

14

Thou most causeless wert forsaken
For a ruin-bringing love.
Death from thee thy love hath taken,
Left alone sad fates to prove.
  Thee thy parent's fatal doom
  Buries in a living tomb.

15

Happy thou hadst thy desire,
But your nuptial tapers set
  Both your houses on a fire,
So from Troy the flame was fetched;
  Thou long-sought thy love did'st find,
  Find (alas) but proved unkind.

16

But thy woes should I awake,
Woes with thee in silence sleeping,
  All the rest would theirs forsake,
Thine alone thought worth the weeping.
  Had not fate cut off thy story,
  Thine had robbed from mine the glory.

17

Yet for many harms of theirs,
And the greatest of mine own
  Upon any of the spheres
Would I might the blame have thrown
  Whilst they of the ills they sent
  Made myself the instrument.

18

Setting at the race's end
As the doubtful combat still,
  Wheresoe'er my wishes bend,
As still bend to one they will,
  There the loss still lights and brought
  Farther mischiefs with it oft.

19

Help to any gave I ever,
Or advice to any lent.

Well to any wisht I never
Where it came to good event.
But O, where most good of all
I desired, most ill did fall.

20

Thou whose harms were doubly mine,
Whose least ill to have redeemed
Willingly I would resign
What my greatest good I deemed
Not alone must wretched be,
But must owe the cause to me.

21

Whilst I gave myself for thee,
Of that gain yet may I boast.
And whilst thou to purchase me
All thy world beside hast lost.
By this match what have we won,
Both undoing and undone.

22

Not that I my woes desire,
Vented thus to make them less,
Or else pity thus require,
So to sweeten my distress.
Those which that had best deserved
Still are in my heart reserved.

23

But I set my griefs to show
Where nor light nor eyes are near.
And I story out my woe
Where there are no ears to hear.
But with silent words unfold
What by me shall ne'er be told.

3:1 *to greet:* this ed. that greetes BL ms. 4:3 *Bred…other:* did not allow a wet nurse to
suckle her baby. 13:4 & 14:5 *friends' parent's:* no apostrophes appear in the ms, so either
could be singular or plural. 14:6 *living tomb:* the mother's womb, where the baby, appar-
ently, dies. 15:4 *fetched:* this ed. fette BL ms. 23:6 *What…told:* the poem may have been
written just before the poet's death.

RACHEL SPEGHT (*later* Proctor)

c. 1597 – 1630 *or later*

Rachel Speght married William Proctor, a cleric, in 1621, and they had two children, Rachel (*b.* 1627) and William (*b.* 1630). Her father was a Calvinist minister and rector of the London churches: St Mary Magdalen, Milk Street and St Clement, Eastcheap. Her mother died not long before her daughter's marriage. In 1617 Rachel published *A mouzell for Melastomus*, a reply to a misogynistic treatise by Joseph Swetnam. She dedicated *Mortalities memorandum, with a dreame prefixed, imaginarie in manner; reall in matter* (1621) to her godmother, Mary Moundeford. Her allegorical dream vision, from which the following extract is taken, shows a female author reviving a medieval form, found earlier in poems such as the *Roman de la Rose* (translated by Chaucer). At the beginning of the poem, the heroine meets Thought and complains of a sickness or grief called Ignorance. What follows is a strong argument in support of education for women, supported by an educated woman's knowledge of the Bible and the works of classical writers. The final 78 lines which follow this extract depict the heroine's battle with 'some monster, or a Devil' that 'on Eve's sex...foamed filthy froth' (misogynist writers like Swetnam) and her reaction to the death of her mother.

from The Dream

What is without the compass of my brain,
My sickness makes me say it cannot be;
What I conceive not, cannot come to pass,
Because for it I can no reason see.
I measure all men's feet by mine own shoe,
And count all well which I appoint or do.

The pestilent effects of my disease
Exceed report, their number is so great;
The evils, which through it I do incur,
Are more than I am able to repeat.   70
Wherefore, good Thought, I sue to thee again,
To tell me how my cure I may obtain.

Quoth she, 'I wish I could prescribe your help;
Your state I pity much and do bewail;
But for my part, though I am much employed,
Yet in my judgement I do often fail.
And therefore I'll commend unto your trial,
Experience, of whom take no denial.

For she can best direct you what is meet
To work your cure and satisfy your mind'.   80
I thanked her for her love and took my leave,

Demanding where I might Experience find.
She told me if I did abroad enquire,
'Twas likely Age could answer my desire.

I sought, I found; she asked me what I would.
Quoth I, 'Your best direction I implore:
For I am troubled with an irksome grief',
Which when I named, quoth she, 'Declare no more:
For I can tell as much as you can say,
And for your cure I'll help you what I may.   90

The only medicine for your malady,
By which, and nothing else, your help is wrought,
Is knowledge, of the which there is two sorts:
The one is good, the other bad and nought;
The former sort by labour is attained,
The latter may without much toil be gained.

But 'tis the good which must effect your cure'.
I prayed her then that she would further show
Where I might have it. 'That I will', quoth she,
'In Erudition's garden it doth grow: 100
And in compassion of your woeful case,
Industry shall conduct you to the place.'

Dissuasion, hearing her assign my help
(And seeing that consent I did detect)
Did many remoraes to me propose,
As dullness and my memory's defect;
The difficulty of attaining lore,
My time, and sex, with many others more,

Which when I heard, my mind was much perplexed,
And as a horse new come into the field,   110
Who with a harquebuz at first doth start,
So did this shot make me recoil and yield.
But of my fear when some did notice take,
In my behalf, they this reply did make.

First quoth Desire, 'Dissuasion, hold thy peace,
These oppositions come not from above'.
Quoth Truth, 'They cannot spring from reason's root,
And therefore now thou shalt no victor prove'.
'No', quoth Industry, 'be assured this:
Her friends shall make thee of thy purpose miss.   120

For with my sickle I will cut away
All obstacles that in her way can grow,
And by the issue of her own attempt,
I'll make thee *labor omnia vincet* know'.
Quoth Truth, 'And since her sex thou do'st object,
Thy folly I by reason will detect.

Both man and woman of three parts consist,
Which Paul doth body, soul, and spirit call;
And from the soul three faculties arise:
The mind, the will, the power; then wherefore shall   130
A woman have her intellect in vain,
Or not endeavour knowledge to attain?

The talent God doth give must be employed;
His own, with vantage, he must have again.
All parts and faculties were made for use;
The God of knowledge nothing gave in vain.
'Twas Mary's choice our Saviour did approve,
Because that she the better part did love.

Cleobulina and Demophila,
With Telesilla, as historians tell,   140
(Whose fame doth live, though they have long been dead)
Did all of them in poetry excel.
A Roman matron that Cornelia hight,
An eloquent and learnèd style did write.

Hypatia in astronomy had skill,
Aspatia was in rhet'ric so expert,
As that Duke Pericles of her did learn;
Areta did devote herself to art,
And by consent (which shows she was no fool),
She did succeed her father in his school.   150

And many others here I could produce,
Who were in science counted excellent;
But these examples which I have rehearsed
To show thy error, are sufficient.'
Thus having said, she turned her speech to me,
That in my purpose I might constant be.

'My friend', quoth she, 'regard not vulgar talk,
For dung-hill cocks at precious stones will spurn,

And swine-like natures prize not crystal streams,
Contemnèd mire and mud will serve their turn. 160
Good purpose seldom oppositions want:
But constant minds Dissuasion cannot daunt.

Shall every blast disturb the sailor's peace?
Or boughs and bushes travellers affright?
True valour doth not start at every noise;
Small combats must instruct for greater fight.
Disdain to be with every dart dismayed;
'Tis childish to be suddenly afraid.

If thou didst know the pleasure of the place
Where knowledge grows, and where thou mayst it gain, 170
Or rather knew the virtue of the plant,
Thou would'st not grudge at any cost or pain
Thou can'st bestow to purchase for thy cure
This plant, by which of help thou shalt be sure.

Let not Dissuasion alter thy intent;
'Tis sin to nip good motions in the head;
Take courage, and be constant in thy course,
Though irksome be the path which thou must tread.
Sick folks drink bitter medicines to be well,
And to enjoy the nut men crack the shell.' 180

When Truth had ended what she meant to say,
Desire did move me to obey her will,
Whereto consenting I did soon proceed
Her counsel and my purpose to fulfil;
And by the help of Industry, my friend,
I quickly did attain my journey's end.

Where being come, Instruction's pleasant air
Refreshed my senses which were almost dead,
And fragrant flowers of sage and fruitful plants
Did send sweet savours up into my head; 190
And taste of science, appetite did move
To augment theory of things above.

There did the harmony of those sweet birds
(Which higher soar with contemplation's wings,
Than barely with a superficial view
Denote the value of created things),

Yield such delight as made me to implore
That I might reap this pleasure more and more.

And as I walked, wand'ring with Desire
To gather that for which I thither came   200
(Which by the help of Industry I found),
I met my old acquaintance, Truth by name,
Whom I requested briefly to declare
The virtue of that plant I found so rare.

Quoth she, 'By it, God's image man doth bear;
Without it, he is but a human shape,
Worse then the Devil, for he knoweth much;
Without it who can any ill escape?
By virtue of it evils are withstood;
The mind without it is not counted good.'   210

Who wanteth knowledge is a scripture fool;
Against the ignorant the prophets pray,
And Hosea threatens judgement unto those
Whom want of knowledge made to run astray.
Without it thou no practice good canst show,
More then by hap, as blind men hit a crow.

True knowledge is the window of the soul,
Through which her objects she doth speculate;
It is the mother of faith, hope, and love;
Without it who can virtue estimate?   220
By it, in grace thou shalt desire grow;
'Tis life eternal God and Christ to know.

104 *detect:* display, reveal. 105 *remoraes:* obstacles. 107 *lore:* learning. 110 *field:* i.e. of
battle. 111 *harquebuz:* gun. 124 *labor omnia vincet:* from Virgil: work conquers all things
(as opposed to the more familiar, *amor* [love] *vincet omnia*). 128 *Paul:* St Paul, I.Thess-
alonians 5:23. 133 *talent:* special gifts, mental ability. 144 *His...again:* He expects a
return for his investment; see Luke 19:23. 136 *God of knowledge:* I. Samuel 2:3. 137
Mary's choice: see Luke 10:42. 139 *Cleobulina:* composer of riddles, renowned for her
genius, learning, and courage; *Demophila:* a name given to the Sibyl of Cumae, the most
famous classical female prophet. 140 *Telesilla:* a lyric poet in the 5th century B.C. who
armed the women of Argos and defended her country against the Lacedaemonians. 143
Cornelia: mother of Tiberius and Caius Gracchus, famous for the writing style of her
letters. 145 *Hypatia:* mathematician and philosopher, renowned for her learning, virtues,
and beauty (died 415 A.D.). 146 *Aspatia:* a teacher of rhetoric who became the mistress
of Pericles. 148 *Areta:* a philosopher, daughter of Aristippus of Cyrene. 176 *motions:*
impulses. 210 *The...good:* see Proverbs 2:10. 211 *wanteth:* lacks. 213-14 *And...astray:*
see Hosea 4: 1-6. 216 *hap:* chance, luck. 218 *speculate:* observe, contemplate.

HESTER WYAT

c. 1600

This poem is reproduced from MS. Rawl. D. 360, fol. 53^r Bodleian Library.
University of Oxford. On the back of the page it is endorsed: 'Mrs Hester
Wyat upon women's writing verse'. The poem has no punctuation in the
original manuscript. Nothing has yet been discovered concerning the life of
Hester Wyat, who may have been a descendant of the poet Sir Thomas
Wyatt (*EMWP*, 153). The poem suggests that the writer lived in rural seclu-
sion (ll.15-23), separated from her 'Friend' (who may have been at Court),
and mistrustful of those around her (ll.17-18). *See also* Mary Wroth's Sonnet
23 (*Pamphilia to Amphilanthus*, First Sequence).

A poem made by a friend of mine in answer to One who asked why she wrote

What makes me write, my dearest Friend, you ask,
For our sex always thought too great a task.
I grant you this yet 'tis no ill spent time
And my thoughts natur'ly fall into rhyme:
Rude and unpolished from my pen they flow,
So artless I my native tongue scarce know.
Learning the wit and judgement must improve,
Refine the verse, each tender passion move,
While me no muse assists nor God of Love;
Like those whose hearts with sudden grief oppressed,   10
No kind friend near on whose loved constant breast
Leaning their drooping heads they may complain,
To groves which no return can make again
They sigh their woes to ease their killing pain.
So whilst in solitude the days I pass
Paper I make my Friend and mind's true glass,
To that myself unbosom free from fear
Of a false woman's tongue or listening ear,
Blessing their fate who your dear sight enjoy,
Pleasures their hours, their happy hours employ.   20
This to us rural nymphs is now denied,
A life which is, you know, my humble share,
Free from ambition, nor yet clogged with care,
Nor need I tell you, Friend, this dismal truth
How vice and folly has possessed our youth,
So empty is our sex, yet so vain grown,
And more debauched the other ne'er were known.

Out of such company what's to be brought?
Scandal or nonsense not one solid thought.
With joy I from these noisy crowds retire   30
And from my thoughts of my own heart inquire,
Should we not to ourselves this great debt pay?
The little time that fleeting life does stay
Were worthless if unthinking thrown away.
Then I my secret thoughts collect and write
Cause this improves me most, does most delight
And whilst with innocence my time I spend,
That soonest leads to the proposed end,
No guilty blush my cheeks dye to impart.
These lines, my Friend, chaste as the author's heart,   40
Happy if they can answer your desire
Though they in flames bright as your eyes expire.

4 *rhyme:* this ed. rime Bodleian ms. 16 *glass:* mirror. 18 *listening:* this ed. lissening Bodleian ms. 20 *Pleasures: EMWP* Plea Bodleian ms. 34 *Were:* this ed. Wear Bodleian ms.

ANNE BRADSTREET (*née* Dudley)
1612–72

Anne Bradstreet, one of the first published poets of the New World, and America's first woman poet writing in English, was born in Northamptonshire, England. Her father was chief steward to the Earl of Lincoln and Anne had free access to the Earl's library. Thomas Dudley encouraged his daughter to further her education. In 1628 she married Simon Bradstreet, at one point an assistant steward to the Earl. In 1630, after her father had been threatened with imprisonment because of his Puritan faith, both families emigrated to America with fellow Puritans to found the Massachusetts Bay Colony. They arrived in Salem and Anne had several homes before settling on a farm in Andover, Massachusetts, where she wrote most of her poetry. After five years of marriage the couple had the first of their eight children. Her father was Governor of Massachusetts and Anne had access to an extensive library until more than eight hundred books were destroyed in a fire (see below). Anne's poetry was, initially, both formal and political, but her reputation grew as a result of her more autobiographical and intimate later works. Emily Dickinson, another Massachusetts poet, may have been influenced by Anne Bradstreet. The following poems are taken from *Several Poems...by a Gentlewoman in New-England, 2nd ed. corrected by the author and enlarged by an addition of several other poems found amongst her papers after her death* (Boston, John Foster, 1678). '...upon the Burning of our House' comes from the first printed edition of the Andover manuscript (*The Works of Anne Bradstreet in prose and verse*, ed. John Harvard Ellis, 1867).

from Contemplations

1

Some time now past in the autumnal tide,
When Phoebus wanted but one hour to bed,
The trees all richly clad, yet void of pride,
Were gilded o'er by his rich golden head.
Their leaves and fruits seemed painted, but was true,
Of green, of red, of yellow, mixèd hue;
Rapt were my senses at this delectable view.

2

I wist not what to wish, yet sure thought I,
If so much excellence abide below,
How excellent is He that dwells on high,
Whose power and beauty by his works we know?
Sure he is goodness, wisdom, glory, light,
That hath this under world so richly dight;
More heaven than earth was here, no winter and no night.

3

Then on a stately oak I cast mine eye,
Whose ruffling top the clouds seemed to aspire;
How long since thou wast in thine infancy?
Thy strength and stature, more thy years admire,
Hath hundred winters past since thou wast born?
Or thousand since thou breakest thy shell of horn?
If so, all these as nought, eternity doth scorn.

4

Then higher on the glistering sun I gazed,
Whose beams were shaded by the leavy tree;
The more I looked, the more I grew amazed,
And softly said, 'What glory's like to thee?'
Soul of this world, this universe's eye,
No wonder some made thee a deity;
Had I not better known, alas, the same had I.

5

Thou, as a bridegroom from thy chamber rushes,
And as a strong man, joys to run a race;
The morn doth usher thee with smiles and blushes;
The earth reflects her glances in thy face.

Birds, insects, animals with vegative,
Thy heart from death and dullness doth revive,
And in the darksome womb of fruitful nature dive.

6

Thy swift annual and diurnal course,
Thy daily straight and yearly oblique path,
Thy pleasing fervor and thy scorching force,
All mortals here the feeling knowledge hath.
Thy presence makes it day, thy absence night,
Quaternal seasons caused by thy might:
Hail creature, full of sweetness, beauty, and delight.

7

Art thou so full of glory that no eye
Hath strength thy shining rays once to behold?
And is thy splendid throne erect so high,
As to approach it, can no earthly mould?
How full of glory then must thy creator be,
Who gave this bright light lustre unto thee?
Admired, adored for ever, be that majesty.

8

Silent alone, where none or saw, or heard,
In pathless paths I lead my wand'ring feet;
My humble eyes to lofty skies I reared
To sing some song, my mazèd muse thought meet.
My great creator I would magnify,
That nature had thus decked liberally;
But Ah, and Ah, again, my imbecility!

9

I heard the merry grasshopper then sing.
The black-clad cricket bear a second part;
They kept one tune and played on the same string,
Seeming to glory in their little art.
Shall creatures abject, thus their voices raise?
And in their kind, resound their Maker's praise,
Whilst I, as mute, can warble forth no higher lays?

1.2 *Phoebus:* Apollo, the sun; 1.3 *void of:* lacking; 1.4 *Were:* Where. 2.1 *wist:* know; 2.6
dight: composed; adorned. 3.6 *shell of horn:* acorn. 4.2 *were:* was. 5.5 *vegative:* the power
of growth. 6.6 *Quaternal:* in groups of four. 7.4 *mould:* mortal. 8.4 *mazèd:* both 'con-
fused' and 'amazed', overwhelmed with wonder. 9.7 *lays:* songs of birds; lyric poem.

The Author to Her Book

Thou ill-formed offspring of my feeble brain,
Who after birth did'st by my side remain,
Till snatched from thence by friends, less wise than true,
Who thee abroad, exposed to public view,
Made thee in rags, halting to th' press to trudge,
Where errors were not lessened (all may judge).
At thy return my blushing was not small,
My rambling brat (in print) should mother call,
I cast thee by as one unfit for light,
Thy visage was so irksome in my sight;   10
Yet being mine own, at length affection would
Thy blemishes amend, if so I could:
I washed thy face, but more defects I saw,
And rubbing off a spot, still made a flaw.
I stretched thy joints to make thee even feet,
Yet still thou run'st more hobbling than is meet;
In better dress to trim thee was my mind,
But nought save home-spun cloth, i' th' house I find.
In this array, 'mongst vulgars may'st thou roam,
In critics' hands, beware thou dost not come;   20
And take thy way where yet thou art not known.
If for thy father asked, say thou hadst none:
And for thy mother, she alas is poor,
Which caused her thus to send thee out of door.

3-6 Bradstreet's first book, *The Tenth Muse*, was published in London by her brother-in-law without her knowledge. There was strong resistance to women writing in the colony. 15 *make...feet:* regularise the poetic metre. 19 *vulgars:* ordinary books; common readers

Before the Birth of One of Her Children

All things within this fading world hath end,
Adversity doth still our joys attend;
No ties so strong, no friends so dear and sweet,
But with death's parting blow is sure to meet.
The sentence past is most irrevocable,
A common thing, yet oh, inevitable.
How soon, my Dear, death may my steps attend,
How soon't may be thy lot to lose thy friend;
We both are ignorant, yet love bids me
These farewell lines to recommend to thee,   10
That when that knot's untied that made us one,

I may seem thine, who in effect am none.
And if I see not half my days that's due,
What nature would, God grant to yours and you;
The many faults that well you know I have,
Let be interred in my oblivious grave;
If any worth or virtue were in me,
Let that live freshly in thy memory,
And when thou feel'st no grief, as I no harms,
Yet love thy dead, who long lay in thine arms: 20
And when thy loss shall be repaid with gains
Look to my little babes, my dear remains.
And if thou love thyself, or loved'st me,
These O protect from step-dame's injury.
And if chance to thine eyes shall bring this verse,
With some sad sighs honour my absent hearse;
And kiss this paper for thy love's dear sake,
Who with salt tears this last farewell did take.

7 *my Dear:* her husband. 8 *friend:* lover; close companion. 11 *that...untied:* their marriage
is dissolved by her death. 13 *half...due:* the Bible gives 'three score years and ten' as
man's allotted span; this suggests Bradstreet was under 35 when the poem was written.
26 *honour...hearse:* recall my passing.

To My Dear and Loving Husband

If ever two were one, then surely we.
If ever man were loved by wife, then thee;
If ever wife was happy in a man,
Compare with me, ye women, if you can.
I prize thy love more than whole mines of gold,
Or all the riches that the East doth hold.
My love is such that rivers cannot quench,
Nor ought but love from thee, give recompense.
Thy love is such I can no way repay,
The heavens reward thee manifold, I pray.
Then while we live, in love let's so persever,
That when we live no more, we may live ever.

8 *ought:* aught, anything. 11 *persever:* persevere.

A Letter to Her Husband, Absent upon Public Employment

My head, my heart, mine eyes, my life, nay more,
My joy, my magazine of earthly store,

If two be one, as surely thou and I,
How stayest thou there, whilst I at Ipswich lie?
So many steps, head from the heart to sever;
If but a neck, soon should we be together:
I, like the earth this season, mourn in black,
My sun is gone so far in's zodiac,
Whom whilst I 'joyed, nor storms, nor frosts I felt,
His warmth such frigid colds did cause to melt.   10
My chilled limbs now numbed lie forlorn;
Return, return sweet Sol from Capricorn;
In this dead time, alas, what can I more
Than view those fruits which through thy heat I bore?
Which sweet contentment yield me for a space,
True living pictures of their father's face.
O strange effect! Now thou art southward gone,
I weary grow, the tedious day so long;
But when thou northward to me shalt return,
I wish my sun may never set, but burn   20
Within the Cancer of my glowing breast,
The welcome house of him my dearest guest.
Where ever, ever stay, and go not thence,
Till nature's sad decree shall call thee hence;
Flesh of thy flesh, bone of thy bone,
I here, thou there, yet both but one.

Title: *Public Employment:* Simon Bradstreet, like her father, was involved with colonial affairs; he became Governor of Massachusetts after her death. 2 *magazine:* store for arms and provisions. 4 *Ipswich:* Ipswich, Massachusetts, their home from 1635/6 to 1646. 8 *My sun:* her husband. 12 *Sol:* sun (as in 8); *Capricorn:* tenth sign of the zodiac (21/22 December to 19/20 January). 14 *those fruits:* their children. 21 *Cancer:* fourth sign of the zodiac (21/22 June to 22/23 July).

Here Follows Some Verses upon the Burning of Our House, July 10th, 1666. Copied Out of a Loose Paper

In silent night when rest I took,
For sorrow near I did not look,
I wakened was with thund'ring noise
And piteous shrieks of dreadful voice.
That fearful sound of 'Fire!' and 'Fire!'
Let no man know is my desire.

I, starting up, the light did spy,
And to my God my heart did cry
To strengthen me in my distress

And not to leave me succourless. 10
Then, coming out, beheld a space,
The flame consume my dwelling place.

And, when I could no longer look,
I blest His name that gave and took,
That laid my goods now in the dust.
Yea, so it was, and so 'twas just.
It was His own, it was not mine;
Far be it that I should repine.

He might of all justly bereft,
But yet sufficient for us left. 20
When by the ruins oft I passed
My sorrowing eyes aside did cast,
And here and there the places spy
Where oft I sat and long did lie.

Here stood that trunk, and there that chest;
There lay that store I counted best:
My pleasant things in ashes lie,
And them behold no more shall I.
Under thy roof no guest shall sit,
Nor at thy table eat a bit. 30

No pleasant tale shall e'er be told,
Nor things recounted done of old.
No candle e'er shall shine in thee,
Nor bridegroom's voice e'er heard shall be.
In silence ever shalt thou lie;
Adieu, Adieu; all's vanity.

Then straight I 'gin my heart to chide,
And did thy wealth on earth abide?
Didst fix thy hope on mould'ring dust?
The arm of flesh didst make thy trust? 40
Raise up thy thoughts above the sky
That dunghill mists away may fly.

Thou hast an house on high erect,
Framed by that mighty Architect,
With glory richly furnishèd,
Stands permanent though this be fled.
It's purchasèd and paid for too
By Him who hath enough to do.

A price so vast as is unknown,
Yet, by His gift, is made thine own.   50
There's wealth enough, I need no more;
Farewell my pelf, farewell my store.
The world no longer let me love,
My hope and treasure lies above.

29 *thy:* addressed to the house. 37 *'gin:* begin. 38 *thy:* addressed to her heart. 39 *mould'ring:* decaying. 44 *that...Architect:* God. 52 *pelf:* property; wealth. 53 *The...love:* Let me no longer love worldly possessions.

MARGARET CAVENDISH (*née* Lucas), Duchess of Newcastle

1623–73

Margaret Cavendish, one of the most eccentric and prolific early woman writers, was born in Colchester, the eighth child of a wealthy couple, Thomas and Elizabeth Lucas. Her father died two years later. Margaret had a limited education but an expansive imagination. In 1642 her family moved to Oxford and she became a Maid of Honour to Queen Henrietta Maria, following the Queen into exile in Paris, where she met William Cavendish, the Marquis of Newcastle, a widower in his 50s with five children. They married in 1645 and lived in Paris, Rotterdam, and Antwerp until the Restoration of Charles II in 1660 when William was made Duke of Newcastle and had some property restored to him. They were a devoted, childless, but happy couple and William encouraged his wife to write and publish. Her first books, *Poems and Fancies*, and *Philosophical Fancies*, appeared in 1653. *The World's Olio* (1655, 1671) is a collection of essays which includes a defence against plagiarism (a charge often, then, directed at women writers). *Philosophical and Physical Opinions* (1655, 1663, 1668), which was dedicated to the universities of Oxford and Cambridge, includes an attack on customs that denied women education and power. *Natures Pictures* (1656, 1671), tales of romantic heroines, also contained the first direct autobiographical account by an English woman writer: 'A True Relation of my Birth, Breeding and Life'. She wrote a biography of her husband, 14 closet dramas, books of orations, letters, and philosophical observations. She published her works in expensive folio editions that she presented to university libraries. Daring in her dress, behaviour, and writing, Margaret Cavendish drew crowds of spectators when she visited London in 1667. She died suddenly, aged 50, and was buried in Westminster Abbey. The poems below are taken from the third edition of *Poems, or several Fancies in Verse...* (1668). Emma L.E. Rees's *Margaret Cavendish: gender, genre, exile* was published by Manchester University Press in 2003.

Of Many Worlds in this World

Just like as in a nest of boxes round,
Degrees of sizes in each box are found:
So, in this world, may many others be,
Thinner and less, and less still by degree:
Although they are not subject to our sense,
A world may be no bigger than two-pence.
Nature is curious, and such works may shape,
Which our dull senses easily escape:
For creatures, small as atoms, may be there,
If every one a creature's figure bear.   10
If atoms four, a world can make, then see
What several worlds might in an ear-ring be:
For millions of those atoms may be in
The head of one small, little, single pin.
And if thus small, then ladies may well wear
A world of worlds, as pendants in each ear.

1 *as in:* unto 1653 ed. 2 *within:* in 1653 ed. 3 *others be:* Worlds more be 1653 ed. 7 *works...shape:* worke may make 1653 ed. 8 *Which:* That 1653 ed.; *senses...escape:* Sense can never finde, but scape 1653 ed. 10 *one:* Atome 1653 ed. 11 *atoms four:* four Atomes 1653 ed. 13 *those:* these 1653 ed. 15 *may...wear:* well may weare 1653 ed.

The Clasp

Give me a free and noble style, that goes
in an uncurbed strain, though wild it shows:
For, though it runs about it cares not where,
It shows more courage than it doth of fear.
Give me a style that Nature frames, not Art;
For Art doth seem to take the pedant's part:
And that seems noble, which is easy, free,
And not bound up with ore-nice pedantry.

Title *Clasp:* metal fastening of a book cover; embrace. 1 *a:* the 1653 ed.; *that goes:* omitted 1653 ed. 2 *in...shows:* Which seems uncurb'd, though it be wild 1653 ed. 3 *For...runs:* Though It runs wild 1653 ed. 6 *pedant's part:* side of the person who overrates book-learning. 8 *And...up:* Not to be bound 1653 ed.; *ore-nice:* over-fastidious.

Nature's Cook

Death is the cook of Nature; and we find
Creatures dressed several ways to please her mind.
Some, Death doth roast with fevers burning hot:

And some he boils, with dropsies, in a pot.
Some are consumed, for jelly, by degrees:
And some, with ulcers, gravy out to squeeze.
Some, as with herbs, he stuffs with gouts and pains:
Others, for tender meat, he hangs in chains.
Some, in the sea, he pickles up, to keep:
Others he, as soused brawn, in wine doth steep.　　　　10
Some, flesh and bones, he with the Pox chops small;
And doth a French fricassee make withall.
Some on grid-irons of calentures are broiled;
And some are trodden down, and so quite spoiled.
But some are baked, when smothered they do die:
Some meat he doth by hectic fevers fry.
In sweat, sometimes, he stews with savoury smell:
An hodge-podge of diseases, he likes well.
Some brains he dresseth with apoplexy,
Or sauce of megrims, swimming plenteously:　　　　20
And tongues he dries with smoke from stomachs ill;
Which, as the second course, he sends up still.
Throats he doth cut, blood-puddings for to make;
And puts them in the guts, which colics rack.
Some hunted are, by him, for deer that's red:
And some, as stall-fed oxen, knocked o' th' head.
Some, singed and scaled for bacon, seem most rare;
When with salt rheum and phlegm they powdered are.

2 *dressed:* prepared. 4 *dropsies:* diseases in which fluid collects in cavities or body tissue.
10 *soused:* pickled; *brawn:* muscle; boar's flesh. 11 *the Pox:* probably syphilis rather than
smallpox. 12 *French:* syphilis was known as the French disease. 13 *grid-irons:* barred metal
cooking utensils; *calentures:* tropical, delirious fevers; broiled: cooked, made very hot.
20 *megrims:* headaches; low spirits. 22 *sends…still:* makes them vomit.

Nature's Officers

Eternity, as usher, goes before;
And Destiny, as porter, keeps the door
Of the great World, who lets Life out and in.
The Fates, her maids, the thread of Life do spin;
Change orders all, with Industry and Care.
Motion, her foot-boy, runneth everywhere.
Time, as her page, doth carry up her train;
But, in his service, he doth little gain.
The Days are the surveyors, which do view
All Nature's works, that are both old and new.

The Seasons four, by turns, their circuits take;
Like judges sit, and distributions make.
The Months, as pen-clerks, write down everything;
Make deeds of gifts, and bonds of all that spring.
Life's office is to pay, and give out all
To her receiver, Death, when he doth call.

4 *Fates:* the three daughters of Zeus who determined a mortal's future: Clotho spun the thread of life, Lachesis allotted destiny and length of life, and Atropos cut the thread of life.

The Soul's Garment

Great Nature clothes the soul, which is but thin,
With fleshy garments, which the Fates do spin;
And, when these garments are grown old and bare,
With sickness torn, Death takes them off with care;
Doth fold them in peace, and quiet rest,
And lays them safe within an earthly chest;
Then scours them well, and makes them sweet and clean,
Fit for the soul to wear those clothes again.

A Woman Dressed by Age

A milk-white hair-lace wound up all her hairs;
And a deaf coif did cover both her ears.
A sober look about her face she ties,
And a dim sight doth cover half her eyes.
About her neck, a kercher of coarse skin,
Which time had crumpled, and worn creases in.
Her gown was turned to melancholy black,
Which loose did hang upon her sides and back.
Her stockings cramps had knit, red worsted gout;
And pains, as garters, tied her legs about.
A pair of palsy-gloves her hands did cover,
With weakness stitched, and numbness trimmed all over.
Her shoes were corns and hard skin sewed together;
Hard skin was soles, and corns the upper leather.
A mantle of diseases laps her round;
And thus she's dressed, till Death her lays i' th' ground.

2 *deaf coif:* deafness, like a close-fitting cap. 5 *kercher:* neckerchief. 9 *worsted:* closely twisted woollen fabric. 11 *palsy-gloves:* gloves of paralysis.

The Common Fate of Books

Books have the worst fate; when they once are read,
They're laid aside, forgotten like the dead.
Under a heap of dust they buried lie,
Within a vault of some small library.
But spiders, which Nature has taught to spin,
For the love and honour of this art, since men
Spin likewise all their writings from their brain,
A lasting web of fame thereby to gain;
They do high altars of thin cobwebs raise,
Their off'rings, flies, a sacrifice of praise.

1 *Books...fate:* The worst Fate Bookes have 1653 ed.; *they...are:* they are once 1653 ed.
5-10 *which...praise:* they, for honour of that Art / Of Spinning, which by Nature they
were taught; / Since Men doe spin their Writings from the Braine, Striving to make a
lasting Web of Fame, / Of Cobwebs thin, high Altars doe they raise, / There offer Flyes,
as sacrifice of praise. 1653 ed.

A Poet I am neither born nor bred;
But to a witty poet marrièd,
Whose brain is fresh and pleasant, as the Spring
Where fancies grow, and where the Muses sing:
There oft I lean my head; and, list'ning, hark,
T'observe his words and all his fancies mark:
And from that garden, flow'rs of fancies take,
Whereof a posie up in verse I make.
Thus I, that have no garden of my own,
There gather flowers that are newly blown.

2 *witty...married:* her husband, William Cavendish, Duke of Newcastle, was a minor poet.

ELIZA

fl. 1652

The following poems were published in the 1652 volume: *Eliza's Babes: or the
Virgins-Offering, being Divine Poems and Meditations written by 'A Lady'*. Eliza's
identity has never been discovered. Everything known about her comes from
her poems.

My Wishes

I wish no wit to wrong my brother,
I wish not wealth to wrong another,
I wish no beauty to enthral,
I wish no worldly wish at all.
I wish from sin God would me bring,
I wish for heaven at my ending.

To a Friend at Court

Retired here content I live,
My own thoughts to me pleasure give.
While thine own actions anger thee,
Sweet quiet thoughts contenteth me.
This blessing sweet retiredness brings,
We envy none, but pity kings.

The Dart

Shoot from above
Thou God of Love,
And with heaven's dart
Wound my blest heart.

Descend sweet life
And end this strife:
Earth would me stay,
But I'll away.

I'll die for love
Of thee above.
Then should I be
Made one with thee.

And let be said
Eliza's dead,
And of love died,
That love defied.

By a bright beam shot from above
She did ascend to her great Love,

And was content of love to die,
Shot with a dart of heaven's bright eye.

2 *Shoot...Love:* Eliza appears to be applying a Petrarchan conceit, associated with the pagan god of love, to her relationship with her Christian God.

The Heart

Two hearts in one breast can there not remain,
The one heart puts the other heart to pain.
My heart I will still keep, take thou thine own,
My heart is happy when disturbed by none.
Without a heart I know you cannot live,
Wherefore your own I freely to you give.
Mine is in heaven and will admit no change
To leave my rest in heaven, on earth to range.
I'd have it written in my happy story,
None had my heart but heaven's great Prince of Glory.
My youth's affection to him I did send,
None can have any but what he will lend.
From mortal thraldom, dear Prince, keep thou me
So though on earth, I as in heaven shall be.

13 *mortal thraldom:* the slavery involved in being human; slavery that causes death.

The Bride

Sith you me ask, why born was I?
I'll tell you, 'twas to heaven to fly,
Nor here to live a slavish life
By being to the world a wife.

When I was born I was set free
From mortals' thraldom here to be
For that great Prince prepared a bride,
That for my love on earth here died.

May not I then earth's thraldom scorn,
Sith for heaven's Prince I here was born?
If matched in heaven I wear a crown,
But earthly thraldom pulls me down.

7 *For...bride:* dedicated to God as a bride of Christ, a nun. 11 *matched:* this ed. match't 1652 ed. joined in marriage; *I...crown:* alluding to her crowning as consort to heaven's Prince and also, perhaps, a martyr or saint's crown.

On Marriage

Lord! if thou hast ordained for me
That I on earth must married be,
As often I have been foretold:
Be not thy will by me controlled.
And if my heart thou dost incline
Children to have, Lord make them thine,
Or never let't be said they're mine.
I shall not like what's not divine.
I no ambition have for earth,
My thoughts are of a higher birth.
The soul's sweet babes do bring no pain,
And they immortalize the name.

The Gift

My Lord, hast thou given me away?
Did I on earth, for a gift stay?
Hath he by prayer of thee gained me,
Who was so strictly knit to thee?

To thee I only gave my heart,
Wouldst thou my Lord from that gift part?
I know thou wouldst deliver me
To none, but one beloved by thee.

But Lord, my heart thou dost not give,
Though here on earth while I do live   10
My body here he may retain,
My heart in heaven, with thee must reign.

Then, as thy gift, let him think me,
Sith I a donage am from thee.
And let him know thou hast my heart,
He only hath my earthly part.

It was my glory I was free
And subject here to none but thee,
And still that glory I shall hold
If thou my spirit dost enfold.   20

It is my bliss I here serve thee,
'Tis my great joy thou lovest me.

14 *Sith:* since; *donage:* bestowal. 22 *joy thou:* this ed. joy; thou 1652 ed.

To a Lady that Bragged of her Children

If thou hast cause to joy in thine,
I have cause too to joy of mine.
Thine did proceed from sinful race,
Mine from the heavenly dew of grace.
Thine at their birth did pain thee bring,
When mine are born, I sit and sing.
Thine doth delight in nought but sin,
My babes' work is to praise heaven's King.

2 *mine:* her poems. 3 *sinful race:* the human race. 6 *sit:* this ed. set 1652 ed.

To General Cromwell

The sword of God doth ever well
I'th hand of virtue! O Cromwell,
But why do I complain of thee?
'Cause thou'rt the rod that scourgeth me?
But if a good child I will be,
I'll kiss the rod and honour thee;
And if thou'rt virtuous as 'tis said,
Thou'lt have the glory when thou'rt dead.

Sith kings and princes scourgèd be,
Whip thou the lawyer from his fee
That is so great, when nought they do,
And we are put off from our due.
But they for their excuse do say,
'Tis from the Law is our delay.
By tyrants' heads those laws were made,
As by the learnèd it is said.
If then from tyrants you'll us free,
Free us from their Law's tyranny.
If not! we'll say the head is pale,
But still the sting lives in the tail.

9 *Sith:* since; *kings...be:* Charles I was executed in 1649. 19 *pale:* dead.

Questions and Answers

Qu. Lord! why have I so much from thee?
An. Th'art child to me.
Qu. But why on earth have I such store?
An. In heaven is more.

<pre>
Qu. Lord I have more than I do need.
An. The poor then feed.
</pre>

Then sith I'm thine,
I'll be divine,
And what I've more
I'll give the poor.

Thine bring both sorrow, pain and fear,
Mine banish from me dreadful care.

11-12 *Thine...care:* perhaps alluding to the first answer and comparing God's human children with her own, i.e. her poems.

To a Friend for Her Naked Breasts

Madam I praise you, 'cause you're free
And you do not conceal from me
What hidden in your heart doth lie,
If I can it through your breasts spy.

Some Ladies will not show their breasts
For fear men think they are undressed,
Or by't their hearts they should discover
They do't to tempt some wanton lover.

They are afraid tempters to be,
Because a curse imposed they see
Upon the tempter that was first,
By an all-seeing God that's just.

But though I praise you have a care
Of that all-seeing eye, and fear,
Lest he through your bare breasts see sin
And punish you for what's within.

AN COLLINS
fl. 1653

An Collins experimented with both form and content in her meditative poems. Only one copy of her sole book, *Divine Songs and Meditacions*, survives in the Huntington Library, San Marino, California. All we know of her life comes from this volume. In the prefatory material she writes that she is 'restrained from bodily employments' and 'through weakness to the house confin'd'. Critics are divided concerning the exact nature of her faith: Calvinist, anti-Calvinist, and Roman Catholic have all been proposed. This poem is taken from an edition by Sidney Gottlieb (*Medieval & Renaissance Texts & Studies*, vol.161, Tempe, Arizona, 1996), who suggests that it might be useful to consider An Collins in relation to 17th-century Quakers. His edition is preferred because it was prepared directly from the Huntington Library copy and supplies the last line as found there. Most reprintings of this poem are taken from facsimile editions that miss out the line, leading editors to conjecture a substitute. Other poems in the volume comment on topical theological and political issues.

Another Song

The winter of my infancy being over-past
I then supposed, suddenly the spring would haste
Which useth every thing to cheer
With invitation to recreation
This time of year.

The sun sends forth his radiant beams to warm the ground,
The drops distil, between the gleams delights abound,
Ver brings her mate the flowery Queen,
The groves she dresses, her art expresses
On every green.   10

But in my spring it was not so, but contrary,
For no delightful flowers grew to please the eye,
No hopeful bud, nor fruitful bough,
No moderate showers which causeth flowers
To spring and grow.

My April was exceeding dry, therefore unkind;
Whence 'tis that small utility I look to find,
For when that April is so dry
(As hath been spoken) it doth betoken
Much scarcity.   20

Thus is my spring now almost past in heaviness,
The sky of pleasures over-cast with sad distress,
For by a comfortless eclipse
Disconsolation and sore vexation,
My blossom nips.

Yet as a garden is my mind enclosed fast
Being to safety so confined from storm and blast

Apt to produce a fruit most rare,
That is not common with every woman
That fruitful are.   30

A love of goodness is the chiefest plant therein,
The second is (for to be brief) dislike to sin.
These grow in spite of misery,
Which grace doth nourish and ease to flourish
Continually.

But evil motions, corrupt seeds, fall here also
Whence spring profaneness as do weeds where flowers grow
Which must supplanted be with speed,
These weeds of error, distrust and terror,
Lest woe succeed.   40

So shall they not molest the plants before expressed,
Which countervails these outward wants, and purchase rest
Which more commodious is for me
Than outward pleasures or earthly treasures
Enjoyed would be.

My little hopes of worldly gain I fret not at,
As yet I do this hope retain; though spring be late
Perhaps my summer-age may be
Not prejudicial, but beneficial
Enough for me.   50

Admit the worst, it be not so, but stormy too,
I'll learn my self to undergo more than I do
And still content myself with this
Sweet meditation and contemplation
Of heavenly bliss,

Which for the saints reserved is, who persevere
In piety and holiness and godly fear,
The pleasures of which bliss divine,
Neither logician nor rhetorician
Can well define.   60

---

1 *see* Song of Solomon 2:11. 2-5: the first letters of each line are cut off in the original.
Most eds. supply 'I then'. 2 *haste:* hast 1653 ed. 6 *ground,:* ground 1653 ed. 8 *Ver:* spring;
flowery Queen: Flora, the goddess of flowers and the spring. 22 *pleasures:* pleasure's
1653 ed. 26: *see* Song of Solomon 4:12-13; *fast:* securely. 42 *countervails:* avails against,
counter-balances. 44 *Than:* Then 1653 ed. 47 *late:* lat 1653 ed. 51 *worst,...so,:* worst...so
1658 ed. Some editors supply 'worst, if it be not so,'.

ELIZABETH MAJOR

fl. 1656

Little is known of Elizabeth Major, whose *Honey on the Rod: Or a Comfortable Contemplation for One in Affliction with Sundry poems on Several Subjects*, was published in 1656 and contains the following acrostic. In her preface to the poems (between pages 160 and 161) Elizabeth relates that her mother died in her infancy, she was brought up by her father until the age of 15 or 16, and that she served in a 'great and honorable family' under a 'wise and vertuous governess' for almost ten years, until she became severely lame and had to return home to her father. She appears to have struggled physically and financially to find a cure, but records that she was not well treated by those professing to have 'skill in lameness' and her health became worse. Elizabeth is described, in Rector Joseph Caryl's preface, as an 'afflicted Gentlewoman'. It has been speculated that she may have belonged to a prominent Hampshire family or have been the daughter of John Major, from Blackfriars in London (Germaine Greer et al., *Kissing the Rod*, 1988). An Elizabeth Major, listed as a servant living in St Dionis Backchurch, is also in the *Index of London Inhabitants Within the Walls*, 1695 (London Record Society, 1966). Although it has been occasionally suggested that *Honey on the Rod* and *Eliza's Babes* (1652) could have been written by the same person, this seems unlikely as their authors' biographical details and poetic styles differ. Elizabeth Major was a seriously devout writer of prose and poetry whose work, although accomplished, lacked the playful qualities found in that of 'Eliza'.

The Author's Prayer: O my blessed Lord and Saviour Jesus Christ, have mercy on thy poor hand-maid, Elizabeth Major.

Oh	gracious God, inhabiting	E ternity,
My	blest redeemer, that hast	L ovingly
Blessed	me with hope, a kingdom to	I nherit,
Lord	of this mercy give an humble	S pirit,
And	grant I pray, I may my life	A mend:
Saviour	'tis thou that canst my soul	B efriend.
Jesus	with grace my guilty soul	E ndue
Christ	promised grace, and thou, O Lord art	T rue;
Have	care of me, deal out with thine own	H and
Mercy	to my poor soul, thou canst com-	M and
On	me a shower of grace, sin to	A void,
Thy	praise to sing, my tongue shall be	I mployed;
Poor,	Lord I am, with fear and care	O ppressed,
Handmaid	to thee I am, in thee I'll	R est.

KATHERINE PHILIPS (*née* Fowler)
1632-64

Katherine Philips, poet, translator, and dramatist, was born into a prosperous London family and educated at Mrs Salmon's school in Hackney, where she met Mary Aubrey (the 'Mrs M.A.' or 'Rosania' of her poems). Her father died in 1642, and when her mother married Sir Richard Phillips of Pembrokeshire in 1646, Katherine lived with them in Wales. In 1648 she married her stepfather's kinsman, James Philips, a local politician and supporter of Cromwell. Katherine was 16: James, 54. They had a son who died in his first month and a daughter who survived. Katherine's Royalist leanings and court contacts helped to save her husband from prosecution after the Restoration. She circulated her poems, in manuscript, to the members of her 'Society of Friendship' (which included her neighbour Anne Owen ('Lucrasia') and some were published with Henry Vaughan's poems and William Cartwright's plays, in 1651. Others appeared in Henry Lawe's *Second Book of Ayres* (1655). Her translation of Corneille's *Pompey* was a success when performed in Dublin in 1663. A pirated edition of her poems went on sale in 1664 and she travelled to London to suppress it. When she died there, of smallpox, in June 1664, she had almost completed a translation of Corneille's *Horace*. It was finished by Sir John Denham and performed in London 1668-69. A volume of her collected poems, *Pompey*, and the unfinished *Horace* was published in 1667. Revered as the 'Matchless Orinda', her admirers included Dryden, Cowley, Aphra Behn, Anne Killigrew and Anne Finch. Her poems can be witty, metaphysical, and philosophical. She successfully reworks John Donne's poetic conceits from a woman's perspective (see below). These poems are taken from *Poems by the most deservedly admired Mrs Katherine Philips, the Matchless Orinda...* (1667). Manuscripts survive in The National Library of Wales and at the University of Texas, Austin. Patrick Thomas's three volume edition: *The Collected Works of Katherine Philips*, was published by Stump Cross Books, 1990-1993.

Friendship's Mystery, To my dearest Lucrasia

1

Come, my Lucrasia, since we see
That miracles men's faith do move,
By wonder and by prodigy
To the dull angry world let's prove
There's a religion in our love.

2

For though we were designed t'agree,
That fate no liberty destroys,
But our election is as free
As angels, who with greedy choice
Are yet determined to their joys.

3

Our hearts are doubled by the loss,
Here mixture is addition grown;
We both diffuse, and both ingross:
And we whose minds are so much one,
Never, yet ever are alone.

4

We court our own captivity
Than thrones more great and innocent;
'Twere banishment to be set free,
Since we wear fetters whose intent
Not bondage is, but ornament.

5

Divided joys are tedious found,
And griefs united easier grow:
We are our selves but by rebound,
And all our titles shuffled so,
Both princes, and both subjects too.

6

Our hearts are mutual victims laid,
While they (such power in friendship lies)
Are altars, priests, and off'rings made:
And each heart which thus kindly dies,
Grows deathless by the sacrifice.

Title: *Mystery:* like John Donne, in 'The Canonization', Philips plays on mystery, mean-
ing both hidden, inexplicable qualities and religious truth divinely revealed. 2.3 *election:*
choosing. 2.5 *determined:* limited. 3.3 *diffuse...ingross:* spread out...condense. 5.5 *Both...
too:* compare Donne's 'The Sun Rising': 'She's all states, and all princes, I'.

Friendship in Emblem, or the Seal.
To my dearest Lucrasia

1

The hearts thus intermixèd speak
A love that no bold shock can break;
For joined and growing both in one,
Neither can be disturbed alone.

2

That means a mutual knowledge too;
For what is't either heart can do,

Which by its panting sentinel
It does not to the other tell?

3

That friendship hearts so much refines,
It nothing but itself designs:
The hearts are free from lower ends,
For each point to the other tends.

4

They flame, 'tis true, and several ways,
But still those flames do so much raise,
That while to either they incline
They yet are noble and divine.

5

From smoke or hurt those flames are free,
From grossness or mortality:
The heart (like Moses' bush presumed)
Warmed and enlightened, not consumed.

6

The compasses that stand above
Express this great immortal love;
For friends, like them, can prove this true,
They are, and yet they are not, two.

7

And in their posture is expressed
Friendship's exalted interest:
Each follows where the other leans,
And what each does, this other means.

8

And as when one foot does stand fast,
And t'other circles seeks to cast,
The steady part does regulate
And make the wand'rer's motion straight:

9

So friends are only two in this,
T' reclaim each other when they miss:
For whosoe'er will grossly fall
Can never be a friend at all.

10

And as that useful instrument
For even lines was ever meant;
So friendship from good angels springs
To teach the world heroic things.

11

As these are found out in design
To rule and measure every line;
So friendship governs actions best,
Prescribing unto all the rest.

12

And as in nature, nothing's set
So just as lines in number met;
So compasses for these b'ing made,
Do friendship's harmony persuade.

13

And like to them, so friends may own
Extension, not division:
Their points, like bodies, separate;
But head, like souls, knows no such fate.

14

And as each part so well is knit,
That their embraces ever fit:
So friends are such by destiny,
And no third can the place supply.

15

There needs no motto to the seal:
But that we may the mind reveal
To the dull eye, it was thought fit
That friendship only should be writ.

16

But as there are degrees of bliss,
So there's no friendship meant by this
But such as will transmit to fame
Lucrasia and Orinda's name.

Title: *To...Lucasia:* dedicated to Anne Lewis (later Owen); the name comes from a
character in William Cartwright's play, *The Lady Errant* (1636). 1.1 *The...thus:* the

design of hearts on the seal of Philips's community of friends. 5.3 *Moses' bush:* see Exodus 3:2. 6.1 *compasses:* geometrical instrument with two connected legs, used to create circles; compare John Donne's 'A Valediction Forbidding Mourning'. 7.4 *this:* each 1664 ed. 9.2 *miss:* avoid, go astray. 11.4 *unto:* law to in two mss versions. 12.2 *in:* and in two mss versions. 12.2-4 *So...persuade:* compasses, as a poetic conceit, demonstrate 'friendship's harmony', just as metre imposes a 'set' pattern in lines of poetry.

To Mrs M.A. Upon Absence

1

'Tis now since I began to die
Four months, yet still I gasping live;
Wrapped up in sorrow do I lie,
Hoping, yet doubting, a reprieve.
Adam from Paradise expelled
Just such a wretched being held.

2

'Tis not thy love I fear to lose,
That will in spite of absence hold;
But 'tis the benefit and use
Is lost, as in imprisoned gold:
Which though the sum be ne'er so great,
Enriches nothing but conceit.

3

What angry star then governs me
That I must feel a double smart,
Prisoner to fate as well as thee;
Kept from thy face, linked to thy heart?
Because my love all love excels,
Must my grief have no parallels?

4

Sapless and dead as winter here
I now remain, and all I see
Copies of my wild state appear,
But I am their epitome.
Love me no more, for I am grown
Too dead and dull for thee to own.

Title: *Mrs. M.A.:* Mrs Mary Aubrey, also known as Rosania. 1.6 *held:* beheld.

Friendship

Let the dull brutish world that know not love
Continue heretics, and disapprove
That noble flame; but the refined know
'Tis all the heaven we have here below.
Nature subsists by love, and they tie
Things to their causes but by sympathy.
Love chains the different elements in one
Great harmony, linked to the heavenly throne.
And as on earth, so the blest choir above
Of saints and angels are maintained by love;   10
That is their business and felicity,
And will be so to all eternity.
That is the ocean, our affections here
Are but streams borrowed from the fountain there.
And 'tis the noblest argument to prove
A beauteous mind, that it knows how to love:
Those kind impressions which fate can't control
Are heaven's mintage on a worthy soul;
For love is all the arts' epitome,
And is the summer of all divinity.   20
He's worse than beast that cannot love, and yet
It is not bought by money, pains or wit;
So no chance nor design can spirits move,
But the eternal destiny of love:
    For when two souls are changed and mixèd so,
It is what they and none but they can do.
And this is friendship, that abstracted flame
Which grovelling mortals know not how to name.
All love is sacred, and the marriage tie
Hath much of honour and divinity;   30
But lust, design, or some unworthy ends
May mingle there, which are despised by friends.
Passion hath violent extremes, and thus
All oppositions are contiguous.
So when the end is served the love will bate,
If friendship make it not more fortunate:
Friendship! that love's elixir, that pure fire
Which burns the clearer 'cause it burns the higher;
For love, like earthly fires (which will decay
If the material fuel be away)   40
Is with offensive smoke accompanied,

And by resistance only is supplied:
But friendship, like the fiery element,
With its own heat and nourishment content,
(Where neither hurt, nor smoke, nor noise is made)
Scorns the assistance of a foreign aid.
Friendship (like heraldry) is hereby known,
Richest when plainest, bravest when alone;
Calm as a virgin, and more innocent
Than sleeping doves are, and as much content   50
As saints in visions; quiet as the night,
But clear and open as the summer's light;
United more than spirits' faculties,
Higher in thoughts than are the eagle's eyes;
What shall I say? When we true friends are grown,
We're like – alas, we're like ourselves alone.

50 *Than:* this ed. then 1667 ed. (and at ll.53-54). 56 *We're:* this ed. W'are 1667 ed.

Upon the graving of her name upon a tree in Barnelmes Walks

Alas how barbarous are we,
Thus to reward the courteous tree,
Who its broad shade affording us,
Deserves not to be wounded thus;
See how the yielding bark complies
With our ungrateful injuries.
And seeing this, say how much then
Trees are more generous than men,
Who by a nobleness so pure
Can first oblige and then endure.

Title: *Barnelmes:* near Barnes, outside London; the place has associations with Sidney, Donne, and Abraham Cowley.

An Answer to Another Persuading a Lady to Marriage

1

Forbear bold youth, all's heaven here,
　　And what you do aver,
To others courtship may appear,
　　'Tis sacrilege to her.

2

She is a public deity,
    And were't not very odd
She should depose herself to be
    A petty household god?

3

First make the sun in private shine,
    And bid the world adieu,
That so he may his beams confine
    In complement to you.

4

But if of that you do despair,
    Think how you did amiss,
To strive to fix her beams which are
    More bright and large than this.

3.4 *In...you:* to make you perfect.

APHRA BEHN (*née* Johnson)
?1640-89

The first female professional writer in England, Aphra Behn, was probably born near Canterbury in 1640, the daughter of a barber, Bartholomew Johnson. Her mother was wet nurse to a Colonel Culpepper, now assumed to be Sir Thomas Culpepper, who later wrote admiringly of Aphra and the poems she wrote from infancy. Described as his 'foster sister' in Culpepper's *Adversaria* (BL Harley ms 7588), she may have gained an education through this association. In 1663 Aphra's father was appointed Lieutenant-General of the colony of Surinam and 36 Caribbean islands, perhaps as a result of pro-Royalist activities to help restore Charles II to the throne, though no evidence of this is known. He died on the journey and the family left Surinam two months later. Soon afterwards Aphra Johnson became Aphra Behn. According to different sources, she may have married a London merchant of Dutch extraction or a German seaman who sailed in the West Indies, but no marriage records have been found – and she never refers to a husband in her writing. She was linked romantically to the dissident, William Scot and to the bisexual lawyer, John Hoyle. It is possible that, seeking to earn an independent living as a playwright, Aphra changed her name, inspired by the dramatist, Ben Jonson – adding the 'h' from her maiden name to his forename. Thomas Killigrew recruited her to spy for Charles II in the Dutch Wars (1666) but she received no payment and was threatened with confinement in a debtors' prison in 1668. Her code-name, Astrea, is also associated with her literary life. Besides writing poetry, she saw eighteen of her plays performed between 1670 and 1689, was a prolific pioneer of the novel, a writer of short stories, a translator, and an editor of miscellanies. She struggled with poverty most of her life, and also with sickness latterly: she wrote to survive. She was the first woman whose writing earned her a burial in Westminster Abbey. Today she is best known for her drama, *The Rover*, her anti-slave novella, *Oroonoko* (1688), and her poetry. These poems come from: *Poems upon several occasions with a Voyage to the Island of Love* (1684), from *Lycidus: or the Lover in Fashion...* (1688), and from *The 3rd & last Miscellany of Poems published by Mrs A. Behn* (1685), respectively.

On a Juniper-Tree, cut down to make Busks

Whilst happy I triumphant stood,
The pride and glory of the wood;
My aromatic boughs and fruit,
Did with all other trees dispute.
Had right by nature to excel,
In pleasing both the taste and smell:
But to the touch I must confess,
Bore an ungrateful sullenness.
My wealth, like bashful virgins, I
Yielded with some reluctancy;   10
For which my value should be more,
Not giving easily my store.
My verdant branches all the year
Did an eternal beauty wear;
Did ever young and gay appear.
Nor needed any tribute pay,
For bounties from the God of Day:
Nor do I hold supremacy,
In all the wood, o'er every tree,
But even those too of my own race   20
That grow not in this happy place.
But that in which I glory most,
And do myself with reason boast,
Beneath my shade the other day,
Young Philocles and Cloris lay;
Upon my root she leaned her head,
And where I grew, he made their bed:
Whilst I the canopy more largely spread.
Their trembling limbs did gently press

The kind supporting yielding grass: 30
Ne'er half so blest as now, to bear
A swain so young, a nymph so fair.
My grateful shade I kindly lent,
And every aiding bough I bent
So low, as sometimes had the bliss,
To rob the shepherd of a kiss,
Whilst he in pleasures far above
The sense of that degree of love
Permitted every stealth I made,
Unjealous of his rival shade. 40
I saw 'em kindle to desire,
Whilst with soft sighs they blew the fire:
Saw the approaches of their joy,
He growing more fierce, and she less coy,
Saw how they mingled melting rays,
Exchanging love a thousand ways.
Kind was the force on every side,
Her new desire she could not hide:
Nor would the shepherd be denied.
Impatient he waits no consent, 50
But what she gave by languishment,
The blessed minute he pursued;
Whilst love, her fear, and shame subdued;
And now transported in his arms,
Yields to the conqueror all her charms.
His panting breast, to hers now joined,
They feast on raptures unconfined;
Vast and luxuriant, such as prove
The immortality of Love.
For who but a divinity, 60
Could mingle souls to that degree;
And melt 'em into ecstasy?
Now, like the phoenix, both expire,
While from the ashes of their fire,
Sprung up a new, and soft desire.
Like charmers, thrice they did invoke
The god! And thrice new vigour took.
Nor had the mystery ended there,
But *Cloris* reassumed her fear,
And chid the swain, for having pressed 70
What she, alas, would not resist:
Whilst he in whom Love's sacred flame,

Before and after was the same,
Fondly implored she would forget
A fault, which he would yet repeat.
From active joys with some they hast,
To a reflection on the past;
A thousand times my covert bless,
That did secure their happiness:
Their gratitude to every tree   80
They pay, but most to happy me.
The shepherdess my bark caressed,
Whilst he my root, Love's pillow, kissed,
And did with sighs their fate deplore,
Since I must shelter them no more;
And if before my joys were such,
In having heard and seen too much,
My grief must be as great and high
When all abandoned I shall be,
Doomed to a silent destiny.   90
No more the charming strife to hear,
The shepherd's vows, the virgin's fear:
No more a joyful looker-on,
Whilst Love's soft battle's lost and won.
With grief I bowed my murmuring head,
And all my crystal dew I shed,
Which did in *Cloris* pity move,
(*Cloris* whose soul is made of Love).
She cut me down, and did translate
My being to a happier state.   100
No martyr for religion died
With half that unconsidering pride;
My top was on that altar laid
Where Love his softest offerings paid,
And was as fragrant incense burned;
My body into busks was turned:
Where I still guard the sacred store,
And of Love's temple keep the door.

---

3 *aromatic...fruit:* juniper berries have a piquant aroma. 8 *ungrateful sullenness:* its prickly
pointed leaves and blue-black berries; *ungrateful:* 1684 ed. unwilling 1680 version, attri-
buted initially to Rochester. 9-10 *My...reluctancy:* both leaves and berries must be crushed
to release the scent; 13-14 *verdant...wear:* it is an evergreen. 18 *Nor...supremacy:* some
varieties of juniper are shrubs. 21 *grow:* 1684 ed. grew 1680 ed. 26 *she lean'd:* 1684 ed.
he plac'd 1680 ed. 27 *their:* 1684 ed. her 1680 ed. 28 *Whilst...spread:* 1684 ed. omitted
1680 ed. 30 *grass:* 1684 ed. moss 1680 ed. 48 *desire:* 1684 ed. desires 1680 ed. 53 *While...*

subdued: 1680 ed. omitted in 1684 ed. 63-65 *Now...desire:* the mythical phoenix rose from the ashes of its funeral pyre with renewed youth. 67 *The...took:* 'And had the *Nymph,* been half so kind,/As was the Shepherd, well inclin'd' follows in 1680 ed. 68 *mystery:* quasi-religious rite *Nor...Mysterie:* 1684 ed. The Myst'ry had not 1680 ed. 74 *Fondly implor'd:* 1684 ed. Humbly implores 1680 ed. 75 *A:* 1684 ed. That 1680 ed. 76 *hast:* have had; *some:* 1684 ed. shame 1680 ed. 78 *my:* 1684 ed. the 1680 ed. 87 *heard...too:* 1684 ed. seen, and heard so 1680 ed. 88 *Grief:* 1684 ed. griefs 1680 ed. 89 *shall be:* 1684 ed. must lye 1680 ed. 91 *Charming:* 1684 ed. Am'rous 1680 ed. 102 *unconsidering:* unthought of. 103 *that:* 1684 ed. the 1680 ed. 103-05 *My...burned:* twigs and branches were burnt in a bonfire, releasing the aroma. 106: *body:* trunk; 107-08 *guard...door:* like the stiff strips in corsets, holding in the women's breasts, beneath which lie their hearts.

To the fair Clarinda, who made Love to me, imagined more than Woman.

Fair lovely Maid, or if that title be
Too weak, too feminine for nobler thee,
Permit a name that more approaches truth:
And let me call thee, lovely charming youth.
This last will justify my soft complaint,
While that may serve to lessen my constraint;
And without blushes I the youth pursue,
When so much beauteous woman is in view.
Against thy charms we struggle but in vain,
With thy deluding form thou giv'st us pain,   10
While the bright nymph betrays us to the swain.
In pity to our sex sure thou wert sent
That we might love, and yet be innocent:
For sure no crime with thee we can commit;
Or if we should – thy form excuses it.
For who, that gathers fairest flowers believes
A snake lies hid beneath the fragrant leaves.

    Thou beauteous wonder of a different kind,
Soft Cloris with the dear Alexis joined;
When e'er the manly part of thee would plead,   20
Thou tempts us with the image of the maid,
While we the noblest passions do extend
The love to Hermes, Aphrodite the friend.

17 *snake...leaves:* in a C16 emblem the serpent hid beneath a strawberry plant. The snake was also an image of the penis. 23 *Hermes...Aphrodite:* the parents of Hermaphroditus, who united the beauty of both sexes when his body was combined with that of the nymph, Salmacis

A Paraphrase on the Lord's Prayer

Our Father,

O wondrous condescension of a God
To poor unworthy sinful flesh and blood!
Lest the high Mystery of Divinity,
Thy sacred title, should too awful be;
Lest trembling prostrates should not freely come,
As to their parent, to their native home;
Lest thy incomprehensible God-head should
Not by dull man be rightly understood;
Thou deignst to take a name that fits our sense,
Yet lessens not thy glorious excellence.

Which art in Heaven,

Thy mercy ended not when thou didst own
Poor lost and out-cast man to be thy Son;
'Twas not enough the Father to dispense,
In Heaven thou gav'st us an inheritance;
A province, where thou'st deigned each child a share;
Advance my tim'rous soul, thou needst not fear,
Thou hast a God! A God and Father! There.

Hallowed be thy Name,

For ever be it; may my pious verse,
That shall thy great and glorious name rehearse,
By singing angels still repeated be,
And tune a song that may be worthy thee;
While all the earth with echoing Heaven shall join
To magnify a being so divine.

Thy Kingdom come,

Prepare my soul 'gainst that triumphant day,
Adorn thy self with all that's heavenly gay,
Put on the garment which no spot can stain,
And with thy God, thy King, and Father reign!
When all the joyful court of Heaven shall be
One everlasting day of jubilee,
Make my soul fit but there to find a room,
Then when thou wilt, Lord let thy Kingdom come.

Thy Will be done

With all submission, prostrate I resign
My soul, my faculties, and will to thine;
For thou, Oh Lord, art holy, wise, and just,
And raising man from forth the common dust
Hast set thy sacred image on his soul,
And shall the pot the potter's hand control?
Poor boasting feeble clay, that error shun;
Submit and let th'Almighty's will be done.

In Earth as it is in Heaven.

For there the angels and the saints rejoice,
Resigning all to the blest heavenly voice;
Behold the Seraphim his will obey,
Wilt thou less humble be, fond man, than they?
Behold the Cherubim and Pow'rs divine,
And all the heavenly host in homage join;
Shall their submission yield, and shall not thine?
Nay, shall even God submit to flesh and blood?
For our redemption, our eternal good,
Shall he submit to stripes, nay even to die
A death reproachful and of infamy?
Shall God himself submit, and shall not I?
Vain, stubborn fool, draw not thy ruin on,
But as in Heaven, on earth God's will be done.

Give us this day our daily Bread,

For oh my God! As boasting as we are,
We cannot live without thy heavenly care;
With all our pride, not one poor morsel's gained,
Till by thy wondrous bounty first obtained;
With all our flattered wit, our fancied sense,
We have not to one mercy a pretence
Without the aid of thy omnipotence.
Oh God, so fit my soul that I may prove
A pitied object of thy grace and love;
May my soul be with heavenly manna fed,
And deign my grosser part thy daily bread.

And forgive us our Trespasses

How prone we are to sin, how sweet were made
The pleasures our resistless hearts invade!
Of all my crimes, the breach of all thy laws,
Love, soft bewitching love, has been the cause!
Of all the paths that vanity has trod,
That sure will soonest be forgiven of God;
If things on earth may be to Heaven resembled,
It must be love, pure, constant, undissembled:
But if to sin by chance the charmer press,
Forgive, O Lord, forgive our trespasses.

As we forgive them that Trespass against us.

Oh that this grateful, little charity,
Forgiving others all their sins to me,
May with my God for mine atoning be.
I've sought around and found no foe in view,
Whom with the least revenge I would pursue:
My God, my God, dispense thy mercies too.

Lead us not into Temptation

Thou but permits it, Lord, 'tis we go on
And give our selves the provocation;
'Tis we, that prone to pleasures which invite,
Seek all the arts to heighten vain delight;
But if without some sin we cannot move,
May mine proceed no higher than to love;
And may thy vengeance be the less severe,
Since thou hast made the object loved so fair.

But deliver us from Evil.

From all the hasty fury passion breeds
And into deaf and blinded error leads,
From words that bear damnation in the sound,
And do the soul as well as honour wound,
That by degrees of madness lead us on
To indiscretion, shame, confusion;
From fondness, lying, and hypocrisy,
From my neglect of what I owe to thee;
From scandal, and from pride, divert my thought,
And from my neighbour grant I covet nought;

From black ingratitude and treason, Lord,
Guard me, even in the least irreverent word.
In my opinion, grant, O Lord, I may
Be guided in the true and rightful way,
And he that guides me may not go astray.
Do thou, oh Lord, instruct me how to know
Not whither, but which way I am to go;
For how should I an unknown passage find,
When my instructing guide himself is blind.
All honour, glory, and all praise be given
To kings on earth, and to our God in Heaven.

           _____ *Amen.*

MARY CHUDLEIGH (*née* Lee)
1656–1710

Lady Mary Chudleigh was a successful poet and essayist. In 1674 she married
George Chudleigh who succeeded to a baronetcy in 1691. They had two sons,
and a daughter who died young. Mary was born in Devon, where she seems to
have lived a solitary and often unhappy life. She published *The Ladies Defence*
in 1701 as a reply to a marriage sermon by the Nonconformist, John Sprint,
which advocated extreme subordination of wives to their husbands. The poet,
Elizabeth Thomas, admired it and became a correspondent. A volume, *Poems
on Several Occasions*, was published in 1703 (with later editions in 1709, 1713,
1722, and 1750). A collection of her moral essays was published in 1710. Her
unpublished plays and translations survive in manuscripts at the Houghton
Library, Harvard, and the Huntington Library, San Marino, California.

from The Ladies' Defence: or a Dialogue between Sir John Brute, Sir William Loveall, Melissa and a Parson

MELISSA:
    Must men command, and we alone obey,
    As if designed for arbitrary sway:
    Born petty monarchs, and, like Homer's gods,
    See all subjected to their haughty nods?
    Narcissus-like, you your own graces view,
    Think none deserve to be admired but you:
    Your own perfections always you adore,   70
    And think all others despicably poor.
    We have our faults, but you are all Divine;
    Wisdom does in your meanest actions shine:
    Just, pious, chaste, from every passion free,

By learning raised above humanity.
For every failure you a covering find:
Rage is a noble bravery of mind
Revenge, a tribute due to injured fame;
And pride, but what transcendent worth does claim.
Cowards are wary, and the dull are grave,   80
Fops are genteel, and hectoring bullies brave:
Such as live high, regardless of expense,
Are generous men, and ever blessed with sense.
Base avarice, frugality you call,
And he's a prudent man who grasps at all:
Who to be rich, does labour, cheat and lie;
Does to himself the sweets of life deny,
And wretched lives that he may wealthy die.
Thus to each vice you give some specious name,
And with bright colours varnish o'er your shame.   90
But unto us is there no deference due?
Must we pay all, and look for none from you?
Why are not husbands taught as well as we;
Must they from all restraints, all laws be free?
Passive obedience you've to us transferred,
And we must drudge in paths where you have erred:
That antiquated doctrine you disown;
'Tis now your scorn, and fit for us alone...   98
[...]

PARSON:
Why all this rage? We merit not your hate;
'Tis you alone disturb the marriage state.
If to your lords you strict allegiance paid,
And their commands submissively obeyed;   180
If like wise Eastern slaves with trembling awe
You watched their looks, and made their will your law,
You would both kindness and protection gain,
And find your duteous care was not in vain.
This, I advised, this, I your sex have taught;
And ought instruction to be called a fault?
Your duty was, I knew, the harder part;
Obedience being a harsh, uneasy art:
The skill to govern, men with ease can learn;
We're soon instructed in our own concern.   190
But you need all the aid that I can give,
To make you unrepining vassals live.

100

Heaven, you must own, to you has been less kind.
You cannot boast our steadiness of mind,
Nor is your knowledge half so unconfined;
We can beyond the bounds of nature see,
And dare to fathom vast Infinity...   197
[...]

But you, not blest with Phoebus' influence,   210
Wither in shades; with nauseous dullness cursed,
Born fools, and by resembling idiots nursed.
Then taught to work, to dance, to sing and play,
And vainly trifle all your hours away,
Proud that you've learnt the little Arts to please,
As being incapable of more than these.
Your shallow minds can nothing else contain,
You were not made for labours of the brain;
Those are the manly toils which we sustain.
We, like the Ancient Giants, stand on high,   220
And seem to bid defiance to the sky,
While you poor worthless insects crawl below,
And less than mites to our exalted reason show.
Yet by compassion for your frailties moved,
I've strove to make you fit to be beloved...   225
[...]

MELISSA:
I've still revered your order as divine;
And when I feel unblemished virtue shine,
When solid learning, and substantial sense,   490
Are joined with unaffected eloquence;
When lives and doctrines of a piece are made,
And holy truths with humble zeal conveyed;
When free from passion, bigotry and pride,
Not swayed by interest, nor to parties tied,
Contemning riches, and abhorring strife,
And shunning all the noisy pomps of life,
You live the awful wonders of your time,
Without the least suspicion of a crime:
I shall with joy the highest deference pay,   500
And heedfully attend to all you say.
From such, reproofs shall always welcome prove,
As being th'effects of piety and love.
But those from me can challenge no respect,
Who on us all without just cause reflect:

101

Who, without mercy, all the sex decry,
And into open defamations fly:
Who think us creatures for derision made,
And the creator with his works upbraid:
What he called Good, they proudly think not so,   510
And with their malice, their profaneness show...

[...]

Those generous few, whom kinder thoughts inspire,
And who the happiness of all desire;
Who wish we were from barbarous usage free,   540
Exempt from toils, and shameful slavery,
Yet let us unreproved, mispend our hours,
And to mean purposes employ our nobler pow'rs.
They think if we our thoughts can but express,
And know but how to work, to dance and dress,
It is enough, as much as we should mind,
As if we were for nothing else designed,
But made, like puppets, to divert mankind.
O that my sex would all such toys despise,
And only study to be good and wise: 550
Inspect themselves, and every blemish find,
Search all the close recesses of the mind,
And leave no vice, no ruling passion there,
Nothing to raise a blush, or cause a fear:
Their memories with solid notions fill,
And let their reason dictate to their will.
Instead of novels, histories peruse,
And for their guides the wiser Ancients choose,
Thro' all the labyrinths of learning go,
And grow more humble, as they more do know.   560
By doing this, they will respect procure,
Silence the men, and lasting fame secure;
And to themselves the best companions prove,
And neither fear their malice, nor desire their love.

66 *Homer's gods:* the classical Greek gods, featured in Homer's *Iliad* and *Odyssey*. Homer himself was venerated as a god by some. 68 *Narcissus-like:* Narcissus fell in love with his own reflection; 71 The colon of the 1701 ed. is replaced by a full-stop here, and also at ll.79, 83, 178, 216. 76 *covering:* concealment. 91 *us:* women. 180 *obeyed;:* this ed. obeyed, 1701 ed. 192 *unrepining...live:* live as uncomplaining, humble dependants; 193 *kind.:* this ed. kind, 1701 ed. 210 *Phoebus:* Apollo, god of the fine arts, medicine, music, poetry and eloquence; his name means shining, bright. 214 *away,:* this ed. away: 1701 ed. 496 *contemning:* despising. 498 *awful:* aweful; commanding great respect. 542 *unreproved:* unrebuked. 549 *despise,:* this ed. despise; 1701 ed.

ANNE WHARTON (*née* Lee)
1659–85

An orphan when she was eleven days old, Anne was brought up by her grandmother, Anne Wilmot, the mother of John Wilmot, Earl of Rochester. Born in Ditchley, Oxfordshire, she had a sister, Ellinora, and appears to have been devoted to her uncle, Rochester, who was twelve years older than herself. She was married to Thomas Wharton when she was 14, having possibly spent some years at court, where her grandmother served the Duchess of York. Her husband had a mistress and a reputation as a rake with expensive hobbies: politics and horses. They had no children. Although the co-heir to her late uncle's fortune (Henry Danvers, Earl of Danby), the inheritance was small when Anne finally received it. Her grandmother fought costly legal battles on her wards' behalf. Anne learned French and Italian and Rochester seems to have encouraged her poetic skills. In poor health since 1672, she may have died as a consequence of syphilis: critics are divided as to whether this could have been contracted before or after her marriage. Anne wrote a verse tragedy, *Love's Martyr*, which exists in manuscript, a translation of Ovid's *Epistles* (more a combination of imaginative paraphrasing and her own innovations than a translation), and 17 poems. Her poetry was published posthumously in different collections and highly praised. These poems are taken from *The Temple of Death, a Poem; written by the Marquess of Normanby...to the which is added several poems of the honourable Madam Wharton* (2nd ed. 1695), and *Penelope to Ulysses* by the Honourable Mrs Wharton *in Ovid's Epistles*, trans. by several hands (8th ed. 1712), respectively.

To Mrs A. Behn,
On what she Writ of The Earl of Rochester

In pleasing transport rapt, my thoughts aspire
With humble verse to praise what you admire:
Few living poets may the laurel claim;
Most pass thro' death, to reach at living fame.
Fame, phoenix like, still rises from a tomb,
But bravely you this custom have o'ercome.
You force an homage from each generous heart,
Such as you always pay to just desert.
You praised him living, whom you dead bemoan,
And now your tears afresh his laurel crown.   10
It is this flight of yours excites my art,
Weak as it is, to take your Muse's part,
And pay loud thanks back from my bleeding heart.
May you in every pleasing grace excel;
May bright Apollo in your bosom dwell;
May yours excel the matchless Sappho's name;
May you have all her wit, without her shame:

Tho' she to honour gave a fatal wound,
Employ your hand to raise it from the ground.
Right its wronged cause with your enticing strain,   20
Its ruined temples try to build again.
Scorn meaner themes, declining low desire,
And bid your Muse maintain a vestal fire.
If you do this, what glory will ensue
To all our sex, to poesy, and you?
Write on, and may your numbers ever flow,
Soft as the wishes that I make for you.

Title *On...Rochester:* a response to Aphra Behn's elegy on the poet John Wilmot, second
Earl of Rochester. Behn wrote a reply to Anne Wharton in verse (see *EMWP*, 378-80).
15 *Apollo:* god of poetry and eloquence, among other things. 16 *Sappho:* the Greek
lyric poet, born in Lesbos, mid-7th century B.C. 17 *shame:* perhaps an allusion to the
unsubstantiated story of Sappho's suicide because of unrequited love for Phaon, or a
reference to her love for her own sex, though this seems not to have been widely pub-
licised despite works like Donne's 'Sapho to Philaenis'. Behn linked herself with Sappho
in her work, 'Of Trees'. 23 *vestal fire:* sacred fire, perpetually burning (in praise of chastity).
26 *numbers:* metrical feet of verses.

from Penelope to Ulysses

Where art thou, my Ulysses, tell me where?
Where dost thou hide thyself t'increase my fear?
None of thy victories to me return,
Apollo's city vanquished, yet I mourn:
Ah! Would it stood, that scene of pomp and pride,
Then I should know where all my hopes reside:
But now, alas! I know not where thou art,   110
My vows are turned and help to break my heart.
What may be, tho' 'tis not, augments my care,
I know not where to limit now my fear;
My sorrows wander in so large a field,
I fear all dangers sea and earth can yield.
Forgive me, dear Ulysses, if sometimes
My eager love dares tax thy heart of crimes.
I sometime think some crafty stranger may
Have made thy absent wand'ring heart a prey;
Where to make sure the vows to her are sworn,   120
Penelope each day is made a scorn.
Thou tell'st her the weak distaff is my care,
I know no art the conqu'ror to ensnare,
The homely duties of a wife I prove,
But never knew to fix a wand'ring love.

When thus I think, I'm filled with deep despairs,
Then straight I rave, and chide away those fears;
I think thou'rt true, and were it in thy pow'r
Ulysses were Penelope's this hour.
My father adds to my insulting fate, 130
Bidding me quit those robes and widowed state;
And laughs to hear me feign some weak excuse,
Rather than all my vows and hopes abuse:
But let him laugh, I'm thine and only thine,
Tho' much I fear Ulysses is not mine;
My fixed resolves at length have conquered him,
He thinks I may be true without a crime.
Slaves I have many who affect to move,
But vainly tempt my fixed and constant love;
Vain, youthful, gay, endued with all those arts 140
Which captive and secure less faithful hearts;
They lord it here o'er all, now thou'rt away,
Thy wealth is theirs, who bless thy kind delay;
All but thy wife to them is made a prey.
Why should I reckon up each hated name,
Hateful to me, and cruel to thy fame?
Pylander, Polypus and Medon here
Are fierce thro' pow'r, I feeble thro' despair.
Why should I name the sly Eurymachus,
The cursed and covetous Altinous? 150
Ulysses, these and more to thy disgrace
Live on thy riches, while thy herds decrease;
The mean Melanthus and poor Irus too
Are ever in the way t'assist the crew,
Whose careless riots all my hopes undo:
Alone upon thy succour we depend,
We are but three, and weakly we defend;
I am a woman, and Laertes old,
Telemachus too young, the foe too bold;
Telemachus nigh lost the other day, 160
For he to Pylos had prepared his way
Against my will, who ne'er could have designed
Parting with th'only pledge you left behind.
O may he live, that when I'm freed by death,
Ulysses' soul may in his bosom breath.
The little family you left behind
Thus pray for him, whom all the gods designed,
Heir to thy wealth and to thy richer mind.

Laertes, 'mongst his foes, is old and weak,
His pow'r decays, in vain his help I seek.   170
Your son may live, the foe may grow less strong,
As yet they're pow'rful and their hopes are young.
Return, my wand'ring Lord, the only scope
Of all our prayers, the end of all our hope;
Return and teach your son, like you, to know
The arts to govern and subdue a foe;
Instruct his tender years for learning fit,
His blood is thine, and thine may be his wit;
Return, and bless Laertes, e're he dies,
With thy dear sight, then close his willing eyes;   180
Return, and bless thy wife, whose youth decays
With shedding tears at thy unkind delays;
Return, Life of our Hopes, Light of our Days.

Title *Penelope* was the loyal wife of Odysseus or Ulysses, King of Ithaca, and mother of Telemachus. Odysseus's long journey home, after fighting in the Trojan War, is the subject of Homer's *Odyssey* and *Penelope to Ulysses* is the first of Ovid's *Heroides*. This extract follows Penelope's expression of her fear that Ulysses is 'false' and has 'all his Vows forsworn' (Ovid's heroine never criticises her husband, nor accuses him of infidelity). 107 *Apollo's city:* Troy. 122 *distaff:* cleft stick for spinning wool or flax. 158 *Laertes:* Odysseus's father.

ANNE KILLIGREW

1660–85

Anne Killigrew was praised by Dryden as being 'Excellent in the two Sister-Arts of Poesie and Painting'. Her uncles, Thomas and William, and her cousin, Thomas, were all dramatists. Her father, Dr Henry Killigrew, was a Royalist and a theologian. Anne was Maid of Honour to Mary of Modena, Duchess of York. She was born and lived in London – where she died from smallpox at the age of 25. Her father published *Poems by Mrs Anne Killigrew* (1685), which includes the following works. Her portrait of James II is in Windsor Castle; two other surviving paintings are privately owned.

On Death

Tell me thou safest end of all our woe,
Why wretched mortals do avoid thee so:
Thou gentle drier o' th' afflicted's tears,
Thou noble ender of the coward's fears;
Thou sweet repose to lovers' sad despair,
Thou calm t' ambition's rough tempestuous care.
If in regard of bliss thou wert a curse,

And then the joys of Paradise art worse;
Yet after man from his first station fell,
And God from Eden Adam did expel, 10
Thou wert no more an evil, but relief;
The balm and cure to ev'ry human grief:
Through thee (what man had forfeited before)
He now enjoys, and ne'er can lose it more.
No subtle serpents in the grave betray,
Worms on the body there, not soul do prey;
No vice there tempts, no terrors there affright,
No coz'ning sin affords a false delight:
No vain contentions do that peace annoy,
No fierce alarms break the lasting joy. 20

Ah, since from thee so many blessings flow,
Such real good as life can never know;
Come when thou wilt, in thy affrighting'st dress,
Thy shape shall never make thy welcome less.
Thou may'st to joy, but ne'er to fear give birth,
Thou best, as well as certain'st thing on earth.
Fly thee? May travellers then fly their rest,
And hungry infants fly the proffered breast.
No, those that faint and tremble at thy name,
Fly from their good on a mistaken fame. 30
Thus childish fear did Israel of old
From plenty and the Promised Land with-hold;
They fancied giants, and refused to go
When Canaan did with milk and honey flow.

18 *coz'ning:* beguiling. 33 *fancied:* conjured up, imagined. 34 *Canaan...flow:* see Exodus 13:5

St John Baptist, Painted by herself in the Wilderness, with Angels appearing to him, and with a Lamb by him

The sun's my fire, when it does shine,
The hollow spring's my cave of wine,
The rocks and woods afford me meat;
This lamb and I on one dish eat:
The neighbouring herds my garments send,
My pallet the kind earth doth lend:
Excess and grandeur I decline,
M'associates only are divine.

Title: *see* Matthew 3:1-4. 6 *pallet:* bed, mattress.

Herodias' Daughter presenting to her Mother St John's Head in a Charger, also Painted by herself

Behold, dear Mother, who was late our fear,
Disarmed and harmless, I present you here;
The tongue tied up, that made all Jewry quake,
And which so often did our greatness shake;
No terror sits upon his awful brow,
Where fierceness reigned, there calmness triumphs now;
As lovers use, he gazes on my face
With eyes that languish, as they sued for grace;
Wholly subdued by my victorious charms,
See how his head reposes in my arms.
Come, join then with me in my just transport,
Who thus have brought the hermit to the court.

Title: *Herodias' Daughter:* Salome, daughter of Herodias and Herod Antipas's brother. Instructed by her mother, she asked her stepfather, Herod, for the head of John the Baptist in a charger as a reward for dancing before him. See Matthew 14: 1-11; *charger:* large flat dish. 3 *Jewry:* the Jewish people. 7 *use:* are accustomed to. 11 *transport:* carrying of the head; indulgence in ecstatic emotion

On my Aunt Mrs A.K.
Drowned under London Bridge in the Queen's Barge, Anno 1641

The darling of a father good and wise,
The virtue, which a virtuous age did prize;
The beauty, excellent even to those were fair,
Subscribed unto, by such as might compare;
The star that 'bove her orb did always move,
And yet the noblest did not hate, but love;
And those who most upon their title stood,
To whom the wronged and worthy did resort,
And held their suits obtained, if only brought;
The highest saint in all the heaven of Court.   10
So noble was her air, so great her mien,
She seemed a friend, not servant to the Queen.
To sin, if known, she never did give way,
Vice could not storm her, could it not betray.
    When angry heaven extinguished her fair light,
It seemed to say, 'Nought's precious in my sight;
As I in waves this paragon have drowned,
The nation next, and King I will confound'.

Title *Queen:* Charles I's queen, Henrietta Maria; *1641:* in the first stages of the Civil War. 9 *suits:* petitions, requests.

ANNE FINCH (*née* Kingsmill),
Countess of Winchilsea
1661–1720

Anne was born at Sydmonton, Hampshire. Her father, Sir William Kingsmill, died when she was five months old: a book of his poetry survives in Lichfield Cathedral Library. In his will he directed that his daughter be educated and Anne read French and Italian as well as English literature. From 1664 to 1671, Anne and her sister, Bridget, were brought up by their grandmother in London: their brother lived with his uncle. In 1671 the sisters joined him at Maidwell in Northamptonshire. At 21, Anne was Maid of Honour to Mary of Modena. (Anne Killigrew belonged to the same court circle.) In 1684 she married Heneage Finch, second son of the second Earl of Winchilsea, and left her post. They had no children. When William and Mary came to the throne in 1688 the couple refused to swear an oath of allegiance to them. Anne's husband (who had been Gentleman of the Bedchamber to James II) was arrested attempting to join James in France and remained in prison for a year. On his release they settled with his nephew, Charles, Earl of Winchilsea, at Eastwell in Kent. Anne began writing poetry in the 1680s and it was published from 1701. Her husband supported her and helped to edit her work from 1690. Her most famous poem, *The Spleen*, a meditation on melancholy, was first printed anonymously, but later her authorship was known and poems appeared in a number of miscellanies. Swift addressed a poem to her in 1709: she also met and corresponded with Alexander Pope. Eventually she was made Lady of the Bedchamber to Queen Anne and in 1712 became Lady Winchilsea on the death of her husband's nephew. These poems come from *Miscellany Poems on Several Occasions, Written by a Lady* [later named as Lady Winchilsea] (1713). She also wrote religious verse in her latter years. Many poems were left unpublished after her death but her reputation revived when Wordsworth praised 'A Nocturnal Rêverie' in 1815 and included her work in an anthology he produced in 1819.

A Nocturnal Rêverie

In such a night, when every louder wind
Is to its distant cavern safe confined;
And only gentle Zephyr fans his wings,
And lonely Philomel, still waking, sings;
Or from some tree, famed for the owl's delight,
She, hollowing clear, directs the wand'rer right:
In such a night, when passing clouds give place,
Or thinly veil the heaven's mysterious face;
When in some river, overhung with green,
The waving moon and trembling leaves are seen;   10
When freshened grass now bears itself upright,
And makes cool banks to pleasing rest invite,
Whence springs the woodbind, and the bramble-rose,

And where the sleepy cowslip sheltered grows;
Whilst now a paler hue the foxglove takes,
Yet chequers still with red the dusky brakes:
When scattered glow-worms, but in twilight fine
Show, trivial beauties watch their hour to shine;
Whilst Salisb'ry stands the test of every light,
In perfect charms and perfect virtue bright: 20
When odours, which declined repelling day,
Thro' temp'rate air uninterrupted stray;
When darkened groves their softest shadows wear,
And falling waters we distinctly hear;
When thro' the gloom more venerable shows
Some ancient fabric, awful in repose,
While sunburnt hills their swarthy looks conceal,
And swelling haycocks thicken up the vale:
When the loosed horse now, as his pasture leads,
Comes slowly grazing thro' th' adjoining meads,   30
Whose stealing pace and lengthened shade we fear,
Till torn-up forage in his teeth we hear:
When nibbling sheep at large pursue their food,
And unmolested kine rechew the cud;
When curlews cry beneath the village-walls,
And to her straggling brood the partridge calls;
Their short-lived jubilee the creatures keep,
Which but endures whilst tyrant-man does sleep:
When a sedate content the spirit feels,
And no fierce light disturbs, whilst it reveals;   40
But silent musings urge the mind to seek
Something, too high for syllables to speak;
Till the free soul to a composedness charmed,
Finding the elements of rage disarmed,
O'er all below a solemn quiet grown,
Joys in th' inferior world, and thinks it like her own:
In such a night let me abroad remain,
Till morning breaks, and all's confused again;
Our cares, our toils, our clamours are renewed,
Or pleasures, seldom reached, again pursued.   50

1 *In…night:* see Shakespeare's *The Merchant of Venice* V.i. 1-2 *every…confined:* Aeolus
ruled the winds by imprisoning them in a cave and releasing them at will (Virgil, *Aeneid* I).
3 *Zephyr:* the west wind. 4 *Philomel:* the nightingale. 13 *woodbind:* climbing plants, esp-
ecially honeysuckle; *bramble-rose:* the sweet-scented white or pink dog-rose; 16 *brakes:*
thickets; 18 *Show,…beauties:* Shew…Beauties 1713 ed. 19 *Salisb'ry:* Anne Tufton, Count-
ess of Salisbury, a close friend of Finch. 34 *kine:* cattle. 37 *jubilee:* time of rejoicing, of
exuberant joy.

To the Nightingale

Exert thy voice, sweet harbinger of spring!
    This moment is thy time to sing,
    This moment I attend to praise,
And set my numbers to thy lays.
    Free as thine shall be my song,
    As thy music, short, or long.
Poets, wild as thee, were born,
    Pleasing best when unconfined,
    When to please is least designed,
Soothing but their cares to rest;   10
    Cares do still their thoughts molest,
    And still th'unhappy poet's breast,
Like thine, when best he sings, is placed against a thorn.

She begins, let all be still!
    Muse, thy promise now fulfil!
Sweet, oh! sweet, still sweeter yet
Can thy words such accents fit,
Canst thou syllables refine,
Melt a sense that shall retain
Still some spirit of the brain,   20
Till with sounds like these it join?
    'Twill not be! Then change thy note;
    Let division shake thy throat.
Hark! Division now she tries;
Yet as far the Muse outflies.
    Cease then, prithee, cease thy tune;
    Trifler, wilt thou sing till June?
Till thy bus'ness all lies waste,
And the time of building's past!
    Thus we poets that have speech,   30
Unlike what thy forests teach,
    If a fluent vein be shown
    That's transcendent to our own,
Criticise, reform, or preach,
Or censure what we cannot reach.

4 *lays:* songs. 23 *division:* a rapid melodic passage.

A Song

Love, thou art best of human joys,
Our chiefest happiness below;
All other pleasures are but toys,
Music without thee is but noise,
And beauty but an empty show.

Heaven, who knew best what man would move,
And raise his thoughts above the brute,
Said, 'Let him be, and let him love;
That must alone his soul improve,
Howe'er philosophers dispute.'

La Passion Vaincue

Done into English with Liberty

On the banks of the Severn, a desperate maid
(Whom some shepherd, neglecting his vows, had betrayed),
Stood resolving to banish all sense of the pain,
And pursue, thro' her death, a revenge on the swain.
'Since the gods and my passion at once he defies;
Since his vanity lives, while my character dies;
No more', did she say, 'will I trifle with fate,
But commit to the waves both my love and my hate.'
And now to comply with that furious desire,
Just ready to plunge, and alone to expire,
Some reflections on death and its terrors untried,
Some scorn for the shepherd, some flashings of pride
At length pulled her back, and she cried, 'Why this strife,
Since the swains are so many, and I've but *one* life?'

Title *Passion...:* Conquered passion. 1 *Severn:* the River Severn that flows through
Gloucestershire.

SARAH EGERTON (*née* Fyge, *later* Field)
1670–1723

Having published *The Female Advocate* (1686), a response to Robert Gould's
...Satyr Against the Pride, Lust and Inconstancy etc. of Woman, Sarah's father
took her from her birth-place, London, to live with relatives in the country.

She was married to an attorney, Edward Field, apparently against her will. He died after a few years, and she then married the Reverend Thomas Egerton, a widower and her second cousin. Her affections lay, however, with Henry Pierce, an attorney's clerk. She, unsuccessfully, sought a divorce on grounds of cruelty in 1704 and her husband sued to gain her previous husband's estate. Rev. Egerton died in 1720. She published *Poems on Several Occasions together with a Pastoral by Mrs S.F.* in 1703.

A Song

How pleasant is love
When forbid or unknown;
Was my passion approved,
It would quickly be gone.

It adds to the charms
When we steal the delight;
Why should love be exposed
Since himself has no sight?

In some sylvan shade
Let me sigh for my swain,
Where none but an echo
Will speak on't again.

Thus silent and soft
I'll pass the time on,
And when I grow weary
I'll make my love known.

To Philaster

Go perjured youth and court what nymph you please,
Your passion now is but a dull disease,
With worn-out sighs deceive some list'ning ear,
Who longs to know how 'tis and what men swear,
She'll think they're new from you, 'cause so to her.
Poor cozened fool, she ne'er can know the charms
Of being first encircled in thy arms,
When all love's joys were innocent and gay,
As fresh and blooming as the newborn day.
Your charms did then with native sweetness flow,   10
The forced-kind complaisance you now bestow,

Is but a false agreeable design,
But you had innocence when you were mine,
And all your words, and smiles, and looks divine.
How proud, methinks, thy mistress does appear
In sullied clothes, which I'd no longer wear;
Her bosom, too, with withered flowers dressed,
Which lost their sweets in my first-chosen breast.
Perjured imposing youth, cheat who you will,
Supply defect of truth with amorous skill;   20
Yet thy address must needs insipid be,
For the first ardour of thy soul was all possessed by me.

7 *arms,:* this ed. arms. 1703 ed. 18 *breast.:* this ed. breast; 1703 ed.

The Emulation

Say tyrant Custom, why must we obey,
The impositions of thy haughty sway?
From the first dawn of life, unto the grave,
Poor womankind's in every state a slave,
The nurse, the mistress, parent and the swain,
For love she must, there's none escape that pain;
Then comes the last, the fatal slavery,
The husband with insulting tyranny
Can have ill manners justified by law;
For men all join to keep the wife in awe.   10
Moses, who first our freedom did rebuke,
Was married when he writ the Pentateuch.
They're wise to keep us slaves, for well they know,
If we were loose, we soon should make them so.
We yield like vanquished kings whom fetters bind,
When chance of war is to usurpers kind:
Submit in form; but they'd our thoughts control,
And lay restraints on the impassive soul:
They fear we should excel their sluggish parts,
Should we attempt the Sciences and Arts;   20
Pretend they were designed for them alone,
So keep us fools to raise their own renown;
Thus priests of old, their grandeur to maintain,
Cried vulgar eyes would sacred laws profane;
So kept the mysteries behind a screen:
Their homage and the name were lost had they been seen:

114

But in this blessed Age, such freedom's given,
That every man explains the will of heaven;
And shall we women now sit tamely by,
Make no excursions in philosophy,   30
Or grace our thoughts in tuneful poetry?
We will our rights in learning's world maintain,
Wit's empire, now, shall know a female reign;
Come all ye fair, the great attempt improve,
Divinely imitate the realms above:
There's ten celestial females govern wit,
And but two gods that dare pretend to it;
And shall these finite males reverse their rules?
No, we'll be wits, and then men must be fools.

2 *sway?:* this ed. sway; 1703 ed. 4 *slave,:* this ed. slave. 1703 ed.; 5 *swain:* lover (here, unusually female). 11 *Moses,:* this ed. Moses 1703 ed. 12 *Pentateuch.:* this ed. Pentateuch; 1703 ed. the first five books of the Old Testament, traditionally ascribed to Moses, who first wrote down the Ten Commandments on tablets of stone. 14 *make...so:* i.e. slaves; *them so:* this ed. them, so 1703 ed. 23 *old,:* this ed. old 1703 ed. 36 *ten...wit:* perhaps Minerva, goddess of wisdom, and the Nine Muses, or the Muses and their mother, Mnemosyne, the personification of memory. 37 *two gods:* Apollo and Mercury. 38 *rules?:* this ed. rules, 1703 ed.

ELIZABETH ROWE (*née* Singer)
1674–1737

Born in Ilchester, Somerset, Elizabeth Rowe, poet and prose writer, lived most of her life in Frome. Her father, Walter, was a dissenting minister who became a prosperous clothier. Elizabeth wrote verse from the age of twelve and, by the time she was 20, was benefiting educationally from her acquaintance with the Thynne family of Longleat. Henry Thynne, son of Viscount Weymouth, taught her French and Italian. Later, she translated the poems of Tasso. She married the scholar, Thomas Rowe (13 years her junior) in 1710, and moved to London. It seems to have been a happy marriage, but Thomas died of consumption in Hampstead in 1715. Elizabeth returned to Frome and eventually inherited property that would have comfortably supported her had she not given half of the income to charity. From 1691 she published her poems anonymously in Athenian Society journals. The editor, John Dunton, published her first book, *Poems on Several Occasions. Written by Philomela* (from which the first two poems are taken) in 1696. After her husband's death she led a life of relative seclusion, and published prose: *Friendship in Death, in Letters from the Dead to the Living* (1728), and *Letters Moral and Entertaining* (1729-32). A Poem in eight books, a *History of Joseph*, was published in 1736. She was buried, with her father, in the meeting-house at Frome. The latter verse appears in some letters and manuscripts which were published posthumously as *Devout Exercises of the Heart* (1737).

To Celinda

I

I can't, Celinda, say, I love,
But rather I adore,
When with transported eyes I view
Your shining merits o'er.

II

A fame so spotless and serene,
A virtue so refined;
And thoughts as great as ere was yet
Grasped by a female mind.

III

There love and honour dressed, in all,
Their genuine charms appear,
And with a pleasing force at once
They conquer and endear.

IV

Celestial flames are scarce more bright
Than those your worth inspires,
So angels love and so they burn
In just such holy fires.

V

Then let's, my dear Celinda, thus
Blest in ourselves contemn
The treacherous and deluding arts
Of those base things called men.

The Reflection

Where glide my thoughts – rash inclinations stay,
And let me think what 'tis you fool away,
Stay ere it be too late, yet stay and take,
A short review of the great Prize at stake.
Oh! stupid folly 'tis eternal Joy,
That I'm about to barter for a toy;

It is my God, O! dreadful hazard, where
Shall I again the boundless loss repair!
It is my Soul, a Soul that cost the blood,
And painful ag'nies of an humbled God.   10
O! blest occasion made me stay to think,
Ere I was hurried off the dang'rous brink,
Should I have took the charming venom in,
And struggled with all these terrors for a sin,
How equal had my condemnation been?

10 *ag'nies:* agonies. 12 *dang'rous:* dangerous. 14 *struggled:* this ed strug'led 1737 ed. coped
1696 ed.

A Thank-Offering for Saving Grace

Mysterious depths of boundless love
My admiration raise:
O God, thy name exalted stands
Above my highest praise.

ELIZABETH THOMAS
1675–1731

Elizabeth struggled against poverty all her life. Her father died when she was
two and his young widow and daughter moved to London. A self-educated
poet and satirist, she never married, although she was engaged to Richard
Gwinnet, a lawyer and amateur author, for 17 years. They waited until he
could support her, but in the meantime Gwinnet became ill. He proposed in
1716 and the marriage was delayed because Elizabeth was nursing her termi-
nally ill mother. Gwinnet died in 1717 and her mother in 1719. In 1699 she
sent two poems to Dryden, who encouraged her and recommended that she
adopt the pen-name, Corinna. She corresponded with several literary figures,
including Lady Mary Chudleigh. In 1722 her volume, *Miscellany Poems,* was
published, from which the following poems are taken. Financial hardship caused
her to sell letters in her possession to Edmund Curll – her own from Dryden
and others, and some from Alexander Pope to her friend Henry Cromwell,
which Cromwell had given her. Curll published these and Pope wrote dis-
paragingly about her in *The Dunciad.* In 1727 Elizabeth was in the Fleet prison
as a result of her debts. The Bishop of Durham acted on her behalf and appealed
for charity for her. In 1730, too poor to leave prison, she published *The Meta-
morphosis of the Town: Or, A View of the Present Fashions.* When she died,
destitute, in her Fleet Street lodgings, in February 1731, she was writing an
autobiography which Curll later published.

The True Effigies of a Certain Squire:
Inscribed to Clemena

Some gen'rous painter now assist my pen,
And help to draw the most despised of men:
Or else, oh Muse, do thou that charge supply,
Thou that art injured too as well as I;
Revenge thyself, with satire arm thy quill;
Display the man, yet own a justice still.

First, paint a large, two-handed, surly clown,
In silver waistcoat, stockings sliding down,
Shoes (let me see) a foot and half in length,
And stoutly armed with sparables for strength.   10
Ascend! and let a silver string appear,
Which seems to cry, 'A golden watch is here:
O'er all a doily stuff, to which belongs
One pocket charged with citron peel and songs:
T'other contains, more necessary far,
A snuffbox, comb, a glass, and handkercher,
Three parts of which hangs dangling by his side,
The fourth is wisely to a button tied:
Just as it was in former days a rule
To tie young children's muckenders at school.   20
Forget not, Muse, gold buttons at the wrist;
Nor Mechlin lace, to shade the clumsy fist:
Two diamond rings thy pencil next must show,
Always in sight like Prim's, the formal beau,
But if rude company their notice spare,
Then draw that hand elated to his ear;
And at one view let diamond ring and golden bob appear.
A steenkirk next, of paltry needle stuff,
Which cost eleven guineas (cheap enough).
Next draw the giant wig of shape profuse,   30
Larger than Foppington's or Overdo's.
The greasy front pressed down with essence lies,
The spreading elf-locks, cover half his eyes;
But when he coughs, or bows, what clouds of powder rise!

Enough, O Muse, thou hast described him right!
Th'emetic's strong, I sicken at the sight:
A fop is nauseating howe'er he's dressed,
But this too fulsome is to be expressed.

Such hideous medley would thy work debase,
Where rake and clown, where ape and knave appear with open face. 40

Yet stay, proceed and paint his awkward bow,
And if thou hast forgot, I'll tell thee how;
Set one leg forward, draw his other back;
Nor let the lump, a booby wallow lack:
His head bend downward, with obsequious quake;
Then quickly raise it, with a spaniel shake.
His honours thus performed, a speech begin
May show th'obliging principles within:
Thy mem'ry to his sense I now confine,
His be the substance, but th'expression thine. 50

'Madam,' cries he, 'Lord, how my soul is moved
To see such silly toys by you approved!
A closet stuffed with books, pray what's your crime,
To superannuate before your time;
And make yourself look old, and ugly in your prime?
Our modern pedants contradict the schools,
For learned ladies are but learned fools.
With ev'ry blockhead's whim ye load your brains,
And for a shadow take a world of pains.
What is't to you what numbers Caesar slew? 60
Or who at Marathon beat the de'il knows who?
Defend me, Fortune, from the wife I hate,
And let not bookish woman be my fate!
For when with rural sports fatigued I come,
And think to rest my wearied limbs at home;
No sooner shall I be retired to bed,
Than she, for one poor word, shall break poor Priscian's head.
Perhaps you'll say, in books you virtue learn,
And, by right reason, Good from Ill discern.
Ha, ha! Believe me, virtue's but pretence 70
To cloak hypocrisy and insolence:
Let woman mind her economic care,
And let the man what he thinks fit prepare:
(What he thinks fit, I say, or please to spend,
For those are fools, that on their wives depend).
Nor need they musty books to pass their time,
There's twenty recreations more sublime.
When tired with work, then let them to the play;
If fair, go visit; if a rainy day,

In cards and chat drive lazy time away.   80
No, hang me if I speak not as I mean;
If on my nuptial day there is not seen
Of all my spouse's books a stately pyre,
Which she herself obediently shall fire;
And oh! Might Europe's learning in that blaze expire.
Now, Madam, pray, the mighty diff'rence show:
I eat, I drink, I sleep as well as you:
I know by custom two and two is four;
My man is honest, then what need I more?
And truly speak it to my joy and praise,   90
I never read six books in all my days.
Nor should my son; for could my wish prevail,
Blest ignorance I'd on my race entail.
Unthinking and unlearned in plenteous ease
My happy heir each appetite should please:
And when chance strikes the last unlucky blow,
Glutted with life, I'd have him boldly go
To try that somewhat, or that naught below.'

How is't, my friend? Can you your spleen contain
At this ignoble wretch, this less than man?   100
Trust me, I'm weary, can repeat no more,
And own this folly worse than when 'twas acted o'er.

Title *Effigies:* portraits, images. 10 *sparables:* headless nails for soles and heels of boots.
13 *doily stuff:* cheap yet genteel woollen fabric for summer wear. 14 *citron:* lemon-like
fruit with thicker skin and less acidic taste. 15 *contains,:* this ed. contains 1722 ed. 16
snuffbox: box for powdered tobacco, taken by sniffing. 20 *muckenders:* handkerchiefs. 21
not,: this ed. not 1722 ed. 22 *Mechlin:* a Belgian town. 27 *bob:* ornamental pendant,
ear-drop. 28 *steenkirk:* neck cloth with long lace ends, passed through a loop or ring.
31 *Foppington:* Lord Foppington in Vanbrugh's *The Relapse*; *Overdo:* Justice Overdo in
Jonson's *Bartholomew Fair*. 33 *elf-locks:* tangled curls. 35 *O Muse,...right!:* this ed. O
Muse!...right, 1722 ed. 44 *a...wallow:* a lout's rolling walk. 51-52 *moved...approved!:*
this ed. mov'd!...approved: 1722 ed. 61 *Marathon:* where the Athenians defeated the
Persians in 490 BC. 67 *break...head:* violate the rules of grammar (Priscian was a Latin
grammarian of Constantinople, 6th century AD). 69 *discern.:* this ed. discern: 1722 ed.
86 *show::* this ed. shew? 1722 ed. 99 *spleen:* ill temper.

The Forsaken Wife

Methinks, 'tis strange, you can't afford
One pitying look, one parting word;
Humanity claims this as due,
But what's humanity to you.

Cruel man! I am not blind,
Your infidelity I find;
Your want of love, my ruin shows
My broken heart, your broken vows:
Yet maugre all your rigid hate,
I will be true in spite of fate;
And one pre-eminence I'll claim,
To be for ever still the same.

Show me a man that dare be true,
That dares to suffer what I do;
That can for ever sigh unheard,
And ever love without regard.
I then will own your prior claim,
To love, to honour, and to fame:
But till that time, my dear, adieu,
I yet superior am to you.

4 *humanity:* lower case this ed. The words *humanity, true, love, honour, fame* and *superior* are totally in upper case in the 1722 ed. 9 *maugre:* in spite of.

MARY WORTLEY MONTAGU
(*née* Pierrepont)
1689–1762

Witty, amusing, and courageous, particularly in relation to the cruel attacks on her character in later years, Lady Mary Wortley Montagu was a poet, essayist, letter-writer and early travel writer. Her mother died when she was a child and she lived in London under her father's supervision and, for a time, with her grandparents near Salisbury. She had a governess and the use of her father's libraries (he was Earl of Kingston in 1690, becoming Duke in 1715). Mary taught herself Latin and began to write in her teenage years. She eloped with the lawyer MP for Huntingdon, Edward Wortley Montagu. They were married in August 1712 and their son was born in May 1713. Her first published work was an essay in *The Spectator* (no.573). After 1714 the family lived in London and Mary had a place in literary society, developing friendships with John Gay and Alexander Pope. She wrote town eclogues, including one entitled 'The Small-Pox', of which she had first-hand experience in 1715, surviving scarred and without eyelashes. In 1716 she accompanied her husband to Turkey, where he had been appointed Ambassador. Her daughter was born in 1718 and they were recalled to London that year. She had her son inoculated for smallpox and helped to popularise the practice. She later came to know the feminist, Mary Astell, and Voltaire. She gave patronage to the poet Edward Young and her second cousin, Henry Fielding. Despite their earlier friendship, in his epic poem *The Dunciad*, Pope referred to Mary with contempt, perhaps because she rejected his amorous advances, or because of irreconcilable political differences. She responded with her own satire to Pope's personal attack and to Swift's general misogyny. From 1739 she lived in Europe, apart from her husband. Horace Walpole published her *Six Town Eclogues With Some Poems* (1747). She returned to London in 1762, where she died of breast cancer, having previously arranged publication of her *Embassy Letters*, which appeared in 1763. *Poetical Works*, from which 'The Lover' (first published in 1747) is taken, was published in 1768. 'Verses written in...Constantinople' is taken from *A New Miscellany of Original Poems, Translations and Imitations*, ed. A. Hammond, 1720. Variant manuscript versions exist in the New York Public Library and at the Harrowby Manuscripts Trust, Stafford (H ms). Isobel Grundy's biography: *Lady Mary Wortley Montagu*, was published by Oxford University Press in 1999.

Verses written in the chiosk at Pera, overlooking Constantinople, Dec. the 26th. 1718

Give me, great God! said I, a little farm,
In summer shady, and in winter warm;
Where a clear spring gives birth to murm'ring brooks,
By nature gliding down the mossy rocks.
Not artfully in leaden pipes conveyed,
Nor greatly falling in a forced cascade,
Pure and unsullied winding thro' the shade:
All-bounteous Heaven has added to my prayer
A softer climate and a purer air.

Our frozen isle now chilling winter binds,   10
Deformed by rains, and rough with blasting winds;
The withered woods grow white with hoary frost,
By driving storms their verdant beauty lost;
The trembling birds their leafless covert shun,
And seek in distant climes a warmer sun:
The water-nymphs their silent urns deplore,
Even Thames benumbed's, a river now no more:
The barren meads no longer yield delight,
By glistring snows made painful to the sight.

Here summer reigns with one eternal smile,   20
Succeeding harvests bless the happy soil.
Fair fertile fields to whom indulgent Heaven
Has every charm of ev'ry season given.
No killing cold deforms the beauteous year,
The springing flowers no coming winter fear.
But as the parent rose decays and dies,
The infant buds with brighter colour rise,
And with fresh sweets the mother's scent supplies.
Near them the violet glows with odours blessed,
And blooms in more than Tyrian purple dressed;   30
The rich jonquils their golden beams display,
And shine in glories emulating day;
The peaceful groves their verdant leaves retain,
The streams still murmur, undefiled with rain,

And tow'ring greens adorn the fruitful plain.
The warbling kind, uninterrupted sing,
Warmed with enjoyments of perpetual spring.

   Here, at my window, I at once survey
The crowded city and resounding sea;
In distant views the Asian mountains rise   40
And lose their snowy summits in the skies:
Above those mountains proud Olympus towers,
The parliamental seat of heavenly powers.
New to the sight, my ravished eyes admire
Each gilded crescent and each antique spire,
The marble mosques, beneath whose ample domes
Fierce warlike sultans sleep in peaceful tombs;
Those lofty structures, once the Christian's boast,
Their names, their beauty, and their honours lost;
Those altars bright with gold and sculpture graced,   50
By barbarous zeal of savage foes defaced;
Sophia alone her ancient name retains,
Tho' unbelieving vows her shrine profanes.
Where holy saints have died in sacred cells,
Where monarchs prayed, the frantic dervish dwells.
How art thou fallen, imperial city, low!
Where are thy hopes of Roman glory now?
Where are thy palaces by prelates raised?
Where priestly pomp in purple lustre blazed,
Where Grecian artists all their skill displayed,   60
Before the happy sciences decayed;
So vast, that youthful kings might here reside,
So splendid to content a patriarch's pride;
Convents where emperors professed of old,
The laboured pillars that their triumphs told;
Vain monuments of them that once were great,
Sunk undistinguished by one common fate.
   One little spot, the tenure small contains,
Of Greek nobility, the poor remains.
Where other Helens with like powerful charms   70
Have once engaged the warring world in arms;
Those names which royal ancestors can boast,
In mean mechanic arts obscurely lost;
Those eyes a second Homer might inspire,
Fixed at the loom, destroy their useless fire.
   Grieved at a view which struck upon my mind

123

The short-lived vanity of humankind,
In gaudy objects I indulge my sight,
And turn where Eastern pomp gives gay delight;
See the vast train in various habits dressed, 80
By the bright scimitar and sable vest,
The proud vizier distinguished o'er the rest,
Six slaves in gay attire his bridle hold,
His bridle rich with gems, his stirrups gold;
His snowy steed adorned with costly pride,
Whole troops of soldiers mounted by his side,
These toss the plumy crest, Arabian courtiers guide,
With artful duty all decline their eyes,
No bellowing shouts of noisy crowds arise,
Silence in solemn state the march attends, 90
Till at the dread divan the slow procession ends.

Yet not these prospects all profusely gay,
The gilded navy that adorns the sea,
The rising city in confusion fair,
Magnificently formed, irregular:
Where woods and palaces at once surprise,
Gardens on gardens, domes on domes arise,
And endless beauties tire the wand'ring eyes;
So soothe my wishes, or so charm my mind,
As this retreat secure from humankind. 100
No knave's successful craft does spleen excite,
No coxcomb's tawdry splendour shocks my sight;
No mob-alarm awakes my female fear,
No praise my mind, nor envy hurts my ear,
Ev'n fame itself can hardly reach me here:
Impertinence with all her tattling train,
Fair-sounding flattery, delicious bane;
Censorious folly, noisy Party-rage,
The thousand tongues with which she must engage,
Who dares have virtue in a vicious age. 110

Title alternatively dated 1717: chiosk: kiosk, a light, open pavilion. 3 *murm'ring brooks:*
1720 ed. a cool brook H ms. 4 *gliding …rocks:* 1720 ed. sliding down a mossy rock H ms.
11 *by:* 1720 ed. with H ms. 13 *beauty:* 1720 ed. beauty's H ms. 16 *silent:* 1720 ed. silenced
H ms. 17 *benumbed's:* 1720 ed. benumbed H ms. 18 *meads…yield:* 1720 ed. meadows
give no more H ms. 19 *glistring snows:* 1720 ed. glistening snow H ms. 21 *Succeeding:*
1720 ed. And double H ms. 23 *ev'ry:* 1720 ed. every H ms given. H ms given, 1720 ed.
27 *colour:* 1720 ed. colours H ms. 32 *glories:* 1720 ed. glory H ms. 33 *peaceful…verdant:*
1720 ed. cheerful…living H ms. 34 *by:* 1720 ed. with H ms. 35 *tow'ring…adorn:* 1720
ed. rising green adorns H ms; 38 *at:* 1720 ed. from H ms. 40 *views the:* view see H ms.
49 *Beauty…Honours:* 1720 ed. glories…beauties H ms. 50 *gold and:* 1720 ed. gold, with

H ms. 52 *name:* 1720 ed. sound H ms. 56 *fallen…low!* H ms fallen imperial city low?
1720 ed. 59 *Where…blazed,* H ms missing line in 1720 ed. 62 *here:* 1720 ed. there H ms.
66 *them:* 1720 ed. men H ms. 68 *tenure small:* 1720 ed. small Fanar H ms. 70 *with:* 1720
ed. show H ms. 71 *Have:* this ed. Has 1720 ed. As H ms. 72 *ancestors:* 1720 ed. ancestry
H ms. 82 *proud Vizier:* 1720 ed. vizier proud H ms high official. 85 *costly:* 1720 ed. lavish
H ms. 87 *toss:* this ed. top 1720 ed. courtiers: 1720 ed. coursers H ms. 88 *artful:* 1720
ed. awful H ms. 99 *sooth…charm:* 1720 ed. soothes…charms H ms. 107 *flattery:* 1720 ed.
flattery's H ms. 110 *dares:* 1720 ed. dare H ms.

The Lover: A Ballad
To Mr C–.

I

At length, by so much importunity pressed,
Take, Molly, at once, the inside of my breast.
This stupid indiff'rence so often you blame
Is not owing to nature, to fear, or to shame:
I am not as cold as a virgin in lead,
Nor is Sunday's sermon so strong in my head:
I know but too well how time flies along,
That we live but few years, and yet fewer are young.

II

But I hate to be cheated, and never will buy
Long years of repentance for moments of joy.
Oh! was there a man (but where shall I find
Good sense and good nature so equally joined?)
Would value his pleasure, contribute to mine;
Not meanly would boast, nor lewdly design,
Not over severe, yet not stupidly vain,
For I would have the power, tho' not give the pain.

III

No pedant, yet learned; no rake helly gay,
Or laughing, because he has nothing to say;
To all my whole sex, obliging and free,
Yet never be fond of any but me;
In public preserve the decorum that's just,
And show in his eyes he is true to his trust;
Then rarely approach, and respectfully bow,
Yet not fulsomely pert, nor foppishly low.

IV

But when the long hours of public are past,
And we meet with champagne and a chicken at last,
May every fond pleasure that moment endear;

Be banished afar both discretion and fear!
Forgetting or scorning the airs of the crowd,
He may cease to be formal, and I to be proud,
Till lost in the joy, we confess that we live,
And he may be rude, and yet I may forgive.

V

And that my delight may be solidly fixed,
Let the friend and the lover be handsomely mixed,
In whose tender bosom my soul may confide,
Whose kindness can soothe me, whose counsel can guide.
From such a dear lover, as here I describe,
No danger should fright me, no millions should bribe;
But till this astonishing creature I know,
As I long have lived chaste, I will keep myself so.

VI

I never will share with the wanton coquette,
Or be caught by a vain affectation of wit.
The toasters and songsters may try all their art,
But never shall enter the pass of my heart.
I loathe the lewd rake, the dressed fopling despise:
Before such pursuers the nice virgin flies:
And as Ovid has sweetly in parable told,
We harden like trees, and like rivers grow cold.

Title *Mr C –.:* possibly Richard Chandler (*c.* 1703-69). III.1 *helly:* devilishly, infernally.
VI.8 see Ovid's *Metamorphoses.*

MARY BARBER

c. 1690–1757

Married to a Dublin woollen draper, Jonathan Swift called Mary Barber 'the
best poetess of both kingdoms'. She claimed to write verse 'chiefly to form the
minds of my children' and published *The Widows Address in Dublin* in 1725 on
behalf of an army officer's widow. A considerable sum was raised for the widow
and Mary, herself, received patronage from Lady Carteret as a result. Other
separately published poems succeeded it. She became one of Swift's circle and
his support enabled her to publish a volume, *Poems on Several Occasions*, by
subscription, in London in 1734. The following poems are taken from this
edition, to which Swift provided a foreword. The poems were a critical success
but not a financial one. After her husband presumably died, she lived in Bath.
In 1738 Swift gave her the manuscript of his *...Genteel and Ingenious Conversation*

to publish and this helped to support her at a time of ill health. She returned to Ireland where her son, Constantine, was a physician, and died there. Several of her poems appeared in *Poems by Eminent Ladies* in 1755.

Conclusion of a Letter to the Rev. Mr C———.

'Tis time to conclude; for I make it a rule
To leave off all writing, when Con. comes from school.
He dislikes what I've written, and says I had better
To send what he calls a *poetical* letter.

To this I replied, 'You are out of your wits;
A letter in verse would put him in fits:
He thinks it a crime in a woman to read –
Then, what would he say, should your counsel succeed?
"I pity poor Barber, his wife's so romantic:
A letter in rhyme! – Why, the woman is frantic!   10
This reading the poets has quite turned her head!
On my life, she should have a dark room, and straw bed.
I often heard say, that St Patrick took care,
No poisonous creature should live in this air:
He only regarded the body, I find;
But Plato considered who poisoned the mind.
Would they'd follow his precepts, who sit at the helm,
And drive poetasters from out of the realm!

Her husband has surely a terrible life;
There's nothing I dread like a verse-writing wife: 20
Defend me, ye powers, from that fatal curse,
Which must heighten the plagues of *for better for worse*!

May I have a wife that will dust her own floor;
And not the fine minx recommended by More.
(That he was a dotard, is granted, I hope,
Who died for asserting the rights of the Pope.)
If ever I marry, I'll choose me a spouse,
That shall *serve* and *obey*, as she's bound by her vows;
That shall, when I'm dressing, attend like a valet;
Then go to the kitchen, and study my palate.   30
She has wisdom enough, that keeps out of the dirt,
And can make a good pudding, and cut out a shirt.
What good's in a dame that will pore on a book?
No – give me the wife that shall save me a cook." '
Thus far I had written – then turned to my son,

To give him advice, ere my letter was done.
'My son, should you marry, look out for a wife,
That's fitted to lighten the labours of life.
Be sure, wed a woman you thoroughly know,
And shun, above all things, a housewifely shrew;   40
That would fly to your study, with fire in her looks,
And ask what you got by your poring on books,
Think dressing of dinner the height of all science,
And to peace, and good humour bid open defiance.

Avoid the fine lady, whose beauty's her care;
Who sets a high price on her shape, and her air;
Who in dress, and in visits, employs the whole day;
And longs for the ev'ning, to sit down to play.

Choose a woman of wisdom, as well as good breeding,
With a turn, or at least no aversion, to reading: 50
In the care of her person, exact and refined;
Yet still, let her principal care be her mind:
Who can, when her family cares give her leisure,
Without the dear cards, pass an evening with pleasure;
In forming her children to virtue and knowledge,
Nor trust, for that care, to a school, or a college:
By learning made humble, not thence taking airs
To despise, or neglect, her domestic affairs:
Nor think her less fitted for doing her duty,
By knowing its reasons, its use, and its beauty.   60

When you gain her affection, take care to preserve it,
Lest others persuade her you do not deserve it.
Still study to heighten the joys of her life;
Nor treat her the worse for her being your wife.
If in judgement she errs, set her right, without pride:
'Tis the province of insolent fools to deride.
A husband's first praise is a Friend and Protector:
Then change not these titles for Tyrant and Hector.
Let your person be neat, unaffectedly clean,
Though alone with your wife the whole day you remain.   70
Choose books, for her study, to fashion her mind,
To emulate those who excelled of her kind.
Be religion the principal care of your life,
As you hope to be blest in your children and wife;
So you, in your marriage, shall gain its true end;
And find, in your wife, a Companion and Friend.'

1 *rule:* this ed. rule, 1734 ed. 2 *Con:* her son, Constantine Barber. 13-16 *St Patrick…*
mind: according to legend, St Patrick drove all snakes from Ireland: Plato excluded poets
from his Republic. 18 *poetasters:* writers of poor verse. 20 *dread:* this ed. dread, 1734
ed. 21 *curse,:* this ed. curse; 1734 ed. 23 *floor,:* this ed. floor; 1734 ed. 24 *minx:* this
ed. minx, 1734 ed. *More:* Barber's own note directs the reader to Sir Thomas More's
advice to his son, but she may have meant More's Latin verses to a friend on the choice
of a wife (published 1713). 26 *died…Pope:* More's loyalty to the Pope at the time of
Henry VIII's divorce from Catherine of Aragon led to a charge of treason and his be-
heading. 57 *airs:* this ed. airs, 1734 ed. 62-68 commas after 'her', 'worse', 'fools', 'praise',
and 'titles' are omitted, this ed. 68 *Hector:* bully.

Stella and Flavia

Stella and Flavia, ev'ry hour,
    Unnumbered hearts surprise:
In Stella's soul lies all her pow'r,
    And Flavia's, in her eyes.

More boundless Flavia's conquests are,
    And Stella's more confined:
All can discern a face that's fair,
    But few a lovely mind.

Stella, like Britain's Monarch, reigns
    O'er cultivated lands;
Like Eastern tyrants, Flavia deigns
    To rule o'er barren sands.

Then boast, fair Flavia, boast your face,
    Your beauty's only store:
Your charms will ev'ry day decrease,
    Each day gives Stella more.

MARY COLLIER
c. 1690 – 1762

The preface to Mary Collier's *Poems on Several Occasions* (1762) describes her
parents as 'poor but honest'. They taught her to read, but she had no other
education and, after her mother's early death, worked as a domestic servant and
field labourer. *The Woman's Labour* (1739) was a vindication of rural working-
class women, who had been criticised in a poem by Stephen Duck, published
in 1736. On the title-page Mary is described as 'now a washer-woman, at
Petersfield in Hampshire'. Duck, a farm labourer, whose poetry won him a
pension from the Queen, later took holy orders and became Rector of Byfleet
in 1752, but drowned himself in 1756. Mary wrote an elegy for him. She

published *The Woman's Labour* at her own cost, so made little profit from it and worked as a washerwoman until she was 63. After that, she managed a farmhouse until, at 70, she retired to a garret in Alton, due to poor health. She never married.

from The Woman's Labour: an Epistle to Mr Stephen Duck; in answer to his late poem, called *The Thresher's Labour*

Immortal Bard! thou fav'rite of the Nine!
Enriched by peers, advanced by Caroline!
Deign to look down on one that's poor and low,
Rememb'ring you yourself was lately so;
Accept these lines: Alas! What can you have
From her, who ever was, and's still a slave?
No learning ever was bestowed on me;
My life was always spent in drudgery:
And not alone; alas! with grief I find,
It is the portion of poor woman-kind.   10
Oft have I thought as on my bed I lay,
Eased from the tiresome labours of the day,
Our first extraction from a mass refined,
Could never be for slavery designed;
Till time and custom by degrees destroyed
That happy state our sex at first enjoyed.
When men had used their utmost care and toil,
Their recompence was but a female smile;
When they by Arts or Arms were rendered great,
They laid their trophies at a woman's feet;   20
They, in those days, unto our sex did bring
Their hearts, their all, a free-will offering;
And as from us their being they derive,
They back again should all due homage give.

Jove, once descending from the clouds, did drop
In show'rs of gold on lovely Danae's lap;
The sweet-tongued poets, in those generous days,
Unto our shrine still offered up their lays:
But now, alas! that Golden Age is past,
We are the objects of your scorn at last.   30
And you, great Duck, upon whose happy brow
The Muses seem to fix the garland now,
In your late *Poem* boldly did declare
Alcides' labours can't with yours compare;

And of your annual task have much to say,
Of threshing, reaping, mowing corn and hay;
Boasting your daily toil, and nightly dream,
But can't conclude your never-dying theme,
And let our hapless sex in silence lie
Forgotten, and in dark Oblivion die;   40
But on our abject state you throw your scorn,
And women wrong, your verses to adorn.
You of hay-making speak a word or two,
As if our sex but little work could do:
This makes the honest farmer smiling say,
He'll seek for women still to make his hay;
For if his back be turned, their work they mind
As well as men, as far as he can find.
For my own part, I many a summer's day
Have spent in throwing, turning, making hay;   50
But ne'er could see what you have lately found,
Our wages paid for sitting on the ground.
'Tis true, that when our morning's work is done,
And all our grass exposed unto the sun,
While that his scorching beams do on it shine,
As well as you, we have a time to dine:
I hope, that since we freely toil and sweat
To earn our bread, you'll give us time to eat.
That over, soon we must get up again,
And nimbly turn our hay upon the plain;   60
Nay, rake and prow it in, the case is clear;
Or how should cocks in equal rows appear?
But if you'd have what you have wrote believed,
I find, that you to hear us talk are grieved:
In this, I hope, you do not speak your mind,
For none but Turks, that ever I could find,
Have mutes to serve them, or did e'er deny
Their slaves, at work, to chat it merrily.
Since you have liberty to speak your mind,
And are to talk, as well as we, inclined,   70
Why should you thus repine, because that we,
Like you, enjoy that pleasing liberty?
What! Would you lord it quite, and take away
The only privilege our sex enjoy?

When ev'ning does approach, we homeward hie,
And our domestic toils incessant ply:

Against your coming home prepare to get
Our work all done, our house in order set;
Bacon and dumpling in the pot we boil,
Our beds we make, our swine we feed the while; 80
Then wait at door to see you coming home,
And set the table out against you come:
Early next morning we on you attend;
Our children dress and feed, their clothes we mend;
And in the field our daily task renew,
Soon as the rising sun has dried the dew.

When harvest comes, into the field we go,
And help to reap the wheat as well as you;
Or else we go the ears of corn to glean;
No labour scorning, be it e'er so mean; 90
But in the work we freely bear a part,
And what we can, perform with all our heart.
To get a living we so willing are,
Our tender babes into the field we bear,
And wrap them in our clothes to keep them warm,
While round about we gather up the corn;
And often unto them our course do bend,
To keep them safe, that nothing them offend:
Our children that are able, bear a share
In gleaning corn, such is our frugal care. 100
When night comes on, unto our home we go,
Our corn we carry, and our infant too;
Weary, alas! But 'tis not worth our while
Once to complain, or *rest at ev'ry Stile*;
We must make haste, for when we home are come,
Alas! We find our work but just begun;
So many things for our attendance call,
Had we ten hands, we could employ them all.
Our children put to bed, with greatest care
We all things for your coming home prepare: 110
You sup, and go to bed without delay,
And rest yourselves till the ensuing day;
While we, alas! But little sleep can have,
Because our froward children cry and rave;
Yet, without fail, soon as day-light doth spring,
We in the field again our work begin,
And there, with all our strength, our toil renew,
Till Titan's golden rays have dried the dew;

Then home we go unto our children dear,
Dress, feed, and bring them to the field with care.   120
Were this your case, you justly might complain
That day nor night you are secure from pain;
Those mighty troubles which perplex your mind,
(*Thistles* before, and *Females* come behind)
Would vanish soon, and quickly disappear,
Were you, like us, encumbered thus with care.
What you would have of us we do not know:
We oft' take up the corn that you do mow;
We cut the peas, and always ready are
In ev'ry work to take our proper share;   130
And from the time that harvest doth begin,
Until the corn be cut and carried in,
Our toil and labour's daily so extreme,
That we have hardly ever *Time to dream*...   134

[...]

[Descriptions of domestic labours, e.g. charing, follow]

But to rehearse all labour is in vain,
Of which we very justly might complain:
For us, you see, but little rest is found;
Our toil increases as the year runs round.
While you to Sisyphus yourselves compare,
With Danaus' daughters we may claim a share;   240
For while *he* labours hard against the hill,
Bottomless tubs of water *they* must fill.

So the industrious bees do hourly strive
To bring their loads of honey to the hive;
Their sordid owners always reap the gains,
And poorly recompense their toil and pains.

1 *the Nine:* the Muses. 2 *Caroline:* his patron, Queen Caroline, consort of George II. 25-26 *Jove...lap:* Danae's father imprisoned her in a brazen tower, but Jupiter (Jove) was so infatuated that he changed himself into a golden shower to reach her. 28 *lays:* songs. 33 *Poem: The Thresher's Labour.* 34 *Alcides:* Hercules, who was set twelve amazing feats of strength to perform. Of the thresher's labours, Duck wrote: 'Scarce Hercules e'er felt such Toils as these' (line 255). 52 *Our...ground:* see Duck's poem, line 175. 61 *prow:* this may be a misprint for 'prong', or it could mean raking it into the shape of a ship's prow. 62 *cocks:* conical heaps of hay. 79 *Bacon...dumpling:* the meal Duck mentions the thresher coming home to (lines 155-56). 64 *I...grieved:* see Duck's poem, lines 163-70. 86 *Soon...dew:* Duck's line 161 has 'hath drunk' rather than 'has dried', but is otherwise the same. 104 *rest...Stile:* in Duck's poem the threshers walk slowly home 'and rest at every Stile' (line 152). 114 *froward:* wayward. 118 *Titan:* Hyperion, one of the Titans and father to Sol, the sun, but often taken by poets for the sun himself. 124 *Thistles... Females:* referring to Duck's poem lines 241-43. 134 *Time...dream:* a response to Duck's

lines 250-53, where the threshers' imaginations re-enact their labours in their dreams. 239 *Sisyphus:* at the end of Duck's poem he compares the threshers' task to that of Sisyphus who, in the Greek myth, was forced continually to push a huge rock up a hill, only to have it roll down again every time it approached the top. 240 *Danaus' daughters:* the 49 daughters of Danaus who, at their father's command, killed their husbands on their wedding nights, were condemned to the eternal punishment of attempting to fill leaking vessels with water. 245 *sordid:* mean.

ARABELLA MORETON
b. after 1690 *and before* 1741

There is some doubt concerning the female author of the following poem. It was first attributed to 'B-ll M-rt-n' in *A New Miscellany...Written Chiefly by Persons of Quality* (?1726). Roger Lonsdale, acknowledging a debt to Mrs E.E. Duncan-Jones (*EWP*, 539), concludes that this was Arabella Moreton, the daughter of Matthew Ducie Moreton, MP for Gloucestershire (1708-13), later Lord Ducie (1720). Arabella died before 1741 and does not seem to have married. The poem also appeared (anonymously) in Ashley Cowper's *Norfolk Poetical Miscellany* (1744) and in the Cowper family miscellany, attributed to Arabella's sister, 'Mrs Pen. Moreton'. The following is taken from the latter text: BL, Add. Ms 28,101.fo.49. R.E. Pritchard attributes the poem to Laetitia Pilkington (*PBEW*, 137).

The Humble Wish

I ask not wit, nor beauty do I crave
Nor wealth, nor pompous titles, wish to have;
But since 'tis doomed, thro' ev'ry state of life;
Whether a daughter – sister – or a wife –
That females must the stronger males obey
And yield perforce to their tyrannic sway;
Since this, I say, is ev'ry woman's fate,
Give me a mind to suit my slavish state.

3 *thro'...state:* BL ms in all degrees 1726? ed. 4 *Whether...wife* –: BL ms (Whether... daughter, sister, or a wife, 1726? ed. 5 *must:* BL ms shall 1726? ed. 6 *sway;:* 1726? ed. sway, BL ms.

MARY JONES
1707–78

In 1752, Ralph Griffiths, in *The Monthly Review* (vol.6), described Mary Jones as the best woman writer since Katherine Philips. She was later invited to become a reviewer for the journal, but declined. She lived in Oxford most of her life, with her brother, Rev. Oliver Jones, Chanter of the Cathedral, and was, accordingly, called 'the Chantress' by Samuel Johnson, who first met her in Oxford. In her teens she translated Italian songs and knew both French and Italian. She may have been a governess for a time, but had close friendships with aristocratic members of the Oxford literary circle. She wrote that her grandfather 'was the first of his particular Branch that ever set up for a Gentleman' and that 'Our real Worth must depend upon Our Selves'. Her broadside ballad, *The Lass of the Hill*, had some success in 1742, and 1,400 subscribers (including the Princess Royal) made publication of her *Miscellanies in Prose and Verse* possible in Oxford in 1750. This collection, from which the following poem is taken, was well received. A selection of her work was included in *Poems by Eminent Ladies* (1755). She lived next to the Wheatsheaf and Anchor in St Aldate's and may have been a post-mistress in Oxford after her brother's death in 1775.

Soliloquy on an Empty Purse

Alas, my purse! how lean and low!
My silken purse! what art thou now!
Once I beheld – but stocks will fall –
When both thy ends had wherewithal.
When I within thy slender fence
My fortune placed, and confidence;
A poet's fortune! – not immense:
Yet, mixed with keys, and coins among,
Chinked to the melody of song.

Canst thou forget, when, high in air,   10
I saw thee fluttering at a fair?
And took thee, destined to be sold,
My lawful purse, to have and hold?
Yet used so oft to disembogue,
No prudence could thy fate prorogue.
Like wax thy silver melted down,
Touch but the brass, and lo! 'twas gone:
And gold would never with thee stay,
For gold had wings, and flew away.

Alas, my purse! yet still be proud,   20
For see the Virtues round thee crowd!
See, in the room of paltry wealth,
Calm Temperance rise, the nurse of health;
And Self-Denial, slim and spare,
And Fortitude, with look severe;
And Abstinence, to leanness prone,

135

And Patience, worn to skin and bone:
Prudence and Foresight on thee wait,
And Poverty lies here in state!
Hopeless her spirits to recruit,   30
For every Virtue is a mute.

Well then, my purse, thy Sabbaths keep;
Now thou art empty, I shall sleep.
No silver sounds shall thee molest,
Nor golden dreams disturb my breast.
Safe shall I walk with thee along,
Amidst temptations thick and strong;
Catched by the eye, no more shall stop
At Wildey's toys, or Pinchbeck's shop;
Nor cheapening Payne's ungodly books,   40
Be drawn aside by pastry-cooks:
But fearless now we both may go
Where Ludgate's mercers bow so low;
Beholding all with equal eye,
Nor moved at – 'Madam, what d'ye buy?'

Away, far hence each worldly care!
Nor dun nor pick-purse shalt thou fear,
Nor flatterer base annoy my ear.
Snug shalt thou travel through the mob,
For who a poet's purse will rob?   50
And softly sweet in garret high
Will I thy virtues magnify;
Outsoaring flatterers' stinking breath,
And gently rhyming rats to death.

14 *disembogue:* pour forth, empty. 15 *prorogue:* postpone. 39 *Wildey's...Pinchbeck's:* fashionable London shops. 47 *dun:* debt collector, pressing creditor.

JANE COLMAN TURELL

1708–35

Jane Turell was born in Boston, New England, the third child of Rev. Benjamin Colman and Jane Clark. Their first two offspring had died, so Jane was, in effect, an only child for seven years. Despite ill health, she read widely. Her father was president of Harvard College and had a large library. He also met, admired, and corresponded with Elizabeth Singer Rowe. A hymn Jane wrote, in January 1718, was reproduced by her husband, Ebenezer Turell, in *Memoirs of the Life & Death of the Pious & Ingenious Mrs Jane Turell...collected chiefly from her own manuscripts...* (1741), which also contains the following poems. Ebenezer, one of her father's theology students, married Jane in 1726. They had four children but only one survived her. The only texts of Jane's that survive are those her husband selected to publish. He noted that she had also written 'Pieces of Wit and Humor', but he chose to omit these. In addition to writing her own poetry, she conducted a lengthy correspondence with her father, kept a diary, paraphrased the Psalms, and composed prayers. According to her husband, Jane was affected greatly by the sudden death of her mother and wrote 'much upon it'. She also constantly struggled with doubts and fears, being tempted to deny God, but died in faith.

[Lines On Childbirth]

Phoebus has thrice his yearly circuit run,
The winter's over, and the summer's done;
Since that bright day on which our hands were joined,
And to Philander I my all resigned.

Thrice in my womb I've found the pleasing strife,
In the first struggles of my infant's life:
But O how soon by Heaven I'm called to mourn,
While from my womb a lifeless babe is torn?
Born to the grave ere it had seen the light,
Or with one smile had cheered my longing sight.   10

Again in travail-pains my nerves are wrecked,
My eye-balls start, my heart strings almost cracked;
Now I forget my pains, and now I press
Philander's image to my panting breast.
Ten days I hold him in my joyful arms,
And feast my eyes upon his infant charms.
But then the King of Terrors does advance,
To pierce its bosom with his iron lance.
Its soul released, upward it takes its flight,
O never more below to bless my sight!   20
Farewell, sweet babes, I hope to meet above,
And there with you sing the Redeemer's love.

And now O gracious Saviour, lend thine ear,
To this my earnest cry and humble prayer,
That when the hour arrives with painful throes,
Which shall my burden to the world disclose;
I may deliverance have, and joy to see
A living child, to dedicate to Thee.

Title: not supplied by the author, though now known as such. Her first child's birth was difficult and she is said to have known nothing of her delivery until two days later. The child died. Her second child lived eleven days. 20 *O:* this ed. Oh 1741 ed. 21 *Farewell,...* *babes,:* this ed. Farewell...babes 1741 ed. 23 *Saviour,:* this ed. Saviour 1741 ed. 25 *throes:* this ed. throws 1741 ed.

To my Muse, December 29, 1725

Come Gentle Muse, and once more lend thine aid,
O bring thy succour to a humble maid!
How often dost thou liberally dispense
To our dull breast thy quick'ning influence!
By thee inspired, I'll cheerful tune my voice,
And Love and sacred Friendship make my choice.
In my pleased bosom you can freely pour,
A greater treasure than Jove's golden shower.
Come now, fair Muse, and fill my empty mind,
With rich ideas, great and unconfined.   10
Instruct me in those secret Arts that lie
Unseen to all but to a Poet's eye.
O let me burn with Sappho's noble fire,
But not like her for faithless man expire.
And let me rival great Orinda's fame,
Or like sweet Philomela's be my name.
Go lead the way, my Muse, nor must you stop,
'Till we have gained Parnassus' shady top:
'Till I have viewed those fragrant soft retreats,
Those fields of bliss, the Muses' sacred seats.   20
I'll then devote thee to fair Virtue's fame,
And so be worthy of a Poet's name.

4 *quick'ning:* life-giving, inspiring. 13 *Sappho:* the Greek lyric poet, born in Lesbos, mid-7th century B.C., see note on p.104. 15 *Orinda:* the poet, Katherine Philips (1632-64). 16 *Philomela:* the poet, Elizabeth Rowe (1674-1737). 18 *Parnassus:* a mountain in Greece, sacred to the Muses.

MARTHA BREWSTER

1710 – *after* 1759

Martha Brewster and her two older siblings were born into a farming family in Lebanon, Connecticut. She married Oliver Brewster, her father's second cousin, in 1732 and settled near Goshen, where their two children, Ruby and Wadsworth, were born. Oliver was a 'sealer of leather' in Bernardstone, Massachusetts from 1775 to 1776, but no record of either his or Martha's death has been found. Martha's volume, *Poems on divers subjects*, from which the following is taken, was published in Boston in 1757 and ran into two editions.

An Acrostic For My Husband

Oh! may propitious Heaven still extend
Lasting delights, to solace thee my friend:
Injoying every lawful sweet below,
Viewing by faith, the fountain whence they flow,
Erected be his throne, within thy heart,
Rule and replenish there, thy every part.

Blest with a vine, whose love and loyalty,
Richer than choicest wine her progeny,
Each like an olive branch adorn thy house,
With the fair transcript of thy loving spouse.
Soft are the charms inviolable bands
Twine round the lover's heart, raptured he stands:
Eternal King that hast these powers given,
Renew our love to Thee, and love us up to Heaven.

3 *Injoying:* now obsolete, combining the meanings of enjoying and enjoining – and supplying the necessary 'I' in Oliver's name!

MARY LEAPOR

1722–46

In *The Gentleman's Magazine* (1784), John Duncombe described Mary Leapor as 'a most extraordinary, uncultivated genius'. Poet and, less successfully, playwright, she was born at Marston St Lawrence, Northamptonshire, where her father was gardener to Sir John Blencowe. Later the family moved to Brackley. She read from an early age and was writing when she was ten or eleven years old. After her mother's death (*c.* 1742), Mary kept house for her father and was a 'cook-maid' in a gentleman's family. Heavily influenced by the poetry of Alexander Pope, Mary was a prolific writer, despite frequent ill health. Bridget Fremantle, a rector's daughter, tried to raise subscriptions to publish a volume of her work, but Mary died of measles before this could be done. Her dying wish was that her poetry should be published for her father's benefit. *The London Magazine* printed one of her poems in 1747 and a volume, *Poems upon Several Occasions*, appeared in April 1748. Subscribers included members of the Blencowe family, the Countess of Hertford, and the poet, Stephen Duck. Samuel Richardson edited and printed a new volume of her poems in 1751. This book, from which the following is taken, included letters by Leapor and a memoir by Bridget Fremantle. A selection of her poetry also appeared in *Poems by Eminent Ladies* (1755).

An Essay on Woman

Woman – a pleasing, but a short-lived flow'r,
Too soft for business, and too weak for pow'r:
A wife in bondage, or neglected maid;
Despised, if ugly; if she's fair – betrayed.
'Tis wealth alone inspires every grace,
And calls the raptures to her plenteous face.
What numbers for those charming features pine,
If blooming acres round her temples twine?
Her lip the strawberry, and her eyes more bright
Than sparkling Venus in a frosty night. 10
Pale lilies fade; and when the fair appears,
Snow turns a negro, and dissolves in tears.
And where the charmer treads her magic toe,
On English ground Arabian odours grow;
Till mighty Hymen lifts his sceptred rod,
And sinks her glories with a fatal nod;
Dissolves her triumphs, sweeps her charms away,
And turns the goddess to her native clay.

But, Artemisia, let your servant sing
What small advantage wealth and beauties bring. 20
Who would be wise, that knew Pamphilia's fate?
Or who be fair, and joined to Sylvia's mate?
Sylvia, whose cheeks are fresh as early day;
As evening mild, and sweet as spicy May:
And yet that face her partial husband tires,
And those bright eyes, that all the world admires.
Pamphilia's wit who does not strive to shun,
Like death's infection, or a dog-day's sun?
The damsels view her with malignant eyes:
The men are vexed to find a nymph so wise – 30
And wisdom only serves to make her know
The keen sensation of superior woe.
The secret whisper, and the list'ning ear,
The scornful eyebrow, and the hated sneer;
The giddy censures of her babbling kind,
With thousand ills that grate a gentle mind,
By her are tasted in the first degree,
Tho' overlooked by Simplicus, and me.
Does thirst of gold a virgin's heart inspire,
Instilled by nature, or a careful sire? 40

140

Then let her quit extravagance and play,
The brisk companion, and expensive tea,
To feast with Cordia in her filthy sty
On stewed potatoes, or on mouldy pie;
Whose eager eyes stare ghastly at the poor,
And fright the beggars from her hated door:
In greasy clouts she wraps her smoky chin,
And holds that pride's a never-pardoned sin.

If this be wealth, no matter where it falls;
But save, ye Muses, save your Mira's walls: 50
Still give me pleasing indolence, and ease;
A fire to warm me, and a friend to please.

Since, whether sunk in avarice, or pride;
A wanton virgin, or a starving bride;
Or wond'ring crowds attend her charming tongue;
Or deemed an idiot, ever speaks the wrong:
Tho' nature armed us for the growing ill,
With fraudful cunning, and a headstrong will;
Yet, with ten thousand follies to her charge,
Unhappy woman's but a slave at large.   60

15 *Hymen:* god of marriage. 19 *Artemisia:* Bridget Fremantle. 30 *wise − :* this ed. wise: 1751 ed. 41-42 *play,...companion,...tea,:* this ed. play;...companion;...tea; 1751 ed. 50 *Mira:* the poet's name for herself.

ELIZABETH TEFT

b. 1723

'Elizabeth Teft of Lincoln' published *Orinthia's Miscellanies* in London in 1747. In 1741, her poem, 'Orinthia's Plea to the Gentlemen of Fortune...', appeared in *The Gentleman's Magazine*, anonymously. In it, she jokingly appealed to them to buy lottery tickets for her to help make her fortune: 'To give the tickets, yours the kindness be,/ And Fortune's to direct the Prize to me!' Several gentlemen took her at her word and replied in verse. Although, as she revealed in July 1742, she had no luck in the lottery and mourned 'her humble state', she said she would 'rest content to be unfortunate'. Very little is known of her life.

On Learning. Desired by a Gentleman

Well, Ignorance, the cause is yet unknown
Why thou'rt confined unto my sex alone.

Why are not girls, as boys, sent forth when young
To learn the Latin, Greek, and Hebrew tongue?
I the first founders of great Rome would know,
Their funeral piles, their mounting eagles too;
Would trace thro' Greece, thro' Athens and old Troy;
For potent wonders give a reason why;
Search out the nature of all things below;
From what great causes dire effects do flow.   10
In conference with deathless Homer be,
Read Virgil's thoughts, and Milton's poetry;
Study the actions of the bravest men,
Copy their worth, and shine as bright as them.
Good, great, and brave, these are such envied charms,
Me, hero-like, a martial spirit warms:
And yet, methinks, I would not be a man,
No, not to put imperial purple on;
I'd rather be the foolish thing I am.
Our sex against you justly may exclaim,   20
To link our knowledge to so short a chain;
Cowards, you fear, had we full lengths to run,
We should eclipse your starlight with our sun.
We in their native dress our thoughts impart,
Yours decked with learning, and adorned with art.
Every error generously excuse:
Consider, Sir, a simple virgin's muse.

10 *flow.:* this ed. flow; 1747 ed. 26 *excuse::* this ed. excuse, 1747 ed.

On Snuff-Taking

Custom, in this small article I find
What strong ascendance thou hast o'er the mind.
My friend's advice the first inducements were:
'Take it', said she, 'it will your spirits cheer.'
All resolute the offered drug to take,
But in the trial sickened with my hate,
By repetition I was brought to bear,
Then rather liked, now love it too, too dear.
Be careful, oh my soul! How thou let'st in
The baneful poison of repeated sin;   10
Never be intimate with any crime,
Lest Custom makes it amiable in time.

2 *were::* this ed. were, 1747 ed.

142

To her sister, who was very fond of London

'Tis strange our sentiments so ill agree,
What's kind of Heaven to you, is Hell to me.
How vast we differ in this one regard!
That which would punish me, would you reward.
The air all smoke, so scorching hot the sun,
Heathens would swear 'twas done by Phaeton.
Your notion must be good, your judgement right;
London may have its charms for the polite.

6 *Phaeton:* the son of Helios, the sun god; he drove the sun chariot perilously near the earth.

MERCY OTIS WARREN
1728–1814

Mercy Otis Warren, Republican poet, playwright, historian, pamphleteer, and essayist, is best known for her three-volume *History of the Rise, Progress and Termination of the American Revolution Interspersed with Biographical, Political, and Moral Observations* (1805). Her plays satirised the counsellors appointed by the British Parliament and included outspoken female characters. Her anti-federalist paper, *Observations on the New Constitution by a Columbian Patriot* (1788) was first attributed to Elbridge Gerry. All her writing was anonymous prior to 1790, the year her *Poems: Dramatic & Miscellaneous* was published. Born Mary Otis, on a large farm in Barnstable, Massachusetts, Mercy was the third of 13 children. Her great-grandfather, John Otis, emigrated to Bear Cove in the Massachusetts Bay Colony on the Mayflower in 1630. Her father was Barnstable's representative to the Massachusetts General Assembly, a judge of the probate court, and a captain of the local militia. She was educated by her brother's tutor and read widely. She married James Warren in 1754. He later became Sheriff of Plymouth county. They had five sons. Both husband and wife criticised public corruption. A book-length study of Mercy, by Alice Brown, was published in 1896.

To Mrs Montagu, Author of 'Observations On the Genius and Writings of Shakespeare'

Will Montagu, whose critic pen adds praise,
Even to a Shakespeare's bold exalted lays;
Who points the faults in sweet Corneille's page,
Sees all the errors of the Gallic stage –
Corrects Voltaire with a superior hand,
Or traces genius in each distant land –

Will she across the Atlantic stretch her eye,
Look o'er the main, and view the western sky;
And there Columbia's infant drama see –
Reflect that Britain taught us to be free;
Survey with candor what she can't approve;
Let local fondness yield to gen'rous love;
And, if fair truth forbids her to commend,
Then let the critic soften to the friend?

The bard of Avon justly bears the meed
Of fond applause, from Tiber to the Tweed;
Each humbler muse at distance may admire,
But none to Shakespeare's fame e'er dare aspire.
And if your isle, where he so long has charmed,
If Britain's sons, when by his mantle warmed,
Have soared in vain to reach his lofty quill,
Nature to paint with true Shakespearean skill –
A sister's hand may wrest a female pen,
From the bold outrage of imperious men.

If gentle Montague my chaplet raise,
Critics may frown, or mild good nature praise;
Secure I'll walk, and placid move along,
And heed alike their censure or their song;
I'll take my stand by famed Parnassus' side,
And for a moment feel a poet's pride.

Plymouth, July 10, 1790

Title *Mrs Montagu:* Elizabeth Montagu (1720-1800), founder of an intellectual and social group later called the 'blue-stockings', whose members included Hannah More and Fanny Burney. *Observations...Shakespeare:* the remaining part of the title of her essay is: 'Compared with the Greek and French dramatic poets with some remarks upon the misrepresentations of Monsieur de Voltaire'. 6 *land –:* this ed. land? 1790 ed. 14 *friend?:* this ed. friend. 1790 ed. 29 *Parnassus:* a mountain in Greece, sacred to the Muses. *Plymouth:* Plymouth, Massachusetts.

CHARLOTTE LENNOX (*née* Ramsay)
1729?–1804

Poet and novelist, Charlotte Lennox, may have been born in Gibraltar in 1729 although, near the end of her life, in correspondence with the Royal Literary Fund, she gave her date of birth as 1720. Her father, James, was an army officer and she spent some of her childhood in the former New York Province, near Albany. She later lived in London, where her *Poems on Several Occasions*

'By a Young Lady' (from which the following poem is taken) was published in 1747. In the same year she married Alexander Lennox, who worked for the publisher, William Strahan, but soon found that she had to support herself and, later, her children. She was not successful on the stage between 1748 and 1750: Horace Walpole called her 'a poetess, and a deplorable actress'. Charlotte appears to have caused some offence through her writing and her behaviour, but Samuel Johnson became her loyal friend, helping to launch her first novel, *Harriet Stuart*, in 1750. Both Samuel Richardson and Johnson assisted the publication of her second novel, *The Female Quixote* (1752), and between 1749 and 1752 various unsuccessful efforts were made to bring about a new collection of her poetry. She was the first to collect Shakespeare's source materials in the three-volume *Shakespear Illustrated* (1753-54). She was also an editor and translator. She separated from her husband in 1792. From 1802 her financial hardship was relieved by payments from the Royal Literary Fund.

from The Art of Coquetry

Let the heaved breast a struggling sigh restrain,
And seem to stop the falling tear with pain.
The youth, who all the soft distress believes,
Soon wants the kind compassion which he gives.
But Beauty, Wit, and Youth may sometimes fail,
Nor always o'er the stubborn soul prevail.
Then let the fair one have recourse to Art,
And, if not vanquish, undermine the Heart.   50
First form your artful looks with studious care,
From mild to grave, from tender to severe.
Oft on the careless youth your glances dart,
A tender meaning let each look impart.
Whene'er he meets your looks, with modest pride
And soft confusion turn your eyes aside,
Let a soft sigh steal out, as if by chance,
Then cautious turn, and steal another glance.
Caught by these arts, with pride and hope elate,
The destined victim rushes on his fate: 60
Pleased, his imagined victory pursues,
And the kind maid with softened glances views;
Contemplates now her shape, her air, her face,
And thinks each feature wears an added grace;
Till gratitude, which first his bosom proves,
By slow degrees is ripened into Love.
'Tis harder still to fix than gain a heart;
What's won by Beauty must be kept by Art.
Too kind a treatment the blest lover cloys,
And oft despair the growing flame destroys: 70

Sometimes with smiles receive him, sometimes tears,
And wisely balance both his hopes and fears.
Perhaps he mourns his ill-requited pains,
Condemns your sway, and strives to break his chains;
Behaves as if he now your scorn defied,
And thinks at least he shall alarm your pride:
But with indifference view the seeming change,
And let your eyes after new conquests range;
While his torn breast with jealous fury burns,
He hopes, despairs, hates, and adores by turns;   80
With anguish now repents the weak deceit,
And powerful Passion bears him to your feet.

LUCY TERRY (Luce Bijah)
1730–1821

Lucy Terry was the first known black American poet. Brought from Africa
to Rhode Island as a slave when she was approximately five years old, she
married a free black man, Abijah Prince, in 1756. Through him, she gained
her freedom. They moved to Vermont in 1764, cultivated land, and raised six
children. Lucy was skilled in rhetoric and, when threatened with dispossession,
she took the case to court and was praised by the Judge for her persuasive
argument. The following poem was created about 1746 and was passed on
verbally until 1855, when Josiah Holland first published it in his *History of
Western Massachusetts* (vol. II, part III, p.360). He comments that she was 'noted
for her wit and shrewdness' (p.359). Another version appeared in *New England
Magazine* (March 1893). The following is taken from Holland's text. The
attack Lucy evokes in such detail took place in a hay meadow near Deerfield,
Massachusetts.

Bars Fight

August, 'twas the twenty-fifth,
Seventeen hundred forty six;
The Indians did in ambush lay,
Some very valiant men to slay,
The names of whom I'll not leave out.
Samuel Allen like a hero fout,
And though he was so brave and bold,
His face no more shall we behold.
Eleazer Hawks was killed outright,
Before he had time to fight, –   10
Before he did the Indians see,

Was shot and killed immediately.
Oliver Amsden he was slain,
Which caused his friends much grief and pain.
Simeon Amsden they found dead,
Not many rods distant from his head.
Adonijah Gillett we do hear
Did lose his life which was so dear.
John Sadler fled across the water,
And thus escaped the dreadful slaughter.   20
Eunice Allen see the Indians coming,
And hopes to save herself by running,
And had not her petticoats stopped her,
The awful creatures had not catched her,
Nor tommy hawked her on her head,
And left her on the ground for dead.
Young Samuel Allen, Oh lack-a-day!
Was taken and carried to Canada.

Title *Bars:* meadow. 6 *fout:* fought.

ANNIS BOUDINOT STOCKTON
1736–1801

Annis Boudinot, poet and dramatist, was the eldest daughter of a merchant
and silversmith from French Huguenot stock. She was born in Darby, Penn-
sylvania, but the family later settled in Princeton, New Jersey. She read widely
and wrote poetry and hymns from her early teens. Her marriage to one of the
signatories of the Declaration of Independence, the lawyer, Richard Stockton,
appears to have been happy. Annis brought up their six children whilst man-
aging the estate in her husband's absences, leading an active social life, and
writing. The gardens of their home, Morven (now 55 Stockton Street, Prince-
ton), were modelled on Pope's garden at Twickenham and have lately been
recreated from details in her poetry and correspondence. When Richard, who
had held Royal appointments before the American Revolution, eventually took
the colonists' part, the family had to flee to Monmouth, New Jersey. In 1776,
he was captured and imprisoned for a month in New York, but was released
following protests from George Washington. Morven was occupied by British
troops. The estate was pillaged and the family's possessions and library burned.
Richard died from cancer early in 1781, having never recovered from the brutal
treatment he received whilst in prison. After his death Annis frequently enter-
tained George and Martha Washington. Several of her poems are addressed to
Washington, who was also her correspondent. Between 1758 and 1793 21 of
her poems were published in a variety of magazines – under 'A.S.', 'Emilia' or
'Amelia'. Several of her manuscripts survive. The following poem was taken

from a manuscript text in Princeton University Library (Stimson Boudinot Collection Folder 42). Another version can be found in an appendix to the Rev. Samuel Stanhope Smith's *Funeral Sermon on the Death of the Hon, Richard Stockton* (1781). A donation of Annis Stockton's copybook to the New Jersey Historical Society in 1985 inspired Carla J. Mulford to collect over a hundred known poems in *Only for the Eye of a Friend: The Poems of Annis Boudinot Stockton* (1995).

An Extempore Ode in a Sleepless Night by a Lady Attending on Her Husband in a Long and Painful Illness

1

Sleep, balmy sleep, has closed the eyes of all,
And darkness reigns o'er this terrestial ball,
But me, ah me! no respite can I gain,
Not one soft slumber cheats this vital pain.

2

All day in secret sighs I've poured my soul,
And now, at night, in floods of sorrow roll;
My downy pillow, used to scenes of grief,
Has lost its power to yield the least relief.

3

Through all the silence of this dreary night,
Made awful by that taper's gloomy light
My aching heart re echoes ev'ry groan,
And makes each sigh, each mortal pang its own.

4

But why should I implore sleep's friendly aid?
O'er me, her poppies shed, no ease impart,
But dreams of dear departing joys invade,
And rack with fears my sad foreboding heart.

5

But vain is prophecy when death's approach,
Through years of pains, has sapped a dearer life,
And makes me, coward like, myself reproach,
That e'er I knew the tender name of wife.

6

Ah, could I take the fate to him assigned
And leave the helpless family their head
How pleased, how peaceful, to my lot resigned,
I'd quit the nurse's station for the bed.

7

O death, thou canker-worm of human joy,
Thou cruel foe to sweet domestic peace,
He soon shall come, that shall thy shafts destroy;
And cause thy dreadful ravages to cease.

8

Yes, the Redeemer comes to wipe the tears,
The briny tears, from every streaming eye,
And death, and sin, and doubts, and fears,
Shall all be lost in endless victory.

6 *roll;:* this ed. roll, Princeton ms (December 1780?).

ELIZABETH MOODY (*née* Greenly)
1737–1814

At the age of 40, Elizabeth Moody married a clergyman, Christopher Lake Moody, 16 years her junior. They lived in Turnham Green and were neighbours of Ralph Griffiths, editor of the *Monthly Review*, to which both contributed. Elizabeth was probably the magazine's first regular female reviewer. Between 1781 and 1788 some of her poems were published anonymously in magazines that included the *General Evening Post* and *The Gentleman's Magazine*: another appeared in a collection by George Miller in 1796. Her volume of poetry, *Poetic Trifles*, from which the following are taken, was published in 1798. The poet's own notes to 'To Darwin...' have been reproduced below.

To a Lady, Who was a great Talker

If your friendship to take I must take too your clack,
That friendship, methinks, I could almost give back;
Yet for worlds would I not with your amity part,
Could you lock up your tongue when you open your heart.

To Dr Darwin,
On Reading His Loves of the Plants

No bard e'er gave his tuneful powers,
Thus to traduce the fame of flowers;
Till Darwin sung his gossip tales,
Of females woo'd by *twenty* males.
Of *plants* so given to amorous pleasure;

Incontinent beyond all measure.
He sings that in botanic schools,
Husbands* adopt licentious rules;
Plurality of wives they wed,
And all they like – they take to bed.   10
That lovers sigh with *secret* love,
And marriage rites clandestine, prove.
That, fanned in groves their mutual fire,
They to some Gretna Green retire.

Linneus things, no doubt, revealed,
Which prudent *plants* would wish concealed;
So free of *families* he spoke,
As must that modest race provoke.
Till he invaded Flora's bowers
None heard of marriage among flowers;   20
Sexual distinctions were unknown;
Discovered by the Swede alone.
He blabbed through all the list'ning groves,
The mystic rites of *flow'ry loves.*
He pried in every blossom's fold,
And all he saw unseemly – told.
Blabbed tales of many a *feeble* swain;*
Unmeet to join in Flora's train;
Unless appointed by her care,
Like Turkish guards to watch the fair.   30
These *vegetable monsters* claim
Alliance with the eunuch's name.
In every herb and tree that grows;
Some frail propensity he shows.

But then in prose Linneus prattles,
And soon forgot is all he tattles.
While memory better pleased retains
The frolics of poetic brains.

So when the Muse with strains like thine
Enchantment breathes through every line;   40
That Reason pausing makes a stand,
Controlled by Fiction's magic hand.
Enamoured we the verse pursue,
And feel each fair delusion true.

Luxuriant thought thy mind o'ergrows;
Such painting from thy pencil flows;
Warm to my sight the visions rise,
And thy rich fancy mine supplies.
Thy themes rehearsing in my bower;
From those I picture ev'ry flower;   50
With thy descriptive forms impressed,
I see them in thy colours dressed;
Rememb'ring all thy lays unfold,
The snow-drop* *freezes* me with *cold*.
I hear the *love-sick* violet's sighs,
And see the hare-bell's *azure eyes*,
See *jealous cowslips* hang their heads,
And *virgin lilies* – pine in beds.
The primrose meets my tinctured view,
Far paler than before – she grew.   60
While woodbines *wanton* seem to twine,
And reeling shoots the *maud'ling** vine*.
If e'er I seek the *cypress* shade,
Whose branches contemplation aid.
Of learned lore my thoughts possessed,
Might dwell on mummies in a chest.
Unperishable chests 'tis said,
Where the Egyptian dead were laid,
Are of the cypress timber made.
And gates of Rome's famed church they say,   70
Defying mould'ring time's decay;
From Constantine to Pope Eugene,
Eleven hundred years were seen,
In perfect state of sound and good,
Formed of this adamantine wood.
Then, Darwin! were it not for thee,
I sure must venerate this tree.
But as his boughs hang o'er my head,
I recollect from you I read,
*His wife he exiles from his bed.**   80

151

Since thus thy fascinating art
So takes possession of the heart,
Go bid thy Muse a wreath prepare,
'To bind some charming Chloe's hair.'
But tune no more thy lyre's sweet powers,
To libel harmless trees and flowers.

Title *Darwin...Plants:* The second (and less serious) part of Erasmus Darwin's poem, *The Botanic Garden* (1789). 8 * See classes of Flowers, Polygamy, Clandestine Marriage, &c. note 1798 ed. 14 *Gretna Green:* Scottish village, close to the border, where runaway couples could have quick, legal marriages (until 1939). 15 *Linneus:* Linnaeus – Carl von Linné (1707-78), Swedish naturalist whose classification system for plants laid the foundations of modern botany. 22 *the Swede:* Linnaeus. 27 * See class – Vegetable Monsters and Eunuchs note 1798 ed. 31 *claim:* this ed. final comma here and at ll. 37, 81 1798 ed. 54 * How snow-drops cold and blue eye'd hare-bells blend/ Their tender tears as o'er the stream they bend;/ The love-sick violet, and the primrose pale,/ Bow their sweet heads and whisper to the gale,/ With secret sighs the virgin lily droops,/ And jealous cowslips hang their tawny cups. *Darwin's Love of the Plants* note 1798 ed. 62 * 'Drink deep, sweet youths,' seductive Vitis cries,/ The maudlin tear-drop glittering in her eyes. Darwin note 1798 ed. 80 * Cupressus dark disdains his dusky bride,/ One dome contains them – but two beds divide. Darwin note 1798 ed.

ANNA SEWARD

1742–1809

Her father, a rector and literary man, became Canon of Lichfield Cathedral and Anna lived in the Bishop's Palace from 1754. An author's note tells that her 'December Morning' sonnet was written in an apartment in the West Front of the Palace that 'looks upon the Cathedral-Area, a green Lawn enciled by Prebendal Houses, which seem white from being rough-cast' – the 'mansions white' of the poem. From 1776 she began to publish. Her successful *Elegy on Captain Cook* (1780) was followed by *Monody on the Death of Major André* (1781), which included a denunciation of George Washington, who later sent an emissary to her to defend his involvement in André's execution for spying. In 1784 she published a 'poetical novel', *Louisa*. Anna was a frequent contributor of verse and prose to major periodicals. Her sonnet on France in *The Gentleman's Magazine* (vol.59, 1789) was one of the first poetic responses to the French Revolution. (Later, like Wordsworth, she became disillusioned by the turn of events.) Her *Collection of Original Sonnets*, from which the other poems are taken, was published in 1799, though the first of these printed here was written in 1782 and the rest in 1789. She also published a *Memoir of Dr Darwin* in 1804. Before her death she negotiated the posthumous publication of her poetry and letters. Walter Scott edited three volumes of her *Poetical Works* in 1810. The 'Swan of Lichfield' never married.

Sonnet XL: December Morning

I love to rise ere gleams the tardy light,
    Winter's pale dawn; – and as warm fires illume,
    And cheerful tapers shine around the room,
    Thro' misty windows bend my musing sight
Where, round the dusky lawn, the mansions white,
    With shutters closed, peer faintly thro' the gloom,
    That slow recedes; while yon grey spires assume,
    Rising from their dark pile, an added height
By indistinctness given. – Then to decree
    The grateful thoughts to God, ere they unfold
    To Friendship or the Muse, or seek with glee
Wisdom's rich page! – O, hours! more worth than gold,
    By whose blest use we lengthen Life, and free
    From drear decays of Age, outlive the Old!

Sonnet LXXI: To the Poppy

While summer roses all their glory yield
    To crown the votary of love and joy,
    Misfortune's victim hails, with many a sigh,
    Thee, scarlet Poppy of the pathless field,
Gaudy, yet wild and lone; no leaf to shield
    Thy flaccid vest that, as the gale blows high,
    Flaps, and alternate folds around thy head. –
So stands in the long grass a love-crazed maid,
Smiling aghast; while stream to every wind
    Her garish ribbons, smeared with dust and rain;
    But brain-sick visions cheat her tortured mind,
And bring false peace. Thus, lulling grief and pain,
    Kind dreams oblivious from thy juice proceed,
    Thou flimsy, showy, melancholy weed.

14 *Thou...weed:* in capitals 1799 ed.

Sonnet XCII: Autumn Leaves

Behold that tree in Autumn's dim decay,
    Stripped by the frequent, chill, and eddying wind;
    Where yet some yellow, lonely leaves we find
    Lingering and trembling on the naked spray,

Twenty, perchance, for millions whirled away!
  Emblem, alas! too just, of human kind!
  Vain man expects longevity, designed
  For few indeed; and their protracted day –
What is it worth that wisdom does not scorn?
  The blasts of sickness, care, and grief appal,
  That laid the friends in dust, whose natal morn
Rose near their own; – and solemn is the call; –
  Yet, like those weak, deserted leaves forlorn,
Shivering they cling to life, and fear to fall!

8 *day* –: this ed. day 1799 ed.

Sonnet
To France on her present exertions

Thou, that where Freedom's sacred fountains play,
Which sprung effulgent, tho' with crimson stains,
On transatlantic shores, and widening plains,
Hast, in their living waters, washed away
Those cankering spots, shed by tyrannic sway
On thy long drooping lilies, English veins
Swell with the tide of exultation gay,
To see thee spurn thy deeply-galling chains.
Few of Britannia's free-born sons forbear
To bless thy Cause; – cold is the heart that breathes
No wish fraternal. – FRANCE, we bid thee
The blessings twining with our civic wreaths,
While Victory's trophies, permanent as fair,
Crown the bright SWORD that LIBERTY unsheaths.

MARY ALCOCK (*née* Cumberland)
c. 1742–98

Mary Alcock was the daughter of Dr Denison Cumberland, a Northamptonshire clergyman who became Bishop of Kilmore, and Joanna, daughter of the scholar, Dr Richard Bentley. Her brother, Richard, was a dramatist. The widow of an Archdeacon, Mary lived in Bath from the early 1780s. In the preface to her posthumously published volume, *Poems*, from which the following text is taken, her niece and editor, Joanna Hughes, writes that her aunt had previously only published her poetry anonymously to raise money to free debtors from prisons in Ilchester and Newgate. The book's list of subscribers includes the

Prince and Princess of Wales with other members of the royal family, bishops, admirals, and literary figures such as Hannah More and William Cowper. Towards the end of the volume Mary tells how she came to write this poem in an attempt to use humour to overcome her genuine disquiet at hearing a young woman request M.G. Lewis's fashionable but disturbing novel, *The Monk* (1796), from a bookseller.

A Receipt for Writing a Novel

Would you a fav'rite novel make,
Try hard your reader's heart to break,
For who is pleased, if not tormented?
(Novels for that were first invented).
'Gainst nature, reason, sense, combine
To carry on your bold design,
And those ingredients I shall mention,
Compounded with your own invention,
I'm sure will answer my intention.
Of love take first a due proportion –
It serves to keep the heart in motion:
Of jealousy a powerful zest,
Of all tormenting passions best;
Of horror mix a copious share,
And duels you must never spare;
Hysteric fits at least a score,
Or, if you find occasion, more;
But fainting fits you need not measure,
The fair ones have them at their pleasure;
Of sighs and groans take no account,
But throw them in to vast amount;
A frantic fever you may add,
Most authors make their lovers mad;
Rack well your hero's nerves and heart,
And let your heroine take her part;
Her fine blue eyes were made to weep,
Nor should she ever taste of sleep;
Ply her with terrors day or night,
And keep her always in a fright,
But in a carriage when you get her,
Be sure you fairly overset her;
If she will break her bones – why let her:
Again, if e'er she walks abroad,
Of course you bring some wicked lord,

Who with three ruffians snaps his prey,
And to a castle speeds away;
There close confined in haunted tower,
You leave your captive in his power,
Till dead with horror and dismay,
She scales the walls and flies away.

Now you contrive the lovers meeting,
To set your reader's heart a beating.
But ere they've had a moment's leisure,
Be sure to interrupt their pleasure;
Provide yourself with fresh alarms
To tear 'em from each other's arms;
No matter by what fate they're parted,
So that you keep them broken-hearted.

A cruel father some prepare
To drag her by her flaxen hair;
Some raise a storm, and some a ghost,
Take either, which may please you most.
But this you must with care observe,
That when you've wound up every nerve
With expectation, hope and fear,
Hero and heroine must disappear.
Some fill one book, some two without 'em,
And ne'er concern their heads about 'em,
This greatly rests the writer's brain,
For any story, that gives pain,
You now throw in – no matter what,
However foreign to the plot,
So it but serves to swell the book,
You foist it in with desperate hook –
A masquerade, a murdered peer,
His throat just cut from ear to ear –
A rake turned hermit – a fond maid
Run mad, by some false loon betrayed –
These stores supply the female pen
Which writes them o'er and o'er again,
And readers likewise may be found
To circulate them round and round.

Now at your fable's close devise
Some grand event to give surprise –

Suppose your hero knows no mother –
Suppose he proves the heroine's brother –
This at one stroke dissolves each tie,
Far as from east to west they fly:
At length when every woe's expended,
And your last volume's nearly ended,
Clear the mistake, and introduce
Some tatt'ling nurse to cut the noose,
The spell is broke – again they meet
Expiring at each other's feet;
Their friends lie breathless on the floor –
You drop your pen; you can no more –
And ere your reader can recover,
They're married – and your history's over.

ANNA LAETITIA BARBAULD
(*née* Aikin)
1743–1825

Born in Kibworth, Leicestershire, both Anna's father and husband were Unitarian ministers. She contributed hymns, anonymously, to her brother John's *Essays on Song-Writing* (1772). In 1773 she successfully published her *Poems* and, with her brother, *Miscellaneous Pieces in Prose*. She married Rochemont Barbauld in 1774 and moved to Palgrave, Suffolk, where the couple ran a boys' boarding-school, as her father had done. Among her publications at this time are *Devotional Pieces* (1775), *Lessons for Children* (1778) and *Hymns in Prose for Children* (1781). When the school closed in 1785 the couple lived in Europe before settling in Hampstead. Arguing against slavery and for religious freedom and equality, she published radical political prose pamphlets from 1790; an enlarged edition of her poems came out in 1792. She also reviewed, wrote essays, and edited poetry collections. In 1802 the Barbaulds moved to Stoke Newington, London, but her husband's mental health declined drastically to the point where he needed to be restrained. He was discovered drowned in 1808. In the meantime Anna edited six volumes of Samuel Richardson's letters (1804) and 50 volumes of *The British Novelists* (1810), which included her own essay, 'On the Origins and Progress of Novel-Writing'. Her poem, *Eighteen Hundred and Eleven*, which was published in 1812 and harshly reviewed, foresaw future challenges to British and European rule. Surprisingly, she was not a supporter of formal education for women. Her niece, Lucy Aikin, published *The Works of Anna Laetitia Barbauld*, with a memoir, in 1825. Anna Barbauld's poetry was praised by contemporaries, particularly Wordsworth and Coleridge. Her range is vast and covers ballads, riddles, elegies, odes, satire, mock-heroic, humorous occasional verse, and classical imitation.

The Rights of Woman

Yes, injured Woman! Rise, assert thy right!
Woman! Too long degraded, scorned, oppressed;
O born to rule in partial Law's despite,
Resume thy native empire o'er the breast!

Go forth arrayed in panoply divine;
That angel pureness which admits no stain;
Go, bid proud Man his boasted rule resign,
And kiss the golden sceptre of thy reign.

Go, gird thyself with grace; collect thy store
Of bright artillery glancing from afar;
Soft melting tones thy thundering cannon's roar,
Blushes and fears thy magazine of war.

Thy rights are empire: urge no meaner claim, –
Felt, not defined, and if debated, lost;
Like sacred mysteries, which withheld from fame,
Shunning discussion, are revered the most.

Try all that wit and art suggest to bend
Of thy imperial foe the stubborn knee;
Make treacherous Man, thy subject, not thy friend,
Thou mayst command, but never canst be free.

Awe the licentious, and restrain the rude;
Soften the sullen, clear the cloudy brow:
Be, more than princes' gifts, thy favours sued;–
She hazards all, who will the least allow.

But hope not, courted idol of mankind,
On this proud eminence secure to stay;
Subduing and subdued, thou soon shalt find
Thy coldness soften, and thy pride give way.

Then, then, abandon each ambitious thought,
Conquest or rule thy heart shall feebly move,
In Nature's school, by her soft maxims taught,
That separate rights are lost in mutual love.

from A Summer Evening's Meditation

...'Tis now the hour
When Contemplation, from her sunless haunts,
The cool damp grotto, or the lonely depth
Of unpierced woods, where wrapped in solid shade   20
She mused away the gaudy hours of noon,
And fed on thoughts unripened by the sun,
Moves forward; and with radiant finger points
To yon blue concave swelled by breath divine,
Where, one by one, the living eyes of heaven
Awake, quick kindling o'er the face of ether
One boundless blaze; ten thousand trembling fires,
And dancing lustres, where th'unsteady eye
Restless, and dazzled wanders unconfined
O'er all this field of glories: spacious field!   30
And worthy of the master: he, whose hand
With hieroglyphics older than the Nile,
Inscribed the mystic tablet; hung on high
To public gaze, and said, adore, O man!
The finger of thy GOD. From what pure wells
Of milky light, what soft o'erflowing urn,
Are all these lamps so filled? These friendly lamps,
For ever streaming o'er the azure deep
To point our path, and light us to our home.
How soft they slide along their lucid spheres!   40
And silent, as the foot of time, fulfil
Their destined courses: Nature's self is hushed,
And, but a scattered leaf, which rustles through
The thick-wove foliage, not a sound is heard
To break the midnight air; tho' the raised ear,
Intensely listening, drinks in every breath.
How deep the silence, yet how loud the praise!
But are they silent all? Or is there not
A tongue in every star that talks with man,
And woos him to be wise; nor woos in vain: 50
This dead of midnight is the noon of thought,
And wisdom mounts her zenith with the stars.
At this still hour the self-collected soul
Turns inward, and beholds a stranger there
Of high descent, and more than mortal rank;
An embryo GOD; a spark of fire divine,
Which must burn on for ages, when the sun,

159

(Fair transitory creature of a day!)
Has closed his golden eye, and wrapped in shades
Forgets his wonted journey thro' the east.   60

Title: Text from 1773 ed. Compare Anne Finch, 'A Nocturnal Rêverie', p.109. 33. *mystic*
tablet: the Universe. 26-49 *see* Psalm 19: 1-3.

HANNAH MORE
1745–1833

Poet, playwright, writer of tracts, didactic novelist – Hannah More was a
successful author in financial terms. She was born in Stapleton, Gloucestershire.
Educated by her father, a schoolmaster, she taught for a time in a school set up
by one of her four sisters in Bristol. Her fiancé, Edward Turner, broke their
engagement several times; he eventually gave Hannah an annuity of £200 and
a bequest in his will instead of marriage. She was able to live independently,
supplementing the annuity with proceeds from her writing, which became
increasingly more pious. David Garrick produced two of her plays at Drury
Lane: *Percy* (1777) and *The Fatal Falsehood* (1779). A friend of the MP,
William Wilberforce, Hannah wrote a number of poems against slavery.
Slavery, A Poem (1788) was the first; it coincided with Wilberforce's efforts
in Parliament to abolish the slave-trade. Fearful of the impact of the French
Revolution, she wrote *Village Politics* (an anti-revolutionary tract) under a
pseudonym, 'Will Chip' in 1792. Her poetry ranged from an ode to Dagon,
Garrick's dog (1777), to *Sensibility* (1782) and the satirical, *Bishop Bonner's
Ghost* (Strawberry Hill Press, 1789). She was also a patron to the poet, Ann
Yearsley, but this did not end harmoniously when Yearsley was denied con-
trol of her own income. Hannah More moved to Wrington, Somerset at the
end of the 1780s and, in 1828, to Clifton, where she died.

from Slavery, A Poem

When'er to Afric's shores I turn my eyes,
Horrors of deepest, deadliest guilt arise;
I see, by more than Fancy's mirror shown,
The burning village, and the blazing town:
See the dire victim torn from social life,
The shrieking babe, the agonizing wife!   100
She, wretch forlorn! is dragged by hostile hands,
To distant tyrants sold, in distant lands!
Transmitted miseries, and successive chains,
The sole sad heritage her child obtains!
Ev'n this last wretched boon their foes deny,

To weep together, or together die.
By felon hands, by one relentless stroke,
See the fond links of feeling Nature broke!
The fibres twisting round a parent's heart,
Torn from their grasp, and bleeding as they part.   110
   Hold, murderers, hold! nor aggravate distress;
Respect the passions you yourselves possess;
Ev'n you, of ruffian heart, and ruthless hand,
Love your own offspring, love your native land.
Ah! Leave them holy Freedom's cheering smile,
The heaven-taught fondness for the parent soil;
Revere affections mingled with our frame,
In every nature, every clime the same;
In all, these feelings equal sway maintain;
In all the love of HOME and FREEDOM reign: 120
And Tempe's vale, and parched Angola's sand,
One equal fondness of their sons command...
[...]

And thou, WHITE SAVAGE! whether lust of gold,   211
Or lust of conquest, rule thee uncontrolled!
Hero, or robber! – by whatever name
Thou plead thy impious claim to wealth or fame;
Whether inferior mischiefs be thy boast,
A petty tyrant rifling Gambia's coast:
Or bolder carnage track thy crimson way,
Kings dispossessed, and Provinces thy prey;
Panting to tame wide earth's remotest bound;
All Cortez murdered, all Columbus found;   220
O'er plundered realms to reign, detested Lord,
Make millions wretched, and thyself abhorred; –
In Reason's eye, in Wisdom's fair account;
Your sum of glory boasts a like amount;
The means may differ, but the end's the same;
Conquest is pillage with a nobler name.
Who makes the sum of human blessings less,
Or sinks the stock of general happiness,
No solid fame shall grace, no true renown,
His life shall blazon, or his memory crown.   230
   Had those advent'rous spirits who explore
Thro' oceans trackless wastes, the far-sought shore;
Whether of wealth insatiate, or of power,
Conquerors who waste, or ruffians who devour:
Had these possessed, O Cook! thy gentle mind,

161

Thy love of arts, thy love of humankind;
Had these pursued thy mild and liberal plan,
DISCOVERERS had not been a curse to man!

220 *Cortez:* Hernando Cortez, who conquered Mexico for Spain; *all...found:* i.e. the Bahamas, Cuba, South America. 235 *Cook:* James Cook (*d.* 1779), who explored the South Pacific islands and claimed Australia for the British in 1770.

SUSANNA BLAMIRE
1747–94

Known as 'The Muse of Cumberland', poet and songwriter, Susanna Blamire, was born near Carlisle. Her father was a yeoman farmer and her mother, Isabella, died when she was seven. After her father's death (*c.* 1758), she and her brothers and sister were brought up by their aunt on a farm near Stokedalewath. Her poem, 'Stoklewath, or the Cumbrian Village', is a response to Goldsmith's 'The Deserted Village' and vividly depicts 18th-century Cumbrian rural life. Susanna was educated at a nearby village school and played the guitar and flageolet as well as writing verse. Having lived for six years with her sister, in the Scottish Highlands, she wrote in Cumbrian and Scottish dialect as well as standard English. Some of her songs were printed anonymously in the 1780s. She never married, and died, aged 47, from a rheumatism-related illness. Dr Henry Lonsdale of Carlisle, who began collecting her verse long after her death, noted that her manuscripts were frequently written on the backs of old letters or recipes. *Poetical Works*, from which this was taken, was published posthumously in Edinburgh (1842).

Wey, Ned, Man!
The subject of this song was actually overheard

'Wey, Ned, man! Thou luiks sae down-hearted,
  Yen wad swear aw thy kindred were dead;
For sixpence, thy Jean and thee's parted, –
  What then, man, ne'er bodder thy head!
There's lasses enow, I'll uphod te,
  And tou may be suin as weel matched;
Tou knows there's still fish i' the river
  As guid as has ever been catched.'

'Nay, Joe! Tou kens nought o' the matter,
  Sae let's hae nae mair o' thy jeer;   10
Auld England's gown's worn till a tatter,
  And they'll nit new don her, I fear.

True liberty never can flourish,
  Till man in his reets is a king, –
Till we tek a tithe pig frae the bishop,
  As he's duin frae us, is the thing.'

'What, Ned! And is this aw that ails thee?
  Mess, lad! Tou deserves maist to hang!
What! Tek a bit lan frae its owner! –
  Is this then thy fine *Reets o' Man?*   20
Tou ploughs, and tou sows, and tou reaps, man,
  Tou cums, and tou gangs, where tou will;
Nowther king, lword, nor bishop, dar touch thee,
  Sae lang as tou dis fwok nae ill!'

'How can tou say sae, Joe! Tou kens, now,
  If hares were as plenty as hops,
I durstn't fell yen for my life, man,
  Nor tek't out o' auld Cwoley's chops:
While girt fwok they ride down my hedges,
  And spang o'er my fields o' new wheat,   30
Nought but ill words I get for my damage; –
  Can ony man tell me *that's reet?*'

'Why, there I mun own the shoe pinches,
  Just there to find faut is nae shame;
Ne'er ak! There's nae hard laws in England,
  Except this bit thing about game:
Man, were we aw equal at mwornin,
  We couldn't remain sae till neet;
Some arms are far stranger than others,
  And some heads will tek in mair leet.   40

Tou couldn't mend laws an' tou wad, man;
  'Tis for other-guess noddles than thine;
Lord help te! Sud beggars yence rule us,
  They'd tek off baith thy cwoat an' mine.
What is't then but law that stands by us,
  While we stand by country and king?
And as to being parfet and parfet,
  I tell thee, there is nae sec thing.'

20 *Reets…Man:* Thomas Paine's political treatise, *The Rights of Man*, was published in
1791-92. 35-36 *There's…game:* only large property owners were allowed to take game.

163

ANNE WILSON

fl. 1778

Anne Wilson's 1,615-line poem, from which the following extract is taken, was published in Newcastle upon Tyne in 1778. It has been seen as an early example of ecofeminist writing (see Bridget Keegan's essay, 'Writing Against the Current: Anne Wilson's "Teisa" and the Tradition of British River Poetry' in *Women's Studies* 31, Summer 2002, pp.267-85) and ranges from providing details of cheesemaking to singing the praises of the drainage system. Her poem suggests that she is a local poet of limited means who appreciated the relationship between the region's people and their land.

from Teisa: a Descriptive Poem of the River Tees, its Towns and Antiquities

We next a beauteous cataract espy,
Amazed where wonder lends her eager eye:
For vast thy height, and rapid is thy course;
From rock sublime, O justly called, High Force! 50
Nature has sure exhausted here her store,
She scarce can add a single beauty more.
From this stupendous height, the streams that flow
Are swiftly changed to flakes of falling snow;
As down its ragged sides they pour along,
Light airy vehicles push each other on:
Time's striking picture, here, methinks, I view;
Ye swollen spheres! He marches on like you;
Bubbles push bubbles, minutes minutes on,
And all, at last, is one promiscuous throng: 60
Ye hasten to salute your parent sea,
And time to meet with round Eternity.
With pleasure here my wond'ring eye could dwell,
While these exhaustless scenes, my Muse should tell,
And all the beauties of this vast cascade:
But artful peasants, lo! a bridge have made;
Whose novelty diverts the wand'ring eye:
Across the flood, from rocks immensely high,
See two strong iron chains their length extend;
On these rebounding links some boards depend, 70
And make a dancing bridge, where peasants go,
Regardless of th'amazing depth below!

Let not the citizen polite, disdain
These peasants, who, each useful art maintain:
Each people to their place kind nature suits,

164

Superintendent o'er her works deputes:
These humble people, who inhabit here,
Have minds, we see, capacious, and as clear
As ye, the great, who lordship o'er them claim:
O when ye take from these a master's name,   80
Do not their honest labour ill requite;
Let not the Sun withdraw his sacred light,
Ere you the wages of industry pay;
For you they drudge throughout the weary day;
For you, what perils here they undergo,
By delving in the dreary mines below:
Oft has the patient miner in the morn,
Left a beloved wife, and babes at home;
Happy in the thoughts of returning eve,
But fate (alas!) does each warm hope deceive;   90
Perhaps, he, by some vapour lost his breath,
His wife and helpless infants mourned his death...

Title: the river Tees rises in the Pennines and flows into the North Sea beyond Middlesbrough. 50 *High Force:* a spectacular waterfall in the Pennine region, near Ettersgill, reputedly the largest (above-ground) continuous fall of water in England. 86 *dreary mines:* the region has a history of lead and coal mining.

CHARLOTTE SMITH (*née* Turner)
1749–1806

Charlotte Smith, poet and novelist, was born into a wealthy London family. Her mother died when she was three and her aunt arranged a limited education for her (until she was twelve). She wrote poetry from the age of six or seven. After her father's re-marriage, Charlotte was married herself, at 15, to Benjamin Smith, the second son of a director of the East India Company. Her husband was extravagant and unable to provide for their twelve children. When he was in prison for debt, she published *Elegiac Sonnets and Other Essays* in 1784, at her own expense: four more editions in the next five years helped her financial situation. Although they later separated (in practice, not law) she gave her husband financial support until his death in 1806. *The Emigrants*, a two-volume narrative poem (1793), and *Beachy Head, with Other Poems* (1807), were not as successful as her first collection, but this was reissued with new work in 1797 as *Elegiac Sonnets, with Additional Sonnets and Other Poems*. She was praised by Burns, Wordsworth, Coleridge and others, though Anna Seward disputed some of the effusive praise her sonnets received in the *Gentleman's Magazine* (1786). Although Charlotte went on to write ten popular novels, and also produced translations and moralistic works for children, she thought of herself primarily as a poet. Loraine Fletcher's very readable *Charlotte Smith: a critical biography* was published by Macmillan in 1998 and Judith Wilson edited a selection of Charlotte's poetry for Carcanet in 2003.

Elegiac Sonnets, No.70. On Being Cautioned against Walking on an Headland Overlooking the Sea, because It Was Frequented by a Lunatic

Is there a solitary wretch who hies
　　To the tall cliff, with starting pace or flow,
And, measuring, views with wild and hollow eyes
　　Its distance from the waves that chide below;
Who, as the sea-born gale with frequent sighs
　　Chills his cold bed upon the mountain turf,
With hoarse, half-uttered lamentation, lies
　　Murmuring responses to the dashing surf?
In moody sadness, on the giddy brink,
　　I see him more with envy than with fear;
He has no *nice felicities* that shrink
　　From giant horrors; wildly wandering here,
He seems (uncursed with reason) not to know
　　The depth or the duration of his woe.

Title: text from the 1797 ed. 1 *hies:* hurries.

from Beachy Head

　　　　…Just beneath the rock
Where Beachy overpeers the channel wave,
Within a cavern mined by wintry tides
Dwelt one, who long disgusted with the world
And all its ways, appeared to suffer life
Rather than live; the soul-reviving gale,
Fanning the bean-field, or the thymy heath,
Had not for many summers breathed on him;
And nothing marked to him the season's change,
Save that more gently rose the placid sea,　　　　680
And that the birds which winter on the coast
Gave place to other migrants; save that the fog,
Hovering no more above the beetling cliffs
Betrayed not then the little careless sheep
On the brink grazing, while their headlong fall
Near the lone Hermit's flint-surrounded home,
Claimed unavailing pity; for his heart
Was feelingly alive to all that breathed;
And outraged as he was, in sanguine youth,
By human crimes, he still acutely felt　　　　690
For human misery.

Wandering on the beach,
He learned to augur from the clouds of heaven,
And from the changing colours of the sea,
And sullen murmurs of the hollow cliffs,
Or the dark porpoises, that near the shore
Gambolled and sported on the level brine
When tempests were approaching: then at night
He listened to the wind; and as it drove
The billows with o'erwhelming vehemence
He, starting from his rugged couch, went forth   700
And hazarding a life, too valueless,
He waded thro' the waves, with plank or pole
Towards where the mariner in conflict dread
Was buffeting for life the roaring surge;
And now just seen, now lost in foaming gulfs,
The dismal gleaming of the clouded moon
Showed the dire peril. Often he had snatched
From the wild billows, some unhappy man
Who lived to bless the hermit of the rocks.
But if his generous cares were all in vain,   710
And with slow swell the tide of morning bore
Some blue swol'n corse to land; the pale recluse
Dug in the chalk a sepulchre – above
Where the dank sea-wrack marked the utmost tide,
And with his prayers performed the obsequies
For the poor helpless stranger.

                    One dark night
The equinoctial wind blew south by west,
Fierce on the shore;-the bellowing cliffs were shook
Even to their stony base, and fragments fell
Flashing and thundering on the angry flood.   720
At day-break, anxious for the lonely man,
His cave the mountain shepherds visited,
Tho' sand and banks of weeds had choked their way –
He was not in it; but his drowned corse
By the waves wafted, near his former home
Received the rites of burial. Those who read
Chiselled within the rock, these mournful lines,
Memorials of his sufferings, did not grieve,
That dying in the cause of charity
His spirit, from its earthly bondage freed,   730
Had to some better region fled for ever.

705 *gulfs:* gulphs 1807 ed. 712 *corse:* corpse.

167

ANNE LINDSAY (*later* Barnard)
1750–1825

Lady Anne Lindsay grew up in Fife and met Samuel Johnson during his tour of Scotland. She later lived in London and the Cape of Good Hope (after her marriage to Andrew Barnard in 1793). The eldest daughter of James Lindsay, 5th Earl of Balcarres, and his wife, Anne Dalrymple, she wrote the following poem to counter the words of an old Scottish song, 'The Bridegroom greets when the Sun gangs down', which she considered to be improper. Written in 1771 and first published in 1776, her poem became very popular in her lifetime though, initially, she concealed her identity as its author. Walter Scott printed a verse from its less popular sequel at the head of Chapter 26 in his novel, *The Pirate* (1821). Later editions included the following note: '...this motto, and the ascription of the beautiful ballad from which it is taken to the Right Honourable Lady Ann Lindsay, occasioned the ingenious authoress's acknowledgement of the ballad, of which the Editor, by her permission, published a small impression, inscribed to the Bannatyne Club'. He published it in 1825, the year she died.

Auld Robin Gray

When the sheep are in the fauld, when the cows come hame,
When a' the weary world to quiet rest are gane,
The woes of my heart fa' in showers frae my ee,
Unkenned by my gudeman, who soundly sleeps by me.

Young Jamie loo'd me weel, and sought me for his bride;
But saving ae crown-piece, he'd naething else beside.
To make the crown a pound, my Jamie gaed to sea;
And the crown and the pound, oh! they were baith for me!

Before he had been gane a twelvemonth and a day,
My father brak his arm, our cow was stown away;   10
My mither she fell sick – my Jamie was at sea –
And auld Robin Gray, oh! he came a-courting me.

My father cou'dna work, my mother cou'dna spin;
I toiled day and night, but their bread I cou'dna win;
And Rob maintained them baith, and wi' tears in his ee,
Said, 'Jenny, oh! for their sakes, will you marry me?'

My heart it said na, and I looked for Jamie back;
But hard blew the winds, and his ship was a wrack:
His ship it was a wrack! Why didna Jenny dee!
Or, wherefore am I spared to cry out, Woe is me!   20

My father argued sair – my mother didna speak,
But she looked in my face till my heart was like to break:
They gied him my hand, but my heart was in the sea;
And so auld Robin Gray, he was gudeman to me.

I hadna been his wife, a week but only four,
When mournfu' as I sat on the stane at my door,
I saw my Jamie's ghaist – I cou'dna think it he,
Till he said, 'I'm come hame, my love, to marry thee!'

O sair, sair did we greet, and mickle say of a';
Ae kiss we took, nae mair – I bad him gang awa.　　　　30
I wish that I were dead, but I'm no like to dee;
For O, I am but young to cry out, Woe is me!

I gang like a ghaist, and I carena much to spin;
I darena think o' Jamie, for that wad be a sin.
But I will do my best a gude wife aye to be,
For auld Robin Gray, oh! he is sae kind to me.

4 *unkenned:* unknown. 6 *crown-piece:* coin worth 5 old shillings or 25 new pence. 10 *stown:* stolen. 21 *sair:* sorrowfully.

ANN YEARSLEY (*née* Cromartie)
1752–1806

Ann lived on Clifton Hill, Bristol. Like her mother before her, she delivered and sold milk, hence her *nom de plume*, 'Lactilla'. Married to a labourer who earned £6 a year, she had six children and her mother to support. In 1783-84 the family almost starved. Although help eventually came, Ann's mother died the following spring. Later that year, through her connection with Hannah More's cook (who provided her with pig-swill), Ann's poetical talent and her poverty came to the lady of the house's attention. Hannah More decided to collect subscriptions to publish a volume of her poetry. *Poems on Several Occasions* (from which *Clifton Hill* is extracted) was a financial success in 1785, but Hannah and the critic and literary patron, Elizabeth Montagu, made themselves trustees of the profits (over £500), and restricted Ann's access to them, believing this to be for her own good. Ann was enraged: bitter arguments followed, some of them in print. The last edition of *Poems on Several Occasions* (1786) and *Poems, on Various Subjects* (1787) both included Hannah More's initial letter, in 1784, to Elizabeth Montagu about Ann ('a genius buried in obscurity'), as well as an account of the subsequent quarrels from Ann's point-of-view. Ann eventually received the money due to her for her book and found a new patron in Frederick Augustus Hervey, Bishop of Derry and Earl of Bristol. In 1788 she published *A Poem on the Inhumanity of the Slave-Trade*. *The Rural Lyre*, which provides the texts of the other poems here, appeared in

1796. Ann also wrote a play, *Earl Goodwin* (performed in 1789), and a Gothic novel, *The Royal Captives* (1795). She ran a circulating library at Bristol Hot Wells from about 1793 and eventually retired to a reclusive existence at Melksham, where she died. She is buried at Clifton. A very accessible volume of her selected poems was edited by Tim Burke for the Cyder Press in 2003.

from Clifton Hill
Written in January 1785

Beneath those heights, lo! balmy springs arise,
To which pale Beauty's faded image flies;
Their kindly powers life's genial heat restore,
The tardy pulse, whose throbs were almost o'er,
Here beats a livelier tune. The breezy air,   130
To the wild hills invites the languid fair:
Fear not the western gale, thou tim'rous maid,
Nor dread its blast shall thy soft form invade;
Tho' cool and strong the quick'ning breezes blow,
And meet thy panting breath, 'twill quickly grow
More strong; then drink the odoriferous draught,
With unseen particles of health 'tis fraught.
Sit not within the threshold of Despair,
Nor plead a weakness fatal to the fair;
Soft term for Indolence, politely given,   140
By which we win no joy from earth or heaven.
Foul Fiend! thou bane of health, fair Virtue's bane,
Death of true pleasure, source of real pain!
Keen exercise shall brace the fainting soul,
And bid her slackened powers more vigorous roll.
    Blame not my rustic lay, nor think me rude,
If I avow Conceit's the grand prelude
To dire disease and death. Your high-born maid,
Whom fashion guides, in youth's first bloom shall fade;
She seeks the cause, th'effect would fain elude,   150
By Death's o'erstretching stride too close pursued,
She faints within his icy grasp, yet stares,
And wonders why the Tyrant yet appears –
Abrupt – so soon – Thine, Fashion, is the crime,
Fell Dissipation does the work of time.
    How thickly clothed, yon rock of scanty soil,
It's lovely verdure scorns the hand of Toil.
Here the deep green, and here the lively plays,
The russet birch, and ever-blooming bays;
The vengeful black-thorn, of wild beauties proud,   160

Blooms beauteous in the gloomy-chequered crowd:
The barren elm, the useful feeding oak,
Whose hamadryad ne'er should feel the stroke
Of axe relentless, 'till twice fifty years
Have crowned her woodland joys, and fruitful cares...

[...]

Low not, ye herds, your lusty Masters bring   200
The crop of Summer; and the genial Spring
Feels for your wants, and softens Winter's rage,
The hoarded hay-stack shall your woes assuage;
Woes summed in one alone, 'tis Nature's call,
That secret voice which fills creation all.
  Beneath this stack Louisa's dwelling rose,
Here the fair Maniac bore three Winters' snows.
Here long she shivered, stiffening in the blast,
The lightnings round their livid horrors cast;
The thunders roar, while rushing torrents pour,   210
And add new woes to bleak affliction's hour;
The heavens lour dismal while the storm descends,
No Mother's bosom the soft maid befriends;
But, frightened, o'er the wilds she swiftly flies,
And drenched with rains, the roofless hay-stack tries.
The morn was fair, and gentle – – sought
These lonely woodlands, friends to sober Thought;
With Solitude, the slow-paced maid is seen
Tread the dark grove, and unfrequented green,
Well – – knew their lurkings; Phoebus shone,   220
While, musing, she pursued the track alone.
O, thou kind friend! Whom here I dare not name,
Who to Louisa's shed of misery came,
Lured by the tale, sighed o'er her beauteous form,
And gently drew her from the beating storm,
Stand forth – defend, for well thou canst, the cause
Of Heaven, and justify its rigid laws;
Yet own that human laws are harshly given,
When they extend beyond the will of Heaven.
Say, can thy pen for that hard duty plead,   230
By which the meek and helpless maid's decreed
To dire seclusion? Snatched from guiltless joys,
To where corroding grief the frame destroys;
Monastic glooms, which active virtue cramp,
Where horrid silence chills the vital lamp;
Slowly and faint the languid pulses beat,

And the chilled heart forgets its genial heat;
The dim sunk eye, with hopeless glance, explores
The solemn aisles, and death-denouncing doors,
Ne'er to be past again. – Now heaves the sigh,   240
Now unavailing sorrows fill the eye:
Fancy once more brings back the long-lost youth
To the fond soul, in all the charms of Truth;
She welcomes the loved image; busy Thought
Portrays the past, with guiltless pleasures fraught;
'Tis momentary bliss, 'tis rapture high,
The heart o'erflows, and all is ecstasy.
Memory! I charge thee yet preserve the shade,
Ah! let not yet the glittering colours fade!
Forbear the cruel future yet to view,   250
When the sad soul must bid a long adieu,
E'en to its fancied bliss – Ah! turn not yet
Thou wretched bankrupt, that must soon forget
This farewell draught of joy: lo! Fancy dies,
E'en the thin phantom of past pleasure flies.
Thought sinks in real woe; too poor to give
Her present bliss, she bids the future live;
The spirit soon quits that fond clasp, for see,
The future offers finished misery.
Hope quite extinct, lo! frantic thro' the aisles   260
She raves, while Superstition grimly smiles.
Th' exhausted mourner mopes, then wildly stalks
Round the drear dome, and seeks the darkest walks.
The glance distracted each sad sister meets,
The sorrow-speaking eye in silence greets
Each death-devoted maid; Louisa here
Runs thro' each various shape of sad despair;
Now swells with gusts of hope, now sick'ning dies;
Alternate thoughts of death and life arise
Within her panting soul; the firm resolve,   270
The new desire, in stronger fears dissolve.
She starts – then seized the moment of her fate,
Quits the lone cloister and the horrid grate,
Whilst wilder horrors to receive her wait;
Muffled, on Freedom's happy plains they stand,
And eager seize her not reluctant hand;
Too late to these mild shores the mourner came,
For now the guilt of flight o'erwhelms her frame:
Her broken vows in wild disorder roll,

And stick like serpents in her trembling soul;   280
Thought, what art thou? of thee she boasts no more,
O'erwhelmed, thou dy'st amid the wilder roar
Of lawless anarchy, which sweeps the soul,
Whilst her drowned faculties like pebbles roll,
Unloosed, uptorn, by whirlwinds of despair,
Each well-taught moral now dissolves in air;
Dishevelled, lo! her beauteous tresses fly,
And the wild glance now fills the staring eye;
The balls, fierce glaring in their orbits move,
Bright spheres, where beamed the sparkling fires of Love,   290
Now roam for objects which once filled her mind,
Ah! long-lost objects they must never find.
Ill starred Louisa! Memory, 'tis a strain,
Which fills my soul with sympathetic pain.
Remembrance, hence, give thy vain struggles o'er,
Nor swell the line with forms that live no more.

Title: *Clifton* was known as a health resort in the 18th century. The hill was the subject
of legend and this poem entwines its historical, social, and natural aspects with the poet's
own experience. 126 *those heights...balmy springs:* St Vincent's rocks...The Hot Wells.
The latter area is where curative springs were found at the foot of these rocks on the
north bank of the Avon. 142 *Foul fiend:* see also *King Lear* III.iv.51, III.vi.8, etc. 163
hamadryad: a nymph who lives and dies with the tree of which she is the spirit. 206
Louisa: a young refugee who, according to Yearsley's note, lived under a hay-stack for
three years 'in a state of distraction', having escaped from a convent where she had been
confined by her father for refusing to marry the man of his choice. 223 *Who...came:*
Hannah More may be meant as she assisted Louisa.

Sonnet to ------.

LO! dreary Winter, howling o'er the waste,
    Imprints the glebe, bids ev'ry channel fill –
His tears in torrents down the mountains haste,
    His breath augments despair, and checks our will!
Yet thy pure flame through lonely night is seen,
To lure the shiv'ring pilgrim o'er the green –
He hastens on, nor heeds the pelting blast:
Thy spirit softly breathes – 'The worst is past;
Warm thee, poor wand'rer, 'mid thy devious way!
    On thy cold bosom hangs unwholesome air;
Ah! pass not this bright fire! Thou long may'st stray
    Ere through the glens one other spark appear.'

Thus breaks thy friendship on my sinking mind,
And lures me on, while sorrow dies behind.

The Indifferent Shepherdess

Colin, why this mistake?
    Why plead thy foolish love?
My heart shall sooner break
    Than I a minion prove;
Nor care I half a rush,
No snare I spread for thee:
Go home, my friend, and blush
For love and liberty.

Remembrance is my own –
    Dominion bright and clear,
Truth there was ever known
    To combat ev'ry care:
One image there imprest
Thro' life shall ever be,
Whilst my innoxious breast
Owns love of liberty.

I ever taught thee how
    To prize the soul entire,
When on the mountain's brow
    I tuned my rural lyre:
Thou servile art and vain,
    Thy love unworthy me!
Away! nor hear my strain,
Of love or liberty.

What arts needs I display
    To woo a soul like thine?
Thou ne'er canst know the way
My mem'ry to confine;
    For my eternal plan
    Is to be calm and free.
Estranged from tyrant man
I'll keep my liberty.

Yon woods their foliage wear,
    Be thou away or nigh;
The warblers of the year
    Instruct me not to sigh:
My tears ne'er roll the steep,

Nor swell the restless sea,
Except for those who sleep
Bereft of liberty.

Slave to commanding eyes!
    Those eyes thou wouldst commend
My judgment must despise –
    My pity is thy friend:
If eyes alone can move
    A swain so dull as thee,
They mean but to reprove
    Thy loss of liberty.

I stray o'er rocks and fields
    Where native beauties shine:
All fettered fancy yields
    Be, Colin, ever thine.
Complain no more! but rove –
    My cheek from crimson free,
Within my native grove
    I'll guard my liberty.

Title: This poem goes one step further than Sir Walter Raleigh's 'The Nymph's Reply to the Shepherd' which is, itself, a reply to Christopher Marlowe's 'The Passionate Shepherd to his Love'. Yearsley's shepherdess, being created by a female poet, portrays her own landscape, largely independent of Marlowe's language, where there is no place for 'tyrant man' at all and certainly no point in him attempting to woo her, since liberty – of mind and body – is her sole love. 1 *Colin:* frequently used name for a rustic lover in pastoral poetry.

PHILLIS WHEATLEY
(*c*. 1753–84)

Phillis Wheatley was the first black writer known to have published a book in the North-American colonies. She was sold into slavery in West Africa and bought, in 1761, in Boston, by Susanna and John Wheatley. Educated with the Wheatley's children, according to John Wheatley, she learnt English quickly and could soon read 'the most difficult parts of the sacred writings'. She learnt Latin and read widely, particularly Ovid, Milton and Pope. Her first known published poem appeared in the Newport, Rhode Island *Mercury* in 1767 and her 'On the Death of Mr George Whitefield' (1770) was published as a broadside in both America and England. This led to a volume, *Poems on Various Subjects, Religious and Moral*, being published in London, in 1773, when Phillis accompanied the Wheatleys on their voyage to England. Her publisher included a letter from John Wheatley endorsing Phillis's authorship, as well as a declaration signed by the Governor, Thomas Hutchinson, and 17 others, 'to assure the world, that the poems specified on the following page, were (as we verily believe) written by Phillis, a young negro girl, who was but a few years since, brought an uncultivated barbarian from Africa, and has ever since been, and now is, under the disadvantage of serving as a slave in a family in this town. She has been examined by some of the best judges, and is thought qualified to write them.' She was freed in 1773 but remained with the Wheatleys. She wrote a poem and a letter of support to George Washington in 1776. He praised her in return and invited her to visit him. When John Wheatley died, in 1778, she married John Peters, a free African-American. They had three children, but none survived and, in 1784, Phillis herself died, in poverty, from complications arising from childbirth. Her poems were reprinted by abolitionists in the 1830s.

To S.M., a Young *African* Painter, on Seeing His Works

To show the lab'ring bosom's deep intent,
And thought in living characters to paint,
When first thy pencil did those beauties give,
And breathing figures learnt from thee to live,
How did those prospects give my soul delight,
A new creation rushing on my sight?
Still, wond'rous youth! each noble path pursue,
On deathless glories fix thine ardent view:
Still may the painter's and the poet's fire
To aid thy pencil, and thy verse conspire!   10
And may the charms of each seraphic theme
Conduct thy footsteps to immortal fame!
High to the blissful wonders of the skies
Elate thy soul, and raise thy wishful eyes.
Thrice happy, when exalted to survey
That splendid city, crowned with endless day,
Whose twice six gates on radiant hinges ring:
Celestial Salem blooms in endless spring.

Calm and serene thy moments glide along,
And may the muse inspire each future song!   20
Still, with the sweets of contemplation blessed,
May peace with balmy wings your soul invest!
But when these shades of time are chased away,
And darkness ends in everlasting day,
On what seraphic pinions shall we move,
And view the landscapes in the realms above?
There shall thy tongue in heavenly murmurs flow,
And there my muse with heavenly transport glow:

176

No more to tell of Damon's tender sighs,
Or rising radiance of Aurora's eyes,   30
For nobler themes demand a nobler strain,
And purer language on th'ethereal plain.
Cease, gentle muse! The solemn gloom of night
Now seals the fair creation from my sight.

29 *Damon:* in classical legend, a Syracusan who stood bail for his friend, Phinitias. The latter returned to save him at the last moment so their names are synonymous with faithful friends. 30 *Aurora:* the goddess of the dawn

To the Right Honourable William, Earl of Dartmouth, His Majesty's Principal Secretary of State for North America

Hail, happy day, when, smiling like the morn,
Fair *Freedom* rose New-England to adorn:
The northern clime beneath her genial ray,
Dartmouth, congratulates thy blissful sway:
Elate with hope her race no longer mourns,
Each soul expands, each grateful bosom burns,
While in thine hand with pleasure we behold
The silken reins, and *Freedom*'s charms unfold.
Long lost to realms beneath the northern skies
She shines supreme, while hated *faction* dies: 10
Soon as appeared the *Goddess* long desired,
Sick at the view, she lanquished and expired;
Thus from the splendors of the morning light
The owl in sadness seeks the caves of night.

No more, *America*, in mournful strain
Of wrongs, and grievance unredressed complain,
No longer shalt thou dread the iron chain,
Which wanton *Tyranny* with lawless hand
Had made, and with it meant t' enslave the land.

Should you, my lord, while you peruse my song,   20
Wonder from whence my love of *Freedom* sprung,
Whence flow these wishes for the common good,
By feeling hearts alone best understood –
I, young in life, by seeming cruel fate
Was snatched from *Afric*'s fancied happy seat:
What pangs excruciating must molest,
What sorrows labour in my parent's breast?
Steeled was that soul and by no misery moved

177

That from a father seized his babe beloved:
Such, such my case. And can I then but pray   30
Others may never feel tyrannic sway?

For favours past, great Sir, our thanks are due,
And thee we ask thy favours to renew,
Since in thy power, as in thy will before,
To sooth the griefs, which thou did'st once deplore.
May heavenly grace the sacred sanction give
To all thy works, and thou for ever live
Not only on the wings of fleeting *Fame*,
Though praise immortal crowns the patriot's name,
But to conduct to heaven's refulgent fane,   40
May fiery coursers sweep th'ethereal plain,
And bear thee upwards to that blest abode,
Where, like the prophet, thou shalt find thy God.

23 *understood –:* this ed. understood, 1773 ed. 40 *fane:* temple.

JANE CAVE (*later* Winscom)
c. 1754–1813

Jane Cave's father was an exciseman and glover from Talgarth, Brecon. He lived beyond 1794, but her mother died in 1777. She seems to have been an Anglican working woman with Methodist sympathies. Jane lived in Bath before 1779, when she left for Winchester, where her *Poems on Various Subjects, Entertaining, Elegiac, and Religious* was published in 1783. (The following poem is from this edition.) Her 2000 subscribers were drawn from towns in the south and west of England, with almost 500 subscriptions coming from Oxford. The Headmaster of Winchester College was a supporter. She married Thomas Winscom, an exciseman from Bristol, where a second, revised edition of her poems was published in 1786. Further editions were published at Shrewsbury (1789) and Bristol (1794), incorporating new poems, including some against the slave trade. The couple had sons but little more is known. Jane died in January 1813, in Newport, Monmouthshire.

Written by the Desire of a Lady, On Building of Castles

Building of castles did commence,
In days of old, for our defence,
And usually erected were,
Adjacent to the seat of war;
Where blood and slaughter did abound,

178

And drenched with gore the thirsty ground;
Where powder, darts, and bullets flew,
Not one relenting passion knew;
But winging through the smoke and fire,
Made thousands groan, bleed, and expire.   10

Castles were built firm and secure,
Wherein some treasure to insure;
With cells and caverns dark, profound,
And walls impregnable around.
Its direful decorations are
The whole artillery of war;
Cannons and muskets, swords and bombs,
Hangers and spears, and fifes and drums.
Bullets, and ev'ry fit supply,
Wherewith t'attack the enemy.   20

Some castles too, of which we hear,
Are fabricated in the air;
But these are of the mental kind,
The sole construction of the mind.
We in these ether castles ride,
With all the equipage of pride,
And in imagination rise,
Superior monarchs of the skies.
One blast this edifice destroys,
Abortive are our promised joys.   30
Our ministry this castle built,
By which the blood of thousands spilt;
Fancied a thousand men or two
Could all America subdue.
But thrice ten thousand crossed the main,
A million's in the contest slain.
Yet, ah! fell castle, direful ill,
America's unconquered still.

Castles are an imperfect plan,
Of that superior creature, – Man.   40
The body is a castle where,
The most intrinsic treasures are;
Well fraught with arms for man's defence
As reason, recollection, sense;
Which if we exercise aright,

Put all our enemies to flight;
Spoil Envy with her pois'nous dart,
And wound Resentment to the heart;
Bid Discontent and Anger fly,
And each unruly passion die;
Subdue Distrust and black Despair,
And substitute Contentment there.
Thus conqu'ring, we superior rise
With shouts of victory to the skies.
Where ev'ry conqueror is blest,
In castles of eternal rest.

8 *Not:* this ed. Nor 1783 ed. 34 *America subdue:* in the American War of Independence
1775-83.

ANNE MacVICAR GRANT
1755–1838

Anne MacVicar, poet, letter writer, travel writer, and essayist, was born in Glasgow. She was the only child of an officer in a Highland regiment and his Highland Scots wife who were posted to America in 1758. Anne lived near Albany, New York, aged three to thirteen, with short periods in more remote outposts. Her mother taught her to read and Catalina Schuyler (from a prominent New York family) helped to provide her with some formal education. The family went back to Scotland in 1768 and never returned after the War of Independence. Their land in Vermont was confiscated and, in 1797, Anne was still attempting to reclaim it. She lived at Fort Augustus from 1773 to 1779, when she married James Grant, a former army chaplain, then minister of a Highland parish at Laggan. Anne learnt to speak Gaelic (she later translated Gaelic poems for Henry Mackenzie) and her twelve children knew it as their first language. When her husband died in 1801 she had eight children to support on a limited pension and supplemented her income by writing. Her *Poems on various subjects...*, from which the following is taken, was published, by subscription, in 1803. She moved to Stirling, then Edinburgh and took in pupils. She published *Letters from the Mountains* in 1806 and a revised volume of poems. *Memoirs of an American Lady* appeared in 1808. The latter included a biography of Catalina Schuyler alongside memories of Anne's childhood: there was a second edition in 1809. In 1811, she published *Essays on the Superstitions of the Highlanders* and, in 1814, her long poem, *Eighteen Hundred and Thirteen* was an optimistic counter-response to Anna Laetitia Barbauld's *Eighteen Hundred and Eleven*. Her only surviving child, John Peter, published her later letters posthumously. The links she made between the Highlanders of Laggan and the Mohawk Native Americans give her writings an unusual dimension.

Written in one of the Duke of Athole's Walks at Blair, after making a clandestine entrance through the river Tilt, then very low: summer 1796.

There I suck the liquid air,
All amidst the gardens fair.
MILTON

Your jealous walls, great Duke, in vain
All access would refuse;
What walls can Highland steps restrain?
What bars keep out the Muse?
Where'er I go I bring with me
'That mountain-nymph, sweet LIBERTY!'

Would you engross each breathing sweet
Yon violet banks exhale?
Or trees with od'rous blooms replete,
That scent th'enamoured gale: 10
Alike they smile on you and me,
Like Nature and sweet Liberty!

While pleasure's fleeting form you trace
In *Mona's* distant isle,
And leave forlorn your native place
Where rural beauties smile:
Congenial see them smile for me,
Then do not grudge my Liberty.

Aeneas passed with branch of gold
The gloomy gates below: 20
And silver branches, I am told,
Can smooth your porter's brow;
But wand'ring Highland folks like me,
Can seldom *purchase* Liberty.

While musing by the Tilt I stood,
And viewed its wand'ring tide,
Uprose a Naiad from the flood,
And beckoning, showed its side:
I took the kindly hint with glee,
And scrambled hard for Liberty. 30

Beneath the bridge's bending arch
My vent'rous steps she led,
Till by yon ancient weeping larch
I laid my wearied head:
While birds methought on every tree
Rejoicing hailed my Liberty!

The leaden gods above the gate
Aghast with wonder stood,
Olympian Jove, his vixen mate,
And all the heathen brood: 40
Bravo! cried thievish MERCURY,
'Tis right to steal sweet Liberty!

Title: *Blair:* family seat of John Murray, fourth Duke of Athole (1755-1830), who entertained Robert Burns there in 1787; *There...fair:* spoken by the attendant spirit in the epilogue to Milton's masque, *Comus* (1634). 6 *mountain-nymph...LIBERTY:* from John Milton's *L'Allegro* (1632). 7 *engross:* monopolise. 14 *Mona's...isle:* in Milton's *Lycidas* (1637), an island between Britain and Ireland, traditionally the home of Druids. It is supposed by some to be the Isle of Man or Anglesey. 19-20 *Aeneas...below:* Trojan prince in classical mythology who was aided on his journey into the underworld by the Sybil of Cumae. 27 *Naiad:* nymph of the river. 41 *MERCURY:* inventor of the lyre (so linked with poets), messenger of the gods, and patron of travellers and thieves.

ANNA YOUNG SMITH
1756-80?

When their mother died, Anna Young and her brother were cared for by their aunt, Elizabeth Graeme Fergusson, also a poet. They lived at Graeme Park near Philadelphia. Anna Young read widely and wrote her poetry under the name 'Sylvia'. She married William Smith in 1775, but died in childbirth when she was about 24. Some of her poems survive in manuscript; others were published in magazines. The following poem was written in 1774 and appeared in *Universal Asylum and Columbian Magazine*, vol.5 (Sept. 1790), 185. A variant text exists in her commonplace book.

On Reading Swift's Works

Ungenerous bard, whom not e'en Stella's charms
Thy vengeful satire of its sting disarms!
Say when thou dipp'st thy keenest pen in gall,
Why must our 'dirt and dullness' fill each line,
Our love of 'follies, our desire to shine?'

Why are we drawn as a whole race of fools,
Unswayed alike by sense or virtue's rules?
Oh! had thy heart with generous candor glowed,
Hadst thou alone on vice thy lash bestowed,
Had there fair Purity her form imprest,
And had the milder virtues filled thy breast;
Thy sprightly page had been by all approved,
And what we now admire, we then had loved.
But thy harsh satire, rude, severe, unjust,
Awakes too oft our anger or disgust.
Such are the scenes which still thy pen engage,
That modesty disdains the shameless page.
'Tis true, we own thy wit almost divine,
And view the diamond 'midst the dunghill shine:
Oh, had it sparkled on the breast of youth,
To charm the sage, and to instruct with truth,
To chase the gloom of ignorance away,
And teach mankind with wisdom to be gay;
Thy perfect style, thy wit serenely bright,
Would shed through distant climes their pleasing light;
Mankind would grateful to thy muse attend,
And after ages hail thee as their friend!
But now, so oft filth chokes thy sprightly fire,
We loathe one instant, and the next admire –
Even while we laugh, we mourn thy wit's abuse,
And while we praise thy talents, scorn their use.

Title: *Swift:* Jonathan Swift (1667-1745). 1 *Stella:* Esther Johnson, with whom Swift had an affectionate relationship: Swift referred to her as 'Stella' in his writing.

GEORGIANA SPENCER,
Duchess of Devonshire
1757-1806

Lady Georgiana Spencer married William Cavendish, 5th Earl of Devonshire in 1774. A beauty in her youth, and a prominent socialite, she was also a letter-writer, the first woman to campaign for a political candidate (1794), and probably a novelist (*The Sylph*, 1780, has been attributed to her). In 1782 she met Lady Elizabeth Foster (Bess), who became her best friend and, later, her husband's mistress, bearing him two children. (Georgiana had three children by her husband and one illegitimate daughter by the future Prime Minister, Charles Grey.) They lived in a *ménage à trois* for almost 25 years and, when Georgiana died, the Duke married Bess. Georgiana suffered from severe migraine attacks that affected her eyes. Her partial blindness appears to have stemmed from these and operations performed on her eyes under primitive conditions. The following poem was written at a time when both Bess's first husband and the wife of her other lover, the Duke of Richmond, had recently died, leaving the pair free to marry. It was sent as a letter to Bess, presumably to persuade her to remain with Georgiana and was first published in 1890. Although she wrote poetry throughout her life, little of it was published. A poem about her journey from Italy to Switzerland in 1793 ('The Passage of the Mountain of St Gothard') appeared in several newspapers and magazines in December 1799.

To Lady Elizabeth Foster,
from Georgiana, Duchess of Devonshire,
when she was apprehensive of losing her eyesight – 1796

The life of the roebuck was mine,
As I bounded o'er valley and lawn;
I watched the gay twilight decline,
And worshipped the day-breaking dawn.

I regret not the freedom of will,
Or sigh, as uncertain I tread;
I am freer and happier still,
When by thee, I am carefully led.

Ere my sight I was doomed to resign,
My heart I surrendered to thee;
Not a thought or an action was mine,
But I saw as thou badst me to see.

Thy watchful affection I wait,
And hang with delight on thy voice;
And dependence is softened by Fate,
Since dependence on thee is my choice.

MARY ROBINSON (*née* Darby)
1758-1800

One of five children, Mary was born in Bristol and educated for a time at the school run by Hannah More's sisters. In her teens she helped her mother run a girls' school in Chelsea: regular financial support from her father was lacking. She attended a finishing school in Marylebone and, through the dancing teacher there, met David Garrick. In 1774 she married Thomas Robinson, an articled clerk who turned out to be a gambler. They fled to Wales to escape his creditors: their daughter was born there in November 1774. Later, the whole family spent ten months in a debtors' prison. Her *Poems* appeared in 1775 in an attempt to better their finances. Mary sent a copy to Georgiana, Duchess of Devonshire, who gave her some assistance. From 1776 to 1780, through her connection with Garrick, Mary acted at Drury Lane. She published *Captivity. A Poem; and Celadon and Lydia. A Tale* in 1777 and her musical farce, *The Lucky Escape*, was performed in 1778. In 1779, following her performance as Perdita in *The Winter's Tale*, she became the mistress of the Prince of Wales (later George IV). When the affair ended, after about a year, she was given an annuity of £500. She had several other affairs, one of which took her to France. Mary returned to England in 1788. In 1791 another volume of *Poems* included members of the Royal family as subscribers. Driven to write by poor health and financial hardship, a second volume followed in 1793. She started writing semi-autobiographical novels in 1792: these include *Vancenza* (1792), *Angelina* (1796) and *The False Friend* (1799). Her cycle of love sonnets, *Sappho and Phaon* (1796), resulted in her being called the 'English Sappho'. Her *Letter to the Women of England, on the Injustice of Mental Subordination* focused on male hypocrisy in relation to the treatment of women. Between 1798 and 1800 she regularly contributed poems to the *Morning Post* under a variety of pseudonyms. *Lyrical Tales* (1800) is influenced by Wordsworth and Coleridge's *Lyrical Ballads*: Coleridge admired Mary's later poetry. Her autobiography was unfinished when she died. The following poem is taken from *Poetical Works* (1806). Paula Byrne's best-selling biography, *Perdita: the life of Mary Robinson*, was published by Harper Collins in 2004.

London's Summer Morning

Who has not waked to list the busy sounds
Of summer's morning, in the sultry smoke
Of noisy London? On the pavement hot
The sooty chimney-boy, with dingy face
And tattered covering, shrilly bawls his trade,
Rousing the sleepy housemaid. At the door
The milk-pail rattles, and the tinkling bell
Proclaims the dustman's office; while the street
Is lost in clouds impervious. Now begins
The din of hackney-coaches, waggons, carts;   10
While tinmen's shops, and noisy trunk-makers,
Knife-grinders, coopers, squeaking cork-cutters,
Fruit barrows, and the hunger-giving cries
Of vegetable vendors, fill the air.
Now every shop displays its varied trade,
And the fresh-sprinkled pavement cools the feet
Of early walkers. At the private door
The ruddy housemaid twirls the busy mop,
Annoying the smart 'prentice, or neat girl,

Tripping with band-box lightly. Now the sun 20
Darts burning splendour on the glittering pane,
Save where the canvas awning throws a shade
On the day merchandize. Now, spruce and trim,
In shops (where beauty smiles with industry),
Sits the smart damsel; while the passenger
Peeps through the window, watching every charm.
Now pastry dainties catch the eye minute
Of humming insects, while the limy snare
Waits to enthral them. Now the lamp-lighter
Mounts the tall ladder, nimbly venturous, 30
To trim the half-filled lamp; while at his feet
The pot-boy yells discordant! All along
The sultry pavement, the old-clothes man cries
In tone monotonous, the side-long views
The area for his traffic: now the bag
Is slyly opened, and the half-worn suit
(Sometimes the pilfered treasure of the base
Domestic spoiler), for one half its worth,
Sinks in the green abyss. The porter now
Bears his huge load along the burning way; 40
And the poor poet wakes from busy dreams,
To paint the summer morning.

1 *list:* hear. 10 *hackney-coaches:* horse-drawn coaches for hire. 32 *pot-boy:* one who serves
and collects the drinking 'pots' in a tavern.

ELIZABETH HANDS

fl. 1789

Elizabeth Hands considered herself to have been 'born in obscurity'. She was
a servant who married a blacksmith and lived near Rugby. She published one
book of poetry: *The Death of Amnon...* (1789), with the help of an assistant
master at Rugby School. Anna Seward was among subscribers to her volume.
Earlier poems appeared under the pseudonym, 'Daphne', in *The Coventry
Mercury*. Her work ranged from humorous ironic verse to pastorals and poems
on serious topics. Her poetry was praised in *The Gentleman's Magazine* (1790).

On an Unsociable Family

O what a strange parcel of creatures are we,
Scarce ever to quarrel, or ever agree;
We all are alone, though at home altogether,

Except to the fire constrained by the weather;
Then one says, ''Tis cold', which we all of us know,
And with unanimity answer, ''Tis so':
With shrugs and with shivers all look at the fire,
And shuffle ourselves and our chairs a bit nigher;
Then quickly, preceded by silence profound,
A yawn epidemical catches around:
Like social companions we never fall out,
Nor ever care what one another's about;
To comfort each other is never our plan,
For to please ourselves, truly, is more than we can.

On the Author's Lying-In, August, 1785

O God, the giver of all joy,
Whose gifts no mortal can destroy,
 Accept my grateful lays:
My tongue did almost ask for death,
But thou did'st spare my lab'ring breath,
 To sing thy future praise.

I live! My God be praised, I live,
And do most thankfully receive,
 The bounty of my life:
I live, still longer to improve,
The fondest husband's tender love,
 To the most happy wife.

I live within my arms to clasp
My infant with endearing grasp,
 And feel my fondness grow:
O God endow her with thy grace,
And heav'nly gifts, to hold a place
 Among thy Saints below.

May she in duty, as she ought,
By thy unerring precepts taught,
 To us a blessing prove:
And thus prepared for greater joys,
May she, with thine elect arise
 To taste the joys above.

Title: *Lying-in:* giving birth.

SARAH WENTWORTH MORTON

1759-1846

Her father (James Apthorp) and her mother (Sarah Wentworth) both belonged to prosperous merchant families and Sarah was well-educated. She began to write poetry when she was ten. Born in Boston, she also lived in Braintree. In 1781 she married Perez Morton, a lawyer, and a patriot in the War of Independence. Her family may have been loyalists but Sarah and her husband moved into the Apthorp home in Boston which prevented it being confiscated. Initially Sarah's manuscripts were read only by a circle of literary friends but from 1788 she published poetry in journals like *The Massachusetts Magazine* under the name 'Philenia' and enjoyed some success. Her first book, *Ouâbi: or the Virtues of Nature...* borrowed from Native American culture and she also touched on political and social issues, but other writing was related to personal sorrows. Her husband had an affair with her sister, Frances, who gave birth to his child, then committed suicide when the affair was revealed. Sarah's own son died after a few hours, and two other children died prematurely. The couple stayed together: Sarah outlived all five of her children and her husband. Her manuscripts survive in the Huntington Library, San Marino, California. Her other works include *Beacon Hill* and *The Virtues of Society*. The following poems are taken from her last publication, *My Mind and its Thoughts* (1823), a collection of poems, sketches, and essays, which was the first to appear with her name on it – and, being proud of her Welsh heritage, she combined her mother's maiden name with her own. 'The African Chief' dates from 1792 and was popular with the anti-slavery movement.

The African Chief

See how the black ship cleaves the main,
　　High bounding o'er the dark blue wave,
Remurmuring with the groans of pain,
　　Deep freighted with the princely slave!

Did all the Gods of Afric sleep,
　　Forgetful of their guardian love,
When the white tyrants of the deep
　　Betrayed him in the palmy grove?

A chief of Gambia's golden shore,
　　Whose arm the band of warriors led,　　　10
Or more – the lord of generous power,
　　By whom the foodless poor were fed.

Does not the voice of reason cry,
　　Claim the first right that nature gave,
From the red scourge of bondage fly,
　　Nor deign to live a burdened slave?

Has not his suffering offspring clung,
     Desponding round his fettered knee;
On his worn shoulder, weeping hung,
     And urged one effort to be free?   20

His wife by nameless wrongs subdued,
     His bosom's friend to death resigned;
The flinty path-way drenched in blood,
     He saw with cold and frenzied mind.

Strong in despair, then sought the plain,
     To heaven was raised his steadfast eye,
Resolved to burst the crushing chain,
     Or mid the battle's blast to die.

First of his race, he led the band,
     Guardless of danger, hurling round,   30
Till by his red avenging hand,
     Full many a despot stained the ground.

When erst Messenia's sons oppressed
     Flew desperate to the sanguine field,
With iron clothed each injured breast,
     And saw the cruel Spartan yield,

Did not the soul to heaven allied,
     With the proud heart as greatly swell,
As when the roman Decius died,
     Or when the Grecian victim fell?   40

Do later deeds quick rapture raise,
     The boon Batavia's William won,
Paoli's time-enduring praise,
     Or the yet greater Washington?

If these exalt thy sacred zeal,
     To hate oppression's mad control,
For bleeding Afric learn to feet,
     Whose Chieftain claimed a kindred soul.

Ah, mourn the last disastrous hour,
     Lift the full eye of bootless grief,   50
While victory treads the sultry shore,
     And tears from hope the captive chief.

189

While the hard race of pallid hue,
Unpracticed in the power to feel,
Resign him to the murderous crew,
The horrors of the quivering wheel,

Let sorrow bathe each blushing cheek,
Bend piteous o'er the tortured slave,
Whose wrongs compassion cannot speak,
Whose only refuge was the grave.   60

Title: an authorial note (*My Mind and its Thoughts*, 277) reads: 'Taken in arms, fighting
for his freedom, and inhumanely butchered by his conquerors! This affecting event was
fully delineated in the various Gazettes of that period'. 33 *Messenia's sons:* made slaves
of Sparta, the Messenians eventually rose up and achieved freedom. 39 *Decius:* a celeb-
rated Roman consul. 40 *Grecian victim:* Leonidas, a valiant king of Lacedaemon, defeated
through treachery. 42 *Batavia:* the Netherlands.

Simple Address to My Home

Safe on the vale's protected breast,
The portals of my mansion rest.
In trembling tenderness of form,
Outlive the hard and hurrying storm –
While on the firm hill's cultured side
Is crushed the seat of taste and pride.

To God the powerless poor belong;
He shields the weak, and smites the strong.
Without his will no sparrow falls,
Whose shelter was thy friendly walls.   10
My HOME – if quiet dwells with thee –
What are the storms of life to me!
So in the frail ark's tranquil view,
The whirlwinds of the deluge blew;
Hurtless they blew – of heaven the care,
The dove of peace still rested there –
Rested – while ruin's darts were hurled,
To strike the chosen of the world.

As yet from earth no joy shall rise
Without the atoning sacrifice –   20
No more thy bordering elms are seen
To fling their arch of darkening green –
And the ripe fruit tree's nectared store
Shall wave its blooming gold no more.

Though not a charm with polished grace
Smile on thy changed and cheerless face,
I love thee – that no passion rude
Profanes thy sacred solitude:-
I love thee, that no envious eye
Regards thee with a passing sigh!   30
I love thee, for the friend sincere
Whose voice of blessing greets me *here*,
But most – that to thy haunts are given
That calm, which looks from earth to heaven.

Not for the fair, the firm, the high,
Does pity come with pleading eye;
Thence are thy faded features dear
To me, as nature's vernal year –
And dear thy wasted form to me –
For all I love must change like thee.   40

Title: Prefaced by: Lines written immediately after the tremendous gale and storm which proved so generally disastrous to life and its possessions, on September 23, 1815 (*My Mind and its Thoughts*, 133). 5 *side:* this ed. side, 1823 ed. 7 *belong;*: this ed. belong, 1823 ed. 19 *rise:* this ed. rise, 1823 ed. 23 *store:* this ed. store, 1823 ed. 27 *rude:* this ed. rude, 1823 ed. 29 *eye:* this ed. eye, 1823 ed. 33 *given:* this ed. given, 1823 ed.

CATHERINE UPTON
fl. 1785

Little is known about Catherine Upton. She lived in Gibraltar for a time and solicited patronage from General Boyd, the Lieutenant Governor. The following is taken from *Miscellaneous Pieces in Prose and Verse by Mrs Upton, Authoress of the Siege of Gibraltar, and Governess of the Ladies Academy No.43, Bartholomew Close. London: printed for and sold by the authoress; T. & G. Egerton, Charing-Cross, and G. Robinson, Paternoster-row. 1785*. In the preface she defends herself from critics of her earlier poem who argued that it was 'badly versed' as one line was a syllable too long. She quotes Dryden and Pope, both of whom take the same liberty, and argues: 'Errors like these (if they can be called such) are forgiven in great Poets and learned men, but not in a <u>woman</u>, who pretends to no learning at all.' She ends: 'I have but little time to write, or correct what I write, and shall ingeniously confess that I send the following sheets into the world, with a view to <u>support my children</u>, not to extend my own fame.'

Epitaph, by desire of a Young Lady, on the Death of her Canary Bird

This simple urn contains within
A beauteous form, that knew no sin:
Contented in his narrow sphere,
He sought no crimes, nor knew a care;
His gentle suit was ne'er denied,
A bounteous hand his wants supplied;
He wished no wealth, nor feared a wrong,
And all his business was – a song.
Ye sons of care contract your plan,
For life itself is but a span.

ELIZA THOMPSON
fl. 1787

The following is taken from *Poems on various subjects* (1787) by 'Miss Eliza Thompson'. The opening recalls Samuel Johnson's *London* (1738), but the poem may also be related, ironically, to a contemporary 'new song' (dated 1790?): 'The Lady's favourite wish' – 'Grant me, kind heaven, a fortune large to spend...' (Cambridge University Library Madden Ballads vol.2, ref. ESTCT201371).

A Wish

Grant me, kind Heaven, some calm retreat,
    Where I may never view distress;
Or grant the means, if you see meet,
    Where-e'er I view't, to make it less.

Can I enjoy e'er from your hands
    One peaceful meal, however scant,
Whilst shivering at my window stands
    A son of Adam, pale with want?

Ah, no! the most luxurious meat,
    The richest wines would quickly pall;
That sight embitter every sweet,
    And every cup would dash with gall.

But if, great God, I ask amiss,
    What might, (if granted) prove a curse;
The only boon I crave is this,
    To suit my feelings to my purse.

JOANNA BAILLIE
1762-1851

The daughter of Dorothea Hunter and a Scottish clergyman who became a
Professor of Divinity, Joanna Baillie was born in Bothwell, Lanarkshire and
was educated in Glasgow. Her sister, Agnes, and her aunt, Anne Hunter, were
also poets. Her brother, Matthew, followed his uncles into the medical pro-
fession and inherited his uncle William Hunter's house in London. On their
father's death his sisters and mother lived there with him until he married in
1791. Later, the three women lived in Hampstead. In *Fugitive Verses* (London,
1840), from which the following are taken, Joanna explains how her first vol-
ume of poems was published anonymously in 1790 and largely went unnoticed.
Several of these poems were reprinted (with revisions) in the later book, which
also gathers together songs first published in George Thomson's *Collection of
Irish, Welch and Scotch Melodies*. Joanna had most success as a dramatist. Her
plays were published and performed (*A Series of Plays: in which it is attempted
to delineate the stronger passions of the mind, 3 vols. 1798-1812, Dramas*, 2 vols,
1836, *The Dramatic and Poetical Works of Joanna Baillie*, 1851). She also pro-
duced an anthology: *Metrical Legends of Exalted Characters* in 1821. Championed
by Sir Walter Scott, Joanna had many literary friends and acquaintances, inc-
luding Anna Laetitia Barbauld, Maria Edgeworth and William Wordsworth.

from A Winter's Day

The cock warm roosting 'mid his feathered mates,
Now lifts his beak and snuffs the morning air,
Stretches his neck and claps his heavy wings,
Gives three hoarse crows, and glad his task is done,
Low chuckling turns himself upon the roost,
Then nestles down again into his place.
The labouring hind, who on his bed of straw
Beneath his home-made coverings, coarse but warm,
Locked in the kindly arms of her who spun them,
Dreams of the gain that next year's crop should bring;   10
Or at some fair, disposing of his wool,
Or by some lucky and unlooked-for bargain,
Fills his skin purse with store of tempting gold,
Now wakes from sleep at the unwelcome call,
And finds himself but just the same poor man
As when he went to rest.
He hears the blast against his window beat
And wishes to himself he were a laird,
That he might lie a-bed. It may not be:
He rubs his eyes and stretches out his arms;   20

Heigh ho! Heigh ho! He drawls with gaping mouth,
Then, most unwillingly creeps from his lair,
And without looking-glass puts on his clothes.
  With rueful face he blows the smothered fire,
And lights his candle at the reddening coal;
First sees that all be right among his cattle,
Then hies him to the barn with heavy tread,
Printing his footsteps on the new-fallen snow.
From out the heaped-up mow he draws his sheaves,
Dislodging the poor red-breast from his shelter   30
Where all the live-long night he slept secure;
But now, affrighted, with uncertain flight,
Flutters round walls, and roof, to find some hole
Through which he may escape.
Then whirling o'er his head, the heavy flail
Descends with force upon the jumping sheaves,
While every rugged wall and neighbouring cot
The noise re-echoes of his sturdy strokes.

[...]

  The varied rousing sounds of industry   122
Are heard through all the village.
The humming wheel, the thrifty housewife's tongue,
Who scolds to keep her maidens to their work,
The wool-card's grating most unmusical!
Issue from every house.
But hark! The sportsman from the neighbouring hedge
His thunder sends! Loud bark the village curs;
Up from her cards or wheel the maiden starts   130
And hastens to the door; the housewife chides,
Yet runs herself to look, in spite of thrift,
And all the little town is in a stir.

7 *hind:* according to the author's note, the word 'does not perfectly express the condition of the person here intended, who is somewhat above a common labourer, – the tenant of a very small farm, which he cultivates with his own hands; a few cows, perhaps a horse, and some six or seven sheep, being all the wealth he possessed. A class of men very common in the west of Scotland, ere political economy was thought of.'

Verses written in February, 1827

Like gleam of sunshine on the mountain's side,
Fair, bright and beautiful, while all beside,
Slope, cliff and pinnacle in shadow lie

Beneath the awning of a wintry sky,
Through loop-hole in its cloudy texture beaming
A cataract of light, so softly streaming, –
Shines one blest deed of ruth when war's grim form
O'er a scourged nation guides his passing storm.

Like verdant islet-spots, that softly peer
Through the dull mist, as morning breezes clear   10
The brooding vapour from the wide-stretched vale,
So in a land where Mammon's cares prevail,
Do frequent deeds of gentle charity
Refresh the moral gazer's mental eye.

Britain, thou art in arms and commerce graced
With many generous acts, that, fairly traced
On thy long annals, give a lustre far
Exceeding those of wealth or trophied war;
And may we not say truthfully of thee,
Thou art a land of mercy? – May it be!   20

What forms are those with lean galled sides? In vain
Their laxed and ropy sinews sorely strain
Heaped loads to draw with lash and goad urged on.
They were in other days, but lately gone,
The useful servants, dearly prized, of those
Who to their failing age give no repose, –
Of thankless, heartless owners. Then full oft
Their arched graceful necks so sleek and soft
Beneath a master's stroking hand would rear
Right proudly, as they neighed his well-known voice to hear. 30

But now how changed! – And what marred things are these,
Starved, hooted, scarred, denied or food or ease;
Whose humbled looks their bitter thraldom show,
Familiar with the kick, the pinch, the blow?
Alas! in this sad fellowship are found
The playful kitten and the faithful hound,
The gallant cock that hailed the morning light,
All now hard-fated mates in woeful plight.

Ah no! a land of mercy is a name
Which thou in all thy glory mayest not claim!   40

But yet there dwell in thee the good, the bold,
Who in thy streets, courts, senates bravely hold
Contention with thy wayward cruelty,
And shall subdue it ere this age glide by.
Meantime as they their manly power exert,
'God speed ye well!' bursts from each kindly heart.
And they *will* speed; for this foul blot of shame
Must be washed out from Britain's honoured name,
And she among enlightened nations stand,
A brave, a merciful and generous land.   50

7-8 *war's...storm:* 1824-27 saw the First Burmese War, with Britain fighting for the control of India. Later in 1827, Britain, France and Russia went to war with Turkey to aid Greece in its War of Independence, 1821-28. 32 *or...or:* neither...nor. 41-50 The RSPCA was founded as the Society for Prevention of Cruelty to Animals in 1824 by 22 reformers, including Richard Martin, MP, and William Wilberforce, MP. It was the first society for animal welfare to be created in the world. Martin's Act, passed by Parliament on 22 July 1822, sought to prevent cruelty to farm animals.

AMELIA OPIE (*née* Alderson)
1769-1853

Amelia, an only child in a Unitarian family, was born and died in Norwich. After her mother died when she was 15, she ran the household for her father, a physician. In her teens she wrote poetry for journals such as the *Monthly Magazine* and *London Magazine*. She published a novel anonymously in 1790 and, from 1801, began publishing volumes of fiction and some poetry (*Poems*, 1802, and *The Warrior's Return*, 1808) under her own name. She married the painter, John Opie, in 1798. He died in 1807 and, in 1825, she ceased to be a novelist when she became a member of the Society of Friends. Her writings reflect her support for the anti-slavery movement and her moral preoccupations but, as the following song shows (from *Poems by Mrs Opie*, 1802), she also had wit and a love of society. Her last work was a collection of poems, *Lays for the Dead* (1833).

Song

I know you false, I know you vain,
Yet still I cannot break my chain:
Though with those lips so sweetly smiling,
Those eyes so bright and so beguiling,
On every youth by turns you smile,
And every youth by turns beguile,
Yet still enchant and still deceive me,
Do all things, fatal fair...but leave me.

Still let me in those speaking eyes
Trace all your feelings as they rise;
Still from those lips in crimson swelling,
Which seem of soft delights the dwelling,
Catch tones of sweetness, which the soul
In fetters ever new control;
Nor let my starts of passion grieve thee...
Though death to stay, 't were death to leave thee.

DOROTHY WORDSWORTH
1771-1855

Diarist, travel writer, letter-writer, and poet, Dorothy Wordsworth was born
at Cockermouth in Cumberland, an only daughter. Parentless at an early age,
she was close to her four brothers, particularly William, who was a year her
elder. In 1795 they set up home together at Racedown, Dorset and moved
later to Alfoxden, Somerset, and Goslar in Germany, settling finally in the
Lake District, at Grasmere and Rydal Mount. She remained with him after
his marriage to Mary Hutchinson in 1802, but was financially independent
due to an annuity from their brother, Richard. Many of her journals were
published posthumously and five of her poems were published with William's
during her lifetime (out of a total of approximately 20). Dorothy also contri-
buted to his *Guide to the Lakes* (1820). She suffered from premature senility
and was cared for by William and, after his death in 1850, by his family. She is
remembered for what Coleridge called, 'her eye watchful in minutest observ-
ation of nature' and her detailed evocations of everyday domestic life. William
clearly owed some of the inspiration for his poems to his sister and her prose
descriptions: in Book XI of *The Prelude* he acknowledges the more general
support that she provided. The following poem is written in her Commonplace
Book and also appears at the end of her journal, February 12, 1831 – September
7, 1833. Dorothy's poems were first collected by Susan M. Levin in *Dorothy
Wordsworth and Romanticism* (Rutgers University Press, 1987).

Thoughts on my sick-bed

And has the remnant of my life
Been pilfered of this sunny Spring?
And have its own prelusive sounds
Touched in my heart no echoing string?

Ah! Say not so – the hidden life
Couchant within this feeble frame
Hath been enriched by kindred gifts,
That, undesired, unsought-for, came

With joyful heart in youthful days
When fresh each season in its round
I welcomed the earliest celandine
Glittering upon the mossy ground;

With busy eyes I pierced the lane
In quest of known and *un*known things,
– The primrose a lamp on its fortress rock,
The silent butterfly spreading its wings,

The violet betrayed by its noiseless breath,
The daffodil dancing in the breeze,
The carolling thrush, on his naked perch,
Towering above the budding trees.

Our cottage-hearth no longer our home,
Companions of Nature were we,
The stirring, the still, the loquacious, the mute –
To all we gave our sympathy.

Yet never in those careless days
When spring-time in rock, field, or bower
Was but a fountain of earthly hope,
A promise of fruits & the *splendid* flower.

No! then I never felt a bliss
That might with *that* compare
Which, piercing to my couch of rest
Came on the vernal air.

When loving friends an offering brought,
The first flowers of the year,
Culled from the precincts of our home,
From nooks to Memory dear.

With some sad thoughts the work was done,
Unprompted and unbidden,
But joy it brought to my *hidden* life,
To consciousness no longer hidden.

I felt a Power unfelt before,
Controlling weakness, languor, pain;
It bore me to the terrace walk
I trod the hills again; –

No prisoner in this lonely room,
I *saw* the green banks of the Wye,
Recalling thy prophetic words,
Bard, Brother, Friend from infancy!

No need of motion, or of strength,
Or even the breathing air:
– I thought of Nature's loveliest scenes;
And with Memory I was there.

MARY TIGHE (*née* Blachford)
1772-1810

Daughter of a founder-member of the Methodist movement in Ireland and a
clergyman who was also a librarian, Mary was born in County Wicklow and
was given an extensive education in classics, languages, music and art. She
married her cousin, Henry Tighe, a member of the Irish Parliament, in 1793,
and the couple moved to London. She developed tuberculosis and spent her
final years in Dublin and Roseanna, County Wicklow. Fifty copies of *Psyche*
were privately published in 1805; it was the only one of her poems to be
widely known during her lifetime. The sensuous poem comprises six cantos
of Spenserian stanzas and tells a version of the story of Cupid and Psyche.
The extract below describes the Island of Pleasure and the Palace and Banquet
of Love, prior to Psyche's marriage to Cupid. In *Visionary Gleam: Forty books
from the Romantic Period* (1996), Jonathan Wordsworth draws attention to
Mary's possible influence on John Keats, who is known to have read her work
before he also adopted Spenserian stanzas for *The Eve of St Agnes* and com-
posed his ode 'To Psyche' and *Endymion*. There are also possible links between
Canto I of her *Psyche* and his 'Ode on a Grecian Urn'. When Mary died, as
well as her poems, she left an unpublished novel, *Selena* (National Library of
Ireland), and a number of diaries. A posthumous volume, *Psyche with Other
Poems* (from which the following cantos are taken), appeared in 1811.

from Psyche; Or The Legend of Love (CANTO 1)

Gently ascending from a silvery flood,   370
Above the palace rose the shaded hill,
The lofty eminence was crowned with wood,
And the rich lawns, adorned by nature's skill,
The passing breezes with their odours fill;
Here ever blooming groves of orange glow,
And here all flowers which from their leaves distil
Ambrosial dew in sweet succession blow,
And trees of matchless size a fragrant shade bestow.

The sun looks glorious mid a sky serene,
And bids bright lustre sparkle o'er the tide;   380
The clear blue ocean at a distance seen
Bounds the gay landscape on the western side,
While closing round it with majestic pride,
The lofty rocks mid citron groves arise;
'Sure some divinity must here reside,'
As tranced in some bright vision, Psyche cries,
And scarce believes the bliss, or trusts her charmed eyes.

When lo! a voice divinely sweet she hears,
From unseen lips proceeds the heavenly sound;
'Psyche approach, dismiss thy timid fears,   390
At length his bride thy longing spouse has found,
And bids for thee immortal joys abound;
For thee the palace rose at his command,
For thee his love a bridal banquet crowned;
He bids attendant nymphs around thee stand
Prompt every wish to serve, a fond obedient band.'

Increasing wonder filled her ravished soul,
For now the pompous portals opened wide,
There, pausing oft, with timid foot she stole
Through halls high domed, enriched with sculptured pride,   400
While gay saloons appeared on either side
In splendid vista opening to her sight;
And all with precious gems so beautified,
And furnished with such exquisite delight,
That scarce the beams of heaven emit such lustre bright.

The amethyst was there of violet hue,
And there the topaz shed its golden ray,
The chrysoberyl, and the sapphire blue
As the clear azure of a sunny day,
Or the mild eyes where amorous glances play;   410
The snow white jasper, and the opal's flame,
The blushing ruby, and the agate grey,
And there the gem which bears his luckless name
Whose death by Phoebus mourned ensured him deathless fame.

There the green emerald, there cornelians glow,
And rich carbuncles pour eternal light,
With all that India and Peru can show,

Or Labrador can give so flaming bright
To the charmed mariner's half dazzled sight:
The coral paved baths with diamonds blaze: 420
And all that can the female heart delight
Of fair attire, the last recess displays,
And all that Luxury can ask, her eye surveys.

Now through the hall melodious music stole,
And self-prepared the splendid banquet stands,
Self-poured the nectar sparkles in the bowl,
The lute and viol touched by unseen hands
Aid the soft voices of the choral bands;
O'er the full board a brighter lustre beams
Than Persia's monarch at his feast commands: 430
For sweet refreshment all inviting seems
To taste celestial food, and pure ambrosial streams.

But when meek Eve hung out her dewy star,
And gently veiled with gradual hand the sky,
Lo! the bright folding doors retiring far,
Display to Psyche's captivated eye
All that voluptuous ease could e'er supply
To sooth the spirits in serene repose:
Beneath the velvet's purple canopy
Divinely formed a downy couch arose, 440
While alabaster lamps a milky light disclose.

Once more she hears the hymeneal strain;
Far other voices now attune the lay;
The swelling sounds approach, awhile remain,
And then retiring faint dissolved away:
The expiring lamps emit a feebler ray,
And soon in fragrant death extinguished lie:
Then virgin terrors Psyche's soul dismay,
When through the obscuring gloom she nought can spy,
But softly rustling sounds declare some Being nigh. 450

Oh, you for whom I write! whose hearts can melt
At the soft thrilling voice whose power you prove,
You know what charm, unutterably felt,
Attends the unexpected voice of Love:
Above the lyre, the lute's soft notes above,
With sweet enchantment to the soul it steals

And bears it to Elysium's happy grove;
You best can tell the rapture Psyche feels
When Love's ambrosial lip the vows of Hymen seals.

Title: *Psyche:* In the mythological tale (first told by Apuleius) the god of love fell in love with mortal Psyche and she with him. Separated through the jealousy of Venus and Psyche's sisters, they were eventually happily reunited after Psyche underwent many dangerous trials. 408 *chrysoberyl:* a yellowish-green gem. 415 *cornelians:* dull red or reddish-white precious stones, like quartz. 442 *hymeneal strains:* the music that accompanies Hymen, god of marriage. 457 *Elysium:* a place or state of absolute happiness where, in classical mythology, the blessed exist after death.

JANE AUSTEN
1775–1817

Now one of England's most popular and revered novelists, Jane Austen is best known next as a letter-writer rather than a poet. Her poetry mainly consists of occasional verses, but these are valuable in showing her wit and humour operating in another genre. Unusually serious, 'To the Memory of Mrs Lefroy...' demonstrates her alliance with Samuel Johnson and the Age of Reason. David Selwyn's *Jane Austen: Collected Poems & Verse of the Austen Family* (Fyfield Books, Carcanet, in association with the Jane Austen Society, 1996) is the source for the texts below. Born in Steventon, Hampshire, Jane Austen was the seventh of eight children. She never married and moved with her family to Bath on her father's retirement, but returned to Hampshire after his death in 1815. She lived at Southampton for a short time, then at Chawton, where she died. (A Library and Study Centre dedicated to early women's writing, 1600-1830, opened in her brother's house there, in July 2003.) She is buried in the Cathedral at Winchester.

To Miss Bigg
previous to her marriage, with some pocket handkerchiefs I had hemmed for her

Cambric! with grateful blessings would I pay
The pleasure given me in sweet employ;
Long may'st thou serve my friend without decay,
And have no tears to wipe, but tears of joy!

Title: Catherine Bigg was the sister of Harris Bigg-Wither, whose marriage proposal Jane accepted on 2 December 1802, but declined the next morning. Catherine married Rev. Herbert Hill in 1808; *handkerchiefs:* this ed. handfs. Ms. 1 *Cambric:* fine white linen, originally from Cambray, Flanders.

On the same occasion – but not sent

Cambric! Thou'st been to me a Good,
And I would bless thee if I could.

Go, serve thy Mistress with delight,
Be small in compass, soft & white;
Enjoy thy fortune, honoured much
To bear her name & feel her touch;
And that thy worth may last for years,
Slight be her colds and few her tears.

6 *bear...name:* perhaps as well as hemming the handkerchiefs, Jane had embroidered her friend's initials on them.

To the Memory of Mrs Lefroy,
who died Dec:ʳ 16. – my Birthday.
– written 1808

The day returns again, my natal day;
What mixed emotions with the thought arise!
Beloved friend, four years have passed away
Since thou wert snatched forever from our eyes.

The day, commemorative of my birth,
Bestowing life and light and hope on me,
Brings back the hour which was thy last on earth.
Oh! bitter pang of torturing memory!

Angelic woman! past my power to praise
In language meet, thy talents, temper, mind,   10
Thy solid worth, thy captivating grace! –
Thou friend and ornament of humankind!

At Johnson's death, by Hamilton 'twas said,
'Seek we a substitute – ah! vain the plan,
No second best remains to Johnson dead –
None can remind us even of the man'.

So we of thee – unequalled in thy race
Unequalled thou, as he the first of men.
Vainly we search around thy vacant place,
We ne'er may look upon thy like again.   20

Come then, fond Fancy, thou indulgent Power,
Hope is desponding, chill, severe to thee!
Bless thou, this little portion of an hour,
Let me behold *her* as she used to be.

203

I see her here, with all her smiles benign,
Her looks of eager love, her accents sweet.
That voice & countenance almost divine!
Expression, harmony, alike complete.

I listen – 'tis not sound alone – 'tis sense,
'Tis genius, taste, and tenderness of soul.   30
'Tis genuine warmth of heart without pretence
And purity of mind that crowns the whole.

She speaks; 'tis eloquence – that grace of tongue
So rare, so lovely! – never misapplied
By her to palliate vice, or deck a wrong,
She speaks & reasons but on Virtue's side.

Hers is the energy of soul sincere.
Her Christian spirit, ignorant to feign,
Seeks but to comfort, heal, enlighten, cheer,
Confer a pleasure, or prevent a pain.   40

Can aught enhance such goodness? – Yes, to me,
Her partial favour from my earliest years
Consummates all. – Ah! give me yet to see
Her smile of love – the vision disappears.

'Tis past & gone – we meet no more below.
Short is the cheat of Fancy o'er the tomb.
Oh! might I hope to equal bliss to go!
To meet thee, Angel, in thy future home!

Fain would I feel an union in thy fate,
Fain would I seek to draw an omen fair   50
From this connection in our earthly date.
Indulge the harmless weakness – Reason, spare. –

Title: *Mrs Lefroy:* Anne Lefroy (1749-1804) died after falling from her horse on Jane
Austen's birthday. An occasional poet and lover of literature, she came (with her hus-
band, the rector of Ashe) to the Steventon neighbourhood in 1783 and, as a woman of 34,
befriended the seven year old Jane. 13 *Hamilton:* 'Single-speech' Hamilton, William
Gerard Hamilton (1729-96), MP for Petersfield, whom Samuel Johnson praised for his
conversational skills. Johnson wrote 'Considerations on the Corn Laws' for him in 1766.
17 *race;:* this ed. semi-colon supplied – and at 23 and 35.

On the Marriage of Miss Camilla Wallop & the Revd. Wake

Camilla, good-humoured, & merry, & small
For a husband was at her last stake;
And having in vain danced at many a Ball
Is now happy to jump at a Wake.

Title: Urania Katharine Camilla Wallop (*b*. 1774) married the elderly Rev. Henry Wake in 1813.

ISABELLA LICKBARROW
1784–1847

Isabella Lickbarrow was born in Kendal, Westmorland. Her schoolteacher father taught his daughters Latin, Greek and French, though, in the preface to her volume, *Poetical Effusions*, published in Kendal in 1814, she suggests that her reading was limited. Her mother died when Isabella was five years old and she lost her father 15 years later. The preface to *Poetical Effusions* (from which the following poem is taken) indicates that she wrote in the little free time she had from domestic labour and decided to publish, at the instigation of 'kind friends', to try to raise money to support her 'orphan sisters'. Her poems had appeared in *The Westmorland Advertiser* since the end of 1811 and the list of subscribers for her first volume included 'W. Wordsworth, Esq. Rydal Mount' and 'De Quincey' of Grasmere. Despite Isabella's struggle against poverty, her sisters suffered from debilitating depression and she could not save them from spending years in an asylum. She died, worn down by overwork and tuberculosis. Her literary reputation has been rescued from obscurity in recent years by critics such as Duncan Wu (who included her in his anthology, *Romantic Women Poets*, 1997). The first collected edition of her poems, compiled by Constance Parrish, was published by the Wordsworth Trust in 2004.

On Esthwaite Lake

O'er Esthwaite's lake, serene and still,
At sunset's silent peaceful hour,
Scarce moved the zephyr's softest breath,
Or sighed along its reedy shore.

The lovely landscape on its sides,
With ev'ning's soft'ning hues imprest,
Shared in the gen'ral calm, and gave
Sweet visions of repose and rest.

Inverted on the waveless flood,
   A spotless mirror smooth and clear,
Each fair surrounding object shone
   In softer beauty imaged there.

Brown hills, and woods of various shades,
   Orchards and sloping meadows green,
Sweet rural seats, and sheltered farms,
   Were in the bright reflector seen.

Ev'n lofty Tilberthwaite from far
   His giant shadow boldly threw,
His rugged, dark, high-tow'ring head
   On Esthwaite's tranquil breast to view.

Struck with the beauty of the scene,
   I cried, Oh! may my yielding breast
Retain but images of peace,
   Like those, sweet lake, on thine impressed.

Ne'er may it feel a ruder gale
   Than that which o'er thy surface spread
When sportive zephyrs briskly play,
   And whisper through thy bord'ring reeds;

When dancing in the solar beam,
   Thy silv'ry waves the margin seek,
With gently undulating flow,
   And there in softest murmurs break.

Vain wish! O'er Esthwaite's tranquil lake,
   A stronger gale full frequent blows,
The soothing prospect disappears,
   The lovely visions of repose.

Title: *Esthwaite Lake:* Esthwaite Water in Cumbria.

LYDIA HUNTLEY SIGOURNEY
1791–1865

Poet, essayist, novelist, children's writer and hymnist, Lydia Huntley Sigourney ('the sweet singer of Hartford'), published over 50 works before her death, including 15 volumes of poetry. An extremely popular writer, and the first American woman poet to support herself by her writing, she was known as 'the American Hemans'. Born in Norwich, Connecticut, her father was care-taker of the Lathrop Estate and his employer took an interest in Lydia, allowing her access to a private library, and assisting with her education. With the help of the Lathrop family, she set up a private school in Hartford, Connecticut, with a friend, in 1814. Her first book, *Moral Pieces in Prose and Verse*, was published in 1815. In 1819, she married hardware merchant and widower, Charles Sigourney, and gave up teaching at his insistence. When his business failed she sold her poems and articles to magazines. A poem-cycle, *Traits of the Aborigines of America* was published in 1822, and her volume, *Poems*, first appeared in 1827. A further volume, *Poems* (1834), from which the following is taken, was reprinted three times. Several of her children died prematurely and death was a prominent theme in her writing, as were political and social issues. She supported abolition, Native American rights, the temperance move-ment, peace societies, and also worked for the deaf and dumb. She travelled in 1840, met Wordsworth and Carlyle, and was presented at the court of Louis Philippe.

Indian Names

'How can the red men be forgotten, while so many of our states and territories, bays, lakes and rivers, are indelibly stamped by names of their giving?'

Ye say they all have passed away,
     That noble race and brave,
That their light canoes have vanished
     From off the crested wave;
That 'mid the forests where they roamed
     There rings no hunter shout,
But their names is on your waters,
     Ye may not wash it out.

'Tis where Ontario's billow
     Like ocean's surge is curled,   10
Where strong Niagra's thunders wake
     The echo of the world.
Where red Missouri bringeth
     Rich tribute from the west,
And Rappahannock swiftly sleeps
     On green Virginia's breast.

Ye say their cone-like cabins,
     That clustered o'er the vale,
Have fled away like withered leaves
     Before the autumn gale,   20

But their memory liveth on your hills,
Their baptism on your shore,
Your everlasting rivers speak
Their dialect of yore.

Old Massachusetts wears it,
Within her lordly crown,
And broad Ohio bears it,
Amid his young renown;
Connecticut hath wreathed it
Where her quiet foliage waves,   30
And bold Kentucky breathed it hoarse
Through all her ancient caves.

Wachuset hides its lingering voice
Within its rocky heart,
And Alleghany graves its tone
Throughout his lofty chart;
Monadnock on his forehead hoar
Doth seal the sacred trust,
Your mountains build their monument,
Though ye destroy their dust.   40

Ye call these red-browed brethren
The insects of an hour,
Crushed like the noteless worm amid
The regions of their power;
Ye drive them from their father's lands,
Ye break of faith the seal,
But can ye from the court of Heaven
Exclude their last appeal?

Ye see their unresisting tribes,
With toilsome step and slow,   50
On through the trackless desert pass,
A caravan of woe;
Think ye the Eternal's ear is deaf?
His sleepless vision dim?
Think ye the *soul's blood* may not cry
From that far land to him?

7-8 *is...it:* the singular seems to have been deliberately used. 15 *Rappahannock:* a river
in Virginia. 33 *Wachuset:* a mountain in Massachusetts. 37 *Monadnock:* a mountain in
New Hampshire.

FELICIA DOROTHEA HEMANS
(*née* Browne)
1793–1835

Felicia Hemans published a volume of poetry almost every year from 1808 until she died. Born in Liverpool, one of six children of an Irish father and Italian-German mother, Felicia was educated by her mother and studied German, Italian, French, Spanish, Portuguese and Latin. She grew up in Wales and was encouraged to write poetry from her childhood. Her first volume, dedicated to the Prince of Wales, was published by her parents and had over 900 subscribers. She married Captain Alfred Hemans in 1812. Just before their fifth son was born, he travelled to Italy and did not return. Earlier, her father had abandoned his family in a similar way when he left for Quebec, so Felicia and her children lived with her sister and mother until the latter's death. Despite initial adverse criticism, she became the most popular woman poet of the 19th century, acclaimed in America as well as Britain. She won The Royal Society of Literature prize for *Dartmoor: a Poem* (1821), and 'Casabianca' ('The boy stood on the burning deck'), first published in 1826, was frequently anthologised. The following poem is from her most successful book, *Records of Woman: with Other Poems* (1828). It was first published in *New Monthly Magazine* vol. 20, 1827. In her poetry Felicia Hemans explored love, fame, domestic responsibility, creativity, heroism and war. She also wrote songs, translations, prose, and drama (*The Vespers of Palermo: a Tragedy*... was performed at the Theatre Royal, Covent Garden in 1823 and, more successfully, in Edinburgh). She was praised by contemporaries, who included Wordsworth, Elizabeth Barrett Browning, Letitia Landon, and George Eliot. She died of tuberculosis in Dublin.

Properzia Rossi

Properzia Rossi, a celebrated female sculptor of Bologna, possessed also of talents for poetry and music, died in consequence of an unrequited attachment. A painting, by Ducis, represents her showing her last work, a basso-relievo of Ariadne, to a Roman knight, the object of her affection, who regards it with indifference.

> – Tell me no more, no more
> Of my soul's lofty gifts! Are they not vain
> To quench its haunting thirst for happiness?
> Have I not loved, and striven, and failed to bind
> One true heart unto me, whereon my own
> Might find a resting-place, a home for all
> Its burden of affections? I depart,
> Unknown, though Fame goes with me; I must leave
> The earth unknown. Yet it may be that death
> Shall give my name a power to win such tears
> As would have made life precious.

I

One dream of passion and of beauty more!
And in its bright fulfilment let me pour
My soul away! Let earth retain a trace
Of that which lit my being, though its race
Might have been loftier far. – Yet one more dream!
From my deep spirit one victorious gleam
Ere I depart! For thee alone, for thee!
May this last work, this farewell triumph be,
Thou, loved so vainly! I would leave enshrined
Something immortal of my heart and mind,   10
That yet may speak to thee when I am gone,
Shaking thine inmost bosom with a tone
Of lost affection; – something that may prove
What she hath been, whose melancholy love
On thee was lavished; silent pang and tear,
And fervent song that gushed when none were near,
And dream by night, and weary thought by day,
Stealing the brightness from her life away –
While thou – Awake! Not yet within me die!
Under the burden and the agony   20
Of this vain tenderness – my spirit, wake!
Ev'n for thy sorrowful affection's sake,
Live! in thy work breathe out! – that he may yet,
Feeling sad mastery there, perchance regret
Thine unrequited gift.

II

              It comes – the power
Within me born, flows back; my fruitless dower
That could not win me love. Yet once again
I greet it proudly, with its rushing train
Of glorious images: – they throng – they press –
A sudden joy lights up my loneliness –   30
I shall not perish all!
               The bright work grows
Beneath my hand, unfolding as a rose,
Leaf after leaf, to beauty; line by line,
I fix my thought, heart, soul, to burn, to shine,
Through the pale marble's veins. It grows – and now
I give my own life's history to thy brow,
Forsaken Ariadne! thou shalt wear

My form, my lineaments; but oh! more fair,
Touched into lovelier being by the glow
    Which in me dwells, as by the summer light   40
All things are glorified. From thee my woe
    Shall yet look beautiful to meet his sight,
When I am passed away. Thou art the mould
Wherein I pour the fervent thoughts, th' untold,
The self-consuming! Speak to him of me,
Thou, the deserted by the lonely sea,
With the soft sadness of thine earnest eye,
Speak to him, lorn one! deeply, mournfully,
Of all my love and grief! Oh! could I throw
Into thy frame a voice – a sweet, and low,   50
And thrilling voice of song! when he came nigh,
To send the passion of its melody
Through his pierced bosom – on its tones to bear
My life's deep feeling, as the southern air
Wafts the faint myrtle's breath – to rise, to swell,
To sink away in accents of farewell,
Winning but one, *one* gush of tears, whose flow
Surely my parted spirit yet might know,
If love be strong as death!

III

                    Now fair thou art,
Thou form, whose life is of my burning heart!   60
Yet all the vision that within me wrought,
    I cannot make thee! Oh! I might have given
Birth to creations of far nobler thought;
    I might have kindled, with the fire of heaven,
Things not of such as die! But I have been
Too much alone; a heart whereon to lean,
With all these deep affections, that o'erflow
My aching soul, and find no shore below;
An eye to be my star, a voice to bring
Hope o'er my path, like sounds that breathe of spring; 70
These are denied me – dreamt of still in vain. –
Therefore my brief aspirings from the chain
Are ever but as some wild fitful song,
Rising triumphantly, to die ere long
In dirge-like echoes.

IV

Yet the world will see

Little of this, my parting work, in thee.
    Thou shalt have fame! Oh, mockery! Give the reed
From storms a shelter – give the drooping vine
Something round which its tendrils may entwine –
    Give the parched flower a rain-drop, and the meed   80
Of love's kind words to woman! Worthless fame!
That in *his* bosom wins not for my name
Th' abiding place it asked! Yet how my heart,
In its own fairy world of song and art,
Once beat for praise! – Are those high longings o'er?
That which I have been can I be no more?
Never, oh! Oh, never more; though still thy sky
Be blue as then, my glorious Italy!
And though the music, whose rich breathings fill
Thine air with soul, be wandering past me still,   90
And though the mantle of thy sunlight streams
Unchanged on forms, instinct with poet-dreams;
Never, Oh, never more! Where'er I move,
The shadow of this broken-hearted love
Is on me and around! Too well *they* know,
    Whose life is all within, too soon and well,
When there the blight hath settled; – but I go
    Under the silent wings of peace to dwell;
From the slow wasting, from the lonely pain,
The inward burning of those words – '*in vain*',   100
    Seared on the heart – I go. 'Twill soon be past.
Sunshine, and song, and bright Italian heaven,
    And thou, oh! thou, on whom my spirit cast
Unvalued wealth – who knowest not what was given
In that devotedness – the sad, and deep,
And unrepaid – farewell! If I could weep
Once, only once, beloved one! on thy breast,
Pouring my heart forth ere I sink to rest!
But that were happiness, and unto me
Earth's gift is *fame*. Yet I was formed to be   110
So richly blessed! With thee to watch the sky,
Speaking not, feeling but that thou wert nigh;
With thee to listen, while the tones of song
Swept even as part of our sweet air along,
To listen silently; with thee to gaze
On forms, the deified of olden days –

This had been joy enough – and hour by hour,
From its glad well-springs drinking life and power,
How had my spirit soared, and made its fame
A glory for thy brow! – Dreams, dreams! – the fire   120
Burns faint within me. Yet I leave my name –
As a deep thrill may linger on the lyre
When its full chords are hushed – awhile to live,
And one day haply in thy heart revive
Sad thoughts of me: – I leave it, with a sound,
A spell o'er memory, mournfully profound;
I leave it, on my country's air to dwell –
Say proudly yet – *'Twas hers who loved me well!'*

Title: *Properzia Rossi:* the only Renaissance woman sculptor known to have worked in marble. Exposition: *Ariadne:* daughter of Minos; she saved Theseus from the Minotaur and they married, but he deserted her when she was pregnant. 50 *voice –:* this ed. voice, 1828 ed. 63 *thought;:* this ed. thought, 1828 ed. 76 *thee.:* this ed. thee, 1828 ed. 116 *days –:* this ed. days, 1828 ed. 126 *profound;:* this ed. profound, 1828 ed.

FIDELIA S.T. HILL (*née* Munkhouse)
1794–1854

Fidelia Hill wrote the first book of poetry by a woman to be published in Australia. The daughter of Richard Hill (a clergyman) and Fidelia Savage, she also wrote under the names Fidelia Savage Thornton Munkhouse and Fidelia Howe. Born in England – in Pontefract, West Yorkshire – she married Robert Keate Hill in London in 1830. They lived in Jamaica before sailing to South Australia, where they landed in 1836. Their ship, the Buffalo, was commanded by Hindmarsh, the first governor. *Poems and Recollections of the Past* (1840), in which the following poem appears, originally raised two hundred subscriptions and had limited circulation. Published in Sydney, its preface identifies the author as 'the *first* who has ventured to lay claim to the title of Authoress, in Sydney'. Fidelia died in Launceston, Tasmania.

Recollections

Yes, South Australia! three years have elapsed
Of dreary banishment, since I became
In thee a sojourner; nor can I choose
But sometimes think on thee; and tho' thou art
A fertile source of unavailing woe,
Thou dost awaken deepest interest still.
Our voyage past, we anchored in that port
Of our New Colony, styled Holdfast Bay:

In part surrounded by the range sublime
Of mountains, with Mount Lofty in their centre: 10
Beautiful mountains, which at even-tide
I oft have gazed upon with raptured sense,
Watching their rose-light hues, as fleeting fast
Like fairy shadows o'er their verdant sides
They mocked the painter's art, and to portray
Defied the utmost reach of poet's skill!
The new year opened on a novel scene,
New cares, new expectations, a new land!
Then toil was cheered, and labour rendered light,
Privations welcomed, every hardship braved,   20
In the blest anticipation of reward:
(Which some indeed deserved, but ne'er obtained)
Some who unceasingly, had lent their aid,
And time, and information, to promote
The interests of the rising Colony –
Still flattering hope on the dark future smiled,
Gilding each object with fallacious dyes,
And picturing pleasure that was not to be!
They bore me to the future Capitol,
Ere yet 'twas more than desert – a few tents,   30
Scattered at intervals 'mid forest trees,
Marked the abode of men. 'Twas a wide waste,
But beauteous in its wildness. – Park-like scenery
Burst on the astonished sight; for it did seem
As tho' the hand of art had nature aided,
Where the broad level walks – and verdant lawns,
And vistas graced that splendid wilderness!
'Twas then they hailed me as the *first* white lady
That ever yet had entered Adelaide.
Can time e'er teach me to forget the sound,   40
Or gratulations that assailed me then,
And cheered me at the moment, or efface
The welcome bland of the distinguished one –
Who fixed the site, and formed the extensive plan
Of that young City? – He hath passed away
To the dark cheerless chambers of the tomb!
But Adelaide if crowned with fortune, shall
To after age perpetuate his name!

One tent was pitched upon the sloping bank
Of the stream Torrens, in whose lucid wave   50

214

Dipped flow'ring shrubs – the sweet mimosa there
Waved its rich blossoms to the perfumed breeze,
High o'er our heads – amid the stately boughs
Of the tall gum tree – birds of brightest hues
Or built their nests, or tuned 'their wood-notes wild,'
Reposing on the rushes, fresh and cool,
Which a loved hand had for my comfort strewed:
This, this methought shall be my happy home!
Here may I dwell, and by experience prove
That tents with love, yield more substantial bliss   60
Than Palaces without it, can bestow.

8 *Holdfast Bay:* an author's note tells that her husband named the bay 'in consequence of the "Rapid" having held to her anchors, during a tremendous gale of wind'. 17 *new year:* 'H.M.S. Buffalo – commanded by Captain Hindmarsh…anchored in Holdfast Bay at the close of the year 1836', author's note. 28 *was…be:* in italics 1840 ed. 55 *their… wild:* from Milton's *L'Allegro.*

JANET HAMILTON (*née* Thomson)
1795–1873

Born in Carshill, Lanarkshire, the daughter of working-class parents, Janet taught herself to read when she was five. According to some accounts, she didn't teach herself to write until she was 54: in others, she wrote poetry as a teenager. Janet Hamilton published her work in a magazine called *Working Man's Friend* from 1850 and her *Poems and Essays* were collected in a volume in 1863. She wrote in both Anglo-Scots and English, mainly focusing on working women, local topics and places, and social and religious issues. She was a close friend of the missionary, William Logan (1813–79). Her *Poems of Purpose and Sketches in Prose* was published in 1865 and *Poems and Ballads* in 1868. She argued that the working man was 'quite as capable of appreciating the treasures…of the best poets, as if he had ascended through all the gradations of learning from the parish school to…the patrician halls of Oxford and Cambridge'. Janet married young and had ten children, teaching each of them to read by the age of five. She lived in the village of Langloan most of her life. She gradually lost her sight and became blind in 1866. Her headstone is inscribed, 'she being dead yet speaketh'.

Oor Location

A hunner funnels bleezin', reekin',
Coal an' ironstane, charrin', smeekin';
Navvies, miners, keepers, fillers,
Puddlers, rollers, iron millers;
Reestit, reekit, raggit laddies,
Firemen, enginemen, an' Paddies;

215

Boatmen, banksmen, rough and rattlin',
'Bout the wecht wi' colliers battlin',
Sweatin, swearin', fechtin', drinkin',
Change-house bells an' gill-stoups clinkin',   10
Police – ready men and willin' –
Aye at han' when stoups are fillin',
Clerks, an' counter-loupers plenty,
Wi' trim moustache and whiskers dainty –
Chaps that winna staun at trifles,
Min' ye they can han'le rifles.
'Bout the wives in oor location,
An' the lasses' botheration,
Some are decent, some are dandies,
An' a gey wheen drucken randies,   20
Aye to neebors' hooses sailin',
Greetin' bairns ahint them trailin',
Gaun for nouther bread nor butter,
Just to drink an' rin the cutter.
Oh, the dreadfu' curse o' drinkin'!
Men are ill, but tae my thinkin',
Leukin through the drucken fock,
There's a Jenny for ilk Jock.
Oh, the dool an' desolation,
An' the havoc in the nation,   30
Wrocht by dirty, drucken wives!
Oh, hoo mony bairnies' lives
Lost ilk year through their neglec'!
Like a millstane roun' the neck
O' the strugglin', toilin' masses
Hing drucken wives and wanton lassies.
To see sae mony unwed mothers
I' sure a shame that taps a' ithers.
   An' noo I'm fairly set a-gaun,
On baith the whisky-shop and pawn;   40
I'll speak my min' – and whatfor no?
Frae whence cums misery, want, an' wo,
The ruin, crime, disgrace an' shame,
That quenches a' the lichts o' hame?
Ye needna speer, the feck ot's drawn
Out o' the change-house an' the pawn.
   Sin and death, as poets tell,
On ilk side the doors o' hell
Wait to haurl mortals in;

Death gets a' that's catcht by sin:
There are doors where death an' sin   50
Draw their tens o' thoosan's in;
Thick and thrang we see them gaun,
First the dram shop, then the pawn;
Owre a' kin's o'ruination,
Drink's the king in oor location.

1 *hunner:* hundred. 4 *Puddlers:* those who stir molten iron. 8 *wecht:* weight. 10 *Change-house:* Ale-house; *gill-stoups:* drinking beakers. 13 *counter-loupers:* someone who leaps over the bar-counter or queue-jumpers? 20 *gey...randies:* a good few drunken revellers. 22 *Greetin':* Crying, weeping. 24 *drink...cutter:* drink and run ship, smuggle a drink. 27 *fock:* folk. 45 *speer:* ask; *feck:* bulk. 55 *Owre...ruination:* Over all kinds of ruin.

SOJOURNER TRUTH (Isabella Bomefree [Baumfree], *later* van Wagener)

1797–1883

Sojourner Truth may never have learned to read or write but, almost six feet tall, she was a memorable orator and a charismatic presence. She spoke so powerfully that her words were passed down in ways that attempted to recreate both her speech and rhetorical drama. Born a slave in Ulster County, New York, in 1827 she escaped with one of daughters. She later courageously fought for and won custody of her only son, Peter, who had been illegally sold. Her first owners were Dutch and she spoke Low Dutch in her childhood, retaining the accent when she learned English. After years of cruel treatment and a succession of slave masters, Mr and Mrs van Wagener bought her, along with her daughter Sophia, to give them their freedom. She was converted to Methodism under their name. She took the name 'Sojourner Truth' after a vision, in 1843, when she became a travelling missionary. Sojourner joined the Massachusetts utopian community, 'The Northampton Association for Education and Industry' and dictated her autobiography, *Narrative of Sojourner Truth* (1850) to her friend, fellow abolitionist, Olive Gilbert. She was called the 'Lybian Sybil' by Harriet Beecher Stowe in *The Atlantic Monthly* (April 1863, 473-81). In 1864 Sojourner met Abraham Lincoln at the White House. She worked tirelessly for women's rights and black rights, actively supported black troops in the Civil War, and committed herself to improving the welfare of former slaves. Over a thousand people are said to have attended her funeral. The following was adapted into poetry by Robyn Bolam, using eye-witness Frances Gage's transcription of the speech Sojourner Truth gave at the Women's Rights Convention in Akron, Ohio, in 1851 (*History of Woman Suffrage*, vol.1, ed. E.C. Stanton, S.B. Anthony, & M.J. Gage, 1881, 115-16). A previous adaptation into poetry by Erlene Stetson (from Arthur Huff Fauset's account of the speech published in his: *Sojourner, God's Faithful Pilgrim*, 1938, 131-33), is reproduced in: *Black Sister: Poetry by Black American Women 1746-1980*, ed. Erlene Stetson (Bloomington, Indiana UP, 1981, 24-25).

A'n't I a Woman?

But what's all this here talkin' about?
That man over there say that woman
needs to be helped into carriages,
and lifted over ditches, and to have
the best place everywhere...
Nobody ever helps *me* into carriages,
or over mud-puddles, or gives *me*
any best place!
And a'n't *I* a woman?

Look at me! Look at my arm! 10
I have ploughed and planted
and gathered into barns –
and no man could head me –
and a'n't *I* a woman?

I could work as much
and eat as much as a man –
when I could get it –
and bear the lash as well,
and a'n't *I* a woman?

I have born thirteen chilern 20
and seen 'em mos' all sold off to slavery,
and when I cried out with my mother's grief,
none but Jesus heard me –
and a'n't *I* a woman?

Then they talks about this thing in the head –
What's this they call it?
That's it honey – intellect.
Now what's that got to do
With women's rights or niggers' rights?

That little man in black, there – 30
He say women can't have as much rights
as men, cause Christ wan't a woman...
Where did your Christ come from?
From God and a woman!
Man had nothin' to do with him!

If the fust woman God ever made
was strong enough
to turn the world upside down, all alone –
these women together
ought to be able to turn it back
and get it rightside up again.
And now they is asking to do it –
the men better let 'em!

40

1 *But...about?:* According to Frances Gage, Sojourner previously commented: 'I tink dat 'twixt de niggers of de Souf and de womin at de Norf, all talkin' 'bout rights, de white men will be in a fix pretty soon.' (p.115). 20 *thirteen chilern:* Sojourner is thought to have been one of 13 children herself, but only five of her own are known. 30 *That... black:* one of the ministers in the church where she was speaking. 32 *wan't:* wasn't.

LETITIA ELIZABETH LANDON
(*later* Maclean)
1802–38

Born in London, Letitia Landon enjoyed early popular success. As 'L' or 'L.E.L.', her poetry appeared in *The Literary Gazette* from 1820. Between 1821 and 1828 she published five volumes: *The Fate of Adelaide...*, *The Improvisatrice...*, *The Troubadour...*, *The Golden Violet*, and *The Venetian Bracelet, The Lost Pleiad, A History of the Lyre, and Other Poems*. An editor for *Fisher's Drawing Room Scrapbook* (1831-38) and author of three novels (1831-37), she also wrote prose for children which included an autobiography. A further volume of poems, *The Vow of the Peacock...* appeared (with her engraved portrait) in 1835 and *The Zenana, and Minor Poems of Letitia Landon* was published posthumously in 1839. The latter includes a Memoir by her friend, Emma Roberts, and her last letter, written the morning of her death (October 15), in which she describes her home and health as 'excellent'. After a broken engagement to the biographer, John Forster, Letitia had secretly married George Maclean, Governor of Cape Coast, in 1838. However, she died two months after her arrival in Africa: her sudden death was announced in newspapers on 1 January 1839. Roberts relates that it was attributed to 'incaution in taking hydrocyanic acid while suffering under an attack of the spasms' and is emphatic that her friend 'never wilfully would have destroyed herself'. 'The Princess Victoria' first appeared in *Fisher's Drawing Room Scrap-book* in 1832 and 'Scenes in London' was published in *The Zenana, and Minor Poems*.

The Princess Victoria

And art thou a Princess? – in sooth, we may well
Go back to the days of the sign and the spell,

When a young queen sat on an ivory throne
In a shining hall, whose windows shone
With colours its crystals caught from the sky,
Or the roof which a thousand rubies dye;
Where the summer garden was spread around,
With the date and the palm and the cedar crowned;
Where fountains played with the rainbow showers,
Touched with the hues of their comrade flowers;   10
Where the tulip and rose grew side by side,
One like a queen, and one like a bride;
One with its own imperial flush,
The other reddening with love's sweet blush;
When silver stuffs for her step were unrolled,
And the citron was served on a plate of gold;
When perfumes arose from pearl caskets filled
With odours from all sweet things distilled;
When a fairy guarded her throne from ill,
And she knew no rule but her own glad will: 20
Those were the days for a youthful queen,
And such, fair Princess, thou should'st have been.

   But now thou wilt fill a weary throne,
What with rights of the people, and rights of thy own:
An ear-trumpet now thy sceptre should be,
Eternal debate is the future for thee.
Lord Brougham will make a six-hours' oration,
On the progress of knowledge, the mind of the nation;
Lord Grey one yet longer, to state that his place
Is perhaps less dear to himself than his race;   30
O'Connell will tell Ireland's griefs and her wrongs,
In speech, the mac-adamized prose of Moore's songs:
Good patience! How weary the young queen will be
Of 'the flower of the earth, and the gem of the sea!'
Mr Hume, with his watchwords 'Retrenchment and Waste',
Will insist that your wardrobe in his care be placed;
The silk he will save! The blonde he will spare –
I wish he may leave Your Grace any to wear.
That feminine fancy, a will of your own,
Is a luxury wholly denied to a throne;   40
And this is your future – how soon time will trace
A change and a sign on that fair and young face!
Methinks the best wish to be offered thee now,
Is – God keep the crown long from that innocent brow!

27 *Lord Brougham:* Henry Peter, Baron Brougham and Vaux (1778-1868), Whig politician and Lord Chancellor of England. 29 *Lord Grey:* Charles Grey (1764-1845), Whig Prime Minister, responsible for the 1832 Reform Act, who supported Catholic emancipation and the abolition of the slave trade. 31 *O'Connell:* Daniel O'Connell, leader of the Irish Catholic Association. 32 *mac-adamized:* rolled like the tough layers of John Loudon McAdam's roads; *Moore's songs:* the popular songs of Irish poet, Thomas Moore (1779-1852). 34 *flower...sea:* 'Wert thou all that I wish thee, great, glorious, and free,/ First flower of the earth and first gem of the sea' from Moore's song, 'Remember Thee'. 35 *Mr Hume:* Joseph Hume (1777-1855), Whig politician and reformer who fought for financial retrenchment, universal suffrage, etc. 37 *blonde:* silk lace of two threads in hexagonal meshes. 44 Victoria became Queen in 1837.

from Scenes in London

IV *The City Churchyard*

I pray thee lay me not to rest
Among these mouldering bones;
Too heavily the earth is prest
By all these crowded stones.

Life is too gay – life is too near –
With all its pomp and toil;
I pray thee do not lay me here,
In such a world-struck soil.

The ceaseless roll of wheels would wake
The slumbers of the dead,
I cannot bear for life to make
Its pathway o'er my head.

The flags around are cold and drear,
They stand apart, alone;
And no one ever pauses here,
To sorrow for the gone.

No: lay me in the far green fields
The summer sunshine cheers;
And where the early wild flower yields
The tribute of its tears.

Where shadows the sepulchral yew,
Where droops the willow tree,
Where the long grass is filled with dew –
Oh! make such grave for me!

And passers-by, at evening's close,
Will pause beside the grave,
And moralize o'er the repose
They fear, and yet they crave.

Perhaps some kindly hand may bring
Its offering to the tomb;
And say, as fades the rose in spring,
So fadeth human bloom.

But here there is no kindly thought
To soothe, and to relieve;
No fancies and no flowers are brought,
That soften while they grieve.

Here Poesy and Love come not –
It is a world of stone;
The grave is bought – is closed – forgot!
And then life hurries on.

Sorrow and beauty – nature – love –
Redeem man's common breath;
Ah! Let them shed the grave above –
Give loveliness to death.

Author's note: If there be one object more material, more revolting, more gloomy than another, it is a crowded churchyard in a city...No one can love London better than I do; but never do I wish to be buried there. It is the best place in the world for a house, and the worst for a grave...

SARA COLERIDGE

1802–52

Born on 22 December 1802, near Keswick, Sara was the daughter of Samuel Taylor Coleridge and his wife, Sarah Fricker. Her uncle, Robert Southey, helped to bring her up, and her friendship with Wordsworth led to her being the subject of his poem, *The Triad*, along with cousins, Dora Wordsworth and Edith Southey. Initially she translated volumes from Latin and 16th-century French, but after her marriage to her cousin, Henry Nelson Coleridge, in 1829, she published *Pretty Lessons in Verse for Good Children* (1834) and a prose tale with lyrics, *Phantasmion: a fairy tale* (1837). They had two children and lived in London, where Henry was a barrister. As her father's literary executor, she began editing and annotating his work, setting aside her own writing to make his literary reputation secure. She worked with her husband on this until his death in 1843, after which she continued as sole editor, publishing editions of *Biographia Literaria, Notes and Lectures upon Shakespeare* and *Essays on his Own Times*, as well as other works. Her own *Memoirs and Letters* were published by her daughter, Edith, in 1873. The following is from Chapter XXVII of *Phantasmion*.

from Phantasmion: a fairy tale

IX *Yon Changeful Cloud*

Yon changeful cloud will soon thy aspect wear –
So bright it grows:– and now, by light winds shaken
O ever seen yet ne'er to be o'ertaken!
Those waving branches seem thy billowy hair.
The cypress glades recall thy pensive air;
Slow rills, that wind like snakes amid the grass,
Thine eye's mild sparkle fling me as they pass,
Yet murmuring cry, 'This fruitless quest forbear'!

Nay e'en amid the cataract's loud storm,
Where foamy torrents from the crags are leaping,
Methinks I catch swift glimpses of thy form,
Thy robe's light folds in airy tumult sweeping;
Then silent are the falls: 'mid colours warm
Gleams the bright maze beneath their splendour sleeping.

ELIZABETH BARRETT BROWNING
1806–61

Born at Coxhoe Hall, Kelloe, County Durham, Elizabeth grew up in Hereford-shire, the eldest of twelve children. Educated by her brother's tutor, she wrote poetry from the age of eight and studied literature, classics, languages and philosophy. Her long poem, *Battle of Marathon*, was privately printed by her father when she was 13. She injured her spine aged 15 and years of illness followed. After adverse financial fortunes and her mother's death in 1828, she lived in Sidmouth, London, and Torquay, returning to London after her brother's tragic drowning. She published three volumes of poetry before her *Poems* (1844). At Wimpole Street she was an invalid and her father did not allow visitors, but she corresponded with the writer Mary Russell Mitford (who gave her a pet dog, Flush), and with others, most importantly, in 1845, with Robert Browning. They married secretly and later lived in Florence. She had a son in 1849. *Sonnets from the Portuguese* (1850) was written in Italy and Elizabeth was proposed for Poet Laureate that year, but the position was given to Tennyson. Two more volumes followed before her verse novel in nine books, *Aurora Leigh*, was published in 1856. *Last Poems* appeared post-humously in 1862. Her topics ranged from love to female creativity to deeply felt social and political concerns, including child labour, slavery, and Italian liberation.

from Sonnets from the Portuguese

XIV

If thou must love me, let it be for nought
Except for love's sake only. Do not say
'I love her for her smile.. her look.. her way
Of speaking gently,.. for a trick of thought
That falls in well with mine, and certes brought
A sense of pleasant ease on such a day' –
For these things in themselves, Belovèd, may
Be changed or change for thee, – and love so wrought,
May be unwrought so. Neither love me for
Thine own dear pity's wiping my cheeks dry,
Since one might well forget to weep who bore
Thy comfort long, and lose thy love thereby.
But love me for love's sake, that evermore
Thou mayest love on through love's eternity.

XXII

When our two souls stand up erect and strong,
Face to face, silent, drawing nigh and nigher,
Until the lengthening wings break into fire
At either curvèd point, – what bitter wrong
Can the earth do to us, that we should not long
Be here contented. – Think. In mounting higher,
The angels would press on us, and aspire
To drop some golden orb of perfect song
Into our deep, dear silence. Let us stay
Rather on earth, Belovèd – where the unfit
Contrarious moods of men recoil away
And isolate pure spirits, and permit
A place to stand and love in for a day,
With darkness and the death-hour rounding it.

XLII

How do I love thee? Let me count the ways.
I love thee to the depth and breadth and height

224

My soul can reach, when feeling out of sight
For the ends of Being and Ideal Grace.
I love thee to the level of everyday's
Most quiet need, by sun and candlelight.
I love thee freely, as men strive for Right;
I love thee purely, as they turn from Praise;
I love thee with the passion put to use
In my old griefs, and with my childhood's faith;
I love thee with a love I seemed to lose
With my lost saints, – I love thee with the breath,
Smiles, tears, of all my life! – and, if God choose,
I shall but love thee better after death.

from Aurora Leigh, FIRST BOOK

Books, books, books!
I had found the secret of a garret-room
Piled high with cases in my father's name,
Piled high, packed large, – where, creeping in and out
Among the giant fossils of my past,
Like some small nimble mouse between the ribs
Of a mastodon, I nibbled here and there
At this or that box, pulling through the gap,
In heats of terror, haste, victorious joy,   840
The first book first. And how I felt it beat
Under my pillow, in the morning's dark,
An hour before the sun would let me read!
My books!
            At last because the time was ripe,
I chanced upon the poets.
                    As the earth
Plunges in fury, when the internal fires
Have reached and pricked her heart, and, throwing flat,
The marts and temples, the triumphal gates
And towers of observation, clears herself
To elemental freedom – thus, my soul,   850
At poetry's divine first finger-touch,
Let go conventions and sprang up surprised,
Convicted of the great eternities
Before two worlds.
                    What's this, Aurora Leigh,
You write so of the poets, and not laugh?
Those virtuous liars, dreamers after dark,

Exaggerators of the sun and moon,
And sooth-sayers in a tea-cup?
                              I write so
Of the only truth-tellers now left to God –
The only speakers of essential truth,   860
Opposed to relative, comparative,
And temporal truths; the only holders by
His sun-skirts, through conventional grey glooms;
The only teachers who instruct mankind
From just a shadow on a charnel-wall,
To find man's veritable stature out,
Erect, sublime, – the measure of a man,
And that's the measure of an angel, says
The apostle. Ay, and while your common men
Build pyramids, gauge railroads, reign, reap, dine,   870
And dust the flaunty carpets of the world
For kings to walk on, or our senators,
The poet suddenly will catch them up
With his voice like a thunder,.. 'This is soul,
This is life, this word is being said in heaven,
Here's God down on us! What are you about?'
How all those workers start amid their work,
Look round, look up, and feel, a moment's space,
That carpet-dusting, though a pretty trade,
Is not the imperative labour after all.   880

My own best poets, am I one with you,
That thus I love you, – or but one through love?
Does all this smell of thyme about my feet
Conclude my visit to your holy hill
In personal presence, or but testify
The rustling of your vesture through my dreams
With influent odours? When my joy and pain,
My thought and aspiration, like the stops
Of pipe or flute, are absolutely dumb
If not melodious, do you play on me,   890
My pipers, – and if, sooth, you did not blow,
Would no sound come? Or is the music mine,
As a man's voice or breath is called his own,
In-breathed by the Life-breather? There's a doubt
For cloudy seasons!
                    But the sun was high
When first I felt my pulses set themselves

For concords; when the rhythmic turbulence
Of blood and brain swept outward upon words,
As wind upon the alders, blanching them
By turning up their under-natures till   900
They trembled in dilation. O delight
And triumph of the poet, – who would say
A man's mere 'yes,' a woman's common 'no,'
A little human hope of that or this,
And says the word so that it burns you through
With a special revelation, shakes the heart
Of all the men and women in the world,
As if one came back from the dead and spoke,
With eyes too happy, a familiar thing
Become divine i' the utterance! While for him   910
The poet, speaker, he expands with joy;
The palpitating angel in his flesh
Thrills inly with consenting fellowship
To those innumerous spirits who sun themselves
Outside of time.
                    O life, O poetry,
– Which means life in life! cognisant of life
Beyond this blood-beat, – passionate for truth
Beyond these senses, – poetry, my life, –
My eagle, with both grappling feet still hot
From Zeus's thunder, who hast ravished me   920
Away from all the shepherds, sheep, and dogs,
And set me in the Olympian roar and round
Of luminous faces, for a cup-bearer,
To keep the mouths of all the godheads moist
For everlasting laughters, – I, myself
Have drunk across the beaker with their eyes!
How those gods look!
                    Enough so, Ganymede.
We shall not bear above a round or two –
We drop the golden cup at Heré's foot
And swoon back to the earth, – and find ourselves   930
Face-down among the pine-cones, cold with dew,
While the dogs bark, and many a shepherd scoffs,
'What's come now to the youth?' Such ups and downs
Have poets.
                    Am I such indeed? The name
Is royal, and to sign it like a queen,
Is what I dare not, – though some royal blood

227

Would seem to tingle in me now and then,
With sense of power and ache, – with imposthumes
And manias usual to the race. Howbeit
I dare not: 'tis too easy to go mad   940
And ape a Bourbon in a crown of straws;
The thing's too common.
                          Many fervent souls
Strike rhyme on rhyme, who would strike steel on steel
If steel had offered, in a restless heat
Of doing something. Many tender souls
Have strung their losses on a rhyming thread,
As children, cowslips:- the more pains they take,
The work more withers. Young men, ay, and maids,
Too often sow their wild oats in tame verse,
Before they sit down under their own vine   950
And live for use. Alas, near all the birds
Will sing at dawn, – and yet we do not take
The chaffering swallow for the holy lark.

---

838 *mastodon:* large extinct elephant-like mammal. 927 *Ganymede:* cupbearer of Zeus, King of the Olympian gods. 929 *Heré:* Hera, wife of Zeus. 938 *impostumes:* swellings.

SARAH LOUISA FORTEN ('ADA')
1814–83

Born in Philadelphia, Pennsylvania, Sarah Louisa Forten was the great-great-granddaughter of a slave. Her father, James Forten, was an active abolitionist, as was her mother, who had a mixture of African, Native American, and European roots. Sarah married Joseph Purvis in 1838. They farmed near Philadelphia and when Joseph died in 1857, Sarah had eight children to support and large debts to settle. She took her youngest children back with her to her parents' home and joined them in their campaign against slavery. She published 15 poems under the pseudonym 'Ada', from *c.* 1831 to 1836, in magazines like the *Liberator* and the *Philanthropist*. Other poems of disputed authorship have also been attributed to her. Some of her poetry was set to music. The following poem appeared in the *Liberator* on 16 April 1831.

The Slave

Our sires who once in freedom's cause,
    Their boasted freedom sought and won,
For deeds of glory gained applause,
    When patriot feelings led them on.

And can their sons now speak with pride,
Of rights for which they bled and died, –
Or while the captive is oppressed,
Think of the wrongs they once redressed?
Oh, surely they have quite forgot,
That bondage once had been their lot;
The sweets of freedom now they know,
They care not for the captive's woe.
The poor wronged slave can bear no part
In feelings dearest to his heart;
He cannot speak on freedom's side,
Nor dare he own a freeman's pride.
His soul is dark, ay dark as night,
O'er which is shed no gleam of light;
A cloud of error, doubt and fear,
O'er him is ever hovering near;
And sad and hard his lot must be,
To know that he can ne'er be free;
To feel that *his* is doomed to be
A life, and death, of slavery.
But will not justice soon arise,
And plead the cause of the despised?
For oh! my country, must it be,
That they still find a foe in thee?

CHARLOTTE BRONTË (Currer Bell)

1816–55

Best known as the author of novels *Jane Eyre*, *The Professor*, *Shirley* and *Villette*, Charlotte Brontë's first published work comprised contributions, with her sisters', to a volume: *Poems by Currer, Ellis, and Acton Bell*, in 1846. The book attracted little attention and only two copies were sold. The following poems are taken from *The Professor by Currer Bell (Charlotte Brontë)...to which are added the Poems of Currer, Ellis, and Acton Bell: now first collected* (1860). Charlotte was the eldest of the three poets, having become the eldest in the family of six, following the early deaths from tuberculosis of her other sisters Maria and Elizabeth. Born in Thornton, Yorkshire, her father was the Church of England clergyman at Haworth from 1820; her mother died in 1821. She was educated at the Clergy Daughters' School, Cowan Bridge (see *Jane Eyre*), at Roe Head School, Mirfield (where she later taught), and at the Pensionnat Heger, Brussels (a source for *The Professor* and *Villette*). When she was in the process of writing *Shirley* (1848), her remaining brother and sisters died within nine months. In 1854 she married her father's curate, the

Rev. Arthur Nicholls, but died while pregnant, ten months later. In 1857, her friend Elizabeth Gaskell wrote *The Life of Charlotte Brontë*. The strength of feeling of Charlotte's heroines, their loneliness, and their passionate struggles to control their lives and be true to their beliefs can be found in her poetry as well as in her novels.

Pilate's Wife's Dream

I've quenched my lamp, I struck it in that start
Which every limb convulsed, I heard it fall –
The crash blent with my sleep, I saw depart
Its light, even as I woke, on yonder wall;
Over against my bed, there shone a gleam
Strange, faint, and mingling also with my dream.

It sank, and I am wrapt in utter gloom;
How far is night advanced, and when will day
Retinge the dusk and livid air with bloom,
And fill this void with warm, creative ray?   10
Would I could sleep again till, clear and red,
Morning shall on the mountain-tops be spread!

I'd call my women, but to break their sleep,
Because my own is broken, were unjust;
They've wrought all day, and well-earned slumbers steep
Their labours in forgetfulness, I trust;
Let me my feverish watch with patience bear,
Thankful that none with me its sufferings share.

Yet, oh, for light! one ray would tranquillise
My nerves, my pulses, more than effort can;   20
I'll draw my curtain and consult the skies:
These trembling stars at dead of night look wan,
Wild, restless, strange, yet cannot be more drear
Than this my couch, shared by a nameless fear.

All black – one great cloud, drawn from east to west,
Conceals the heavens, but there are lights below;
Torches burn in Jerusalem, and cast
On yonder stony mount a lurid glow.
I see men stationed there, and gleaming spears;
A sound, too, from afar, invades my ears.   30

230

Dull, measured, strokes of axe and hammer ring
From street to street, not loud, but through the night
Distinctly heard – and some strange spectral thing
Is now upreared – and, fixed against the light
Of the pale lamps, defined upon that sky,
It stands up like a column, straight and high.

I see it all – I know the dusky sign –
A cross on Calvary, which Jews uprear
While Romans watch; and when the dawn shall shine
Pilate, to judge the victim, will appear –   40
Pass sentence – yield Him up to crucify;
And on that cross the spotless Christ must die.

Dreams, then, are true – for thus my vision ran;
Surely some oracle has been with me,
The gods have chosen me to reveal their plan,
To warn an unjust judge of destiny:
I, slumbering, heard and saw; awake I know,
Christ's coming death, and Pilate's life of woe.

I do not weep for Pilate – who could prove
Regret for him whose cold and crushing sway   50
No prayer can soften, no appeal can move;
Who tramples hearts as others trample clay,
Yet with a faltering, an uncertain tread,
That might stir up reprisal in the dead.

Forced to sit by his side and see his deeds;
Forced to behold that visage, hour by hour,
In whose gaunt lines the abhorrent gazer reads
A triple lust of gold, and blood, and power;
A soul whom motives fierce, yet abject, urge
Rome's servile slave, and Judah's tyrant scourge.   60

How can I love, or mourn, or pity him?
I, who so long my fettered hands have wrung;
I, who for grief have wept my eye-sight dim;
Because, while life for me was bright and young,
He robbed my youth – he quenched my life's fair ray –
He crushed my mind, and did my freedom slay.

And at this hour – although I be his wife –
He has no more of tenderness from me
Than any other wretch of guilty life;
Less, for I know his household privacy –   70
I see him as he is – without a screen;
And, by the gods, my soul abhors his mien!

Has he not sought my presence, dyed in blood –
Innocent, righteous blood, shed shamelessly?
And have I not his red salute withstood?
Aye, when, as erst, he plunged all Galilee
In dark bereavement – in affliction sore,
Mingling their very offerings with their gore.

Then came he – in his eyes a serpent-smile,
Upon his lips some false, endearing word,   80
And through the streets of Salem clanged the while,
His slaughtering, hacking, sacrilegious sword –
And I, to see a man cause men such woe,
Trembled with ire – I did not fear to show.

And now, the envious Jewish priests have brought
Jesus – whom they in mock'ry call their king –
To have, by this grim power, their vengeance wrought;
By this mean reptile, innocence to sting.
Oh! could I but the purposed doom avert,
And shield the blameless head from cruel hurt!   90

Accessible is Pilate's heart to fear,
Omens will shake his soul, like autumn leaf;
Could he this night's appalling vision hear,
This just man's bonds were loosed, his life were safe,
Unless that bitter priesthood should prevail,
And make even terror to their malice quail.

Yet if I tell the dream – but let me pause.
What dream? Erewhile the characters were clear,
Graved on my brain – at once some unknown cause
Has dimmed and raised the thoughts, which now appear,   100
Like a vague remnant of some by-past scene; –
Not what will be, but what, long since, has been.

I suffered many things – I heard foretold
A dreadful doom for Pilate, – lingering woes,
In far, barbarian climes, where mountains cold
Built up a solitude of trackless snows,
There he and grisly wolves prowled side by side,
There he lived famished – there, methought, he died;

But not of hunger, nor by malady;
I saw the snow around him, stained with gore;   110
I said I had no tears for such as he,
And, lo! my cheek is wet – mine eyes run o'er;
I weep for mortal suffering, mortal guilt,
I weep the impious deed, the blood self-spilt.

More I recall not, yet the vision spread
Into a world remote, an age to come –
And still the illumined name of Jesus shed
A light, a clearness, through the unfolding gloom –
And still I saw that sign, which now I see,
That cross on yonder brow of Calvary.   120

What is this Hebrew Christ? To me unknown
His lineage – doctrine – mission; yet how clear
Is God-like goodness in his actions shewn,
How straight and stainless is his life's career!
The ray of Deity that rests on him,
In my eyes makes Olympian glory dim.

The world advances; Greek or Roman rite
Suffices not the inquiring mind to stay;
The searching soul demands a purer light
To guide it on its upward, onward way;   130
Ashamed of sculptured gods, Religion turns
To where the unseen Jehovah's altar burns.

Our faith is rotten, all our rites defiled,
Our temples sullied and, methinks, this man,
With his new ordinance, so wild and mild,
Is come, even as He says, the chaff to fan
And sever from the wheat; but will his faith
Survive the terrors of tomorrow's death?

*   *   *   *   *   *

233

I feel a firmer trust – a higher hope
Rise in my soul – it dawns with dawning day;   140
Lo! on the Temple's roof – on Moriah's slope
Appears at length that clear and crimson ray
Which I so wished for when shut in by night;
Oh, opening skies, I hail, I bless your light!

Part, clouds and shadows! Glorious Sun appear!
Part, mental gloom! Come insight from on high!
Dusk dawn in heaven still strives with daylight clear,
The longing soul, doth still uncertain sigh.
Oh! to behold the truth – that sun divine,
How doth my bosom pant, my spirit pine!   150

This day, Time travails with a mighty birth;
This day, Truth stoops from heaven and visits earth;
Ere night descends I shall more surely know
What guide to follow, in what path to go;
I wait in hope – I wait in solemn fear,
The oracle of God – the sole – true God – to hear.

Title: Pilate's wife was traditionally named Claudia Procula or Procla; she was a Jewish
proselyte at the time of the crucifixion, but is later said to have converted to Christianity.
81 *Salem:* the seat of the kingdom of Melchizedek, identified with Jerusalem (Genesis
xiv.18). 114 *blood self-spilt:* there is a tradition that Pilate committed suicide (Eusebius
Historia Ecclesiastica II).

Evening Solace

The human heart has hidden treasures,
In secret kept, in silence sealed; –
The thoughts, the hopes, the dreams, the pleasures,
Whose charms were broken if revealed.
And days may pass in gay confusion,
And nights in rosy riots fly,
While, lost in Fame's or Wealth's illusion,
The memory of the Past may die.

But there are hours of lonely musing,
Such as in evening silence come,
When, soft as birds their pinions closing,
The heart's best feelings gather home.
Then in our souls there seems to languish
A tender grief that is not woe;

And thoughts that once wrung groans of anguish,
Now cause but some mild tears to flow.

And feelings, once as strong as passions,
Float softly back – a faded dream;
Our own sharp griefs and wild sensations,
The tale of others' sufferings seem.
Oh! when the heart is freshly bleeding,
How longs it for that time to be,
When, through the mist of years receding,
Its woes but live in reverie!

And it can dwell on moonlight glimmer,
On evening shade and loneliness;
And, while the sky grows dim and dimmer,
Feel no untold and strange distress –
Only a deeper impulse given
By lonely hour and darkened room,
To solemn thoughts that soar to heaven
Seeking a life and world to come.

EMILY BRONTË (Ellis Bell)
1818-48

Two years younger than her sister, Charlotte, and two years older than Anne,
Emily Brontë received less formal education than her elder sister, spending
much of her early life in her father's library or on the Yorkshire moors. She
attended Roe Head School for about three months before she sickened for
home and returned there. Her sister Anne took her place at the school and
Emily developed a close bond with her brother, Branwell, on his return from
London. In 1837, when Branwell became an usher at a boys' school, Emily
also found employment in a school near Halifax. Her knowledge of Law Hill
School and the surrounding area was later used in writing *Wuthering Heights*.
She appears to have stayed there just over a year. Emily accompanied Charlotte
to Brussels in 1842, but returned to Haworth after ten months when their
aunt died. She remained at the Parsonage and wrote much of her poetry in
this period. The sisters' joint collection appeared in 1846 and included 21 of
her poems: she is known to have written over 200. Wuthering Heights was
published in December 1847. Branwell died of tuberculosis in September
1848 and Emily, of the same cause, in the December. In 1850 Charlotte pub-
lished *Selections from Poems by Ellis Bell*. An edition of *Wuthering Heights and
Agnes Grey...with a biographical notice of the authors, a selection of their literary
remains, & a preface by Currer Bell* also appeared in 1850. This volume con-
tained eighteen previously unpublished poems, including 'Stanzas', which is
not known in manuscript.

Remembrance

Cold in the earth – and the deep snow piled above thee,
Far, far, removed, cold in the dreary grave!
Have I forgot, my only Love, to love thee,
Severed at last by Time's all-severing wave?

Now, when alone, do my thoughts no longer hover
Over the mountains, on that northern shore,
Resting their wings where heath and fern-leaves cover
Thy noble heart for ever, ever more?

Cold in the earth – and fifteen wild Decembers,
From those brown hills, have melted into spring:
Faithful, indeed, is the spirit that remembers
After such years of change and suffering!

Sweet Love of youth, forgive, if I forget thee,
While the world's tide is bearing me along;
Other desires and other hopes beset me,
Hopes which obscure, but cannot do thee wrong!

No later light has lightened up my heaven,
No second morn has ever shone for me;
All my life's bliss from thy dear life was given,
All my life's bliss is in the grave with thee.

But, when the days of golden dreams had perished,
And even Despair was powerless to destroy;
Then did I learn how existence could be cherished,
Strengthened, and fed without the aid of joy.

Then did I check the tears of useless passion –
Weaned my young soul from yearning after thine;
Sternly denied its burning wish to hasten
Down to that tomb already more than mine.

And, even yet, I dare not let it languish,
Dare not indulge in memory's rapturous pain;
Once drinking deep of that divinest anguish,
How could I seek the empty world again?

To Imagination

When weary with the long day's care,
  And earthly change from pain to pain,
And lost, and ready to despair,
  Thy kind voice calls me back again:
Oh, my true friend! I am not lone,
  While thou canst speak with such a tone!

So hopeless is the world without;
  The world within I doubly prize;
Thy world, where guile, and hate, and doubt,
  And cold suspicion never rise;
Where thou, and I, and Liberty,
  Have undisputed sovereignty.

What matters it, that, all around
  Danger, and guilt, and darkness lie,
If but within our bosom's bound
  We hold a bright, untroubled sky,
Warm with ten thousand mingled rays
  Of suns that know no winter days?

Reason, indeed, may oft complain
  For Nature's sad reality,
And tell the suffering heart how vain
  Its cherished dreams must always be;
And Truth may rudely trample down
  The flowers of Fancy, newly-blown:

But, thou art ever there, to bring
  The hovering vision back, and breathe
New glories o'er the blighted spring,
  And call a lovelier Life from Death,
And whisper, with a voice divine,
  Of real worlds, as bright as thine.

I trust not to thy phantom bliss,
  Yet, still, in evening's quiet hour,
With never-failing thankfulness,
  I welcome thee, Benignant Power;
Sure solacer of human cares,
  And sweeter hope, when hope despairs!

The Old Stoic

Riches I hold in light esteem,
   And Love I laugh to scorn;
And lust of fame was but a dream,
   That vanished with the morn:

And if I pray, the only prayer
   That moves my lips for me
Is, 'Leave the heart that now I bear,
   And give me liberty!'

Yes, as my swift days near their goal,
   'Tis all that I implore;
In life and death, a chainless soul,
   With courage to endure.

Stanzas

Often rebuked, yet always back returning
   To those first feelings that were born with me,
And leaving busy chase of wealth and learning
   For idle dreams of things which cannot be:

To-day, I will seek not the shadowy region,
   Its unsustaining vastness waxes drear;
And visions rising, legion after legion,
   Bring the unreal world too strangely near.

I'll walk, but not in old heroic traces,
   And not in paths of high morality,
And not among the half-distinguished faces,
   The clouded forms of long-past history.

I'll walk where my own nature would be leading:
   It vexes me to choose another guide:
Where the grey flocks in ferny glens are feeding;
   Where the wild wind blows on the mountain-side.

What have those lonely mountains worth revealing?
   More glory and more grief than I can tell:
The earth that wakes *one* human heart to feeling
   Can centre both the worlds of Heaven and Hell.

No coward soul is mine

No coward soul is mine
No trembler in the world's storm-troubled sphere
I see Heaven's glories shine
And faith stands equal arming me from fear.

O God within my breast,
Almighty, ever-present Deity!
Life – that in me has rest,
As I – undying life – have power in thee!

Vain are the thousand creeds
That move men's hearts: unutterably vain;
Worthless as withered weeds,
Or idlest froth amid the boundless main,

To waken doubt in one
Holding so fast by thine infinity;
So surely anchored on
The steadfast rock of immortality.

With wide-embracing love
Thy spirit animates eternal years,
Pervades and broods above,
Changes, sustains, dissolves, creates, and rears.

Though Earth and moon were gone,
And suns and universes ceased to be,
And thou wert left alone,
Every existence would exist in thee.

There is not room for Death,
Nor atom that his might could render void:
Thou – thou art Being and Breath,
And what thou art may never be destroyed.

Charlotte prefaced this poem with, 'The following are the last lines my sister Emily
ever wrote'.

ELIZA COOK

1818–89

Now considered a feminist prose writer but a sentimental poet, Eliza Cook was self-educated and began to publish poetry at 15. Born in Southwark, London, the youngest of eleven children, she later lived in Peckham, and on a small farm in Horsham, Sussex. *Lays of a Wild Harp* was published in 1835 and *Melaia and Other Poems* in 1838. She continued to contribute poetry to magazines like the *Literary Gazette* and wrote, monthly, between 1849 and 1854, on contemporary women's issues in *Eliza Cook's Journal* – a publication that outsold Charles Dickens' *Household Words*. A collection of her songs appeared in 1850 and *New Echoes and Other Poems* in 1864. *Diamond Dust* (1865) was a collection of aphorisms. Eliza never married, preferred to wear masculine dress, and was passionately attached to the performer, Charlotte Cushman. The following is from her *Melaia and Other Poems*.

Oh! Dear to Memory Are Those Hours

OH! dear to memory are those hours
When every pathway led to flowers;
When sticks of peppermint possessed
A sceptre's power o'er the breast,
And heaven was round us while we fed
On rich ambrosial gingerbread.
I bless the days of Infancy,
When stealing from my mother's eye,
Elysian happiness was found
On that celestial field – the ground;
When we were busied, hands and hearts:
In those important things, dirt tarts.
Don't smile; for sapient, full-grown Man
Oft cogitates some mighty plan;
And, spell-bound by the bubble dream,
He labours till he proves the scheme
About as useful and as wise
As manufacturing dirt pies.
For many a change on Folly's bells
Quite equals dust and oyster-shells.

Then shone the meteor rays of Youth;
Eclipsing quite the lamp of Truth;
And precious those bright sunbeams were;
That dried all tears, dispersed all care;
That shed a stream of golden joy,

Without one shadow of alloy:
Oh! ne'er in mercy strive to chase
Such dazzling phantoms from their place
However trifling, mean, or wild,
The deeds may seem of youth or child;
While they still leave untarnished soul,
The iron rod of stern control
Should be but gentle in its sway;
Nor rend the magic veil away.

I doubt if it be kind or wise,
To quench the light in opening eyes:
By preaching fallacy and woe
As all that we can meet below.
I ne'er respect the ready tongue
That augurs sorrow to the young;
That aptly plays a sibyl's part,
To promise nightshade to the heart.
Let them exult! their laugh and song
Are rarely known to last too long.
Why should we strive with cynic frown
To knock their fairy castles down?
We know that much of pain and strife
Must be the common lot of life:
We know the World *is* dark and rough
But Time betrays that soon enough.

GEORGE ELIOT
(Mary Ann Cross, *née* Evans)
1819–80

Born Mary Ann Evans at South Farm, Arbury, Warwickshire, George Eliot
was the daughter of an Evangelical Protestant land agent. After her mother
died in 1836 she grew very close to her father and moved to Coventry with
him in 1841, but their relationship became strained in 1842 when, as a result
of her theological explorations, she challenged orthodox Christian beliefs and
refused to go to church. In 1849 he died and she lived in Geneva for a while.
She moved to London in 1850, working on the *Westminster Review* with the
editor, John Chapman. In 1853 she formed a relationship with George Henry
Lewes who, although separated from his wife, was not free to marry again.
They lived together from 1854 until his death in 1878: while friends accepted
the situation, others (including her immediate family, particularly her brother,

Isaac) ostracised her. In 1857 she adopted the pseudonym, 'George Eliot', when she began to publish her fiction. Eight months before her death in 1880, she married John Cross, a friend 20 years her junior: this repaired the rift with her brother. George Eliot published two volumes of poetry: *The Spanish Gypsy* (1868), a closet drama, and *The Legend of Jubal and Other Poems* (1874). The following sonnet sequence (first published in the latter) dates from 1869 and particularly relates to her most apparently autobiographical work, *The Mill on the Floss*. Best known for her novels *Adam Bede* (1859), *The Mill on the Floss* (1860), *Middlemarch* (1871-72) and *Daniel Deronda* (1876), George Eliot also produced *Scenes from Clerical Life* (1858), *Romola* (1863) and *Felix Holt the Radical* (1866), as well as essays and translations.

Brother and Sister

I

I cannot choose but think upon the time
When our two lives grew like two buds that kiss
At lightest thrill from the bee's swinging chime,
Because the one so near the other is.

He was the elder and a little man
Of forty inches, bound to show no dread,
And I the girl that puppy-like now ran,
Now lagged behind my brother's larger tread.

I held him wise, and when he talked to me
Of snakes and birds, and which God loved the best,
I thought his knowledge marked the boundary
Where men grew blind, though angels knew the rest.

If he said 'Hush!' I tried to hold my breath;
Wherever he said 'Come!' I stepped in faith.

II

Long years have left their writing on my brow,
But yet the freshness and the dew-fed beam
Of those young mornings are about me now,
When we two wandered toward the far-off stream

With rod and line. Our basket held a store
Baked for us only, and I thought with joy
That I should have my share, though he had more,
Because he was the elder and a boy.

The firmaments of daisies since to me
Have had those mornings in their opening eyes,
The bunchèd cowslip's pale transparency
Carries that sunshine of sweet memories,

And wild-rose branches take their finest scent
From those blest hours of infantine content.

III

Our mother bade us keep the trodden ways,
Stroked down my tippet, set my brother's frill,
Then with the benediction of her gaze
Clung to us lessening, and pursued us still

Across the homestead to the rookery elms,
Whose tall old trunks had each a grassy mound,
So rich for us, we counted them as realms
With varied products: here were earth-nuts found,

And here the Lady-fingers in deep shade;
Here sloping toward the Moat the rushes grew,
The large to split for pith, the small to braid;
While over all the dark rooks cawing flew,

And made a happy strange solemnity,
A deep-toned chant from life unknown to me.

IV

Our meadow-path had memorable spots:
One where it bridged a tiny rivulet,
Deep hid by tangled blue Forget-me-nots;
And all along the waving grasses met

My little palm, or nodded to my cheek,
When flowers with upturned faces gazing drew
My wonder downward, seeming all to speak
With eyes of souls that dumbly heard and knew.

Then came the copse, where wild things rushed unseen,
And black-scathed grass betrayed the past abode
Of mystic gypsies, who still lurked between
Me and each hidden distance of the road.

A gypsy once had startled me at play,
Blotting with her dark smile my sunny day.

V

Thus rambling we were schooled in deepest lore,
And learned the meanings that give words a soul,
The fear, the love, the primal passionate store,
Whose shaping impulses make manhood whole.

Those hours were seed to all my after good;
My infant gladness, through eye, ear, and touch,
Took easily as warmth a various food
To nourish the sweet skill of loving much.

For who in age shall roam the earth and find
Reasons for loving that will strike out love
With sudden rod from the hard year-pressed mind?
Were reasons sown as thick as stars above,

  'Tis love must see them, as the eye sees light:
  Day is but Number to the darkened sight.

VI

Our brown canal was endless to my thought;
And on its banks I sat in dreamy peace,
Unknowing how the good I loved was wrought,
Untroubled by the fear that it would cease.

Slowly the barges floated into view
Rounding a grassy hill to me sublime
With some Unknown beyond it, whither flew
The parting cuckoo toward a fresh spring time.

The wide-arched bridge, the scented elder-flowers,
The wondrous watery rings that died too soon,
The echoes of the quarry, the still hours
With white robe sweeping-on the shadeless noon,

  Were but my growing self, are part of me,
  My present Past, my root of piety.

VII

Those long days measured by my little feet
Had chronicles which yield me many a text;
Where irony still finds an image meet
Of full-grown judgments in this world perplexed.

One day my brother left me in high charge,
To mind the rod, while he went seeking bait,
And bade me, when I saw a nearing barge,
Snatch out the line, lest he should come too late.

Proud of the task, I watched with all my might
For one whole minute, till my eyes grew wide,
Till sky and earth took on a strange new light
And seemed a dream-world floating on some tide –

    A fair pavilioned boat for me alone
    Bearing me onward through the vast unknown.

VIII

But sudden came the barge's pitch-black prow,
Nearer and angrier came my brother's cry,
And all my soul was quivering with fear, when lo!
Upon the imperilled line, suspended high,

A silver perch! My guilt that won the prey,
Now turned to merit, had a guerdon rich
Of songs and praises, and made merry play,
Until my triumph reached its highest pitch

When all at home were told the wondrous feat,
And how the little sister had fished well.
In secret, though my fortune tasted sweet,
I wondered why this happiness befell.

    'The little lass had luck,' the gardener said:
    And so I learned, luck was with glory wed.

IX

We had the self-same world enlarged for each
By loving difference of girl and boy:
The fruit that hung on high beyond my reach
He plucked for me, and oft he must employ

A measuring glance to guide my tiny shoe
Where lay firm stepping-stones, or call to mind
'This thing I like my sister may not do,
For she is little, and I must be kind.'

Thus boyish Will the nobler mastery learned
Where inward vision over impulse reigns,
Widening its life with separate life discerned,
A Like unlike, a Self that self restrains.

His years with others must the sweeter be
For those brief days he spent in loving me.

X

His sorrow was my sorrow, and his joy
Sent little leaps and laughs through all my frame;
My doll seemed lifeless and no girlish toy
Had any reason when my brother came.

I knelt with him at marbles, marked his fling
Cut the ringed stem and make the apple drop,
Or watched him winding close the spiral string
That looped the orbits of the humming top.

Grasped by such fellowship my vagrant thought
Ceased with dream-fruit dream-wishes to fulfil;
My aëry-picturing fantasy was taught
Subjection to the harder, truer skill

That seeks with deeds to grave a thought-tracked line,
And by 'What is,' 'What will be' to define.

XI

School parted us; we never found again
That childish world where our two spirits mingled
Like scents from varying roses that remain
One sweetness, nor can evermore be singled.

Yet the twin habit of that early time
Lingered for long about the heart and tongue:
We had been natives of one happy clime
And its dear accent to our utterance clung.

Till the dire years whose awful name is Change
Had grasped our souls still yearning in divorce,
And pitiless shaped them in two forms that range
Two elements which sever their life's course.

But were another childhood world my share,
I would be born a little sister there.

III 2 *tippet:* a long narrow band of cloth attached to dress, head-dress or sleeve. 9 *Lady-fingers:* perhaps kidney vetch.

JULIA WARD HOWE
1819–1910

Julia Ward Howe was born in New York City, the fourth of seven children. Her father was a Wall Street banker and she was educated privately. She moved to Boston after her marriage, in 1843, to Samuel Gridley Howe and they had six children. A social reformer as well as a poet, for a time Julia published an abolitionist newspaper, *The Commonwealth*, with her husband, was a founding member of the American Woman's Suffrage Association, and the first President of the American branch of the Woman's International Peace Association (1871). She founded and went on to edit the Woman's Journal in 1870 and was the first woman to be elected to the American Academy of Arts and Letters in 1908. Her first volume of poems, *Passion Flowers* (1854) was published anonymously. Other works include *Words for the Home* (1857), a play, *Leonora* (1857), *A Trip to Cuba* (1860), *Later Lyrics* (1866), and *From Sunset Ridge: Poems Old and New* (1899), from which the following poem is taken. It was first published in *Atlantic Monthly* in February 1862 and was set to an old folk tune also used for 'John Brown's Body', becoming a Civil War song of the Union Army. She also wrote *Sex and Education* (1874), *Modern Society* (1881), *Margaret Fuller* (1883), *Is Polite Society Polite?* (1895), and two books of memoirs, *Reminiscences* (1899) and *At Sunset* (1910), before dying of pneumonia at Newport, Rhode Island, aged 91 years.

Battle-Hymn of the Republic

Mine eyes have seen the glory of the coming of the Lord:
He is trampling out the vintage where the grapes of wrath are stored;
He hath loosed the fateful lightning of His terrible swift sword:
    His truth is marching on.

I have seen Him in the watch-fires of a hundred circling camps;
They have builded Him an altar in the evening dews and damps;
I can read His righteous sentence by the dim and flaring lamps:
    His day is marching on.

I have read a fiery gospel writ in burnished rows of steel:
'As ye deal with my contemners, so with you my grace shall deal;
Let the Hero, born of woman, crush the serpent with his heel,
　　　Since God is marching on.'

He has sounded forth the trumpet that shall never call retreat;
He is sifting out the hearts of men before His judgment-seat:
Oh, be swift, my soul, to answer Him! Be jubilant, my feet!
　　　Our God is marching on.

In the beauty of the lilies Christ was born across the sea,
With a glory in his bosom that transfigures you and me:
As he died to make men holy, let us die to make men free,
　　　While God is marching on.

7 *His:* this ed. his 1899 ed.　14 *His:* this ed. his 1899 ed.　15 *Oh,:* this ed. Oh! 1899 ed.

ANNE BRONTË (Acton Bell)
1820–49

The youngest of the surviving Brontë sisters, Anne was first educated at home in Haworth and later, for two years, at Roe Head School. With Emily, she produced juvenilia about an imaginary kingdom, Gondal, from 1831. She wrote a large number of poems but the first collection, shared with her sisters in 1846, was not successful. The following poems appeared in it. Less well known than her sisters, Charlotte and Emily, Anne also took risks in her writing. Her first novel, *Agnes Grey* (1847), drew on the sisters' experiences as governesses. Anne was a governess to the Ingham family at Blake Hall in 1839, but her subsequent post with the Robinson family, near York, was curtailed when her brother, Branwell, also became a tutor there. After his affair with Mrs Robinson, Anne left her employment and he followed. Her second novel, *The Tenant of Wildfell Hall* (1848), shocked readers with its strong language and vivid depictions of alcoholism, based on what she had seen of Branwell's addiction. Anne died of tuberculosis at Scarborough, where Charlotte, the only other surviving sibling, had taken her in hope of a recovery. In 1850 Charlotte republished *Agnes Grey* with Emily's *Wuthering Heights* and nine of Anne's poems (seven previously unpublished). *The Complete Poems of Anne Brontë*, edited by Clement Shorter, first appeared in 1921.

Home

How brightly glistening in the sun
　　The woodland ivy plays!
While yonder beeches from their barks
　　Reflect his silver rays.

248

That sun surveys a lovely scene
From softly smiling skies;
And wildly through unnumbered trees
The wind of winter sighs:

Now loud, it thunders o'er my head,
And now in distance dies.
But give me back my barren hills
Where colder breezes rise;

Where scarce the scattered, stunted trees
Can yield an answering swell,
But where a wilderness of heath
Returns the sound as well.

For yonder garden, fair and wide,
With groves of evergreen,
Long winding walks, and borders trim,
And velvet lawns between;

Restore to me that little spot,
With grey walls compassed round,
Where knotted grass neglected lies,
And weeds usurp the ground.

Though all around this mansion high
Invites the foot to roam,
And though its halls are fair within –
Oh, give me back my HOME!

Past Days

'Tis strange to think, there was a time
When mirth was not an empty name,
When laughter really cheered the heart,
And frequent smiles unbidden came,
And tears of grief would only flow
In sympathy for others' woe;

When speech expressed the inward thought,
And heart to kindred heart was bare,
And Summer days were far too short
For all the pleasures crowded there,
And silence, solitude, and rest,
Now welcome to the weary breast –

249

Were all unprized, uncourted then,
And all the joy one spirit showed,
The other deeply felt again;
And friendship like a river flowed,
Constant and strong its silent course,
For nought withstood its gentle force:

When night, the holy time of peace,
Was dreaded as the parting hour;
When speech and mirth at once must cease,
And Silence must resume her power;
Though ever free from pains and woes,
She only brought us calm repose.

And when the blessed dawn again
Brought daylight to the blushing skies,
We woke, and not *reluctant* then,
To joyless *labour* did we rise;
But full of hope, and glad and gay,
We welcomed the returning day.

If This be All

O God! if this indeed be all
        That Life can show to me;
If on my aching brow may fall
        No freshening dew from Thee,

If with no brighter light than this
        The lamp of hope may glow,
And I may only dream of bliss,
        And wake to weary woe;

If friendship's solace must decay,
        When other joys are gone,
And love must keep so far away,
        While I go wandering on, –

Wandering and toiling without gain,
        The slave of others' will,
With constant care and frequent pain,
        Despised, forgotten still;

Grieving to look on vice and sin,
Yet powerless to quell
The silent current from within,
The outward torrent's swell;

While all the good I would impart,
The feelings I would share,
Are driven backward to my heart,
And turned to wormwood there;

If clouds must ever keep from sight
The glories of the Sun,
And I must suffer Winter's blight,
Ere Summer is begun:

If Life must be so full of care,
Then call me soon to Thee;
Or give me strength enough to bear
My load of misery.

JEAN INGELOW
1820–97

Poet, novelist, and writer for children, Jean was born in Boston, Lincolnshire. She was the eldest of nine children. The family moved when her father encountered difficulties in his banking career and she finally settled in London. She never married and lived with her family all her life. Under the pseudonym 'Orris', Jean published verses and stories in magazines; some were later illustrated by John Millais. Her first book of poetry, *A Rhyming Chronicle of Incidents and Feelings* was published in 1850 and a novel, *Allerton and Dreux*, in 1851. Her next, *Poems* (1863), brought recognition, generated numerous editions, and is reputed to have sold 200,000 copies. 'Songs of Seven' was included in this and was later also issued in a separate illustrated volume in 1866 and 1881. It comprises seven poems, spaced seven years apart in the life-span of a woman – so 'Romance' is associated with the age of 14. Other memorable poems that helped to make her famous are 'The High Tide on the Coast of Lincolnshire (1571)' and 'Divided'. Jean became a member of the Portfolio Society in 1860; other contemporary poets who attended included Adelaide Procter. She was a friend of Ruskin, Longfellow and Tennyson. *A Story of Doom and Other Poems: Second Series* came out in 1874 and *Poems: Third Series*, in 1885. Other works of fiction (for children and adults) were successful and her story, *Mopsa the Fairy* (1869), became a children's classic.

Seven Times Two – Romance

You bells in the steeple, ring, ring out your changes,
  How many soever they be,
And let the brown meadow-lark's note as he ranges
  Come over, come over to me.

Yet birds' clearest carol by fall or by swelling
  No magical sense conveys,
And bells have forgotten their old art of telling
  The fortune of future days.

'Turn again, turn again,' once they rang cheerily,
  While a boy listened alone;
Made his heart yearn again, musing so wearily
  All by himself on a stone.

Poor bells! I forgive you; your good days are over,
  And mine, they are yet to be;
No listening, no longing shall aught, aught discover
  You leave the story to me.

The foxglove shoots out of the green matted heather
  And hangeth her hoods of snow;
She was idle, and slept till the sunshiny weather:
  O children take long to grow.

I wish, and I wish that the spring would go faster,
  Nor long summer bide so late;
And I could grow on like the foxglove and aster,
  For some things are ill to wait.

I wait for the day when dear hearts shall discover,
  While dear hands are laid on my head;
'The child is a woman, the book may close over,
  For all the lessons are said.'

I wait for my story – the birds cannot sing it,
  Not one, as he sits on the tree;
The bells cannot ring it, but long years, O bring it!
  Such as I wish it to be.

DOROTHEA MARIA OGILVY OF CLOVA

1823–95

Dorothea Maria Ogilvy lived at Balnaboth, in north-east Scotland. Her father was MP for the county of Angus. Greatly attached to her local area, Dorothea's Scots and Anglo-Scots poetry was more successful than the poems she wrote in English. Her published works include *Poems* in 1865 (written with her husband); *Willie Wabster's Wooing and Wedding on the Braes of Angus* (1868), *My Thoughts: Poems* (1870), and *Poems...second edition* (1873). She also wrote *The Book of Highland Minstrelsy* (1860) and *The Angler: a Day by the River Dee* (1865). She is buried in Cortachy.

The Weary Spinnin O't

Sittin spinnin, sittin spinnin
    A' the lea-lang day,
Hearin the bit burnie rinnin,
    And the bairns at play.
I'm sweir to get my leg let loose,
To do a turn aboot the hoose;
Oh, amna I a waefu wife
To spin awa my threid of life?
Spinnin, spinnin, ever spinnin,
Never endin, aye beginnin;   10
Hard at wark wi hand and fuit,
Oh, the weary spinnin o't!

Sittin spinnin, sittin spinnin,
    Vow but I am thrang,
My wee pickle siller winnin,
    Croonin some auld sang.
Leese me o my spinnin-wheel,
Gie's us a' oor milk and meal;
Weet or dry, or het or cauld,
I maun spin till I grow auld.   20
Spinnin, spinnin, ever spinnin,
Never endin, aye beginnin,
Hard at wark wi hand and fuit
At the weary spinnin o't.

Sittin spinnin, sittin spinnin,
    Sic a wear and tear,
Taps of tow for wabs o linen,
    Till my heid is sair.
Mony a wiselike wab I've spun,

253

Spreid and sortit I the sun;
Puirtith cauld is ill to bear;
Mony bairns bring mickle care.
Spinnin, spinnin, ever spinnin,
Never endin, aye beginning,
Hard at wark wi hand and fuit,
Oh! the weary spinnin o't!

2 *lea:* a variable length of yarn. 3 *burnie:* small stream. 5 *sweir:* grieved. 14 *Vow:*
exclamation used for emphasis, probably 'I vow'; *thrang:* busy, pressed. 15 *pickle siller:*
small amount of silver. 17 *Leese:* release. 26 *Sic:* such. 27 *Taps of tow:* rush baskets
of flax fibre for spinning; *wabs:* webs. 31 *Puirtith:* poverty. 32 *mickle:* great.

PHOEBE CARY

1824–71

Phoebe Cary was a skilful parodist and a witty poet who also, at times, veered
towards sentimental verse. She was born near Cincinnati, Ohio. Her education
was limited but she wrote poetry in her teens and published a hymn when she
was 18. Phoebe moved from the country to New York and, with her sister,
Alice, she published *Poems of Alice and Phoebe Cary* in 1850. Previously their
work had been included in *The Female Poets of America*, which Rufus Griswold
brought out in 1849. Phoebe's *Poems and Parodies* (from which 'Jacob' is taken)
appeared in 1854, and *Poems of Faith, Hope, and Love*, which includes 'Women',
was published in 1868. Posthumous collections of the sisters' works were
published in 1873 and 1877.

Jacob

He dwelt among 'apartments let',
    About five stories high;
A man I thought that none would get,
    And few would even try.

A boulder, by a larger stone
    Half hidden in the mud,
Fair as a man when only one
    Is in the neighbourhood.

He lived unknown, and few could tell
    When Jacob was not free;
But he has got a wife, – and O!
    The difference to me!

Title: a parody of one of Wordsworth's 'Lucy' poems: 'She Dwelt Among Untrodden
Ways'.

Women

'Tis a sad truth, yet 'tis a truth
That does not need the proving:
They give their hearts away, unasked,
And are not loved for loving.

Striving to win a little back,
For all they feel they hide it;
And lips that tremble with their love,
In trembling have denied it.

Sometimes they deem the kiss and smile
Is life and love's beginning;
While he who wins the heart away,
Is satisfied with winning.

Sometimes they think they have not found
The right one for their mating;
And go on till the hair is white,
And eyes are blind with waiting.

And if the mortal tarry still,
They fill their lamps, undying;
And till the midnight wait to hear
The 'Heavenly Bridegroom' crying.

For while she lives, the best of them
Is less a saint than woman;
And when her lips ask love divine,
Her heart asks love that's human!

LUCY LARCOM
1824–93

Born in Beverly, Massachusetts, Lucy was the ninth of ten children. Her father,
a retired shipmaster, died when she was nine, then her mother moved the
family to Lowell and ran a boarding house for mill girls. Lucy became one of
these herself when she was eleven. She began as a 'bobbin girl' and was later
employed as a book-keeper in the cloth room of the mill. She contributed to
publications produced by the mills, such as the *Lowell Offering*. In 1846 Lucy
moved to Illinois and later attended the Monticello Seminary there. In 1854
she came back to Massachusetts to teach. After 1862 she supported herself

mainly by her writing and editing work. A writer for children as well as a poet and editor, Lucy never married nor had children of her own. Her published works include: *Poems* (1869), *An Idyl of Work* (1875), *Wild Roses of Cape Ann and Other Poems* (1881), *Lucy Larcom's Poetical Works* (1884), *A New England Girlhood, Outlined from Memory* (1892), and a book of criticism, *Landscape in American Poetry* (1879). She died in Boston. In 'Weaving', her allusions to Tennyson's 'The Lady of Shalott' (1833) help to draw politics, literature, her strong religious faith, and her own work experience forcefully together. Both texts are taken from her *Poems* (1869).

Unwedded

Behold her there in the evening sun,
    That kindles the Indian Summer trees
To a separate burning bush, one by one,
    Wherein the Glory Divine she sees!

Mate and nestlings she never had:
    Kith and kindred have passed away;
Yet the sunset is not more gently glad,
    That follows her shadow, and fain would stay.

For out of her life goes a breath of bliss,
    And a sunlike charm from her cheerful eye,   10
That the cloud and the loitering breeze would miss;
    A balm that refreshes the passer-by.

'Did she choose it, this single life?'
    Gossip, she saith not, and who can tell?
But many a mother, and many a wife,
    Draws a lot more lonely, we all know well.

Doubtless she had her romantic dream,
    Like other maidens, in May-time sweet,
That flushes the air with a lingering gleam,
    And golden's the grass beneath her feet: –   20

A dream unmoulded to visible form,
    That keeps the world rosy with mists of youth.
And holds her in loyalty close and warm,
    To her fine ideal of manly truth.

'But is she happy, a woman, alone?'
    Gossip, alone in this crowded earth,
With a voice to quiet its hourly moan,
    And a smile to heighten its rarer mirth?

There are ends more worthy than happiness:
  Who seeks it, is digging joy's grave, we know.   30
The blessed are they who but live to bless;
  She found out that mystery, long ago.

To her motherly, sheltering atmosphere,
  The children hasten from icy homes:
The outcast is welcome to share her cheer;
  And the saint with a fervent benison comes.

For the heart of woman is large as man's;
  God gave her his orphaned world to hold,
And whispered through her His deeper plans
  To save it alive from the outer cold.   40

And here is a woman who understood
  Herself, her work, and God's will with her,
To gather and scatter His sheaves of good,
  And was meekly thankful, though men demur.

Would she have walked more nobly, think,
  With a man beside her, to point the way,
Hand joining hand in marriage-link?
  Possibly, Yes: it is likelier, Nay.

For all men have not wisdom and might:
  Love's eyes are tender, and blur the map;   50
And a wife will follow by faith, not sight,
  In the chosen footprint, at any hap.

In the comfort of home who is gladder than she?
  Yet, stirred by no murmur of 'might have been',
Her heart as a carolling bird soars free,
  With the song of each nest she has glanced within.

Having the whole, she covets no part:
  Hers is the bliss of all blessed things.
The tears that unto her eyelids start,
  Are those which a generous pity brings;   60

Or the sympathy of heroic faith
  With a holy purpose, achieved or lost.
To stifle the truth is to stop her breath,
  For she rates a lie at its deadly cost.

Her friends are good women and faithful men,
    Who seek for the True, and uphold the Right;
And who shall proclaim her the weaker, when
    Her very presence puts sin to flight?

'And dreads she never the coming years?'
    Gossip, what are the years to her?   70
All winds are fair, and the harbor nears,
    And every breeze a delight will stir.

Transfigured under the sunset trees,
    That wreathe her with shadowy gold and red,
She looks away to the purple seas,
    Whereon her shallop will soon be sped.

She reads the hereafter by the here:
    A beautiful Now, and a better To Be:
In life is all sweetness, in death no fear. –
    You waste your pity on such as she.   80

76 *shallop:* a light open boat.

Weaving

All day she stands before her loom;
    The flying shuttles come and go:
By grassy fields, and trees in bloom,
    She sees the winding river flow,
And fancy's shuttle flieth wide,
And faster than the waters glide.

Is she entangled in her dreams,
    Like that fair weaver of Shalott,
Who left her mystic mirror's gleams,
    To gaze on light Sir Lancelot?   10
Her heart, a mirror sadly true,
Brings gloomier visions into view.

'I weave, and weave, the livelong day:
    The woof is strong, the warp is good:
I weave, to be my mother's stay;
    I weave, to win my daily food:
But ever as I weave,' saith she,
'The world of women haunteth me.

The river glides along, one thread
        In nature's mesh, so beautiful!   20
The stars are woven in; the red
        Of sunrise; and the rain-cloud dull.
Each seems a separate wonder wrought;
Each blends with some more wondrous thought.

So, at the loom of life, we weave
        Our separate shreds, that varying fall,
Some stained, some fair; and, passing, leave
        To God the gathering up of all,
In that full pattern, wherein man
Works blindly out the eternal plan.   30

In his vast work, for good or ill,
        The undone and the done he blends,
With whatsoever woof we fill,
        To our weak hands His might He lends,
And gives the threads beneath His eye
The texture of eternity.

Wind on, by willow and by pine,
        Thou blue, untroubled Merrimack!
Afar, by sunnier streams than thine,
        My sisters toil, with foreheads black;   40
And water with their blood this root,
Whereof we gather bounteous fruit.

There be sad women, sick and poor;
        And those who walk in garments soiled:
Their shame, their sorrow, I endure;
        By their defect my hope is foiled:
The blot they bear is on my name;
Who sins, and I am not to blame?

And how much of your wrong is mine,
        Dark women slaving at the South?   50
Of your stolen grapes I quaff the wine;
        The bread you starve for fills my mouth:
The beam unwinds, but every thread
With blood of strangled souls is red.

If this be so, we win and wear
        A Nessus-robe of poisoned cloth;

Or weave them shrouds they may not wear, –
Fathers and brothers falling both
On ghastly, death-sown fields, that lie
Beneath the tearless Southern sky.   60

Alas! the weft has lost its white.
It grows a hideous tapestry,
That pictures war's abhorrent sight: –
Unroll not, web of destiny!
Be the dark volume left unread, –
The tale untold, – the curse unsaid!'

So up and down before her loom
She paces on, and to and fro,
Till sunset fills the dusty room,
And makes the water redly glow,   70
As if the Merrimack's calm flood
Were changed into a stream of blood.

Too soon fulfilled, and all too true
The words she murmured as she wrought!
But, weary weaver, not to you
Alone was war's stern message brought:
'Woman!' it knelled from heart to heart,
'Thy sister's keeper know thou art!'

8 *that...Shalott:* Tennyson's Lady of Shalott, who was forced, under threat of an un-
known curse, to weave constantly and only view the outside world through a mirror;
when Sir Lancelot 'flashed' singing into her 'crystal mirror' as he passed by, she left
her loom to look at him, left her room, and died 'in her song' just as her boat reached
Camelot. 14 *woof...warp:* on a loom the warp comprises threads strung lengthwise to
be woven through by threads forming the woof. 38 *Merrimack:* a river that flowed
through Lowell, Massachusetts. 55 *Nessus-robe:* in classical mythology, when Nessus,
the centaur, carried Deianira (Hercules' wife) over the River Evenus, he tried to rape
her and Hercules shot him with a poisoned arrow. In apparent repentance, Nessus told
her to smear Hercules' tunic with his blood if she ever needed to renew his love and,
years later, when Deianira believed Hercules' affections were straying, she sent him a
tunic stained with Nessus' blood. It contained poison and caused Hercules to die in
great pain. 78 *'Thy...art!'* see Genesis 4:8.

ADELINE D.T. WHITNEY (*née* Train)
1824–1906

Adeline Dutton Train Whitney was born in Boston, Massachusetts, the
daughter of a merchant and ship owner and his wife, Adeline Dutton, from
New Hampshire. She was educated, from 13 to 18, at a private school in

Boston and also spent a year at boarding school. She married Seth Dunbar Whitney, a wool and leather trader, in 1843. They lived in Milton, Massachusetts and had four children, only three of whom grew to adulthood. She began to write novels and advisory books for young women when her children were grown up. Her collection of poems, *Mother Goose for Grown Folks*, from which the following are taken, was first published in 1860 and reissued 15 times between 1861 and 1912. *Pansies* followed in 1873, *Holy Tides* in 1886, *Daffodils* in 1887, and *White Memories* in 1893. Whitney's quirky humour takes her on a variety of philosophical excursions, one of which draws attention to many kinds of oppression, including, as she sees it, the debt male writers owe (but rarely acknowledge) to women.

Brahmic

If a great poet think he sings,
Or if the poem think it's sung,
They do but sport the scattered plumes
That Mother Goose aside hath flung.

Far or forgot to me is near:
Shakespeare and Punch are all the same;
The vanished thoughts do reappear,
And shape themselves to fun or fame.

They use my *quills*, and leave me out,
Oblivious that I wear the *wings*;
Or that a Goose has been about,
When every little gosling sings.

Strong men may strive for grander thought,
But, six times out of every seven,
My old philosophy hath taught
All they can master this side heaven.

6 *Punch:* the popular magazine.

Pickle Peppers

'Peter Piper picked a peck of pickle peppers;
And a peck of pickle peppers Peter Piper picked;
If Peter Piper picked a peck of pickle peppers
Where's the peck of pickle peppers Peter Piper picked?'

Poor Peter toiled his life away,
That afterward the world might say
'Where is the peck of peppers he

Did gather so industriously?'
The peppers are embalmed in metre, –
But who, alas! inquires for Peter?
In sun or storm, by night and day,
Scant time for sleep, and none for play,
Still the poor fool did nothing reck,
If only he might pick his peck:
And what result from all hath sprung,
But just to bite somebody's tongue?
Or, – Lady Fortune playing fickle, –
Get someone in a precious pickle?

Threescore and Ten

'How many miles to Babylon?
   Threescore and ten.
Can I get there by candle-light?
   Yes, and back again.'

How many miles of the weary way?
   Threescore miles and ten.
Where shall I be at the end of the day?
   You shall be back again.

You shall prove it all in the lifelong round;
   The joy, and the pain and the sinning;
And at candle-light your soul shall be found
   Back – at its new beginning.

Down in his grave the old man lies;
   In from the earthward wild,
At the open door of paradise
   Enters a little child.

ADELAIDE ANNE PROCTER
1825–64

One of the most popular poets of her day and beyond it (reputedly more so than Tennyson by 1877, according to Rebecca Stott, *WWIE*, 514), Adelaide was the daughter of a solicitor (poet) and a London salon hostess. Her parents' circle included Charles Dickens and Robert Browning. She submitted her poems to Dickens' *Household Words* under the pseudonym 'Mary Berwick' and Dickens did not, at first, know her true identity. She subsequently contributed 57 poems to his journal over ten years. These were collected in *Legends and Lyrics* (1858), from which 'A Woman's Question' is taken. Texts of the other two poems come from this collection's second series in 1861: it ran into twelve editions. In 1851 she converted to Catholicism and published *A Chaplet of Verses* in 1861 to benefit a Catholic refuge. She is also known as a writer of songs and hymns. Dickens praised her work in his introduction to her 1866 volume of poems. Adelaide died of tuberculosis and her complete works were published in 1905. Gill Gregory's *The Life and Work of Adelaide Procter: poetry, feminism, and fathers*, was published by Ashgate in 1998.

A Woman's Question

Before I trust my Fate to thee,
    Or place my hand in thine,
Before I let thy Future give
    Colour and form to mine,
Before I peril all for thee, question thy soul tonight for me.

I break all slighter bonds, nor feel
    A shadow of regret:
Is there one link within the Past,
    That holds thy spirit yet?
Or is thy Faith as clear and free as that which I can pledge to thee?

Does there within thy dimmest dreams
    A possible future shine,
Wherein thy life could henceforth breathe,
    Untouched, unshared by mine?
If so, at any pain or cost, oh, tell me before all is lost.

Look deeper still. If thou canst feel,
    Within thy inmost soul,
That thou hast kept a portion back,
    While I have staked the whole:
Let no false pity spare the blow, but in true mercy tell me so.

Is there within thy heart a need
    That mine cannot fulfil?
One chord that any other hand
    Could better wake or still?
Speak now – lest at some future day my whole life wither and decay.

Lives there within thy nature hid
   The demon-spirit Change,
Shedding a passing glory still
   On all things new and strange? –
It may not be thy fault alone – but shield my heart against thy own.

Couldst thou withdraw thy hand one day
   And answer to my claim,
That Fate, and that to-day's mistake,
   Not thou, – had been to blame?
Some soothe their conscience thus: but thou wilt surely warn and
     save me now.

Nay, answer *not* – I dare not hear,
   The words would come too late;
Yet I would spare thee all remorse,
   So, comfort thee, my Fate –
Whatever on my heart may fall – remember, I *would* risk it all!

Envy

He was the first always: Fortune
   Shone bright in his face.
I fought for years; with no effort
   He conquered the place:
We ran; my feet were all bleeding,
   But he won the race.

Spite of his many successes
   Men loved him the same;
My one pale ray of good fortune
   Met scoffing and blame.
When we erred, they gave him pity,
   But me – only shame.

My home was still in the shadow,
   His lay in the sun:
I longed in vain: what he asked for
   It straightway was done.
Once I staked all my heart's treasure,
   We played – and he won.

Yes; and just now I have seen him,
　　Cold, smiling, and blest,
Laid in his coffin. God help me!
　　While he is at rest,
I am cursed still to live:- even
　　Death loved him the best.

A Woman's Last Word

Well – the links are broken,
　　All is past;
This farewell, when spoken,
　　Is the last.
I have tried and striven
　　All in vain;
Such bonds must be riven,
　　Spite of pain,
And never, never, never
　　Knit again.

So I tell you plainly,
　　It must be:
I shall try, not vainly,
　　To be free;
Truer, happier chances
　　Wait me yet,
While you, through fresh fancies,
　　Can forget; –
And life has nobler uses
　　Than Regret.

All past words retracing,
　　One by one,
Does not help effacing
　　What is done.
Let it be. Oh, stronger
　　Links can break!
Had we dreamed still longer
　　We could wake, –
Yet let us part in kindness
　　For Love's sake.

Bitterness and sorrow
Will at last,
In some bright to-morrow,
Heal their past;
But future hearts will never
Be as true
As mine was – is ever,
Dear, for you......
...Then must we part, when loving
As we do?

FRANCES ELLEN WATKINS HARPER
1825-1911

Frances Ellen Watkins was orphaned aged three. She was born in Baltimore, Maryland, and her mother was a free black woman. She was brought up and educated by her aunt and uncle who ran a school for free black people in Baltimore. At 14 she worked as a domestic servant. In 1850 Frances moved to Ohio and taught sewing at a school. Involved in the anti-slavery movement, she became a lecturer for the Maine Anti-Slavery Society, travelled as an anti-slavery orator, and wrote for abolitionist journals and newspapers. When John Brown was tried and convicted for leading the uprising at Harper's Ferry in 1859, Frances offered support to his family and stayed with his wife until his execution. She was a member of the American Woman Suffrage Association, the National Council of Negro Women, and the National Council of Women. Her first volume of poems, *Forest Leaves* (1845), ran into 20 editions and, in 1854, she published *Poems on Miscellaneous Subjects*, which was reissued seven times. By 1872, when she brought out *Sketches of Southern Life* (from which the following is taken), there were reputedly 50,000 copies of her first four books in print. She married Fenton Harper in 1860. He was a widower with three children and they lived on a farm near Columbus, Ohio. Fenton died in 1864, leaving children and debts. Frances continued to recite her poetry during her anti-slavery speeches – and to publish. *Moses: a Story of the Nile* appeared in 1869; she wrote novels that included *Iola Leroy* (1892), and more poetry: *The Martyr of Alabama and Other Poems* (1894) and *Atlanta Offering...* (1895). Her *Complete Poems*, edited by Maryemma Graham, was issued in 1988.

Aunt Chloe

I remember, well remember,
That dark and dreadful day,
When they whispered to me, 'Chloe,
Your children's sold away!'

It seemed as if a bullet
Had shot me through and through,
And I felt as if my heart-strings
Was breaking right in two.

And I says to cousin Milly,
'There must be some mistake;
Where's Mistus?' In the great house crying –
Crying like her heart would break.

'And the lawyer's there with Mistus;
Says he's come to 'ministrate,
'Cause when master died he just left
Heap of debt on the estate.

And I thought 'twould do you good
To bid your boys good-bye –
To kiss them both and shake their hands,
And have a hearty cry.

Oh! Chloe, I knows how you feel,
'Cause I'se been through it all;
I thought my poor old heart would break
When master sold my Saul.'

Just then I heard the footsteps
Of my children at the door,
And I rose right up to meet them,
But I fell upon the floor.

And I heard poor Jakey saying,
'Oh, mammy, don't you cry!'
And I felt my children kiss me
And bid me, both, good-bye.

Then I had a mighty sorrow,
Though I nursed it all alone;
But I wasted to a shadow,
And turned to skin and bone.

But one day dear uncle Jacob
(In heaven he's now a saint)
Said, 'Your poor heart is in the fire,
But child you must not faint.'

Then I said to uncle Jacob,
   If I was good like you,
When the heavy trouble dashed me
   I'd know just what to do.

Then he said to me, 'Poor Chloe,
   The way is open wide:'
And he told me of the Saviour,
   And the fountain in His side.

Then he said 'Just take your burden
   To the blessed Master's feet;
I takes all my troubles, Chloe,
   Right unto the mercy-seat.'

His words waked up my courage,
   And I began to pray,
And I felt my heavy burden
   Rolling like a stone away.

And a something seemed to tell me,
   You will see your boys again –
And that hope was like a poultice
   Spread upon a dreadful pain.

And it often seemed to whisper,
   Chloe, trust and never fear;
You'll get justice in the kingdom,
   If you do not get it here.

ELIZABETH SIDDAL

1829–62

Born Elizabeth Eleanor Siddall, Lizzie Siddal was 20 when Walter Deverell,
the Pre-Raphaelite painter, discovered her in a milliner's shop in Cranbourne
Alley near London's Leicester Square. She later became one of the most famous
models for the Pre-Raphaelite Brotherhood, sitting for William Holman Hunt,
John Everett Millais and Dante Gabriel Rossetti. Rossetti tutored her in drawing
and she went on to pursue her own painting career. She had, apparently, begun
to write poetry before she met him. They became 'engaged' in 1851 but he
was reluctant to marry. In 1857 she moved out of London and, in 1860, she
appealed to John Ruskin for help, perhaps due to her laudanum dependency.

When Rossetti knew her situation he took her to Hastings for a holiday and they were married there. She had a stillborn daughter in 1861 and ten months later took an overdose of laudanum. The inquest gave a verdict of accidental death, but some believe it was deliberate, largely because of her depression and Rossetti's rumoured infidelities. She is buried in Highgate Cemetery. None of her poems was published during her lifetime. Rossetti copied out six poems after her death and William Michael Rossetti incorporated 15 of them into the collection of Pre-Raphaelite letters and memoirs that he compiled between 1895 and 1906. 'Dead Love' is taken from *Ruskin: Rossetti: Pre-Raphaelitism: Papers 1854-1862*, ed. W. M. Rossetti (1899), 151-52, and 'Early Death', from *Some Reminiscences of William Michael Rossetti* (1906) vol.1, 196-97. In 1978 the first collected edition of Lizzie's poems was published by the Wombat Press, ed. Roger C. Lewis and Mark Samuels Lasner. Manuscripts are held in the Ashmolean Museum, Oxford.

Dead Love

Oh never weep for love that's dead
    Since love is seldom true,
But changes his fashion from blue to red,
    From brightest red to blue,
And love was born to an early death
    And is so seldom true.

Then harbour no smile on your loving face
    To win the deepest sigh;
The fairest words on truest lips
    Pass on and surely die;
And you will stand alone, my dear,
    When wintry winds draw nigh.

Sweet, never weep for what cannot be,
    For this God has not given;
If the merest dream of love were true,
    Then, sweet, we should be in heaven;
And this is only earth, my dear,
    Where true love is not given.

Early Death

Oh grieve not with thy bitter tears
The life that passes fast:
The gates of heaven will open wide,
And take me in at last.

Then sit down meekly at my side,
And watch my young life flee:
Then solemn peace of holy death
Come quickly unto thee.

But, true love, seek me in the throng
Of spirits floating past;
And I will take you by the hands,
And know thee mine at last.

HELEN HUNT JACKSON (*née* Fiske)
1830–85

Helen Marie Fiske was born in Amherst, Massachusetts. After her parents both died of tuberculosis – her mother in 1844, and her father, a professor at Amherst College, in 1847 – she lived with relatives. She was educated in schools at Ipswich and New York and, as a child, she played with Emily Dickinson. Helen married Edward Bissell Hunt in 1851 but, by 1865, her husband and two sons had tragically died. She began writing to help her to deal with her grief, and to support herself. Her first volume, *Verses*, appeared in 1870. In 1875 she married William Sharpless Jackson and they settled in Colorado Springs, where she campaigned for Native American rights. In 1881, she published *A Century of Dishonor*, which exposed US government betrayals and helped bring about the foundation of the Indian Rights Association. Her novel, *Ramona* (1884), was on the same theme and an earlier novel, *Mercy Philbrick's Choice* (1876) is believed to be based on her acquaintance with Emily Dickinson. Further collections of her poetry are *Sonnets and Lyrics* (1886), *A Calendar of Sonnets* (1891) and *Poems* (1892). The following are taken from the latter, but the text for 'October' is the 1891 *Calendar*... Helen Hunt Jackson was also a writer of travel books and works for children, under pseudonyms such as 'H.H', 'Saxe Holm', and 'Rip Van Winkle'.

Poppies on the Wheat

Along Ancona's hills the shimmering heat,
A tropic tide of air with ebb and flow
Bathes all the fields of wheat until they glow
Like flashing seas of green, which toss and beat
Around the vines. The poppies lithe and fleet
Seem running, fiery torchmen, to and fro
To mark the shore.
           The farmer does not know
That they are there. He walks with heavy feet,

Counting the bread and wine of autumn's gain,
But I, – I smile to think that days remain
Perhaps to me in which, though bread be sweet
No more, and red wine warm my blood in vain,
I shall be glad remembering how the fleet,
Lithe poppies ran like torchmen with the wheat.

1 *Ancona:* Ancona, Italy, on the Adriatic coast.

In Time of Famine

'She has no heart,' they said, and turned away,
Then, stung so that I wished my words might be
Two-edged swords, I answered low: –
                                    'Have ye
Not read how once when famine held fierce sway
In Lydia, and men died day by day
Of hunger, there were found brave souls whose glee
Scarce hid their pangs, who said, "Now we
Can eat but once in two days; we will play
Such games on those days when we eat no food
That we forget our pain."
                                    Thus they withstood
Long years of famine; and to them we owe
The trumpets, pipes, and balls which mirth finds good
Today, and little dreams that of such woe
They first were born.
                                    That woman's life I know
Has been all famine. Mock now if ye dare,
To hear her brave sad laughter in the air.'

Two Truths

'Darling', he said, 'I never meant
To hurt you;' and his eyes were wet.
'I would not hurt you for the world:
Am I to blame if I forget?'

'Forgive my selfish tears!' she cried,
'Forgive! I knew that it was not
Because you meant to hurt me, sweet, –
I knew it was that you forgot!'

271

But all the same, deep in her heart
Rankled this thought, and rankles yet, –
'When love is at its best, one loves
So much that he cannot forget.'

October

The month of carnival of all the year,
When Nature lets the wild earth go its way
And spend whole seasons in a single day.
The spring-time holds her white and purple dear;
October, lavish, flaunts them far and near;
The summer charily her reds doth lay
Like jewels on her costliest array;
October, scornful, burns them on a bier.
The winter hoards his pearls of frost in sign
Of kingdom: whiter pearls than winter knew,
Or Empress wore, in Egypt's ancient line,
October, feasting 'neath her dome of blue,
Drinks at a single draught, slow filtered through
Sunshiny air, as in a tingling wine!

EMILY DICKINSON
1830–86

America's most famous and, for many, most original woman poet was born
(like Helen Hunt Jackson), in Amherst, Massachusetts in 1830. Now consid-
ered a lyric genius, she wrote poetry from her teenage years but led an out-
wardly unexceptional life. Educated at Amherst Academy and South Hadley
(Mount Holyoke) Female Seminary, she never married. Her older brother,
Austin, married Emily's close friend, Susan Gilbert. Their father was a lawyer
and, having no economic need to publish her work, she stayed mostly at home
in Amherst throughout her life, living in relative seclusion with her younger
sister, Lavinia, after their mother's death in 1882. She wrote approximately
1,789 extraordinary poems, some of which were sent to family and friends. She
also copied them into her own little booklets or 'fascicle bundles'. Some were
first written on advertising fliers, wrapping paper, or old letters (*RWF*, 1999,
3). Several were sent, from 1862 onwards, to Thomas Wentworth Higginson
in response to his article in the *Atlantic Monthly* giving practical advice to those
seeking publication, but though their correspondence continued, he did not
encourage her to publish. However, he and Mabel Loomis Todd assisted Lavinia
when she began the process of publishing Emily's poetry posthumously. Their
1890 selection did not accurately reproduce Emily's poems as Higginson's

editing involved substitutions of words and punctuation as well as alterations to line breaks and metre. Even so, her work was well received and further editions followed. Before her death, several poems had been published, anonymously, in newspapers and elsewhere: these were submitted by friends, not Emily herself. (*RWF*, 1999, 4). Emily wrote her last poems in April 1886 and the last of all appears to have been a tribute to her friend from childhood, Helen Hunt Jackson, who had died a few months earlier. Mabel Loomis Todd published Emily's letters in 1894. The first reliable edition of her *Complete Poems* was edited by Thomas H. Johnson in 1955. The *Complete Letters* appeared in 1958. The following poems are from *The Poems of Emily Dickinson: reading edition*, ed. R.W. Franklin (The Belknap Press of Harvard University Press, 1999). R.W. Franklin has also edited an excellent variorum edition of the complete poems.

I'm Nobody! Who are you?
Are you – Nobody – too?
Then there's a pair of us!
Don't tell! they'd advertise – you know!

How dreary – to be – Somebody!
How public – like a Frog –
To tell one's name – the livelong June –
To an admiring Bog!

Written in late 1861, this poem was published in 1891 with the first two words of line 4 as the last 2 of line 3 – and with 'day' substituted for 'June' in line 7.

Wild nights – Wild nights!
Were I with thee
Wild nights should be
Our luxury!

Futile – the winds –
To a Heart in port –
Done with the Compass –
Done with the Chart!

Rowing in Eden –
Ah – the Sea!
Might I but moor – tonight –
In thee!

Written in late 1861; published in 1891.

I felt a Funeral, in my Brain,
And Mourners to and fro
Kept treading – treading – till it seemed
That Sense was breaking through –

And when they all were seated,
A Service, like a Drum –
Kept beating – beating – till I thought
My mind was going numb –

And then I heard them lift a Box
And creak across my Soul
With those same Boots of Lead, again,
Then Space – began to toll,

As all the Heavens were a Bell,
And Being, but an Ear,
And I, and Silence, some strange Race
Wrecked, solitary, here –

And then a Plank in Reason, broke,
And I dropped down, and down –
And hit a World, at every plunge,
And Finished knowing – then –

Probably written in summer 1862.

After great pain, a formal feeling comes –
The Nerves sit ceremonious, like Tombs –
The stiff Heart questions 'was it He, that bore',
And 'Yesterday, or Centuries before'?

The Feet, mechanical, go round –
A Wooden way
Of Ground, or Air, or Ought –
Regardless grown,
A Quartz contentment, like a stone –

This is the Hour of Lead –
Remembered, if outlived,
As Freezing persons, recollect the Snow –
First – Chill – then Stupor – then the letting go –

Written *c*. 1862.

274

I had been hungry, all the Years –
My Noon had Come – to dine –
I trembling drew the Table near –
And touched the Curious Wine –

'Twas this on Tables I had seen –
When turning, hungry, Home
I looked in Windows, for the Wealth
I could not hope – for Mine –

I did not know the ample Bread –
'Twas so unlike the Crumb
The Birds and I, had often shared
In Nature's – Dining Room –

The Plenty hurt me – 'twas so new –
Myself felt ill – and odd –
As Berry – of a Mountain Bush –
Transplanted – to the Road –

Nor was I hungry – so I found
That Hunger – was a way
Of Persons Outside Windows –
The entering – takes away –

Written c. 1862.

This was a Poet –
It is That
Distills amazing sense
From Ordinary Meanings –
And Attar so immense

From the familiar species
That perished by the Door –
We wonder it was not Ourselves
Arrested it – before –

Of Pictures, the Discloser –
The Poet – it is He –
Entitles Us – by Contrast –
To ceaseless Poverty –

275

Of Portion – so unconscious –
The Robbing – could not harm –
Himself – to Him – a Fortune –
Exterior – to Time –

Written late 1862.

Because I could not stop for Death –
He kindly stopped for me –
The Carriage held but just Ourselves –
And Immortality.

We slowly drove – He knew no haste
And I had put away
My labor and my leisure too,
For His Civility –

We passed the School, where Children strove
At Recess – in the Ring –
We passed the Fields of Gazing Grain –
We passed the Setting Sun –

Or rather – He passed Us –
The Dews drew quivering and Chill –
For only Gossamer, my Gown –
My Tippet – only Tulle –

We paused before a House that seemed
A Swelling of the Ground –
The Roof was scarcely visible –
The Cornice – in the Ground –

Since then – 'tis Centuries – and yet
Feels shorter than the Day
I first surmised the Horses' Heads
Were toward Eternity –

Written in late 1862.

'Tis not that Dying hurts us so –
'Tis Living – hurts us more –
But Dying – is a different way –
A kind behind the Door –

276

The Southern Custom – of the Bird –
That ere the Frosts are due –
Accepts a better Latitude –
We – are the Birds – that stay.

The Shiverers round the Farmers' doors –
For whose reluctant Crumb –
We stipulate – till pitying Snows
Persuade our Feathers Home.

Probably written in Spring 1863. 9 *Farmers'*: original ms letter; Farmer's Fascicle 28
(H134).

I heard a Fly buzz – when I died –
The Stillness in the Room
Was like the Stillness in the Air –
Between the Heaves of Storm –

The Eyes around – had wrung them dry –
And Breaths were gathering firm
For that last Onset – when the King
Be witnessed – in the Room –

I willed my Keepsakes – Signed away
What portion of me be
Assignable – and then it was
There interposed a Fly –

With Blue – uncertain – stumbling Buzz –
Between the light – and me –
And then the Windows failed – and then
I could not see to see –

Written in Summer 1863.

We do not play on Graves –
Because there isn't Room –
Besides – it isn't even – it slants
And People come –

And put a Flower on it –
And hang their faces so –
We're fearing that their Hearts will drop –
And crush our pretty play –

277

And so we move as far
As Enemies – away –
Just looking round to see how far
It is – Occasionally –

Probably written in Summer 1863. 2-3 *isn't:* this ed. is'nt RWF, 1999, 269.

The Brain – is wider than the Sky –
For – put them side by side –
The one the other will contain
With ease – and You – beside –

The Brain is deeper than the sea –
For – hold them – Blue to Blue –
The one the other will absorb –
As Sponges – Buckets – do –

The Brain is just the weight of God –
For – Heft them – Pound for Pound –
And they will differ – if they do –
As Syllable from Sound –

Probably written in Summer 1863.

I started Early – Took my Dog –
And visited the Sea –
The Mermaids in the Basement
Came out to look at me –

And Frigates – in the Upper Floor
Extended Hempen Hands –
Presuming Me to be a Mouse –
Aground – upon the Sands –

But no Man moved Me – till the Tide
Went past my simple Shoe –
And past my Apron – and my Belt
And past my Bodice – too –

And made as He would eat me up –
As wholly as a Dew
Upon a Dandelion's Sleeve –
And then – I started – too –

And He – He followed – close behind –
I felt His Silver Heel
Upon my Ankle – Then My Shoes
Would overflow with Pearl –

Until We met the Solid Town –
No One He seemed to know –
And bowing – with a Mighty look –
At me – The Sea withdrew –

Probably written in the latter half of 1863. 8, 15, 19 *upon:* this ed. opon RWF, 1999, 293.

I cannot live with You –
It would be Life –
And Life is over there –
Behind the Shelf

The Sexton keeps the key to –
Putting up
Our Life – His Porcelain –
Like a Cup –

Discarded of the Housewife –
Quaint – or Broke –
A newer Sevres pleases –
Old Ones crack –

I could not die – with You –
For One must wait
To shut the Other's Gaze down –
You – could not –

And I – Could I stand by
And see You – freeze –
Without my Right of Frost –
Death's privilege?

Nor could I rise – with You –
Because Your Face
Would put out Jesus' –
That New Grace

Glow plain – and foreign
On my homesick eye –
Except that You than He
Shone closer by –

They'd judge Us – How –
For You – served Heaven – You know,
Or sought to –
I could not –

Because You saturated sight –
And I had no more eyes
For sordid excellence
As Paradise

And were You lost, I would be –
Though my Name
Rang loudest
On the Heavenly fame –

And were You – saved –
And I – condemned to be
Where You were not –
That self – were Hell to Me –

So We must meet apart –
You there – I – here –
With just the Door ajar
That Oceans are – and Prayer –
And that White Sustenance –
Despair –

Probably written in the latter part of 1863.

I had no time to Hate –
Because
The Grave would hinder me –
And Life was not so
Ample I
Could finish – Enmity –

Nor had I time to Love –
But since

280

Some Industry must be –
The little Toil of Love –
I thought
Be large enough for Me –

Written late 1863.

My Life had stood – a Loaded Gun –
In Corners – till a Day
The Owners passed – identified –
And carried Me away –

And now We roam in Sovereign Woods –
And now We hunt the Doe –
And every time I speak for Him –
The Mountains straight reply –

And do I smile, such cordial light
Upon the Valley glow –
It is as a Vesuvian face
Had let its pleasure through –

And when at Night – Our good Day done –
I guard My Master's Head –
'Tis better than the Eider Duck's
Deep Pillow – to have shared –

To foe of His – I'm deadly foe –
None stir the second time –
On whom I lay a Yellow Eye –
Or an emphatic Thumb –

Though I than He – may longer live
He longer must – than I –
For I have but the power to kill,
Without – the power to die –

Written in late 1863. 10 *upon:* this ed. opon RWF, 1999, 341.

The Life we have is very great.
The Life that we shall see
Surpasses it, we know, because
It is Infinity.

But when all space has been beheld
And all Dominion shown
The smallest Human Heart's extent
Reduces it to none.

Written in October 1870.

Abraham to kill him
Was distinctly told –
Isaac was an Urchin –
Abraham was old –

Not a hesitation –
Abraham complied –
Flattered by Obeisance
Tyranny demurred –

Isaac – to his Children
Lived to tell the tale –
Moral – with a Mastiff
Manners may prevail.

Written c. 1874. 1 *Abraham…him:* see Genesis 22:2-18.

The Pile of Years is not so high
As when you came before
But it is rising every Day
From recollection's Floor
And while by standing on my Heart
I still can reach the top
Efface the mountain with your face
And catch me ere I drop

Written c. 1874.

The Robin is a Gabriel
In humble circumstances –
His Dress denotes him socially,
Of Transport's Working Classes –
He has the punctuality
Of the New England Farmer –
The same oblique integrity,

A Vista vastly warmer –
A small but sturdy Residence,
A Self denying Household,
The Guests of Perspicacity
Are all that cross his Threshold –
As covert as a Fugitive,
Cajoling Consternation
By Ditties to the Enemy
And Sylvan Punctuation –

Written *c.* 1880. 1 *Robin:* the American robin, a migratory thrush, is twice as big as the British bird of this name.

Meeting by Accident,
We hovered by design –
As often as a Century
An error so divine
Is ratified by Destiny,
But Destiny is old
And economical of Bliss
As Midas is of Gold –

Written *c.* 1882.

Who has not found the Heaven – below –
Will fail of it above –
For Angels rent the House next ours,
Wherever we remove –

Written *c.* 1883.

My life closed twice before its close;
It yet remains to see
If Immortality unveil
A third event to me,

So huge, so hopeless to conceive
As these that twice befell.
Parting is all we know of heaven,
And all we need of hell.

Undated.

To make a prairie it takes a clover and one bee,
One clover, and a bee,
And revery.
The revery alone will do,
If bees are few.

Undated.

CHRISTINA GEORGINA ROSSETTI
1830-94

Renowned for her religious verse (and as author of the carol known as 'In the bleak mid-winter'), Christina Rossetti was also an unconventional, experimental poet who explored sexual and social issues in oblique ways. The sensuous and enigmatic *Goblin Market* has proved to be a fascinating riddle of desire for generations of readers. She was born and died in London, the youngest child of an English mother and Italian father. Her eldest brother, Dante Gabriel Rossetti of the Pre-Raphaelite Brotherhood, was a poet and painter; her brother William Michael, a critic and editor; and her sister, Maria, a Dante scholar and writer on religion. Christina's first book, *Verses*, was printed privately on her grandfather's press in 1847. Under the pseudonym, Ellen Alleyne, her poetry appeared in the Pre-Raphaelite journal, *The Germ*, in 1850. In 1862, Macmillan published *Goblin Market and Other Poems*. (Dante Gabriel suggested the present title as an improvement on her first choice: 'A Peep at the Goblins'.) *The Prince's Progress and Other Poems* followed in 1866. *A Pageant and Other Poems* (1881) contains impressive sonnet sequences, and she concentrated powerfully on religious poetry in her last volume, *Verses*, in 1893. Despite ill-health, she taught for short periods and, from 1860-70, worked in a house of charity, run by Anglican nuns for unmarried mothers. She never married, although her name was linked romantically with the painter, James Collinson, and the linguist, Charles Bagot Cayley. Christina Rossetti, a playful children's poet, also wrote short stories, religious prose, and an autobiographical novella, *Maude* (1897). The text for 'Amor Mundi' and 'Amen' is *Goblin Market, The Prince's Progress and Other Poems* (1875). The other poems are taken from *Goblin Market and Other Poems*, 2nd ed. (1865).

Goblin Market

Morning and evening
Maids heard the goblins cry:
'Come buy our orchard fruits,
Come buy, come buy:
Apples and quinces,
Lemons and oranges,

Plump unpecked cherries,
Melons and raspberries,
Bloom-down-cheeked peaches,
Swart-headed mulberries,   10
Wild free-born cranberries,
Crab-apples, dewberries,
Pine-apples, blackberries,
Apricots, strawberries; –
All ripe together
In summer weather, –
Morns that pass by,
Fair eves that fly;
Come buy, come buy:
Our grapes fresh from the vine,   20
Pomegranates full and fine,
Dates and sharp bullaces,
Rare pears and greengages,
Damsons and bilberries,
Taste them and try:
Currants and gooseberries,
Bright-fire-like barberries,
Figs to fill your mouth,
Citrons from the South,
Sweet to tongue and sound to eye;   30
Come buy, come buy.'

Evening by evening
Among the brookside rushes,
Laura bowed her head to hear,
Lizzie veiled her blushes:
Crouching close together
In the cooling weather,
With clasping arms and cautioning lips,
With tingling cheeks and finger tips.
'Lie close,' Laura said,   40
Pricking up her golden head:
'We must not look at goblin men,
We must not buy their fruits:
Who knows upon what soil they fed
Their hungry thirsty roots?'
'Come buy,' call the goblins
Hobbling down the glen.
'Oh,' cried Lizzie, 'Laura, Laura,

You should not peep at goblin men.'
Lizzie covered up her eyes,   50
Covered close lest they should look;
Laura reared her glossy head,
And whispered like the restless brook:
'Look, Lizzie, look, Lizzie,
Down the glen tramp little men.
One hauls a basket,
One bears a plate,
One lugs a golden dish
Of many pounds weight.
How fair the vine must grow   60
Whose grapes are so luscious;
How warm the wind must blow
Through those fruit bushes.'
'No,' said Lizzie: 'No, no, no;
Their offers should not charm us,
Their evil gifts would harm us.'
She thrust a dimpled finger
In each ear, shut eyes and ran:
Curious Laura chose to linger
Wondering at each merchant man.   70
One had a cat's face,
One whisked a tail,
One tramped at a rat's pace,
One crawled like a snail,
One like a wombat prowled obtuse and furry,
One like a ratel tumbled hurry skurry.
She heard a voice like voice of doves
Cooing all together:
They sounded kind and full of loves
In the pleasant weather.   80

    Laura stretched her gleaming neck
Like a rush-imbedded swan,
Like a lily from the beck,
Like a moonlit poplar branch,
Like a vessel at the launch
When its last restraint is gone.

    Backwards up the mossy glen
Turned and trooped the goblin men,
With their shrill repeated cry,

'Come buy, come buy.'   90
When they reached where Laura was
They stood stock still upon the moss,
Leering at each other,
Brother with queer brother;
Signalling each other,
Brother with sly brother.
One set his basket down,
One reared his plate;
One began to weave a crown
Of tendrils, leaves and rough nuts brown   100
(Men sell not such in any town);
One heaved the golden weight
Of dish and fruit to offer her:
'Come buy, come buy,' was still their cry.
Laura stared but did not stir,
Longed but had no money:
The whisk-tailed merchant bade her taste
In tones as smooth as honey,
The cat-faced purred,
The rat-paced spoke a word   110
Of welcome, and the snail-paced even was heard;
One parrot-voiced and jolly
Cried 'Pretty Goblin' still for 'Pretty Polly'; –
One whistled like a bird.

    But sweet-tooth Laura spoke in haste:
'Good folk, I have no coin;
To take were to purloin:
I have no copper in my purse,
I have no silver either,
And all my gold is on the furze   120
That shakes in windy weather
Above the rusty heather.'
'You have much gold upon your head,'
They answered all together:
'Buy from us with a golden curl.'
She clipped a precious golden lock,
She dropped a tear more rare than pearl,
Then sucked their fruit globes fair or red:
Sweeter than honey from the rock,
Stronger than man-rejoicing wine,   130
Clearer than water flowed that juice;

287

She never tasted such before,
How should it cloy with length of use?
She sucked and sucked and sucked the more
Fruits which that unknown orchard bore;
She sucked until her lips were sore;
Then flung the emptied rinds away
But gathered up one kernel-stone,
And knew not was it night or day
As she turned home alone. 140

    Lizzie met her at the gate
Full of wise upbraidings:
'Dear, you should not stay so late,
Twilight is not good for maidens;
Should not loiter in the glen
In the haunts of goblin men.
Do you not remember Jeanie,
How she met them in the moonlight,
Took their gifts both choice and many,
Ate their fruits and wore their flowers 150
Plucked from bowers
Where summer ripens at all hours?
But ever in the noonlight
She pined and pined away;
Sought them by night and day,
Found them no more but dwindled and grew grey;
Then fell with the first snow,
While to this day no grass will grow
Where she lies low:
I planted daisies there a year ago 160
That never blow.
You should not loiter so.'
'Nay, hush,' said Laura:
'Nay, hush, my sister:
I ate and ate my fill,
Yet my mouth waters still;
Tomorrow night I will
Buy more;' and kissed her:
'Have done with sorrow;
I'll bring you plums tomorrow 170
Fresh on their mother twigs,
Cherries worth getting;
You cannot think what figs

My teeth have met in,
What melons icy-cold
Piled on a dish of gold
Too huge for me to hold,
What peaches with a velvet nap,
Pellucid grapes without one seed:
Odorous indeed must be the mead   180
Whereon they grow, and pure the wave they drink
With lilies at the brink,
And sugar-sweet their sap.'

Golden head by golden head,
Like two pigeons in one nest
Folded in each other's wings,
They lay down in their curtained bed:
Like two blossoms on one stem,
Like two flakes of new-fall'n snow,
Like two wands of ivory   190
Tipped with gold for awful kings.
Moon and stars gazed in at them,
Wind sang to them lullaby,
Lumbering owls forbore to fly,
Not a bat flapped to and fro
Round their rest:
Cheek to cheek and breast to breast
Locked together in one nest.

Early in the morning
When the first cock crowed his warning,   200
Neat like bees, as sweet and busy,
Laura rose with Lizzie:
Fetched in honey, milked the cows,
Aired and set to rights the house,
Kneaded cakes of whitest wheat,
Cakes for dainty mouths to eat,
Next churned butter, whipped up cream,
Fed their poultry, sat and sewed;
Talked as modest maidens should:
Lizzie with an open heart,   210
Laura in an absent dream,
One content, one sick in part;
One warbling for the mere bright day's delight,
One longing for the night.

At length slow evening came:
They went with pitchers to the reedy brook;
Lizzie most placid in her look,
Laura most like a leaping flame.
They drew the gurgling water from its deep;
Lizzie plucked purple and rich golden flags,   220
Then turning homewards said: 'The sunset flushes
Those furthest loftiest crags;
Come, Laura, not another maiden lags.
No wilful squirrel wags,
The beasts and birds are fast asleep.'
But Laura loitered still among the rushes
And said the bank was steep.

And said the hour was early still,
The dew not fall'n, the wind not chill;
Listening ever, but not catching   230
The customary cry,
'Come buy, come buy,'
With its iterated jingle
Of sugar-baited words:
Not for all her watching
Once discerning even one goblin
Racing, whisking, tumbling, hobbling;
Let alone the herds
That used to tramp along the glen,
In groups or single,   240
Of brisk fruit-merchant men.

Till Lizzie urged, 'O Laura, come;
I hear the fruit-call, but I dare not look:
You should not loiter longer at this brook:
Come with me home.
The stars rise, the moon bends her arc,
Each glowworm winks her spark,
Let us get home before the night grows dark:
For clouds may gather
Though this is summer weather,   250
Put out the lights and drench us through;
Then if we lost our way what should we do?'

Laura turned cold as stone
To find her sister heard that cry alone,

That goblin cry,
'Come buy our fruits, come buy.'
Must she then buy no more such dainty fruit?
Must she no more such succous pasture find,
Gone deaf and blind?
Her tree of life drooped from the root: 260
She said not one word in her heart's sore ache;
But peering through the dimness, nought discerning,
Trudged home, her pitcher dripping all the way;
So crept to bed, and lay
Silent till Lizzie slept;
Then sat up in a passionate yearning,
And gnashed her teeth for baulked desire, and wept
As if her heart would break.

Day after day, night after night,
Laura kept watch in vain   270
In sullen silence of exceeding pain.
She never caught again the goblin cry:
'Come buy, come buy;'–
She never spied the goblin men
Hawking their fruits along the glen:
But when the noon waxed bright
Her hair grew thin and grey;
She dwindled, as the fair full moon doth turn
To swift decay and burn
Her fire away.   280

One day remembering her kernel-stone
She set it by a wall that faced the south;
Dewed it with tears, hoped for a root,
Watched for a waxing shoot,
But there came none;
It never saw the sun,
It never felt the trickling moisture run:
While with sunk eyes and faded mouth
She dreamed of melons, as a traveller sees
False waves in desert drouth   290
With shade of leaf-crowned trees,
And burns the thirstier in the sandful breeze.

She no more swept the house,
Tended the fowls or cows,

Fetched honey, kneaded cakes of wheat,
Brought water from the brook:
But sat down listless in the chimney-nook
And would not eat.

Tender Lizzie could not bear
To watch her sister's cankerous care   300
Yet not to share.
She night and morning
Caught the goblins' cry:
'Come buy our orchard fruits,
Come buy, come buy': –
Beside the brook, along the glen,
She heard the tramp of goblin men,
The voice and stir
Poor Laura could not hear;
Longed to buy fruit to comfort her,   310
But feared to pay too dear.
She thought of Jeanie in her grave,
Who should have been a bride;
But who for joys brides hope to have
Fell sick and died
In her gay prime,
In earliest Winter time,
With the first glazing rime,
With the first snow-fall of crisp Winter time.

Till Laura dwindling   320
Seemed knocking at Death's door:
Then Lizzie weighed no more
Better and worse;
But put a silver penny in her purse,
Kissed Laura, crossed the heath with clumps of furze
At twilight, halted by the brook:
And for the first time in her life
Began to listen and look.

Laughed every goblin
When they spied her peeping: 330
Came towards her hobbling,
Flying, running, leaping,
Puffing and blowing,
Chuckling, clapping, crowing,

Clucking and gobbling,
Mopping and mowing,
Full of airs and graces,
Pulling wry faces,
Demure grimaces,
Cat-like and rat-like,   340
Ratel – and wombat-like,
Snail-paced in a hurry,
Parrot-voiced and whistler,
Helter skelter, hurry skurry,
Chattering like magpies,
Fluttering like pigeons,
Gliding like fishes,–
Hugged her and kissed her:
Squeezed and caressed her:
Stretched up their dishes,   350
Panniers, and plates:
'Look at our apples
Russet and dun,
Bob at our cherries,
Bite at our peaches,
Citrons and dates,
Grapes for the asking,
Pears red with basking
Out in the sun,
Plums on their twigs;   360
Pluck them and suck them,
Pomegranates, figs.'–

    'Good folk,' said Lizzie,
Mindful of Jeanie:
'Give me much and many': –
Held out her apron,
Tossed them her penny.
'Nay, take a seat with us,
Honour and eat with us,'
They answered grinning: 370
'Our feast is but beginning.
Night yet is early,
Warm and dew-pearly,
Wakeful and starry:
Such fruits as these
No man can carry;

Half their bloom would fly,
Half their dew would dry,
Half their flavour would pass by.
Sit down and feast with us,   380
Be welcome guest with us,
Cheer you and rest with us.'–
'Thank you,' said Lizzie: 'But one waits
At home alone for me:
So without further parleying,
If you will not sell me any
Of your fruits though much and many,
Give me back my silver penny
I tossed you for a fee.'–
They began to scratch their pates,   390
No longer wagging, purring,
But visibly demurring,
Grunting and snarling.
One called her proud,
Cross-grained, uncivil;
Their tones waxed loud,
Their looks were evil.
Lashing their tails
They trod and hustled her,
Elbowed and jostled her,   400
Clawed with their nails,
Barking, mewing, hissing, mocking,
Tore her gown and soiled her stocking,
Twitched her hair out by the roots,
Stamped upon her tender feet,
Held her hands and squeezed their fruits
Against her mouth to make her eat.

    White and golden Lizzie stood,
Like a lily in a flood,–
Like a rock of blue-veined stone   410
Lashed by tides obstreperously,–
Like a beacon left alone
In a hoary roaring sea,
Sending up a golden fire,–
Like a fruit-crowned orange-tree
White with blossoms honey-sweet
Sore beset by wasp and bee,–
Like a royal virgin town

Topped with gilded dome and spire
Close beleaguered by a fleet   420
Mad to tug her standard down.

One may lead a horse to water,
Twenty cannot make him drink.
Though the goblins cuffed and caught her,
Coaxed and fought her,
Bullied and besought her,
Scratched her, pinched her black as ink,
Kicked and knocked her,
Mauled and mocked her,
Lizzie uttered not a word;   430
Would not open lip from lip
Lest they should cram a mouthful in:
But laughed in heart to feel the drip
Of juice that syrupped all her face,
And lodged in dimples of her chin,
And streaked her neck which quaked like curd.
At last the evil people,
Worn out by her resistance,
Flung back her penny, kicked their fruit
Along whichever road they took,   440
Not leaving root or stone or shoot;
Some writhed into the ground,
Some dived into the brook
With ring and ripple,
Some scudded on the gale without a sound,
Some vanished in the distance.

In a smart, ache, tingle,
Lizzie went her way;
Knew not was it night or day;
Sprang up the bank, tore thro' the furze,   450
Threaded copse and dingle,
And heard her penny jingle
Bouncing in her purse,
Its bounce was music to her ear.
She ran and ran
As if she feared some goblin man
Dogged her with gibe or curse
Or something worse:
But not one goblin skurried after,

Nor was she pricked by fear; 460
The kind heart made her windy-paced
That urged her home quite out of breath with haste
And inward laughter.

She cried, 'Laura,' up the garden,
'Did you miss me?
Come and kiss me.
Never mind my bruises,
Hug me, kiss me, suck my juices
Squeezed from goblin fruits for you,
Goblin pulp and goblin dew. 470
Eat me, drink me, love me;
Laura, make much of me;
For your sake I have braved the glen
And had to do with goblin merchant men.'

Laura started from her chair,
Flung her arms up in the air,
Clutched her hair:
'Lizzie, Lizzie, have you tasted
For my sake the fruit forbidden?
Must your light like mine be hidden, 480
Your young life like mine be wasted,
Undone in mine undoing
And ruined in my ruin,
Thirsty, cankered, goblin-ridden?'–
She clung about her sister,
Kissed and kissed and kissed her:
Tears once again
Refreshed her shrunken eyes,
Dropping like rain
After long sultry drouth; 490
Shaking with aguish fear, and pain,
She kissed and kissed her with a hungry mouth.

Her lips began to scorch,
That juice was wormwood to her tongue,
She loathed the feast:
Writhing as one possessed she leaped and sung,
Rent all her robe, and wrung
Her hands in lamentable haste,
And beat her breast.

Her locks streamed like the torch   500
Borne by a racer at full speed,
Or like the mane of horses in their flight,
Or like an eagle when she stems the light
Straight toward the sun,
Or like a caged thing freed,
Or like a flying flag when armies run.

Swift fire spread through her veins, knocked at her heart,
Met the fire smouldering there
And overbore its lesser flame;
She gorged on bitterness without a name: 510
Ah! fool, to choose such part
Of soul-consuming care!
Sense failed in the mortal strife:
Like the watch-tower of a town
Which an earthquake shatters down,
Like a lightning-stricken mast,
Like a wind-uprooted tree
Spun about,
Like a foam-topped waterspout
Cast down headlong in the sea,   520
She fell at last;
Pleasure past and anguish past,
Is it death or is it life?

Life out of death.
That night long Lizzie watched by her,
Counted her pulse's flagging stir,
Felt for her breath,
Held water to her lips, and cooled her face
With tears and fanning leaves:
But when the first birds chirped about their eaves,   530
And early reapers plodded to the place
Of golden sheaves,
And dew-wet grass
Bowed in the morning winds so brisk to pass,
And new buds with new day
Opened of cup-like lilies on the stream,
Laura awoke as from a dream,
Laughed in the innocent old way,
Hugged Lizzie but not twice or thrice;
Her gleaming locks showed not one thread of grey,   540

Her breath was sweet as May
And light danced in her eyes.

Days, weeks, months, years
Afterwards, when both were wives
With children of their own;
Their mother-hearts beset with fears,
Their lives bound up in tender lives;
Laura would call the little ones
And tell them of her early prime,
Those pleasant days long gone   550
Of not-returning time:
Would talk about the haunted glen,
The wicked, quaint fruit-merchant men,
Their fruits like honey to the throat
But poison in the blood;
(Men sell not such in any town:)
Would tell them how her sister stood
In deadly peril to do her good,
And win the fiery antidote:
Then joining hands to little hands   560
Would bid them cling together,
'For there is no friend like a sister
In calm or stormy weather;
To cheer one on the tedious way,
To fetch one if one goes astray,
To lift one if one totters down,
To strengthen whilst one stands.'

22 *bullaces:* wild plums. 75 *wombat...furry:* Dante Gabriel Rossetti owned two wombats
and appears to have had an obsessive fascination with the creatures, drawing them in
unusual contexts and elevating them to a kind of cult status among his followers (see
R.T. Wells, *Wombats,* 1998). Rossetti's frontispiece illustration to *Goblin Market* depicts
a goblin with a wombat's face. 76 *ratel:* African and Indian nocturnal honey-badger.

Remember
Sonnet

Remember me when I am gone away,
    Gone far away into the silent land;
    When you can no more hold me by the hand,
Nor I half turn to go yet turning stay.
Remember me when no more day by day

You tell me of our future that you planned:
Only remember me; you understand
It will be late to counsel then or pray.
Yet if you should forget me for a while
And afterwards remember, do not grieve:
For if the darkness and corruption leave
A vestige of the thoughts that once I had,
Better by far you should forget and smile
Than that you should remember and be sad.

Song

When I am dead, my dearest,
    Sing no sad songs for me;
Plant thou no roses at my head,
    Nor shady cypress tree:
Be the green grass above me
    With showers and dewdrops wet;
And if thou wilt, remember,
    And if thou wilt, forget.

I shall not see the shadows,
    I shall not feel the rain;
I shall not hear the nightingale
    Sing on, as if in pain:
And dreaming through the twilight
    That doth not rise nor set,
Haply I may remember,
    And haply may forget.

Amor Mundi

'Oh where are you going with your love-locks flowing
    On the west wind blowing along this valley track?'
'The downhill path is easy, come with me an it please ye,
    We shall escape the uphill by never turning back.'

So they two went together in glowing August weather,
    The honey-breathing heather lay to their left and right;
And dear she was to doat on, her swift feet seemed to float on
    The air like soft twin pigeons too sportive to alight.

'Oh what is that in heaven where grey cloud-flakes are seven,
    Where blackest clouds hang riven just at the rainy skirt?'
'Oh that's a meteor sent us, a message dumb, portentous,
    An undeciphered solemn signal of help or hurt.'

'Oh what is that glides quickly where velvet flowers grow thickly,
    Their scent comes rich and sickly?' – 'A scaled and hooded worm.'
'Oh what's that in the hollow, so pale I quake to follow?'
    'Oh that's a thin dead body which waits the eternal term.'

'Turn again, O my sweetest, – turn again, false and fleetest:
    This beaten way thou beatest I fear is hell's own track.'
'Nay, too steep for hill-mounting; nay, too late for cost-counting:
    This downhill path is easy, but there's no turning back.'

Amen

It is over.   What is over?
        Nay, now much is over truly! –
Harvest days we toiled to sow for;
    Now the sheaves are gathered newly,
    Now the wheat is garnered duly.

It is finished.   What is finished?
    Much is finished known or unknown:
Lives are finished; time diminished;
    Was the fallow field left unsown?
    Will these buds be always unblown?

It suffices.   What suffices?
    All suffices reckoned rightly:
Spring shall bloom where now the ice is,
    Roses make the bramble sightly,
    And the quickening sun shine brightly,
    And the latter wind blow lightly,
    And my garden teem with spices.

The Thread of Life

1

The irresponsive silence of the land,
    The irresponsive sounding of the sea,
    Speak both one message of one sense to me: –

300

Aloof, aloof, we stand aloof, so stand
Thou too aloof bound with the flawless band
    Of inner solitude; we bind not thee;
    But who from thy self-chain shall set thee free?
What heart shall touch thy heart? What hand thy hand? –
And I am sometimes proud and sometimes meek,
    And sometimes I remember days of old
When fellowship seemed not so far to seek
    And all the world and I seemed much less cold,
    And at the rainbow's foot lay surely gold,
And hope felt strong and life itself not weak.

2

Thus am I mine own prison. Everything
    Around me free and sunny and at ease:
    Or, if in shadow, in a shade of trees
Which the sun kisses, where the gay birds sing
And where all winds make various murmuring;
    Where bees are found, with honey for the bees;
    Where sounds are music, and where silences
Are music of an unlike fashioning.
Then gaze I at the merrymaking crew,
    And smile a moment and a moment sigh
Thinking: Why can I not rejoice with you?
    But soon I put the foolish fancy by:
I am not what I have nor what I do;
    But what I was I am, I am even I.

3

Therefore myself is that one only thing
    I hold to use or waste, to keep or give;
    My sole possession every day I live,
And still mine own despite Time's winnowing.
Ever mine own, while moons and seasons bring
    From crudeness ripeness mellow and sanative;
    Ever mine own, till Death shall ply his sieve;
And still mine own, when saints break grave and sing.
And this myself as king unto my King
    I give, to Him Who gave Himself for me;
Who gives Himself to me, and bids me sing
    A sweet new song of His redeemed set free;
He bids me sing: O death, where is thy sting?
    And sing: O grave, where is thy victory?

The World

By day she woos me, soft, exceeding fair:
  But all night as the moon so changes she;
  Loathsome and foul with hideous leprosy
And subtle serpents gliding in her hair.
By day she woos me to the outer air,
  Ripe fruits, sweet flowers, and full satiety:
But through the night a beast she grins at me,
A very monster void of love and prayer.
By day she stands a lie: by night she stands
  In all the naked horror of the truth
With pushing horns and clawed and clutching hands.
Is this a friend indeed; that I should sell
  My soul to her, give her my life and youth,
Till my feet, cloven too, take hold on hell?

ADAH ISAACS MENKEN (*née* McCord)

c. 1835–68

Adah Isaacs Menken (a.k.a. Adelaide McCord and Ada Bertha Théodore) had a short but dramatic life, involving four marriages, the loss of two children, and a couple of publicised affairs. Conflicting biographical details led to confusion concerning her early years but, in 1990, John Cofran published 'The Identity of Adah Isaacs Menken: A Theatrical Mystery Solved' in *Theatre Survey* (vol. 31) and it now seems likely that she was born to Irish parents in Memphis, Tennessee. She began a career on the stage in New Orleans and married Alexander Isaac Menken in Livingston, Texas. She converted to Judaism and published poems and articles on Jewish concerns in the *Cincinnati Israelite*, but the couple separated in 1859, obtaining a rabbinical diploma of divorce. Adah later travelled to New York and married John Carmel Heenan but, after claims by her first husband that she was not free to remarry, her second husband deserted her when she was pregnant with a son who was to die in infancy. Her passionate poem, 'Judith', seems to have been written at this time. In New York she mixed with Walt Whitman and his circle. As a journalist, she wrote admiringly about his work and also continued her stage career, becoming notorious for playing the leading male role in a dramatisation of Byron's *Mazeppa*, wearing only a body stocking and loin cloth. In this role she successfully toured America and Europe but collapsed in Paris and died a few months afterwards. The following is taken from *Infelicia*, her only known volume of poems, published eight days after her death. Her topics are Jewish and women's issues and, influenced by Whitman, she was an early practitioner of free verse.

Judith

'Repent, or I will come unto thee quickly, and will fight thee with the sword of my mouth.' – Revelation ii.16

I

Ashkelon is not cut off with the remnant of a valley.
Baldness dwells not upon Gaza.
The field of the valley is mine, as it is clothed in verdure.
The steepness of Baal-perazim is mine;
And the Philistines spread themselves in the valley of Rephaim.
They shall yet be delivered into my hands.
For the God of Battles has gone before me!
The sword of the mouth shall smite them to dust.
I have slept in the darkness –
But the seventh angel woke me, and giving me a sword   10
of flame, points to the blood-ribbed cloud, that lifts his
reeking head above the mountain.
Thus I am the prophet.
I see the dawn that heralds to my waiting soul the advent of power.
    Power that will unseal the thunders!
    Power that will give voice to graves!
      Graves of the living;
      Graves of the dying;
      Graves of the sinning;
      Graves of the loving;   20
      Graves of despairing;
And oh! graves of the deserted!
These shall speak, each as their voices shall be loosed.
And the day is dawning.

II

Stand back, ye Philistines!
Practice what ye preach to me;
I heed ye not, for I know ye all.
Ye are living burning lies, and profanation to the garments
which with stately steps ye sweep your marble palaces.
Your palaces of Sin, around which the damning evidence of guilt hangs
like a reeking vapor.
Stand back!
I would pass up the golden road of the world.
A place in the ranks awaits me.
I know that ye are hedged on the borders of my path.

Lie and tremble, for ye well know that I hold with
iron grasp the battle axe.
Creep back to your dark tents in the valley.
Slouch back to your haunts of crime.
Ye do not know me, neither do ye see me.   40
But the sword of the mouth is unsealed, and ye coil
yourselves in slime and bitterness at my feet.
I mix your jeweled heads, and your gleaming eyes,
and your hissing tongues with the dust.
My garments shall bear no mark of ye.
When I shall return this sword to the angel, your foul
blood will not stain its edge.
It will glimmer with the light of truth, and the strong arm shall rest.

III

Stand back!
I am no Magdalene waiting to kiss the hem of your garment.   50
It is mid-day.
See ye not what is written on my forehead?
I am Judith!
I wait for the head of my Holofernes!
Ere the last tremble of the conscious death-agony shall
have shuddered, I will show it to ye with the long black
hair clinging to the glazed eyes, and the great mouth
opened in search of voice, and the strong throat all hot
and reeking with blood, that will thrill me with wild
unspeakable joy as it courses down my bare body and   60
dabbles my cold feet!
My sensuous soul will quake with the burden of so much bliss.
Oh, what wild passionate kisses will I draw up from that bleeding mouth!
I will strangle this pallid throat of mine on the sweet blood!
I will revel in my passion.
At midnight I will feast on it in the darkness.
For it was that which thrilled its crimson tides of reckless passion
through the blue veins of my life, and made them leap up in the wild
sweetness of Love and agony of Revenge!
I am starving for this feast.   70
Oh forget not that I am Judith!
And I know where sleeps Holofernes.

Title: In the apocryphal *Book of Judith*, this rich Israelite widow saved Bethulia from
Nebuchadnezzar's army by cutting off the head of his general, Holofernes, while he slept.
10 *seventh angel:* see Revelation 8-12. 50 *Magdalene:* Mary Magdalene; repentant woman.

HARRIET PRESCOTT SPOFFORD
1835–1921

Harriet Prescott was born in Calais, Maine and was educated in Massachusetts and New Hampshire. She started to publish stories to help support her parents and was assisted by Thomas Wentworth Higginson, the editor of *Atlantic Monthly*. Her short stories and Gothic romances were popular in the early 1860s, though she always considered her poetry to be of greater value. She married Richard Spofford, a lawyer (and poet), in 1865. They had one child who died in infancy. When Richard died in 1888, Harriet continued to write. Her works include *The Amber Gods* (1863), *Azarian* (1864), *Scarlet Poppy and Three Heroines of New England Romance* (1894), *A Master Spirit* (1896), *An Inheritance* (1897), and *Old Madame and Other Tragedies* (1900). Her poetry collections are *Poems* (1882) and *In Titian's Garden and Other Poems* (1897) from which the following are taken.

Pomegranate-Flowers

The street was narrow, close, and dark,
    And flanked with antique masonry,
The shelving eaves left for an ark
    But one long strip of summer sky.
    But one long line to bless the eye –
    The thin white cloud lay not so high,
    Only some brown bird, skimming nigh,
    From wings whence all the dew was dry
Shook down a dream of forest scents,
Of odorous blooms and sweet contents,   10
    Upon the weary passers-by.

Ah, few but haggard brows had part
    Below that street's uneven crown,
And there the murmurs of the mart
    Swarmed faint as hums of drowsy noon.
With voices chiming in quaint tune
From sun-soaked hulls long wharves adown,
The singing sailors rough and brown
Won far melodious renown,
Here, listening children ceasing play,   20
And mothers sad their well-a-way,
    In this old breezy sea-board town.

Ablaze on distant banks she knew,
    Spreading their bowls to catch the sun,

Magnificent Dutch tulips grew
   With pompous color overrun.
By light and snow from heaven won
   Their misty web azaleas spun;
   Low lilies pale as any nun,
     Their pensile bells rang one by one;   30
And spicing all the summer air
Gold honeysuckles everywhere
   Their trumpets blew in unison.

Than where blood-cored carnations stood
   She fancied richer hues might be,
Scents rarer than the purple hood
   Curled over in the fleur-de-lis.
   Small skill in learned names had she,
   Yet whatso wealth of land or sea
     Had ever stored her memory,   40
   She decked its varied imagery
Where, in the highest of the row
Upon a sill more white than snow,
   She nourished a pomegranate-tree.

Some lover from a foreign clime,
   Some roving gallant of the main,
Had brought it on a gay spring-time,
   And told her of the nacar stain
   The thing would wear when bloomed again.
   Therefore all garden growths in vain   50
   Their glowing ranks swept through her brain,
   The plant was knit by subtile chain
To all the balm of Southern zones,
The incenses of Eastern thrones,
   The tinkling hem of Aaron's train.

The almond shaking in the sun
   On some high place ere day begin,
Where winds of myrrh and cinnamon
   Between the tossing plumes have been,
   It called before her, and its kin   60
   The fragrant savage balaustine
   Grown from the ruined ravelin
   That tawny leopards couch them in;
But this, if rolling in from seas

It only caught the salt-fumed breeze,
  Would have a grace they might not win.

And for the fruit that it should bring,
  One globe she pictured, bright and near,
Crimson, and throughly perfuming
  All airs that brush its shining sphere.   70
In its translucent atmosphere
Afrite and Princess reappear, –
Through painted panes the scattered spear
Of sunrise scarce so warm and clear, –
And pulped with such a golden juice,
Ambrosial, that one cannot choose
But find the thought most sumptuous cheer.

Of all fair women she was queen,
  And all her beauty, late and soon,
O'ercame you like the mellow sheen   80
  Of some serene autumnal noon.
Her presence like a sweetest tune
Accorded all your thoughts in one.
Than last year's alder-tufts in June
Browner, yet lustrous as a moon
Her eyes glowed on you, and her hair
With such an air as princes wear
  She trimmed black-braided in a crown.

A perfect peace prepared her days,
  Few were her wants and small her care,   90
No weary thoughts perplexed her ways,
  She hardly knew if she were fair.
Bent lightly at her needle there
In that small room stair over stair,
All fancies blithe and debonair
She deftly wrought on fabrics rare,
All clustered moss, all drifting snow,
All trailing vines, all flowers that blow,
  Her daedal fingers laid them bare.

Still at the slowly spreading leaves   100
  She glanced up ever and anon,
If yet the shadow of the eaves
  Had paled the dark gloss they put on.

But while her smile like sunlight shone,
  The life danced to such blossom blown
That all the roses ever known,
  Blanche of Provence, Noisette, or Yonne,
Wore no such tint as this pale streak
That damasked half the rounding cheek
  Of each bud great to bursting grown.   110

And when the perfect flower lay free,
  Like some great moth whose gorgeous wings
Fan o'er the husk unconsciously,
  Silken, in airy balancings, –
  She saw all gay dishevellings
  Of fairy flags, whose revellings
  Illumine night's enchanted rings.
So royal red no blood of kings
She thought, and Summer in the room
Sealed her escutcheon on their bloom,   120
  In the glad girl's imaginings.

Now, said she, in the heart of the woods
  The sweet south-winds assert their power,
And blow apart the snowy snoods
  Of trilliums in their thrice-green bower.
  Now all the swamps are flushed with dower
  Of viscid pink, where, hour by hour,
  The bees swim amorous, and a shower
  Reddens the stream where cardinals tower.
Far lost in fern of fragrant stir   130
Her fancies roam, for unto her
  All Nature came in this one flower.

Sometimes she set it on the ledge
  That it might not be quite forlorn
Of wind and sky, where o'er the edge,
  Some gaudy petal, slowly borne,
  Fluttered to earth in careless scorn,
  Caught, for a fallen piece of morn
  From kindling vapors loosely shorn,
  By urchins ragged and wayworn,   140
Who saw, high on the stone embossed,
A laughing face, a hand that tossed
  A prodigal spray just freshly torn.

308

What wizard hints across them fleet, –
These heirs of all the town's thick sin,
Swift gypsies of the tortuous street,
With childhood yet on cheek and chin!
What voices dropping through the din
An airy murmuring begin, –
These floating flakes, so fine and thin,   150
Were they and rock-laid earth akin?
Some woman of the gods was she,
The generous maiden in her glee?
And did whole forests grow within?

A tissue rare as the hoar-frost,
White as the mists spring dawns condemn,
The shadowy wrinkles round her lost,
She wrought with branch and anadem,
Through the fine meshes netting them,
Pomegranate-flower and leaf and stem.   160
Dropping it o'er her gold-stitched hem,
Some duchess through the court should sail
Hazed in the cloud of this white veil,
As when a rain-drop mists a gem.

Her tresses once when this was done,
– Vanished the skein, the needle bare, –
She dressed with wreaths vermilion
Bright as a trumpet's dazzling blare.
Nor knew that in Queen Dido's hair,
Loading the Carthaginian air,   170
Ancestral blossoms flamed as fair
As any ever hanging there.
While o'er her cheek their scarlet gleam
Shot down a vivid varying beam,
Like sunshine on a brown-bronzed pear.

And then the veil thrown over her,
The vapor of the snowy lace
Fell downward, as the gossamer
Tossed from the autumn winds' wild race
Falls round some garden-statue's grace.   180
Beneath, the blushes on her face
Fled with the Naiad's shifting chase
When flashing through a watery space.

And in the dusky mirror glanced
A splendid phantom, where there danced
    All brilliances in paler trace.

A spicery of sweet perfume,
    As if from regions rankly green
And these rich hoards of bud and bloom,
    Lay every waft of air between.
Out of some heaven's unfancied screen
The gorgeous vision seemed to lean.
The Oriental kings have seen
Less beauty in their daïs-queen,
And any limner's pencil then
Had drawn the eternal love of men,
    But twice Chance will not intervene.

For soon with scarce a loving sigh
    She lifts it off half unaware,
While through the clinging folds held high,
    Arachnean in a silver snare
    Her rosy fingers nimbly fare,
    Till gathered square with dainty care.
    But still she leaves the flowery flare
    – Such as Dame Venus' self might wear –
Where first she placed them, since they blow
More bounteous color hanging so,
    And seem more native to the air.

Anon the mellow twilight came
    With breath of quiet gently freed
From sunset's felt but unseen flame.
    Then by her casement wheeled in speed
    Strange films, and half the wings indeed
    That steam in rainbows o'er the mead,
    Now magnified in mystery, lead
    Great revolutions to her heed.
And leaning out, the night o'erhead,
Wind-tossed in many a shining thread,
    Hung one long scarf of glittering brede.

Then as it drew its streamers there,
    And furled its sails to fill and flaunt
Along fresh firmaments of air
    When ancient morn renewed his chant, –

190

200

210

220

She sighed in thinking on the plant
Drooping so languidly aslant;
Fancied some fierce noon's forest-haunt
Where wild red things loll forth and pant,
Their golden ant[h]ers wave, and still
Sigh for a shower that shall distil
The largess gracious nights do grant.   230

The oleanders in the South
Drape gray hills with their rose, she thought,
The yellow-tasselled broom through drouth
Bathing in half a heaven is caught.
Jasmine and myrtle flowers are sought
By winds that leave them fragrance-fraught.
To them the wild bee's path is taught,
The crystal spheres of rain are brought,
Beside them on some silent spray
The nightingales sing night away,   240
The darkness wooes them in such sort.

But this, close shut beneath a roof,
Knows not the night, the tranquil spell,
The stillness of the wildwood ouphe,
The magic dropped on moor and fell.
No cool dew soothes its fiery shell,
Nor any star, a red sardel,
Swings painted there as in a well.
Dyed like a stream of muscadel
No white-skinned snake coils in its cup   250
To drink its soul of sweetness up,
A honeyed hermit in his cell.

No humming-bird in emerald coat,
Shedding the light, and bearing fain
His ebon spear, while at his throat
The ruby corselet sparkles plain,
On wings of misty speed astain
With amber lustres, hangs amain,
And tireless hums his happy strain;
Emperor of some primeval reign,   260
Over the ages sails to spill
The luscious juice of this, and thrill
Its very heart with blissful pain.

As if the flowers had taken flight
  Or as the crusted gems should shoot
From hidden hollows, or as the light
  Had blossomed into prisms to flute
  Its secret that before was mute,
  Atoms where fire and tint dispute,
No humming-birds here hunt their fruit.   270
No burly bee with banded suit
Here dusts him, no full ray by stealth
Sifts through it stained with warmer wealth
  Where fair fierce butterflies salute.

Nor night nor day brings to my tree,
  She thought, the free air's choice extremes,
But yet it grows as joyfully
  And floods my chamber with its beams,
  So that some tropic land it seems
  Where oranges with ruddy gleams,   280
And aloes, whose weird flowers the creams
Of long rich centuries one deems,
Wave through the softness of the gloom, –
And these may blush a deeper bloom
  Because they gladden so my dreams.

The sudden street-lights in moresque
  Broke through her tender murmuring,
And on her ceiling shades grotesque
  Reeled in a bacchanalian swing.
  Then all things swam, and like a ring   290
  Of bubbles welling from a spring
Breaking in deepest coloring
Flower-spirits paid her minist'ring.
Sleep, fusing all her senses, soon
Fanned over her in drowsy rune
  All night long a pomegranate wing.

48 *nacar:* bright orange red. 55 *Aaron's train:* Aaron, brother of Moses was the first High
Priest. See Exodus 30–31. 72 *Afrite:* in Arabian mythology, a powerful evil jinnee, demon
or giant monster. 99 *daedal:* from Daedalus, an ingenious artist. 158 *anadem:* garland.
169 *Queen Dido:* a valiant but abandoned woman according to Virgil and Ovid. 182
Naiad: nymph of river or spring. 201 *Arachnean:* Arachne, an expert with a needle, who
pitted her skills against those of the goddess Minerva, and lost. She hanged herself in
despair and Minerva changed her into a spider. 219 *brede:* braid. 228 *anters:* anthers,
the parts of the stamen with pollen. 244 *ouphe:* elf. 249 *muscadel:* muscadines are musk-
flavoured grapes and muscatel is the strong sweet wine made from them: this word
combines both. 286 *moresque:* Moorish in design, i.e. in North African style.

A Winter's Night

Come, close the curtains, and make fast the door,
  Pile high the logs, and let the happy room
  Red as the rose on wall and ceiling bloom,
And bring your golden flagons forth and pour
Full drinking of some ancient summer's store
  Of spice and sweetness, while to ruddy gloom
  The fire falls. And lest one hear sound of doom
Let music sing old ditties o'er and o'er.

Yet shall you never make the door so fast
  That no moan echo on the song, no shape
  Dull the wine's fragrance and the blaze obscure
And breathe the dark chill of the outer blast,
  Till you shall turn and shudder to escape
  The awful phantom of the hungry poor!

AUGUSTA WEBSTER (*née* Davies)

1837–94

Augusta was born in Poole, Dorset. Her father was a Vice-Admiral and she
had an unconventional childhood. She attended Cambridge School of Art and
was also educated in Paris and Geneva. She married Thomas Webster, a soli-
citor, in 1867 and they moved to London. Augusta campaigned for women's
rights and equal educational opportunities. Her first volume of poetry, *Blanche
Lisle and Other Poems* was published in 1860 under the pseudonym, 'Cecil
Home' – as was *Lilian Gray* (1864), and her novel, *Lesley's Guardians* (1864).
Later works appeared under her own name: *Dramatic Studies* (1866), *A Woman
Sold and Other Poems* (1867), and *Portraits* (1870), which provides the text for
Circe. Her decision not to begin each line of her blank verse with a capital
letter was seen as eccentric and makes *Portraits* look ahead of its time. She
wrote about the poet's craft, and the concerns of married women in *A House-
wife's Opinions* (1879). Augusta was a reviewer and essay writer for the *Athenaeum*
and the *Examiner*. Expert in the dramatic monologue, she also wrote verse
dramas, such as *Disguises* (1879), *In a Day* (1882) and *The Sentence* (1887).
Augusta's poetry was admired by Christina Rossetti and she is now considered
to be a major Victorian poet. Her sonnet sequence, *Mother and Daughter*, edited
by William Michael Rossetti (1895), was unfinished when she died.

from Circe

What fate is mine who, far apart from pains
and fears and turmoils of the cross-grained world,

dwell, like a lonely god, in a charmed isle   60
where I am first and only, and, like one
who should love poisonous savours more than mead,
long for a tempest on me and grow sick
of resting, and divine free carelessness!
Oh me, I am a woman, not a god;
yea, those who tend me even are more than I,
my nymphs who have the souls of flowers and birds
singing and blossoming immortally.

Ah me! these love a day and laugh again,
and loving, laughing, find a full content;   70
but I know nought of peace, and have not loved.

Where is my love? Does someone cry for me,
not knowing whom he calls? Does his soul cry
for mine to grow beside it, grow in it?
Does he beseech the gods to give him me,
the one unknown rare woman by whose side
no other woman thrice as beautiful
should once seem fair to him; to whose voice heard
in any common tones no sweetest sound
of love made melody on silver lutes,   80
or singing like Apollo's when the gods
grow pale with happy listening, might be peered
for making music to him; whom once found
there will be no more seeking anything?

Oh love, oh love, oh love, art not yet come
out of the waiting shadows into life?
Art not yet come after so many years
that I have longed for thee? Come! I am here.

Not yet. For surely I should feel a sound
of his far answering if now in the world   90
he sought me who will seek me – oh ye gods
will he not seek me? Is it all a dream?
Will there be never never such a man?
Will there be only these, these bestial things
who wallow in my styes, or mop and mow
among the trees, or munch in pens and byres,
or snarl and filch behind their wattled coops;
these things who had believed that they were men?

Nay, but he *will* come. Why am I so fair,
and marvellously minded, and with sight   100
that flashes suddenly on hidden things,
as the gods see who do not need to look?
Why wear I in my eyes that stronger power
than basilisks, whose gaze can only kill,
to draw men's souls to me to live or die
as I would have them? Why am I given pride
that yet longs to be broken, and this scorn,
cruel and vengeful, for the lesser men
who meet the smiles I waste for lack of him
and grow too glad? Why am I who I am,   110
but for the sake of him whom fate will send
one day to be my master utterly,
that he should take me, the desire of all,
whom only he in the world could bow to him?

Oh sunlike glory of pale glittering hairs,
bright as the filmy wires my weavers take
to make me golden gauzes; oh deep eyes,
darker and softer than the bluest dusk
of August violets, darker and deep
like crystal fathomless lakes in summer noons;   120
oh sad sweet longing smile; oh lips that tempt
my very self to kisses; oh round cheeks,
tenderly radiant with the even flush
of pale smoothed coral; perfect lovely face
answering my gaze from out this fleckless pool;
wonder of glossy shoulders, chiselled limbs;
should I be so your lover as I am,
drinking an exquisite joy to watch you thus
in all a hundred changes through the day,
but that I love you for him till he comes,   130
but that my beauty means his loving it?

Oh, look! a speck on this side of the sun,
coming – yes, coming with the rising wind
that frays the darkening cloud-wrack on the verge
and in a little while will leap abroad,
spattering the sky with rushing blacknesses,
dashing the hissing mountainous waves at the stars.
'Twill drive me that black speck a shuddering hulk
caught in the buffeting waves, dashed impotent

from ridge to ridge, will drive it in the night   140
with that dull jarring crash upon the beach,
and the cries for help and the cries of fear and hope.

And then to-morrow they will thoughtfully,
with grave low voices, count their perils up,
and thank the gods for having let them live
and tell of wives or mothers in their homes,
and children, who would have such loss in them
that they must weep, and maybe I weep too,
with fancy of the weepings had they died.
And the next morrow they will feel their ease   150
and sigh with sleek content, or laugh elate,
Tasting delights of rest and revelling,
music and perfumes, joyaunce for the eyes
of rosy faces, and luxurious pomps,
the savour of the banquet and the glow
and fragrance of the wine-cup; and they'll talk
how good it is to house in palaces
out of the storms and struggles, and what luck
strewed their good ship on our accessless coast.
Then the next day the beast in them will wake,   160
and one will strike and bicker, and one swell
with puffed-up greatness, and one gibe and strut
in apish pranks, and one will line his sleeve
with pilfered booties, and one snatch the gems
out of the carven goblets as they pass;
one will grow mad with fever of the wine,
and one will sluggishly besot himself,
and one be lewd, and one be gluttonous;
and I shall sickly look, and loathe them all.

Title: *Circe:* Ulysses came to the enchantress's island on his way home from the Trojan War and Circe turned his companions into swine. He was immune to her transforming potions and stayed with her a year. 107 *scorn,:* this ed. scorn 1870 ed. 108 *vengeful,:* this ed. vengeful 1870 ed. 125 *from out:* this ed. out from 1870 ed. 165 *pass;* this ed. pass, 1870 ed.

Love's Mourner, XI

'Tis men who say that through all hurt and pain
    The woman's love, wife's, mother's, still will hold,
    And breathes the sweeter and will more unfold
For winds that tear it, and the sorrowful rain.

So in a thousand voices has the strain
  Of this dear patient madness been retold,
  That men call women's love. Ah! they are bold,
Naming for love that grief which *does* remain.

Love faints that looks on baseness face to face:
  Love pardons all; but by the pardonings dies,
  With a fresh wound of each pierced through the breast.
And there stand pityingly in Love's void place
  Kindness of household wont familiar-wise,
  And faith to Love – faith to our dead at rest.

Mother and Daughter, XIV

To love her as to-day is so great bliss
  I needs must think of morrows almost loth,
  Morrows wherein the flower's unclosing growth
Shall make my darling other than she is.
The breathing rose excels the bud I wis,
  Yet bud that will be rose is sweet for both;
  And by-and-by seems like some later troth
Named in the moment of a lover's kiss.

Yes, I am jealous, as of one now strange
  That shall instead of her possess my thought,
Of her own self made new by any change,
  Of her to be by ripening morrows brought.
My rose of women under later skies!
Yet, ah! My child with the child's trustful eyes!

Mother and Daughter, XV

That some day Death who has us all for jest
  Shall hide me in the dark and voiceless mould,
  And him whose living hand has mine in hold,
Where loving comes not nor the looks that rest,
Shall make us nought where we are known the best,
  Forgotten things that leave their track untold
  As in the August night the sky's dropped gold –
This seems no strangeness, but Death's natural hest.

But looking on the dawn that is her face
  To know she too is Death's seems misbelief;

317

She should not find decay, but, as the sun
Moves mightier from the veil that hides his place,
Keep ceaseless radiance. Life is Death begun:
But Death and her! That's strangeness passing grief.

Mother and Daughter, XVI

She will not have it that my day wanes low,
    Poor of the fire its drooping sun denies,
    That on my brow the thin lines write good-byes
Which soon may be read plain for all to know,
Telling that I have done with youth's brave show;
    Alas! And done with youth in heart and eyes,
    With wonder and with far expectancies,
Save but to say 'I knew such long ago'.

She will not have it. Loverlike to me,
    She with her happy gaze finds all that's best,
She sees this fair and that unfretted still,
    And her own sunshine over all the rest:
So she half keeps me as she'd have me be,
And I forget to age, through her sweet will.

MATHILDE BLIND

1841–96

Mathilde Blind was a poet, biographer, essayist, editor, novelist, and transla-
tor. Born in Mannheim, Germany, she came to England with her family after
1849, having first lived briefly in Belgium. Her father was a Jewish banker
called Cohen, but she took the name of her mother's second husband, Karl
Blind, a political writer and activist. Mathilde attended a number of schools
and was expelled as an atheist in 1859; she never married, was extremely
independent, and travelled throughout Britain and Europe alone, venturing
as far as Egypt. She published biographies of Percy Bysshe Shelley (1872),
George Eliot (1883) and Madame Roland (1886), and edited Byron's poems
and letters (1886). Her poetry first appeared under the pseudonym, 'Claude
Lake' in 1867; later work was inspired by her travels in Scotland: *The Prophecy
of St Oran* (1881) and *The Heather on Fire* (1886), and further afield, *Birds of
Passage: Songs of the Orient and Occident* (1895). *The Ascent of Man* (1889) is
unique for its handling of Darwinian theory. Other volumes include: *Dramas in
Miniature* (1891) and *Songs and Sonnets* (1893). A complete *Poetical Works* was
edited by Arthur Symons in 1900. The text for 'Saving Love' is *Songs and
Sonnets* (1893); 'Sphinx-Money' and 'The Agnostic' are from *Birds of Passage*
(1895).

Saving Love

Would we but love what will not pass away!
    The sun that n each morning shines as clear
    As when it rose first on the world's first year;
The fresh green leaves that rustle on the spray.
The sun will shine, the leaves will be as gay
    When graves are full of all our hearts held dear,
    When not a soul of those who loved us here,
Not one, is left us – creatures of decay.

Yea, love the Abiding in the Universe
Which was before, and will be after us.
    Nor yet for ever hanker and vainly cry
For human love – the beings that change or die;
Die – change – forget: to care so is a curse,
Yet cursed we'll be rather than not care thus.

Sphinx-Money

Where Pyramids and temple-wrecks are piled
    Confusedly on camel-coloured sands,
    And the mute Arab motionlessly stands,
Like some swart god who never wept or smiled, –
I picked up mummy relics of the wild
    (And sea-shells once with clutching baby hands),
    And felt a wafture from old Motherlands,
And all the morning wonder of a Child

To find Sphinx-money. So the Bedouin calls
    Small fossils of the waste. Nay, poet's gold;
    'Twill give thee entrance to those rites of old,
When hundred-gated Thebes, with storied walls,
    Gleamed o'er her Plain, and vast processions rolled
To Amon-Ra through Karnak's pillared halls

14 *Karnak:* a village on the Nile near Luxor, with spectacular ruins of the Temple of Ammon (supreme god of Egyptians in the Theban region) on the site of ancient Thebes.

The Agnostic

Not in the hour of peril, thronged with foes,
    Panting to set their heel upon my head, –

319

Or when alone from many wounds I bled
Unflinching beneath Fortune's random blows;
Not when my shuddering hands were doomed to close
The unshrinking eyelids of the stony dead; –
Not then I missed my God, not then – but said:
'Let me not burden God with all man's woes!'

But when resurgent from the womb of night
Spring's Oriflamme of flowers waves from the Sod;
When peak on flashing Alpine peak is trod

By sunbeams on their missionary flight;
When heaven-kissed Earth laughs, garmented in light; –
That is the hour in which I miss my God.

10 *Oriflamme:* blaze of colour.

ADA CAMBRIDGE (*later* Cross)
1844-1926

Ada Cambridge was born in England and grew up in Norfolk, but emigrated
to Australia when she married Rev. George Frederick Cross. Now celebrated
as an Australian poet and novelist, she initially lived a rural life in Victoria as
an Anglican clergyman's wife, but began to publish stories in 1873, while caring
for her children. *A Married Man* (1890) was one of more than 20 novels; Ada
also wrote two volumes of reminiscences (including *Thirty Years in Australia*,
1903), short stories, several hymns, and two collections of poetry: *The Manor
House and Other Poems* (1875), and *The Hand in the Dark and Other Poems*
(1913), from which the following are taken.

Honour

Me let the world disparage and despise –
    This virtuous world that loves its gilded chains,
    Its mean successes and its sordid gains,
Its pleasant vice and profitable lies;
Let its strong hand my rebel deeds chastise,
    The rebel blood that surges in my veins,
    And deal me all due penalties and pains,
And make me hideous in my neighbours' eyes.

But let me fall not in mine own esteem,
    My poor deceit or selfish greed debased.
    Let me be clean from secret sin and shame,

Know myself true, though only false I seem –
Know myself worthy, howsoe'er disgraced –
Know myself right, though all the world should blame.

Vows

What worth are promises? We can pretend
　　To constant passion and a life-long trust,
　　As to all decorous virtues, if we must;
But you and I will speak the truth, my friend.
And can we say what fickle fate will send
　　To lift us up or grind us into dust? –
What bloom of growth or waste of moth and rust
Shall be our portion ere the final end?
No laws, no oaths can free-born souls confine.
When vows have force, the treasured thing whereon
They stamped their pledge is neither yours nor mine,
Wishing to go, it is already gone.
When faith and love need bolts upon the door,
Then faith is faith and love is love no more.

MICHAEL FIELD
(Katherine Harris Bradley, 1846-1914
and Edith Emma Cooper, 1862-1913)

'Michael Field' was the name of shared authorship used by Katherine Bradley and her niece, Edith Cooper, for their collaborative writings. Together they wrote over twenty five plays and eight collections of poetry. Katherine was educated at Newnham College Cambridge and the Collège de France in Paris. When her older sister became an invalid after the birth of Edith's younger sister, she devoted herself to caring for the elder niece. Katherine and Edith moved to Bristol in 1878, both attended classes in classics and philosophy at University College, became involved in the movement for women's suffrage, and began to publish poetry. In 1875, Katherine published a volume of her own verse under the name *Arran Leigh: The New Minnesinger*. In 1881, *Bellerophôn and Other Poems*, a joint volume, appeared under the names Arran and Isla Leigh, and in 1884, they published two tragedies, *Calirrhöe* and *Fair Rosamund*, under the joint name, Michael Field. These were not performed but received praise as the promising work of a new writer. Popular interest waned when they were identified as related spinsters. However, Robert Browning and George Meredith continued to encourage them: their acquaintances also included Oscar Wilde and George Moore. They moved to Reigate in 1888 and travelled in Europe, meeting Browning in Italy. They settled in Richmond in 1899 and lived there until their deaths from cancer, less than a year apart. They both converted to Catholicism in 1907 and religion plays a large part in their later works, although their early writing, with its pagan and sensuous elements, is most highly valued today. *Long Ago* (1889) is based on Sappho's fragments, inspired by H.T. Wharton's *Sappho* (1885). He was the first to collect all of Sappho's fragments in an English translation. No other poetic versions of the fragments that inspired the following poems were cited by Wharton. Other volumes by Michael Field include *Underneath the Bough* (1893), *Wild Honey from Various Thyme: Poems* (1908), *Mystic Trees* (1913) and *Poems of Adoration* (1912). A manuscript of their journal, *Works and Days*, is in the British Library.

from Long Ago

XXIX

Στᾶθι κἄντα φίλος . . . .
καὶ τὰν ἐπ᾽ ὄσσοις ἀμπέτασον χάριν.

When through thy breast wild wrath doth spread
And work thy inmost being harm,
Leave thou the fiery word unsaid,
    Guard thee; be calm.

Closed be thy lips: where Love perchance
Lies at the door to be thy guest,
Shall there be noise and dissonance?
    Quiet were best.

Apollo, when they do thee wrong,
Speechless thou tak'st the golden dart:
I will refrain my barking tongue,
    And strike the heart.

Motto: 'Stand face to face, friend...and unveil the grace in thine eyes' (Wharton, 80)

XXXV

Ἄλλα, μὴ μεγαλύνεο δακτυλίω πέρι.

Come, Gorgo, put the rug in place,
    And passionate recline;
I love to see thee in thy grace,
    Dark, virulent, divine.
But wherefore thus thy proud eyes fix
    Upon a jewelled band?
Art thou so glad the sardonyx
    Becomes thy shapely hand?

322

Bethink thee! 'Tis for such as thou
    Zeus leaves his lofty seat;
'Tis at thy beauty's bidding how
    Man's mortal life shall fleet;
Those fairest hands – dost thou forget
    Their power to thrill and cling?
O foolish woman, dost thou set
    Thy pride upon a ring?

Motto: 'Foolish woman, pride not thyself on a ring' (Wharton, 84)

XXXVI

Οὐκ οἶδ' ὅττι θέω · δύο μοι τὰ νοήματα.

Yea, gold is son of Zeus: no rust
    Its timeless light can stain;
The worm that brings man's flesh to dust
    Assaults its strength in vain:
More gold than gold the love I sing,
A hard, inviolable thing.

Men say the passions should grow old
    With waning years; my heart
Is incorruptible as gold,
    'Tis my immortal part:
Nor is there any god can lay
On love the finger of decay.

Motto: 'I know not what to do; my mind is divided'. (Wharton, 84)

AGNES MARCHBANK (*later* Marshall)

b. 1846

Agnes was born in Edinburgh. Her father drowned in a shipping disaster (the Orion) and her mother moved with her young daughter to Moffat in the Southern Scottish Highlands. Agnes married the Rev. George Alston Marshall, a minister of Mount Park Free Church, Greenock. She returned to live with her mother in Edinburgh when he died, and began to write – under her maiden name. Her poems and stories were published in newspapers like the *People's Journal*, *People's Friend*, etc. She published several volumes of tales, including: *Some Edinburgh Bohemians* (1891), *An Angel's Visit and a Guid Tocher* (1892), *Ruth*

Farmer (1896) and *Betsy Bingham* (1897). A collection of poetry, *Songs of Labour, Home, and Country*, which included 'Limpin' Kate', appeared in 1892. Her main strength is her ability to capture local characters and scenes in popular narrative verse, often with wry humour. She also published *The Covenanters of Annandale* (1895) and *Upper Annandale: Its History and Traditions* (1901). Some of this biographical material is taken from: *Modern Scottish Poets*, vol. 15 (Brechin, D.H. Edwards, 1893), which also contains a selection of Agnes' verse.

Limpin' Kate

O Limpin' Kate cam o'er the lea,
An' blithesome face, I wow, had she;
Aul' John keeked roon the hoose en' to see
    The lass that got the siller.

'If I be auld I hae nae ties,
I'm elder and a laird likewise;
O, lassie, tak' and ne'er despise,
    John o' Girshaw, the miller.'

But Kate laughed oot and said 'Na, na,
An' auld man wud be sune awa';   10
And micht spend or he gaed it a',
    For nursin' tak's some siller.'

The smith keeked frae the smiddy door –
A thing he never did afore –
Richt after Kate, and then he swore
    He'd put the question till her.

'Na, na', said Kate, 'I ken your plan,
I little need a thriftless man,
Ye'd let the smiddy fire out whaun
    Ye'd get me an' my siller.'   20

The weaver rose frae oot his thrums,
An' doon to Newton Carse he comes,
Draws in his chair and hechs and hums,
    And glowers as he would kill her.

But Katie was nae feared, no she,
Even when he said, 'Ye maun tak' *me*,
Or I'll blaw oot my brains and dee';
    She thoucht, 'He wants my siller.'

And then she said, 'What's a' your haste?
Ye ne'er thocht I was to your taste?
Ance, when Kate needed help the maist,
    Ye were richt saucy till her.'

O mony a ane cam coortin' Kate,
But aye she said, 'Ye come ower late;
An' aul' maid's is a blessful state
    When she has got some siller.

The weaver sune would seal my doom,
The smith would leave my pouches toom;
And a' my life would be in gloom,
    If ance I wed the miller.

Na, I'll just end as I began,
I've gat the wit o' ony man –
I'll tak' the comfort while I can,
    O' my wee bit o' siller.'

30

40

1 *lea:* field. 3 *keeked:* peeped. 4 *siller:* silver. 21 *thrums:* threads. 38 *toom:* empty.

MARY HANNAY FOOTT (*née* Black)
1846–1918

Mary was born in Glasgow and arrived in Melbourne, Australia, in 1853. She was educated at art school and became a teacher. After her marriage, she moved to south-west Queensland and, when her husband died, worked as a journalist. She was Social and Literary Editor of the *Queenslander* from 1884. 'Where the Pelican Builds' (dated 5 March 1881) is one of the most famous bush ballads in 19th-century Australian literature. The following poems are both taken from her collection, *Morna Lee and Other Poems*, 2nd ed. (London & Brisbane, Gordon & Gotch, 1890). Mary died at Bundaberg.

The Clever Cat

There was a cat called William –
    The poorest ever seen;
He would not go a-mousing –
    He played the tambourine.

His family would not feed him –
    This lazy little cat –
But out of doors they turned him;
    There seemed no way but that.

So on and on he wandered
  Till he to Catland came,
And there he met a Princess –
  Felina was her name.

She had the loveliest whiskers;
  Her eyes were emerald green.
She fell in love with William –
  All for his tambourine!

For her delight was dancing
  And there was none to play.
'Strike up!' she straight commanded
  When William came that way.

All day she danced. At sunset
  Poor William at her feet
Fell down and said, 'Pray may I
  Have something now to eat?'

'To eat? Of course! – What ho, there!'
  (Felina had no bell,
But when she called her servants
  Her sweet voice did as well.)

Then tortoiseshells and tabbies
  Tripped o'er each other's tails;
All scurrying from the kitchen
  With cream-cakes and stewed snails.

Now after this they brought him
  Six dinners every day –
And 'mouse' was never mentioned.
  His brothers came to stay.

For *they* had heard of Catland
  Where William's word was law.
And by-and-by Felina
  Bestowed on him her paw.

There *is* a cat called William –
  The fattest ever seen;
He need not go a-mousing –
  He plays the tambourine!

Where the Pelican Builds

[The unexplored parts of Australia are sometimes spoken of by the bush-men of Western Queensland as the home of the pelican, a bird whose nesting place, so far as the writer knows, is seldom, if ever found.]

The horses were ready, the rails were down,
    But the riders lingered still, –
      One had a parting word to say,
    And one had his pipe to fill.
Then they mounted, one with a granted prayer,
    And one with a grief unguessed.
      'We are going' they said, as they rode away –
    'Where the pelican builds her nest!'

They had told us of pastures wide and green,
    To be sought past the sunset's glow;
      Of rifts in the ranges by opal lit;
    And gold 'neath the river's flow.
And thirst and hunger were banished words
    When they spoke of that unknown West;
      No drought they dreaded, no flood they feared,
    Where the pelican builds her nest!

The creek at the ford was but fetlock deep
    When we watched them crossing there;
      The rains have replenished it thrice since then
    And thrice has the rock lain bare.
But the waters of Hope have flowed and fled,
    And never from blue hill's breast
      Come back – by the sun and the sands devoured –
    Where the pelican builds her nest!

ALICE MEYNELL (*née* Thompson)
1847–1922

Born in Barnes, Alice Thompson travelled widely in Europe during her early years. Her father, a friend of Charles Dickens, gave Alice and her sister a good education. Her mother, Christiana, was a concert pianist. The family settled in London in 1864, where Alice began to write poetry. She followed her mother in converting to Catholicism. Her first volume, *Preludes*, was praised by Tennyson, Christina Rossetti, George Eliot and Ruskin. It appeared under the name

A.C. Thompson in 1875, and was illustrated by her sister, Elizabeth (who later became a celebrated war artist). Alice married Wilfrid Meynell in 1877: they had eight children, seven surviving. Together, the couple edited several literary journals. Alice was a prolific essayist and published her work widely in journals that included the *National Observer*, the *Spectator* and the *Pall Mall Gazette*. She was made President of the Society of Women Journalists in 1897. Her other publications include: *The Rhythm of Life and Other Essays* (1893), *William Holman Hunt: His Life and Work* (1893), *The Spirit of Place and Other Essays* (1899), *John Ruskin* (1900) and *Mary, the Mother of Jesus* (1912). Alice was a pacifist who supported non-militant suffragism, travelled in Europe and America (where she completed a lecture tour, 1901-02), and was twice nominated for Poet Laureate (in 1895 and 1913). Her later collections of poetry include *Other Poems* (1896), *Later Poems* (1902), *Poems* (1913), *The Shepherdess and Other Verses* (1914), *Poems on the War* (1916), and *A Father of Women and Other Poems* (1917). Her *Last Poems* appeared posthumously in 1923. The following are taken from *Poems* (1921).

Renouncement

I must not think of thee; and, tired yet strong,
   I shun the thought that lurks in all delight –
   The thought of thee – and in the blue Heaven's height,
And in the sweetest passage of a song.

Oh, just beyond the fairest thoughts that throng
   This breast, the thought of thee waits, hidden yet bright;
   Yet it must never, never come in sight;
I must stop short of thee the whole day long.

But when sleep comes to close each difficult day,
   When night gives pause to the long watch I keep,
   And all my bonds I needs must loose apart,

Must doff my will as raiment laid away, –
   With the first dream that comes with the first sleep
   I run, I run, I am gathered to thy heart.

Maternity

One wept whose only child was dead,
   New-born, ten years ago.
'Weep not; he is in bliss', they said.
   She answered, 'Even so.

Ten years ago was born in pain
A child, not now forlorn.
But oh, ten years ago, in vain,
A mother, a mother was born.'

EMMA LAZARUS
1849–87

One of seven children, Emma Lazarus was born into a long-established Jewish family in New York City and grew up in downtown Manhattan. She sent a copy of her first volume, *Poems and Translations: Written between the Ages Fourteen and Sixteen* (1867), to Ralph Waldo Emerson, who she visited later, in Concord. Her second book, *Admetus and Other Poems* (1871), was favourably received in both America and England. *Songs of a Semite* (1882) established her as an outspoken poet on Jewish issues. From 1880, persecution of Jews led to attrocities in Russia and elsewhere: Emma was in personal contact with some of the thousands who fled to New York. She revered George Eliot as the writer 'who did most among the artists of our day towards elevating and enobling the spirit of Jewish nationality' (from the dedication to her play, *The Dance to Death*). Emma also wrote a novel, *Alide* (1874), and translated Heinrich Heine's poems (1881). 'The New Colossus' was published in 1883 for an auction at the Art Loan Fund Exhibition to support the Bartholdi Pedestal Fund for the Statue of Liberty. In 1886 the statue was erected in New York Harbour and in 1901 Emma's poem was inscribed on a bronze plaque at its base. *The Poems of Emma Lazarus*, from which these poems are taken, was published in 1889, two years after her early death from cancer. Emma had visited England and France in her last years and was there in the summer of 1887, but she died in New York. Gary Eiselein edited *Emma Lazarus: selected poems and other writings* for Broadview Press in 2002.

The New Colossus

Not like the brazen giant of Greek fame,
With conquering limbs astride from land to land;
Here at our sea-washed, sunset gates shall stand
A mighty woman with a torch, whose flame
Is the imprisoned lightning, and her name
Mother of Exiles. From her beacon-hand
Glows world-wide welcome; her mild eyes command
The air-bridged harbor that twin cities frame.
'Keep, ancient lands, your storied pomp!' cries she
With silent lips. 'Give me your tired, your poor,
Your huddled masses yearning to breathe free,
The wretched refuse of your teeming shore.
Send these, the homeless, tempest-tost to me,
I lift my lamp beside the golden door!'

The New Ezekiel

What, can these dead bones live, whose sap is dried
  By twenty scorching centuries of wrong?
Is this the House of Israel, whose pride
  Is as a tale that's told, an ancient song?
Are these ignoble relics all that live
  Of psalmist, priest, and prophet? Can the breath
Of very heaven bids these bones revive,
  Open the graves and clothe the ribs of death?

Yea, Prophesy, the Lord hath said. Again
  Say to the wind, Come forth and breathe afresh,
Even that they may live upon these slain,
  And bone to bone shall leap, and flesh to flesh.
The Spirit is not dead, proclaim the word,
  Where lay dead bones, a host of armed men stand!
I ope your graves, my people, saith the Lord,
  And I shall place you living in your land.

HENRIETTA CORDELIA RAY
1849–1916

One of seven children, Henrietta was born in New York City, the daughter
of Charles Bennett Ray, a former blacksmith and Congregational minister,
and his second wife, Charlotte. Her sister, also Charlotte, was the first black
woman lawyer in the District of Columbia. Henrietta was awarded a Master
of Pedagogy from New York City University and taught English in New
York schools for thirty years. She never married. The daughter of an active
abolitionist, she wrote an ode to Lincoln which was read at the unveiling of
the Freedman's Monument in Washington D.C. in 1876 and helped to launch
her career as a poet. She published two volumes of poetry, *Sonnets* (1893) and
Poems (1910), from which the following is taken.

The Vision of Eve

When from the gates of Paradise fair Eve
Turned her reluctant steps with saddest mien,
A sense prophetic stayed her blinding tears,
And thus she yearning cried, her sobs between:
'Could I but see adown the coming days!
Yet, though I may not win that boon, alas!
One question haunts me with resistless charm,
What will my daughters be when aeons pass?'

She bowed her head, then as with rev'rence spoke:
'A hope has seized my spirit, e'en though late
It cometh. Ay! And will my fault be less
By what they may achieve of good or great?
Are all my cherished longings to be vain?
I cannot know what grander purpose lies
Beyond the misty verge that bounds my view.'
She ceased, with supplication in her eyes.

Again we see the Mother of mankind,
Yet not discrowned and mournful as of yore;
From amethystine battlements she leans,
Wide-eyed with wonder and admiring awe.
Far past the planets, past the swinging stars,
Past worlds on worlds that spin in ether there,
Her glances wander to the circling earth,
Lying below swathed by the purpling air.

Lo! What is it she sees? Forms like to hers,
When erst she paced fair Eden's flow'ry courts;
But on each brow there sits a something new,
A something mystical. Is it the thoughts'
Deep impress which the centuries have left?
The seal of alternating joy and woe,
Of care and grief, anon of hope and love,
Marked by the ages as they come and go?

And ever on and on the glances rove
Of our first mother. Now the marble yields
In Eve-like contours 'neath the skilful touch
Of one; another well the sceptre wields;
And one self-poised, regnant in dignity,
In philosophic councils holds the sway.
Upon the battlefield, one kneels to stanch
The crimson life-blood as it ebbs away.

And thus the dreamer spoke: 'Are these my kin,
And has the world so grown since those sweet days
In glorious Paradise when Time was young?
Are these my daughters who with sweeping gaze,
Can scan the sheeny Heavens for a sign
Of God's deep wisdom writ upon the skies?
Are these indeed my children, all my own?
What strange, enchanting visions meet my eyes?'

She hears the rhythmic strains of one who caught
The Muse's most majestic melodies;
The lofty heights, the shining altitudes
Her latest children climb, with pride she sees.
'Ah! My prophetic hopes were not in vain,'
Cried Mother Eve with eager eyes aglow;
'Yet could I dream of this when Time began?
The deeds my daughters dare I could not know.'

She paused, and soon her rapt soliloquy
Died like a zephyr o'er a leafy lawn;
She gazed once more from jewelled battlements
Far down the firmament, e'en as the Dawn
Blushed in the east; and when the magic hues
Began in mimic warfare to engage,
Throughout the spheres a chiming measure thrilled, –
The vibrant music of the newer age!

Title: In Milton's *Paradise Lost*, Adam is allowed a vision of the future while Eve sleeps: here, the vision is solely Eve's and Adam is not present.

ETHELWYN WETHERALD
1857–1940

Agnes Ethelwyn Wetherald was born at Rockwood, Ontario. Her parents were Quakers and her father, the Rev. William Wetherald, founded the Rockwood Academy. Ethelwyn was also educated at the Friends' Boarding School, Union Springs, New York, and at Pickering College. In 1887 she collaborated with G. Mercer Adam and published a novel, *The Algonquin Maiden*. Ethelwyn worked as a journalist for the *Toronto Globe* and was also a freelance writer. Eventually one of Canada's first published women poets, she contributed poems, stories, and reflections to a variety of journals (including the *New England Magazine*) from *c.*1892. Her first volume of poetry, *The House of the Trees and Other Poems* (which provides the texts for the following poems), was published in 1895. Her second poetry collection, *Tangled in Stars*, appeared in 1902, and others followed, including *The Radiant Road* (1904), *The Last Robin* (1907) and *Lyrics and Sonnets* (1931). She provided an introduction to the *Collected Poems of Isabella Valancy Crawford* (1905). Latterly, Ethelwyn lived on a farm in Pelham Township, Weland County, Ontario.

The Sound of the Axe

With the sound of an axe on the light wind's tracks
For my only company,

And a speck of sky like a human eye
Blue, bending over me,

I lie at rest on the low moss pressed,
Whose loose leaves downward drip;
As light they move as a word of love
Or a finger to the lip.

'Neath the canopies of the sunbright trees
Pierced by an Autumn ray,
To rich red flakes the old log breaks
In exquisite decay.

While in the pines where no sun shines
Perpetual morning lies.
What bed more sweet could stay her feet,
Or hold her dreaming eyes?

No sound is there in the middle air
But sudden wings that soar,
As a strange bird's cry goes drifting by –
And then I hear once more

That sound of an axe till the great tree cracks,
Then a crash comes as if all
The winds that through its bright leaves blew
Were sorrowing in its fall.

The Fields of Dark

The wreathing vine within the porch
Is in the heart of me,
The roses that the noondays scorch
Shall burn in memory;
Alone at night I quench the light,
And without star or spark
The grass and trees press to my knees,
And flowers throng the dark.

The leaves that loose their hold at noon
Drop on my face like rain,
And in the watches of the moon
I feel them fall again.
By day I stray how far away

To stream and wood and steep,
But on my track they all come back
To haunt the vale of sleep.

The fields of light are clover-brimmed,
Or grassed or daisy-starred,
The fields of dark are softly dimmed,
And safely twi-light barred;
But in the gloom that fills my room
I cannot fail to mark
The grass and trees about my knees,
The flowers in the dark.

ISABELLA VALANCY CRAWFORD
1850–87

Isabella Valancy Crawford was probably Canada's first major woman poet. Her obituary notices suggest that her work was well-received in Britain, America, and Canada, particularly in her home town, Toronto, but she is often described as being largely unrecognised during her lifetime. Born in Dublin, Isabella was brought to Canada as a child by her family. She lived in Paisley, Lakefield, and Peterborough, before moving to Toronto with her invalid mother, after the death of her father and all ten siblings. Her stories and poems appeared in a number of newspapers (such as the *Toronto Mail*) and in American magazines. In 1879 she began to contribute to the *Toronto Globe* and *Toronto Evening Telegram*. Attempts to publish in literary journals failed. She started her writing career to provide additional support, but her first volume of poetry, *Old Spookses' Pass, Malcolm's Katie, and Other Poems* (1884) was privately published and not a financial success. She died prematurely of heart failure and her *Collected Poems* was published posthumously in 1905.

Said the Canoe

My masters twain made me a bed
Of pine-boughs resinous, and cedar;
Of moss, a soft and gentle breeder
Of dreams of rest; and me they spread
With furry skins and, laughing, said:
'Now she shall lay her polished sides
As queens do rest, or dainty brides,
Our slender lady of the tides!'

My masters twain their camp-soul lit;
Streamed incense from the hissing cones;

Large crimson flashes grew and whirled;
Thin golden nerves of sly light curled
Round the dun camp; and rose faint zones,
Half way about each grim bole knit,
Like a shy child that would bedeck
With its soft clasp a Brave's red neck,
Yet sees the rough shield on his breast,
The awful plumes shake on his crest,
And, fearful, drops his timid face,
Nor dares complete the sweet embrace.

Into the hollow hearts of brakes-
Yet warm from sides of does and stags
Passed to the crisp, dark river-flags –
Sinuous, red as copper-snakes,
Sharp-headed serpents, made of light,
Glided and hid themselves in night.

My masters twain the slaughtered deer
Hung on forked boughs with thongs of leather:
Bound were his stiff, slim feet together,
His eyes like dead stars cold and drear.
The wandering firelight drew near
And laid its wide palm, red and anxious,
On the sharp splendour of his branches,
On the white foam grown hard and sere
    On flank and shoulder.
Death – hard as breast of granite boulder-
    Under his lashes
Peered thro' his eyes at his life's grey ashes.

My masters twain sang songs that wove –
As they burnished hunter-blade and rifle –
A golden thread with a cobweb trifle,
Loud of the chase and low of love:

'O Love! art thou a silver fish,
Shy of the line and shy of gaffing,
Which we do follow, fierce, yet laughing,
Casting at thee the light-winged wish?
And at the last shall we bring thee up
From the crystal darkness, under the cup
    Of lily folden
    On broad leaves golden?

'O Love! art thou a silver deer
With feet as swift as wing of swallow,
While we with rushing arrows follow?
And at the last shall we draw near
And o'er thy velvet neck cast thongs
Woven of roses, stars and songs –
    New chains all moulden
    Of rare gems olden?'

They hung the slaughtered fish like swords
    On saplings slender; like scimitars,
    Bright, and ruddied from new-dead wars,
Blazed in the light the scaly hordes.

They piled up boughs beneath the trees,
    Of cedar web and green fir tassel.
    Low did the pointed pine tops rustle,
The camp-fire blushed to the tender breeze.

The hounds laid dewlaps on the ground
    With needles of pine, sweet, soft and rusty,
    Dreamed of the dead stag stout and lusty;
A bat by the red flames wove its round.

The darkness built its wigwam walls
    Close round the camp, and at its curtain
    Pressed shapes, thin, woven and uncertain
As white locks of tall waterfalls.

TORU DUTT

1856-77

Toru Dutt was a remarkable Indian poet who wrote her poetry in English,
combined European influences in her treatment of the sonnet form, and wrote
evocatively about India. She experimented with free verse and traditional lyrics,
was fascinated by the mythology of her own country, yet was also inspired by
the French symbolists and was fluent in their language before she learnt English.
Born in Calcutta, the youngest of three children in a high-caste Hindu family,
she was educated in India, France, Italy and England. Her father, Govin
Chunder Dutt, also wrote poetry. Her family converted to Christianity when
she was six years old and her mother, Kshetramoni, translated *The Blood of
Jesus* into Bengali. Toru attended lectures for women at Cambridge for a
short time with her sister, Aru, and was also trained in music. In 1873 she
returned to Bengal and studied Sanskrit. She translated poetry from French

to English in *A Sheaf Gleaned in French Fields* (1876) and transformed familiar Hindustani legends (including that of the heroine Savitri) in *Ancient Ballads and Legends of Hindustan*, published posthumously by Edmund Gosse in 1882. The following poems are from this volume. Her novel, *Le Journal de Mademoiselle d'Avers*, was published in 1879, and another, *Bianca, or The Young Spanish Maiden*, remained incomplete at her death, but was subsequently serialised in the *Bengal Magazine* (which had previously published her critical essays). At the age of 21, Toru died of tuberculosis, a disease that had already claimed her brother and sister.

Baugmaree

A sea of foliage girds our garden round,
But not a sea of dull unvaried green,
Sharp contrasts of all colours here are seen;
The light-green graceful tamarinds abound
Amid the mango clumps of green profound,
And palms arise, like pillars gray, between;
And o'er the quiet pools the seemuls lean,
Red, – red, and startling like a trumpet's sound.
But nothing can be lovelier than the ranges
Of bamboos to the eastward, when the moon
Looks through their gaps, and the white lotus changes
Into a cup of silver. One might swoon
Drunken with beauty then, or gaze and gaze
On a primeval Eden, in amaze.

Title: *Baugmaree*, where the Dutt family had a garden residence, is on the outskirts of Calcutta. 4 *tamarinds:* large, tropical trees with dark green leaves, fragrant yellow flowers, streaked red, and fruit used for cooling drinks and medicines. 7 *seemuls:* local name for silk-cotton trees.

Our Casuarina Tree

Like a huge python, winding round and round
The rugged trunk, indented deep with scars,
Up to its very summit near the stars,
A creeper climbs, in whose embraces bound
No other tree could live. But gallantly
The giant wears the scarf, and flowers are hung
In crimson clusters all the boughs among,
Whereon all day are gathered bird and bee;
And oft at nights the garden overflows
With one sweet song that seems to have no close,
Sung darkling from our tree, while men repose.

When first my casement is wide open thrown
   At dawn, my eyes delighted on it rest;
   Sometimes, and most in winter, – on its crest
A grey baboon sits statue-like alone
   Watching the sunrise; while on lower boughs
His puny offspring leap about and play;
And far and near kokilas hail the day;
And to their pastures wend our sleepy cows;
And in the shadow, on the broad tank cast   20
By that hoar tree, so beautiful and vast,
The water-lilies spring, like snow enmassed.

But not because of its magnificence
   Dear is the Casuarina to my soul:
   Beneath it we have played; though years may roll,
O sweet companions, loved with love intense,
   For your sakes, shall the tree be ever dear!
Blent with your images, it shall arise
In memory, till the hot tears blind mine eyes!
   What is that dirge-like murmur that I hear
Like the sea breaking on a shingle-beach?
It is the tree's lament, an eerie speech,
That haply to the unknown land may reach.

Unknown, yet well-known to the eye of faith!
   Ah, I have heard that wail far, far away
   In distant lands, by many a sheltered bay,
When slumbered in his cave the water-wraith
   And the waves gently kissed the classic shore
Of France or Italy, beneath the moon,
When earth lay trancèd in a dreamless swoon: 40
   And every time the music rose, – before
Mine inner vision rose a form sublime,
Thy form, O Tree, as in my happy prime
I saw thee, in my own loved native clime.

Therefore I fain would consecrate a lay
   Unto thy honour, Tree, beloved of those
   Who now in blessed sleep, for aye, repose,
Dearer than life to me, alas, were they!
   Mayst thou be numbered when my days are done
With deathless trees – like those in Borrowdale,
Under whose awful branches lingered pale

'Fear, trembling Hope, and Death, the skeleton,
And Time the shadow'; and though weak the verse
That would thy beauty fain, oh fain rehearse,
May Love defend thee from Oblivion's curse.

Title: a tree with leafless branches, jointed so that it resembles huge horse-tails. 18 *kokila:* a kind of cuckoo, a song-bird. 46-47 *those...sleep:* probably her brother, Abju, who died in 1865, and her sister, Aru, who she lost in 1874. *50 those...Borrowdale:* Toru was influenced by Wordsworth's poem, 'Yew-Trees', set in Borrowdale in the Lake District, which focuses on the trees' huge, intertwining trunks. *52-53 'Fear...shadow':* she is quoting from Wordsworth's poem.

The Tree of Life

Broad daylight, with a sense of weariness!
Mine eyes were closed, but I was not asleep,
My hand was in my father's, and I felt
His presence near me. Thus we often passed
In silence, hour by hour. What was the need
Of interchanging words when every thought
That in our hearts arose, was known to each,
And every pulse kept time? Suddenly there shone
A strange light, and the scene as sudden changed.
I was awake:– It was an open plain
Illimitable, – stretching, stretching – oh, so far!
And o'er it that strange light, – a glorious light
Like that the stars shed over fields of snow
In a clear, cloudless, frosty winter night,
Only intenser in its brilliance calm.
And in the midst of that vast plain, I saw,
For I was wide awake, – it was no dream,
A tree with spreading branches and with leaves
Of divers kinds, – and dead silver and live gold,
Shimmering in radiance that no words may tell!
Beside the tree an Angel stood; he plucked
A few small sprays, and bound them round my head.
Oh, the delicious touch of those strange leaves!
No longer throbbed my brows, no more I felt
The fever in my limbs – 'And oh', I cried,
'Bind too my father's forehead with these leaves'.
One leaf the Angel took and therewith touched
His forehead, and then gently whispered 'Nay!'
Never, oh never had I seen a face

More beautiful than that Angel's, or more full
Of holy pity and of love divine,
Wondering I looked awhile, – then, all at once
Opened my tear-dimmed eyes – when lo! The light
Was gone – the light as of the stars when snow
Lies deep upon the ground. No more, no more,
Was seen the Angel's face. I only found
My father watching patient by my bed,
And holding in his own, close-prest, my hand.

LIZETTE WOODWORTH REESE

1856-1935

Born a twin, in Huntingdon (later, Waverly), Maryland, of a Welsh father and
a German mother, Lizette, like her three sisters and brother, was bilingual.
Educated locally and at a Baltimore High School, she became a teacher of
English and German, and taught for another 45 years. She published her first
poem at 18 and a poetry collection, *A Branch of May*, from which the following
are taken, came out in 1887. Her other volumes include: *A Handful of Lavender*
(1891), *A Quiet Road* (1896), *A Wayside Lute* (1909), *Spicewood* (1920), *Wild
Cherry* (1923), *Selected Poems* (1926), *A Victorian Village* (1929), *White April
and Other Poems* (1930), and *Pastures and Other Poems* (1933). Her work focuses
mainly on nature, the lives of women, the art of poetry, and loss. Nine of her
14 books were written after she retired from teaching, and her reputation con-
tinued to grow in her old age with her readings, lectures and new writing. She
visited England in 1903, 1921 and 1926, and met Walter de la Mare, with
whom she corresponded. Lizette became ill in November 1935, whilst in Nor-
folk, Virginia for a poetry reading and died in hospital on 17 December. Her
work had a big impact on American lyric poetry and both Edna St Vincent
Millay and Sara Teasdale were influenced by her.

After the Rain

Dripping the hollyhocks beneath the wall,
Their fires half quenched, a smouldering red;
A shred of gold upon the grasses tall,
A butterfly is hanging dead.

A sound of trickling waters, like a tune
Set to sweet words; a wind that blows
Wet boughs against a saffron sky; all June
Caught in the breath of one white rose.

Early September

The swallows have not left us yet, praise God!
And bees still hum, and gardens hold the musk
Of white rose and of red; firing the dusk
By the old wall, the hollyhocks do nod,
And pinks that send the sweet East down the wind.
And yet, a yellowing leaf shows here and there
Among the boughs, and through the smoky air –
That hints the frost at dawn – the wood looks thinned.
The little half-grown sumachs, all as green
As June last week, now in the crackling sedge,
Colored like wine burn to the water's edge.
We feel, at times, as we had come unseen
Upon the aging Year, sitting apart,
Grief in his eyes, some ache at his great heart.

A. MARY F. ROBINSON
(*later* Darmesteter, *later* Duclaux)
1857–1944

Mary Robinson was born at Leamington Spa, Warwickshire: she was educated
in Belgium, Italy, and at University College, London. Her first volume of poems,
A Handful of Honeysuckle, was published in 1878. She married James Darmes-
teter, a Professor of Persian, in 1888, and they lived in Paris. After he died,
in 1894, Mary translated his works. She married Émile Duclaux in 1904 and
moved to Olmet. Her poems were published under all three names and titles
include: *Songs, Ballads, and a Garden Play* (1889), and *Retrospect and Other
Poems* (1893), from which the following is taken, *Collected Poems* (1902), and
Images & Meditations (1923). She was also a novelist and critic: her work on
Emily Brontë appeared in 1883.

The Bookworm

The whole day long I sit and read
    Of days when men were men indeed
    And women knightlier far:
I fight with Joan of Arc; I fall
With Talbot; from my castle-wall
    I watch the guiding star...

But when at last the twilight falls
And hangs about the book-lined walls

And creeps across the page,
Then the enchantment goes, and I
Close up my volumes with a sigh
    To greet a narrower age.

Home through the pearly dusk I go
And watch the London lamplight glow
    Far off in wavering lines:
A pale grey world with primrose gleams,
And in the West a cloud that seems
    My distant Apennines.

O Life! So full of truths to teach,
Of secrets I shall never reach,
    O world of Here and Now;
Forgive, forgive me, if a voice,
A ghost, a memory be my choice
    And more to me than Thou!

CONSTANCE C.W. NADEN
1858–89

Constance Caroline Woodhill Naden was born in Edgbaston, Birmingham. An only child, her mother died within two weeks of her birth and she was brought up by her grandparents. She was educated at a local Unitarian school and at the Birmingham and Midlands Institute, where she studied botany. From 1881 she attended courses at Mason College and was a member of the Birmingham Natural History Society. Using her inheritance from her grandmother, she travelled to Constantinople, Palestine, Egypt and India, returning to settle in London in 1888. Constance lectured on women's suffrage and was a friend of Elizabeth Garrett Anderson. A prize-winning essayist on scientific subjects, she also published two volumes of poetry: *Songs and Sonnets of Springtime* (1881) and *A Modern Apostle, The Elixir of Life, and Other Poems* (1887). The complete edition of her poems, from which the following is taken, appeared in 1894. She died prematurely, following an operation, and is buried in Birmingham.

The Pantheist's Song of Immortality

Bring snow-white lilies, pallid heart-flushed roses,
    Enwreathe her brow with heavy scented flowers;
In soft undreaming sleep her head reposes,
    While, unregretted, pass the sunlit hours.

Few sorrows did she know – and all are over;
  A thousand joys – but they are all forgot:
Her life was one fair dream of friend and lover;
  And were they false – ah, well, she knows it not.

Look in her face and lose thy dread of dying;
  Weep not, that rest will come, that toil will cease:
Is it not well, to lie as she is lying,
  In utter silence, and in perfect peace?

Canst thou repine that sentient days are numbered?
  Death is unconscious Life, that waits for birth;
So didst thou live, while yet thy embryo slumbered,
  Senseless, unbreathing, e'en as heaven and earth.

Then shrink no more from Death, though Life be gladness,
  Nor seek him, restless in thy lonely pain:
The law of joy ordains each hour of sadness,
  And firm or frail, thou canst not live in vain.

What though thy name by no sad lips be spoken,
  And no fond heart shall keep thy memory green?
Thou yet shalt leave thine own enduring token,
  For earth is not as though thou ne'er hadst been.

See yon broad current, hasting to the ocean,
  Its ripples glorious in the western red:
Each wavelet passes, trackless; yet its motion
  Has changed for evermore the river bed.

Ah, wherefore weep, although the form and fashion
  Of what thou seemest fades like sunset flame?
The uncreated Source of toil and passion
  Through everlasting change abides the same.

Yes, thou shalt die: but these almighty forces,
  That meet to form thee, live for evermore:
They hold the suns in their eternal courses,
  And shape the tiny sand-grains on the shore.

Be calmly glad, thine own true kindred seeing
  In fire and storm, in flowers with dew impearled;
Rejoice in thine imperishable being,
  One with the Essence of the boundless world.

E(DITH) NESBIT
(*later* Bland, *later* Tucker)
1858–1924

As E. Nesbit she wrote children's classics such as *The Phoenix and the Carpet* (1904) and *The Railway Children* (1906), but Edith Nesbit was also a poet and adult novelist. The youngest of six children, she was born in London. After her father's death the family lived in Europe and returned to England when she was thirteen. Edith's stories and poems were probably first published in journals from 1876. She married a bank clerk, Hubert Bland, in 1880. Both were members of the Fabian Society. They had four children and Edith also raised two of her husband's illegitimate offspring. Bland died in 1914 and she married Thomas Terry Tucker, a marine engineer, in 1917. They moved to Kent, where she later died of cancer. 'The Moors' is taken from *Lays and Legends* (1886), and 'Among his Books', from *Leaves of Life* (1888). Her other poetry collections include *A Pomander of Verse* (1895), *Songs of Love and Empire* (1898) and *Ballads and Lyrics of Socialism, 1883-1908* (1908). In all, she published 15 children's novels, nine for adults (including *The Red House*, 1902), and more than 40 other volumes, writing as Fabian Bland when collaborating with her first husband.

The Moors

Not in rich glebe and ripe, green garden only
   – Does Summer weave her sweet, resistless spells,
But in high hills, and moorlands waste and lonely,
   The vast enchantment of her presence dwells.
Wide sky, and sky-wide waste of thyme and heather,
   Perpetual sleepy hum of golden bees –
If you and I were only there together,
   Free from the weight of all your garden's trees!

The north is mine; though bred by elm and meadow,
   Pines, torrents, rocks and moors my heart loves best;
I love the plover's wail, the cleft hill's shadow,
   The sun-browned grass that is the sky-lark's nest.
Ah, yes! You too I love, dear, wistful pleader,
   You most I love, dear, southern rose, half-blown,
And rather lounge with you beneath your cedar,
   Than greet the moor's wide heaven-on-earth alone.

Among His Books

A silent room – grey with a dusty blight
    Of loneliness;
A room with not enough of light
    Its form to dress.

Books enough though! The groaning sofa bears
    A goodly store –
Books on the window-seat, and on the chairs,
    And on the floor.

Books of all sorts of soul, all sorts of age,
    All sorts of face –   10
Black-letter, vellum, and the flimsy page
    Of commonplace.

All bindings, from the cloth whose hue distracts
    One's weary nerves,
To yellow parchment, binding rare old tracts
    It serves – deserves.

Books on the shelves, and in the cupboard books,
    Worthless and rare –
Books on the mantelpiece – wheree'er one looks
    Books everywhere!   20

Books! Books! The only things in life I find
    Not wholly vain.
Books in my hands – books in my heart enshrined –
    Books in my brain.

My friends are they: for children and for wife
    They serve me too;
For these alone, of all dear things in life,
    Have I found true.

They do not flatter, change, deny, deceive –
    Ah no – not they!   30
The same editions which one night you leave
    You find next day.

You don't find railway novels where you left
    Your Elzevirs!
Your Aldines don't betray you – leave bereft
    Your lonely years!

And yet this common book of Common Prayer
    My heart prefers,
Because the names upon the fly-leaf there
    Are mine and hers.   40

It's a dead flower that makes it open so –
    Forget-me-not –
The Marriage Service...well, my dear, you know
    Who first forgot.

Those were the days when in the choir we two
    Sat – used to sing –
When I believed in God, in love, in you –
    In everything.

Through quiet lanes to church we used to come,
    Happy and good,   50
Clasp hands through sermon, and go slowly home
    Down through the wood.

Kisses? A certain yellow rose no doubt
    That porch still shows,
Whenever I hear kisses talked about
    I smell that rose!

No – I don't blame you – since you only proved
    My choice unwise,
And taught me books should trusted be and loved,
    Not lips and eyes!   60

And so I keep your book – your flower – to show
    How much I care
For the dear memory of what, you know,
    You never were.

---

34 *Elzevirs:* beautiful books, printed by the Elzevir family at Leyden, Amsterdam, Utrecht and The Hague from 1583 to 1712. 35 *Aldines:* books printed in Venice by Aldus Manutius, 1449-1515, who produced the first printed editions of many Greek authors.

CHARLOTTE PERKINS GILMAN
(*formerly* Stetson)
1860–1935

Best known as a feminist author, novelist, and short story writer, Charlotte also wrote approximately 500 poems. She began life in Hartford, Connecticut, as Charlotte Anna Perkins. Her father, Frederic Beecher Perkins, left his family when Charlotte and her brother, Thomas, were very young: although he maintained contact, they had to manage largely without him. Charlotte was educated at Rhode Island School of Design to become a commercial artist and teacher. She married Charles Stetson, an artist, in 1884. Their daughter, Katherine, was born in 1885. Diagnosed as suffering from depression in 1886, Charlotte was forbidden to write, draw or paint by Dr S. Weir Mitchell. She eventually left her husband and took her daughter with her to California to fend for herself: her experiences helped to produce her most famous short story, *The Yellow Wall-paper* (1892). She divorced Stetson in 1894. He later married her best friend, Grace Channing, and Katherine lived with them in New York. Charlotte continued to write (journalism, feminist theory, fiction, and poetry). Her poetry collection, *In this Our World*, first appeared at this time (the following are taken from the 1895 edition). *Women and Economics* was published in 1898. In 1900 Charlotte married her cousin, George Gilman, a lawyer. She published, edited, and wrote for her own feminist journal, *The Forerunner* (1909–16), produced volumes such as *Concerning Children* (1900), *What Diantha Did* (1910) and *Herland* (1915), as well as lecturing on feminist issues. She was diagnosed with breast cancer in 1932 and her husband died in 1934. The following year, whilst living with her daughter and grandchildren, she took an overdose of chloroform. Charlotte Perkins Gilman is remembered for her wit and remarkably modern feminist views. Her writing played an important part in the Feminist Movement at the beginning of the 20th century.

The Prophets

Time was we stoned the Prophets. Age on age
When men were strong to serve, the world hath slain them.
People are wiser now; they waste no rage –
The Prophets entertain them!

Pioneers

Long have we sung our noble pioneers,
Vanguard of progress! Heralds of the time!
Guardians of industry and art sublime!
Leaders of man down all the brightening years.

To them the danger – to their wives the tears –
  While we sit safely in the city's grime
  In old-world trammels of distress and crime,
Playing with words and thoughts, with doubts and fears.

Children of axe and gun! Ye take today
  The baby steps of man's first feeblest age!
  While we, thought-seekers of the printed page,
We lead the world down its untrodden way!
Ours the drear wastes and leagues of empty waves,
The lonely deaths, the undiscovered graves.

She Walketh Veiled and Sleeping

  She walketh veiled and sleeping,
  For she knoweth not her power;
  She obeyeth but the pleading
  Of her heart and the high leading
  Of her soul, unto this hour.
  Slow advancing, halting, creeping,
  Comes the Woman to the Hour! –
  She walketh veiled and sleeping
  For she knoweth not her power.

BETTINA WALKER

fl. 1890

Bettina Walker's first love was music. Her book, *My Musical Experiences* (1890),
gives the personal reminiscences of 'a pianoforte student' and charts her
friendship with Franz Liszt and other renowned musicians. She tells how the
first nine years of her life were spent 'in a remote country village, to which no
news from the outward world ever seemed to come', and expresses her love
of nature and, from the age of five, her dedication to music. She came from
a middle-class family, was well-educated through governesses and her father's
library, and benefited from singing and piano lessons, although she lost her
singing voice as a result of straining it. Her volume, *Songs and Sonnets*, was
published in London in 1893.

Too Late

Long weary hours I toiled indoors today,
  While from a brake close by the blackbird's song
  Came welling so deliciously along

The odorous air, that I was fain to lay
My task aside – let Nature have her way,
    And in the woodlands wandering glad and free,
    Drink in at every pore the melody,
The life, the joy, the sweetness of the May.
But something stern and strenuous in me said,
'Not till thy work is done may'st thou arise,
And pull the honeyed blossoms of the Spring.'
So I forebore – and now, with drooping head,
I mark the day's last glimmer vanishing
'Mid utter silence in the western skies.

AMY LEVY

1861–89

Amy Levy was born and died in London. She was the first Jewish woman to matriculate at Newnham College, Cambridge and her first volume of poetry, *Xantippe and Other Verse*, was published there in 1881. In 1875 her ballad, 'Ida Grey', had come out in the *Pelican Magazine* and 'Euphemia, a Sketch', in the *Victoria Magazine* in 1880. 'Xantippe' first appeared in the *Dublin University Magazine*. After leaving Cambridge, Amy travelled in Europe and wrote on Jewish issues. *A Minor Poet and Other Poems* was published in 1884 and her novel, *Reuben Sachs*, in 1888. Amy was a friend of Oscar Wilde and Olive Schreiner. She published other fiction, articles, and some critical essays, including one on the poet, James Thomson, and another on the poetry of Christina Rossetti. Her work was well-received in the literary world. A *London Plane-Tree and Other Verse* appeared posthumously, following her suicide in 1889. 'At a Dinner Party' comes from this volume. Although known to suffer from bouts of depression, speculation was aroused by the manner of Amy's early death, but the true circumstances have never been ascertained.

Xantippe

(A fragment)

What, have I waked again? I never thought
To see the rosy dawn, or even this grey,
Dull, solemn stillness, ere the dawn has come.
The lamp burns low; low burns the lamp of life:
The still morn stays expectant, and my soul,
All weighted with a passive wonderment,
Waiteth and watcheth, waiteth for the dawn.
Come hither maids; too soundly have ye slept
That should have watched me; nay, I would not chide –

Oft have I chidden, yet I would not chide 10
In this last hour; – now all should be at peace.
I have been dreaming in a troubled sleep
Of weary days I thought not to recall;
Of stormy days, whose storms are hushed long since;
Of gladsome days, of sunny days; alas!
In dreaming, all their sunshine seemed so sad,
As though the current of the dark To-Be
Had flowed, prophetic, through the happy hours.
And yet, full well, I know it was not thus;
I mind me sweetly of the summer days, 20
When, leaning from the lattice, I have caught
The fair, far glimpses of a shining sea:
And nearer, of tall ships which thronged the bay,
And stood out blackly from a tender sky
All flecked with sulphur, azure, and bright gold;
And in the still, clear air have heard the hum
Of distant voices; and methinks there rose
No darker fount to mar or stain the joy
Which sprang ecstatic in my maiden breast
Than just those vague desires, those hopes and fears, 30
Those eager longings, strong, though undefined,
Whose very sadness makes them seem so sweet.
What cared I for the merry mockeries
Of other maidens sitting at the loom?
Or for sharp voices, bidding me return
To maiden labour? Were we not apart, –
I and my high thoughts, and my golden dreams,
My soul which yearned for knowledge, for a tongue
That should proclaim the stately mysteries
Of this fair world, and of the holy gods? 40
Then followed days of sadness, as I grew
To learn my woman-mind had gone astray,
And I was sinning in those very thoughts –
For maidens, mark, such are not woman's thoughts –
(And yet, 'tis strange, the gods who fashion us
Have given us such promptings)......
                         Fled the years,
Till seventeen had found me tall and strong,
And fairer, runs it, than Athenian maids
Are wont to seem; I had not learnt it well –
My lesson of dumb patience – and I stood 50
At Life's great threshold with a beating heart,

And soul resolved to conquer and attain....
Once, walking 'thwart the crowded market place,
With other maidens, bearing in the twigs
White doves for Aphrodite's sacrifice,
I saw him, all ungainly and uncouth,
Yet many gathered round to hear his words,
Tall youths and stranger-maidens – Socrates –
I saw his face and marked it, half with awe,
Half with a quick repulsion at the shape......   60
The richest gem lies hidden furthest down,
And is the dearer for the weary search;
We grasp the shining shells which strew the shore,
Yet swift we fling them from us; but the gem
We keep for aye and cherish. So a soul,
Found after weary searching in the flesh
Which half repelled our senses, is more dear,
For that same seeking, than the sunny mind
Which lavish Nature marks with thousand hints
Upon a brow of beauty. We are prone   70
To overweigh such subtle hints, then deem,
In after disappointment, we are fooled......
And when, at length, my father told me all,
That I should wed me with great Socrates,
I, foolish, wept to see at once cast down
The maiden image of a future love,
Where perfect body matched the perfect soul.
But slowly, softly did I cease to weep;
Slowly I 'gan to mark the magic flash
Leap to the eyes, to watch the sudden smile   80
Break round the mouth, and linger in the eyes;
To listen for the voice's lightest tone –
Great voice, whose cunning modulations seemed
Like to the notes of some sweet instrument.
So did I reach and strain, until at last
I caught the soul athwart the grosser flesh.
Again of thee, sweet Hope, my spirit dreamed!
I, guided by his wisdom and his love,
Led by his words, and counselled by his care,
Should lift the shrouding veil from things which be,   90
And at the flowing fountain of his soul
Refresh my thirsting spirit......
                  And indeed,
In those long days which followed that strange day

When rites and song, and sacrifice and flow'rs,
Proclaimed that we were wedded, did I learn,
In sooth, a-many lessons; bitter ones
Which sorrow taught me, and not love inspired,
Which deeper knowledge of my kind impressed
With dark insistence on reluctant brain;-
But that great wisdom, deeper, which dispels   100
Narrowed conclusions of a half-grown mind,
And sees athwart the littleness of life
Nature's divineness and her harmony,
Was never poor Xantippe's......
                                        I would pause
And would recall no more, no more of life,
Than just the incomplete, imperfect dream
Of early summers, with their light and shade,
Their blossom-hopes, whose fruit was never ripe;
But something strong within me, some sad chord
Which loudly echoes to the later life,   110
Me to unfold the after-misery
Urges, with plaintive wailing in my heart.
Yet, maidens, mark; I would not that ye thought
I blame my lord departed, for he meant
No evil, so I take it, to his wife.
'Twas only that the high philosopher,
Pregnant with noble theories and great thoughts,
Deigned not to stoop to touch so slight a thing
As the fine fabric of a woman's brain –
So subtle as a passionate woman's soul.   120
I think, if he had stooped a little, and cared,
I might have risen nearer to his height,
And not lain shattered, neither fit for use
As goodly household vessel, nor for that
Far finer thing which I had hoped to be......
Death, holding high his retrospective lamp,
Shows me those first, far years of wedded life,
Ere I had learnt to grasp the barren shape
Of what the Fates had destined for my life.
Then, as all youthful spirits are, was I   130
Wholly incredulous that Nature meant
So little, who had promised me so much.
At first I fought my fate with gentle words,
With high endeavours after greater things;
Striving to win the soul of Socrates,

Like some slight bird, who sings her burning love
To human master, till at length she finds
Her tender language wholly misconceived,
And that same hand whose kind caress she sought,
With fingers flippant flings the careless corn...... 140
I do remember how, one summer's eve,
He, seated in an arbour's leafy shade,
Had bade me bring fresh wine-skins......

                    As I stood
Ling'ring upon the threshold, half concealed
By tender foliage, and my spirit light
With draughts of sunny weather, did I mark
An instant, the gay group before mine eyes.
Deepest in shade, and facing where I stood,
Sat Plato, with his calm face and low brows,
Which met above the narrow Grecian eyes; 150
The pale, thin lips just parted to the smile,
Which dimpled that smooth olive of his cheek.
His head a little bent, sat Socrates,
With one swart finger raised admonishing,
And on the air were borne his changing tones.
Low lounging at his feet, one fair arm thrown
Around his knee (the other, high in air
Brandished a brazen amphor, which yet rained
Bright drops of ruby on the golden locks
And temples with their fillets of the vine), 160
Lay Alcibiades the beautiful.
And thus, with solemn tone, spake Socrates:
'This fair Aspasia, which our Pericles
Hath brought from realms afar, and set on high
In our Athenian city, hath a mind,
I doubt not, of a strength beyond her race;
And makes employ of it, beyond the way
Of women nobly gifted: woman's frail –
Her body rarely stands the test of soul;
She grows intoxicate with knowledge; throws 170
The laws of custom, order, 'neath her feet,
Feasting at life's great banquet with wide throat.'
Then sudden, stepping from my leafy screen,
Holding the swelling wine-skin o'er my head,
With breast that heaved, and eyes and cheeks aflame,
Lit by a fury and a thought, I spake:

'By all great powers around us! can it be
That we poor women are empirical?
That gods who fashioned us did strive to make
Beings too fine, too subtly delicate, 180
With sense that thrilled response to ev'ry touch
Of nature's and their task is not complete?
That they have sent their half-completed work
To bleed and quiver here upon the earth?
To bleed and quiver, and to weep and weep,
To beat its soul against the marble walls
Of men's cold hearts, and then at last to sin!'
I ceased, the first hot passion stayed and stemmed
And frighted by the silence: I could see,
Framed by the arbour foliage, which the sun 190
In setting softly gilded with rich gold,
Those upturned faces, and those placid limbs;
Saw Plato's narrow eyes and niggard mouth,
Which half did smile and half did criticise,
One hand held up, the shapely fingers framed
To gesture of entreaty – 'Hush, I pray,
Do not disturb her; let us hear the rest;
Follow her mood, for here's another phase
Of your black-browed Xantippe......'
                                          Then I saw
Young Alcibiades, with laughing lips 200
And half-shut eyes, contemptuous shrugging up
Soft, snowy shoulders, till he brought the gold
Of flowing ringlets round about his breasts.
But Socrates, all slow and solemnly,
Raised, calm, his face to mine, and sudden spake:
'I thank thee for the wisdom which thy lips
Have thus let fall among us: prithee tell
From what high source, from what philosophies
Didst cull the sapient notion of thy words?'
Then stood I straight and silent for a breath, 210
Dumb, crushed with all that weight of cold contempt;
But swiftly in my bosom there uprose
A sudden flame, a merciful fury sent
To save me; with both angry hands I flung
The skin upon the marble, where it lay
Spouting red rills and fountains on the white;
Then, all unheeding faces, voices, eyes,
I fled across the threshold, hair unbound –

White garment stained to redness – beating heart
Flooded with all the flowing tide of hopes   220
Which once had gushed out golden, now sent back
Swift to their sources, never more to rise......
I think I could have borne the weary life,
The narrow life within the narrow walls,
If he had loved me; but he kept his love
For this Athenian city and her sons;
And, haply, for some stranger-woman, bold
With freedom, thought, and glib philosophy......
Ah, me! the long, long weeping through the nights,
The weary watching for the pale-eyed dawn   230
Which only brought fresh grieving: then I grew
Fiercer, and cursed from out my inmost heart
The Fates which marked me an Athenian maid.
Then faded that vain fury; hope died out;
A huge despair was stealing on my soul,
A sort of fierce acceptance of my fate, –
He wished a household vessel – well! 'twas good,
For he should have it! He should have no more
The yearning treasure of a woman's love,
But just the baser treasure which he sought.   240
I called my maidens, ordered out the loom,
And spun unceasing from the morn till eve;
Watching all keenly over warp and woof,
Weighing the white wool with a jealous hand.
I spun until, methinks, I spun away
The soul from out my body, the high thoughts
From out my spirit; till at last I grew
As ye have known me, – eye exact to mark
The texture of the spinning; ear all keen
For aimless talking when the moon is up,   250
And ye should be a-sleeping; tongue to cut
With quick incision, 'thwart the merry words
Of idle maidens......
                          Only yesterday
My hands did cease from spinning; I have wrought
My dreary duties, patient till the last.
The gods reward me! Nay, I will not tell
The after years of sorrow; wretched strife
With grimmest foes – sad Want and Poverty; –
Nor yet the time of horror, when they bore
My husband from the threshold; nay, nor when   260

355

The subtle weed had wrought its deadly work.
Alas! alas! I was not there to soothe
The last great moment; never any thought
Of her that loved him – save at least the charge,
All earthly, that her body should not starve......
You weep, you weep; I would not that ye wept,
Such tears are idle; with the young, such grief
Soon grows to gratulation, as, 'her love
Was withered by misfortune; mine shall grow
All nurtured by the loving,' or, 'her life   270
Was wrecked and shattered – mine shall smoothly sail.'
Enough, enough. In vain, in vain, in vain!
The gods forgive me! Sorely have I sinned
In all my life. A fairer fate befall
You all that stand there......
                            Ha! the dawn has come;
I see a rosy glimmer – nay! it grows dark;
Why stand ye so in silence? throw it wide,
The casement, quick; why tarry? – give me air –
O fling it wide, I say, and give me light!

Title: *Xantippe*, as the wife of Socrates, had a reputation for being ill-humoured and
shrewish. One view supposed that Socrates married her to use her impertinence as a
test for his patience. Here, Amy Levy allows her to tell her own story. 55 *Aphrodite:* in
Greek mythology, the goddess of love and fertility. 158 *amphor:* a Greek two-handled
vessel. 161 *Alcibiades:* nephew of Pericles, who was educated by Socrates and, later,
became a famous Athenian general. 163 *Aspasia:* famous for her personal charms,
Aspasia taught eloquence in Athens and Socrates was proud to be her scholar. Pericles
of Athens was formerly her pupil. She later became his mistress, and then his wife.

At a Dinner Party

With fruit and flowers the board is decked,
   The wine and laughter flow;
I'll not complain – could one expect
   So dull a world to know?

You look across the fruit and flowers,
   My glance your glances find. –
It is our secret, only ours,
   Since all the world is blind.

MARY COLERIDGE

1861-1907

Mary Elizabeth Coleridge was the great-great niece of Samuel Taylor Coleridge and Sara Coleridge was her great aunt. Tennyson, Browning, Millais and Ruskin were family friends. Mary was educated at home in London and learnt French, Italian, German, Greek and Hebrew. She also studied the works of Renaissance dramatists in the British Museum, travelled in Europe, and painted. She taught at the Working Women's College from 1895 to 1907. Mary wrote poetry from a young age and is now best remembered for it, but she started her publishing career with articles and a novel, *The Seven Sleepers of Ephesus* (1893). Her second novel, *The King with Two Faces* (1897), based on King Gustav III of Sweden, brought her recognition. Mary completed five novels, many critical essays, including a collection, *Non Sequitur* (1900), and a life of Holman Hunt (1908). Her first volume of poetry, *Fancy's Following*, appeared in 1896 under the pseudonym 'Anodos', meaning 'Wanderer'. An enlarged edition came out as *Fancy's Guerdon* in 1897. She died at Harrogate, apparently of appendicitis, and her collected poems were published posthumously, in 1908, edited by Henry Newbolt.

To Memory

Strange Power, I know not what thou art,
Murderer or mistress of my heart.
I know I'd rather meet the blow
Of my most unrelenting foe
Than live – as now I live – to be
Slain twenty times a day by thee.

Yet, when I would command thee hence,
Thou mockest at the vain pretence,
Murmuring in mine ear a song
Once loved, alas! forgotten long;
And on my brow I feel a kiss
That I would rather die than miss.

Not Yet

Time brought me many another friend
    That loved me longer.
New love was kind, but in the end
    Old love was stronger.

Years come and go. No New Year yet
Hath slain December.
And all that should have cried – 'Forget!'
Cries but – 'Remember!'

The White Women

Where dwell the lovely, wild white women folk,
    Mortal to man?
They never bowed their necks beneath the yoke,
They dwelt alone when the first morning broke
    And Time began.

Taller are they than man, and very fair,
    Their cheeks are pale,
At sight of them the tiger in his lair,
The falcon hanging in the azure air,
    The eagles quail.

The deadly shafts their nervous hands let fly
    Are stronger than our strongest – in their form
Larger, more beauteous, carved amazingly,
And when they fight, the wild white women cry
    The war-cry of the storm.

Their words are not as ours. If man might go
    Among the waves of Ocean when they break
And hear them – hear the language of the snow
Falling on torrents – he might also know
    The tongue they speak.

Pure are they as the light; they never sinned,
    But when the rays of the eternal fire
Kindle the West, their tresses they unbind
And fling their girdles to the Western wind,
    Swept by desire.

Lo, maidens to the maidens then are born,
    Strong children of the maidens and the breeze,
Dreams are not – in the glory of the morn,
Seen through the gates of ivory and horn –
    More fair than these.

358

And none may find their dwelling. In the shade
Primeval of the forest oaks they hide.
One of our race, lost in an awful glade,
Saw with his human eyes a wild white maid,
And gazing, died.

Title: Newbolt notes that the poem is 'from a legend of Malay, told by Hugh Clifford'.

EMILY PAULINE JOHNSON
(Tekahionwake)
1861-1913

Born on the Six Nation reserve in Brant county, Ontario, Emily Pauline Johnson
was one of four children of a Mohawk chief and a Bristol-born English Quaker,
who had emigrated as a child. She had limited formal schooling but read widely,
encouraged by her mother – especially English poetry. When her father died
in 1884 she wrote for financial support and, in 1892, a dramatised reading of
her native heritage poems proved so successful that she began a career as a
public performer, reviving her great-grandfather's name, Tekahionwake. Her
first volume, *The White Wampum*, from which the following are taken, was
published in London in 1895 after a popular run of performances in the cap-
ital's society drawing rooms the previous summer. She came back to England
in 1906 and 1907, and also toured Canada and the United States, performing in
both evening and native dress. An expert canoeist, she had a wide knowledge
of native culture, though she has been criticised for perpetuating the stereo-
types of her age. Ill-health forced her to retire to Vancouver in 1909. Her other
publications include: *Canadian Born* (1903), *Legends of Vancouver* (1911), *Flint
and Feather* (1912), and a collection of adventure stories, *The Shagganappi*
(1913). Another collection, *The Moccasin Maker*, appeared after her death.

Ojistoh

I am Ojistoh, I am she, the wife
Of him whose name breathes bravery and life
And courage to the tribe that calls him chief.
I am Ojistoh, his white star, and he
Is land, and lake, and sky – and soul to me.

Ah! but they hated him, those Huron braves,
Him who had flung their warriors into graves,
Him who had crushed them underneath his heel,
Whose arm was iron, and whose heart was steel
To all – save me, Ojistoh, chosen wife
Of my great Mohawk, white star of his life.

Ah! but they hated him, and councilled long
With subtle witchcraft how to work him wrong;
How to avenge their dead, and strike him where
His pride was highest, and his fame most fair.
Their hearts grew weak as women at his name:
They dared no war-path since my Mohawk came
With ashen bow, and flinten arrow-head
To pierce their craven bodies; but their dead
Must be avenged. Avenged? They dared not walk
In day and meet his deadly tomahawk;
They dared not face his fearless scalping knife;
So – Niyoh! – then they thought of me, his wife.

O! evil, evil face of them they sent
With evil Huron speech: 'Would I consent
To take of wealth? be queen of all their tribe?
Have wampum ermine?' Back I flung the bribe
Into their teeth, and said, 'While I have life
Know this – Ojistoh is the Mohawk's wife.'

Wah! how we struggled! But their arms were strong.
They flung me on their pony's back, with thong
Round ankle, wrist, and shoulder. Then upleapt
The one I hated most: his eye he swept
Over my misery, and sneering said,
'Thus, fair Ojistoh, we avenge our dead.'

And we two rode, rode as a sea wind-chased,
I, bound with buckskin to his hated waist,
He, sneering, laughing, jeering, while he lashed
The horse to foam, as on and on we dashed.
Plunging through creek and river, bush and trail,
On, on we galloped like a northern gale.
At last, his distant Huron fires aflame
We saw, and nearer, nearer still we came.

I, bound behind him in the captive's place,
Scarcely could see the outline of his face.
I smiled, and laid my cheek against his back:
'Loose thou my hands,' I said. 'This pace let slack.
Forget we now that thou and I are foes.
I like thee well, and wish to clasp thee close;
I like the courage of thine eye and brow;
I like thee better than my Mohawk now.'

He cut the cords; we ceased our maddened haste.
I wound my arms about his tawny waist;
My hand crept up the buckskin of his belt;
His knife hilt in my burning palm I felt;
One hand caressed his cheek, the other drew
The weapon softly – 'I love you, love you,'
I whispered, 'love you as my life.'
And – buried in his back his scalping knife.

Ha! how I rode, rode as a sea wind-chased,
Mad with sudden freedom, mad with haste,
Back to my Mohawk and my home, I lashed
That horse to foam, as on and on I dashed.
Plunging thro' creek and river, bush and trail,
On, on I galloped like a northern gale.
And then my distant Mohawk's fires aflame
I saw, as nearer, nearer still I came,
My hands all wet, stained with a life's red dye,
But pure my soul, pure as those stars on high –
'My Mohawk's pure white star, Ojistoh, still am I.'

23 *Niyoh:* 'God, in the Mohawk language' [author's note].

In the Shadows

I am sailing to the leeward,
Where the current runs to seaward
    Soft and slow,
Where the sleeping river grasses
Brush my paddle as it passes
    To and fro.

On the shore the heat is shaking
All the golden sands awaking
    In the cove;
And the quaint sand-piper, winging
O'er the shallows, ceases singing
    When I move.

On the water's idle pillow
Sleeps the overhanging willow,
    Green and cool;

Where the rushes lift their burnished
Oval heads from out the tarnished
　　Emerald pool.

Where the very silence slumbers,
Water lilies grow in numbers,
　　Pure and pale;
All the morning they have rested,
Amber crowned, and pearly crested,
　　Fair and frail.

Here impossible romances,
Indefinable sweet fancies,
　　Cluster round;
But they do not mar the sweetness
Of this still September fleetness
　　With a sound.

I can scarce discern the meeting
Of the shore and stream retreating,
　　So remote;
For the laggard river, dozing,
Only wakes from its reposing
　　Where I float.

Where the river mists are rising,
All the foliage baptizing
　　With their spray;
There the sun gleams far and faintly,
With a shadow soft and saintly,
　　In its ray.

And the perfume of some burning
Far-off brushwood, ever turning
　　To exhale
All its smoky fragrance dying,
In the arms of evening lying,
　　Where I sail.

My canoe is growing lazy,
In the atmosphere so hazy,
　　While I dream;
Half in slumber I am guiding,
Eastward indistinctly gliding
　　Down the stream.

LOUISE IMOGEN GUINEY

1861-1920

Born in Roxbury, Massachusetts, into an Irish Catholic family, Louise Imogen
Guiney began writing in an attempt to support herself and her mother after
her father's death in 1877. In 1894, when her writing was insufficiently profit-
able, she became postmistress of Auburndale, but was forced to resign three
years and two breakdowns later, due to anti-Catholic, anti-Irish reactions in the
community. She continued to write whilst working in Boston Public Library
(1899-1901) and, although she received a degree of recognition, her work was
not very popular. Louise always had to struggle. Having travelled in Europe
and Britain, she settled in Oxford in 1901. A poet and critic, her publications
include: *Songs at the Start* (1884), *The White Sail* (1887), from which 'The
Water-text' is taken, *A Roadside Harp* (1893), *Oxford and London: XXIV
Sonnets* (1895), *The Martyrs' Idyl and Shorter Poems* (1899) – which contains
the text of 'Deo Optimo Maximo' – and *Happy Ending: The Collected Lyrics
of Louise Imogen Guiney* (1909). She died in poverty at Chipping Campden,
Gloucestershire.

The Water-Text

Watching my river marching overland,
By mighty tides transfigured and set free, –
My river, lapped in idle-hearted mirth,
Made at a touch a glory to the earth,
And leaving, wheresoever falls his hand,
The balm and benediction of the sea, –

O soon, I know, the hour whereof we dreamed,
The saving hour miraculous, arrives!
When, ere to darkness winds our sordid course,
Some glad, new, potent, concecrating force
Shall speed us, so uplifted, so redeemed,
Along the old worn channel of our lives.

Deo Optimo Maximo

All else for use, one only for desire;
Thanksgiving for the good, but thirst for Thee:
Up from the best, whereof no man need tire,
Impel thou me.

Delight is menace, if Thou brood not by,
Power is a quicksand, Fame a gathering jeer.

Oft as the morn, (thou none of earth deny
These three are dear),

Wash me of them, that I may be renewed,
Nor wall in clay mine agonies and joys:
O close my hand upon Beatitude!
Not on her toys.

Title: the motto of the Benedictine religious order: 'For God the best and greatest'.

MAY KENDALL
1861-1943

Born Emma Goldworth Kendall, in Bridlington, Yorkshire, May first collab-
orated with Andrew Lang to produce *That Very Mab* (1885), a collection of
satirical essays and poems. She wrote three novels, including *Such is Life* (1889),
and published two volumes of poetry, *Dreams to Sell* (1887) and *Songs from
Dreamland* (1894). She worked for B. Seebohm Rowntree in York for many
years as a researcher and writer. She also published essays and poems in
Quaker journals, such as *The Friend*. May lived in Monkgate, York and is
buried in an unmarked grave in the city cemetery.

Woman's Future

Complacent they tell us, hard hearts and derisive,
    In vain is our ardour: in vain are our sighs:
Our intellects, bound by a limit decisive,
    To the level of Homer's may never arise.
We heed not the falsehood, the base innuendo,
    The laws of the universe, these are our friends.
Our talents shall rise in a mighty crescendo,
    We trust Evolution to make us amends!

But ah, when I ask you for food that is mental,
    My sisters, you offer me ices and tea!
You cherish the fleeting, the mere accidental,
    At cost of the True, the Intrinsic, the Free.
Your feelings, compressedin Society's mangle,
    Are vapid and frivolous, pallid and mean.
To slander you love; but you don't care to wrangle:
    You bow to Decorum, and cherish Routine.

Alas, is it woolwork you take for your mission,
Or Art that your fingers so gaily attack?
Can patchwork atone for the mind's inanition?
Can the soul, oh my sisters, be fed on a *plaque*?
Is this your vocation? My goal is another,
And empty and vain is the end you pursue.
In antimacassars the world you may smother;
But intellect marches o'er them and o'er you.

On Fashion's vagaries your energies strewing,
Devoting your days to a rug or a screen,
Oh, rouse to a life work – do something worth doing!
Invent a new planet, a flying-machine.
Mere charms superficial, mere feminine graces,
That fade or that flourish, no more you may prize;
But the knowledge of Newton will beam from your faces,
The soul of a Spencer will shine in your eyes.

ENVOY
Though jealous exclusion may tremble to own us,
Oh, wait for the time when our brains shall expand!
When once we're enthroned, you shall never dethrone us –
The poets, the sages, the seers of the land!

JESSIE MACKAY

1864-1938

Jessie Mackay was born on a sheep station near the Rakaia Gorge, Canterbury, New Zealand. She was educated at home and in Christchurch, where she trained as a teacher. She taught for many years with an interlude as a journalist in Dunedin between 1898 and 1902, and returned to journalism in 1904, when her health prevented her from teaching. Jessie was a columnist for the *Otago Witness* for 30 years and became an editor of the *Canterbury Times* after 1906. She never married. A supporter of women's suffrage and feminist concerns, she also campaigned for other causes, including temperance and penal reform. Of Scottish descent, she believed in home rule for Scotland and Ireland and visited these countries in 1921, along with England and Europe. She valued Maori culture, retold Maori mythology in her poetry, and focused on issues of social justice in relation to New Zealand life and opportunities for women. Her first volume of poetry, *The Spirit of the Rangatira and Other Poems* (from which the following satire is taken) was published in Melbourne in 1889, and *The Sitter on the Rail and Other Poems*, in 1891. *From the Maori Sea* appeared in 1908, *Land of the Morning*, in 1909, *The Bride of the Rivers and Other Verses*, in 1926, and *Vigil*, in 1935. The poet, Blanche Baughan, was her close friend.

The Charge at Parihaka

Yet a league, yet a league
    Yet a league onward,
Straight to the Maori Pah
    Marched the Twelve Hundred.
'Forward the Volunteers!
Is there a man who fears?'
Over the ferny plain
    Marched the Twelve Hundred!

'Forward!' the Colonel said;
Was there a man dismayed?
No, for the heroes knew
    There was no danger.
Theirs not to reckon why,
Theirs not to bleed or die,
Theirs but to trample by:
    Each dauntless ranger.

Pressmen to right of them.
Pressmen to left of them,
Pressmen in front of them,
    Chuckled and wondered.
Dreading their country's eyes,
Long was the search and wise,
Vain, for the pressmen five
Had, by a slight device,
    Foiled the Twelve Hundred.

Gleamed all their muskets bare,
Fright'ning the children there,
Heroes to do and dare,
Charging a village, while
    Maoridom wondered.
Plunged in potato fields,
Honour to hunger yields.
Te Whiti and Tohu
Bearing not swords or shields,
Questioned nor wondered,
Calmly before them sat;
    Faced the Twelve Hundred.

20

Children to right of them,
Children to left of them,
Women in front of them,   40
    Saw them and wondered;
Stormed at with jeer and groan,
Foiled by the five alone,
Never was trumpet blown
    O'er such a deed of arms.
Back with their captives three
Taken so gallantly,
    Rode the Twelve Hundred.

When can their glory fade?
Oh! The wild charge they made,
    New Zealand wondered
Whether each doughty soul,
Paid for the pigs he stole:
    Noble Twelve Hundred!

Title: In November 1881 over a thousand New Zealand colonial government troops
marched on the Maori settlement, Parihaka, to capture leaders Te Whiti O Rongomai
and Tohu Kakahi. Both preached non-violent resistance and believed in peaceful co-
habitation with the Europeans, provided Maori land ownership was respected. No Maori
took up arms: their leaders were taken prisoner and later exiled until 1883. Many others
were imprisoned and never returned. The peaceful settlement was plundered and des-
troyed. This poem parodies Tennyson's 'The Charge of the Light Brigade' and was set
to music for a choir in 1994 (commissioned by the Australian Song Company). 3 *Pah:*
originally a native fort, then a Maori village. 27 *children:* the soldiers were met by sing-
ing children.

DORA SIGERSON (*later* Shorter)
1866–1918

Dora Sigerson was born in Dublin. Her mother wrote poetry and fiction and
her father was a historian and translator of Irish poetry. In 1895 she married
the critic and editor, Clement Shorter, and moved to London. Having con-
tributed many poems to journals in Britain and America, her first volume,
Verses, was published in 1893. A prolific writer, particularly praised for her
ballads, her other titles include *The Fairy Changeling and Other Poems* (1897),
My Lady's Slipper and Other Poems (1898), *Ballads and Poems* (1899), from
which 'Ireland' is taken, *The Woman Who Went to Hell, and Other Ballads and
Lyrics* (1902), *Collected Poems* (1907), *New Poems* (1912), and *Love of Ireland,
Poems and Ballads* (1916). A friend of Katharine Tynan, Alice Furlong and
W.B. Yeats, Dora was deeply affected by the political events of Easter 1916
and the subsequent executions.

Ireland

'Twas the dream of a God,
　　And the mould of His hand,
That you shook 'neath His stroke,
That you trembled and broke
　　To this beautiful land.

Here He loosed from His hand
　　A brown tumult of wings,
Till the wind on the sea
Bore the strange melody
　　Of an island that sings.

He made you all fair,
　　You in purple and gold,
You in silver and green,
Till no eye that has seen
　　Without love can behold.

I have left you behind
　　In the path of the past,
With the white breath of flowers,
With the best of God's hours,
　　I have left you at last.

MARY COLBORNE-VEEL
1863–1923

Mary Caroline Colborne-Veel was born in Christchurch, New Zealand. She was
educated at home and contributed poetry and essays to a variety of Australian,
English and other journals, including the *Canterbury Weekly Press*. Her poetry
collection, *The Fairest of the Angels and Other Verse*, from which the following
poem is taken, was published in London in 1894. *Poems and Prose* came out in
1898 and, in 1924, Jessie Mackay edited *A Little Anthology of Mary Colborne-
Veel*.

Her Secret

She moves sedate, through garden ways
　　Or ancient parlours cool and shady;
Content in quiet length of days,
　　A typical old maiden lady.

With soul as snowy as the lace
    That lappets o'er her faded tresses,
And sweet as violet's fragrant trace
    That haunts her quaintly fashioned dresses.
One single crime her heart within,
    In quiet hours of meditation
Must be confessed, a hidden sin
    To stir that soul to trepidation.

For when in maiden age one stands
    Left neither soured nor broken-hearted,
Tradition this at least demands! –
    Nor faithful to some long departed:
When midst the records of the years
    One finds no sign to sorrow over;
No yellowing letters stained with tears,
    No least remembrance of a lover!
Hidden in sacredness apart,
    No withering blossoms loved and guarded –
What wonder that the saintliest heart
    Should feel the slightest bit defrauded?

Dear is the ancient maiden dame
    To maiden belles of modern dances;
And girlish fantasies they frame
    Of long-past, ever-fresh romances.
And if they deem such history
    She treasures, safe from rash intrusion –
She would not tell the whitest lie,
    Yet still, she fosters the delusion.
A smile, a sigh, is all they ask
    To furnish hints for fancy's weaving;
She takes her tender soul to task
    For such unparalleled deceiving!

'What changed her fate? and how, and when?'
    'What crossing chanced of love and duty?'
'She scarce was wondrous fair, but then,
    Is every married dame a beauty?'
'Tis strange how brightest maids will love
    A passing woefulness to borrow:
They treasure happier thoughts above,
    This mystery of secret sorrow.

Their hearts are fluttering to condole
With grief such tenderest pity moving –
And she a gentle lonely soul,
That no one ever thought of loving!

BLANCHE BAUGHAN
1870–1958

Blanche Edith Baughan was born in Putney, Surrey, the youngest of six chil-
dren. She attended Royal Holloway College and was the first member of the
college to be awarded a first-class University of London honours degree in
Classics. Her social work in East London in the early 1890s indicated a concern
with the welfare of the poor, sick or imprisoned which was to last throughout
her life. Blanche also supported women's suffrage. She travelled to Germany,
Switzerland, Norway and Sweden, but returned to England to nurse her mother
and teach Greek. When she was about 30 she travelled to Wellington, New
Zealand, and later visited the Pacific islands and South Africa. She came back
to New Zealand to live at Hawke's Bay, Chorlton, and, from about 1910 to
1930, near Sumner, Christchurch. Between 1915 and 1922 Blanche visited
California, England, and India. In 1930 she moved to Akaroa, where she often
provided shelter for former prisoners and others in need. Her first two volumes
of poetry, *Verses* (1898) and *Reuben and Other Poems* (1903), were published in
London. From *Shingle-Short and other Verses* (1908), which includes *Maui's
Fish*, her writing was published in New Zealand. Other volumes include *Brown
Bread from a Colonial Oven* (1912), *Studies in New Zealand Scenery* (1916),
Glimpses of New Zealand Scenery (1922), *Poems from the Port Hills, Christchurch*
(1923), *Arthur's Pass and the Otira Gorge* (1925) and *People in Prison* (1936).

Maui's Fish
(After the Maori Legend)

Maui, the Fisher, would have gone fishing
In the canoe with the sons of his mother;
He had a thought in his head.
But these Brothers begrudged him.
'He is young and audacious', they grumbled, 'and wilful;
We are not too sure of his birth and his breeding;
His cunning is great, and his tricks are perdition;
What law does he follow? What reverence is his?
He will trick us, perchance he will wreck, peradventure may drown
    us –
He surely will scare us!' said they.   10
'Bide thou here', said these clever and cautious old brothers of Maui;
And forth on the broad breast of Ocean

370

Pushed the canoe, and were off
To their old fishing ground.

Maui the Fisher paced on the sea-beach,
Thinking...thinking...
Working the while at the fish-hook he held in his fingers:
A very old bone he was carving and fitting,
And paving its hollow with blue-and-green *paua*,
Paua, purple-and-blue in the sun as the shimmering water,   20
In the sea-water, bright as the sun.
'Can I sail in the sea-weed?' says Maui;
And a fine tuft of hair he set on it,
Thinking...thinking...
And twisted a stout line upon it –
And behold! there he ended his toil and his thinking together!
'Ha, ha, ha!' laughs Maui the Fisher,
And looks out to sea!

Late that night, when these Brothers, safe back from their fishing,
Wearied with toil, snug and rounded with supper,   30
Snored in the *wharé*,
Maui, the youngest, still hungry on purpose,
Alert and attentive – *Hush!*
Crept from the side of them – *Hush!*
From the warm *wharé* creeps out, to the darkness,
Out, to the cold, lonely beach:
Finds the canoe, and there, under the bottom-boards,
Ha! in he crawls, and lies close.
Huge is the night, and the loneliness gruesome and terrible,
Sharp howls the wind, the old Sea moans there over his shoulder –   40
As a widow, a mother, they wail, at a death, at a *tangi*;
And the Darkness was dreadful all round, a deep darkness of Death!
'Laugh, O my heart!' murmurs Maui,
And waits for the Dawn.

And at Dawn come his Brothers, intent on their old daily duty –
In their old fishing-ground to catch fish.
And they look to their tiller, they look to their paddles,
But, under those sound boards amidship, what need to examine?
(Aha!)
'Now, where is our Maui, our fisher of fishers, this morning?   50
Full belly, sound sleeper, is simply out-witted', they chuckle;
Then out on the laughing blue Ocean
Push forth their canoe, and are off

To their old fishing-ground –
To their old fishing-ground, indeed?
Maui is with them! Oho!

Paddle and paddle, paddle and paddle...
They had gone a long way,
To the first place for casting the hooks they were nearly arrived,
When Maui no more can keep silence. *Ho, ho! and Ha, ha!* –   60
Up pops his head at their horrified feet!
An earthquake! As huts in an earthquake,
Hither and thither they topple and tumble and sprawl.
Were they startled, those wary old Brothers? They nearly upset the canoe!
Were they vext? They were far from the land!
Now this way and that, as a *weka*, that peers for provision,
With faces wrath-wrinkled as mud-holes are wrinkled in summer,
They twisted their eyes and their necks, staying still on their paddles,
And piteously asked of each other:
'O Friends! What shall we do?   70
If we go on, and he with us', they said, 'he will surely upset us,
If we go back, it is far – and what fish for our supper?'
'Cast him out!' whispers one. 'If we do, by some craft he will catch us –
Remember the noosing of *Ra*', they reply, 'Remember the Theft of the Fire
(Fire, like Maui, perturbing and mischievous: true, 'tis a relish to fish) –
Who is safe from him? What shall we do?'
So they toss back and forth in the unsteady hold of their purpose,
Like river-waves, reaching the sea, but the tide flooding in.

Well, now, Maui had pity upon them.
'Let me paddle', says Maui, 'or steer!'   80
But Oh, no, no, no!
'If he paddle', say they, 'we are dead! he will surely capsize us;
If he steer, – we are wrecked on some rock;
If we go on, misadventures are bound to befall us;
Back – one is fallen already, since where are our fish?
And, drowned – alas, he would drown us!'
So, like men out at sea without paddles, they toss in a torment.
Till Maui had pity upon them again, and he said,
'Lo, in your confusion but now, how the waves were splashed over!
Keep me – to bale the canoe'.   90
Then speechless they sat, looking one at the rest,
Till one hopefully said,
'Well, he cannot do much with a baler!'
So then, o'er the bright lips of Ocean, up-bursting with laughter,

These Brothers went cautiously steering and paddling,
While Maui (a shell was his baler),
Baled out the canoe.

Now, pay attention! Behold,
Every shellful he baled from the boat, lo it was but a shellful,
Till, throwing it over, he stretched it- no longer mere shellfuls,   100
Murmuring *karakias*, secretly chanting enchantments,
Seas! he threw seas overboard.
The water spread...spread..., the land faded, faded...and faded...
'Hold! Stop!' cried the Brothers. 'Where are we?
Far, far past our fishing-ground! Put back, and quickly!' they cry.
'Ah, not yet!' Maui pleads, 'O my Brothers, a little way further!
I know of a place where the fish are as fern in the forest,
So many! and fat as fat pigeons, and sweeter than berry-fed pigeons,
        those fish!
Let us on!' And his tongue was of oil, and his words as a feast in the
        cooking;
(He knew what they wished) and their ears and their hearts were
        bemused.   110
On, onward they went:
Paddle and paddle, paddle and paddle and paddle...
The Sun looking on from the North, and Maui still baling and baling.
Till once more spake the Brothers:
'No man hath fished here since the days of our fathers; here anchor!'
'Not yet, Ah, not yet!' Maui said; 'A canoe's length, a little way further!
Ah, Brothers, those fish! So immense
That one piece of one fish will most nobly provide for our supper,
So bold, they will race to the hook, and two castings will fill us,
The wink of an eye see us full'.   120
Aha! Bright was his bait, and he knew what he wanted,
By the ear and the stomach he caught them, these Brothers, these fish!

Paddle on, paddle on, paddle on...
Now the land is gone from their gaze;
To the edge of the world they are come!
Now the Sea was their world,
And the Sun from the opposite side looked upon them,
He looked from the West, and their spirits grew dark,
Their hearts rolled in their breasts!
'Never man can have fished here before. Let us anchor!' they pleaded;   130
And Maui said, 'Anchor and fish!'
For he knew where he was, and he knew he was where he would be.

373

Oh! Oh, those fish!...Enough! It was even as he said –
So many! so large! and they surely desired to get eaten!
Lo! At the cast of the hook, how they came flocking, and flocking!
Two castings apiece, and behold! the canoe, it was full!
Great then were the hearts of these Brothers! They said,
'It is well! And now let us for home.'
But Maui said humbly, 'O Brothers!
Here is one without fish. Behold, I have had neither share of the sport
      or the spoil.   140
Lend me a hook, O Brother! – Brother! Lend me thy hook'
(To one and another he said it). But they taunted him, all, and refused.
'Fishers have hooks, not the maggot that hides in the timber.'
'Canst thou fish with a hook, little Trickster, indeed? but try fishing without!'
'Yet will I fish, answers Maui, and lo! lo! the wonder.
They murmur admiring, in envy they muse, and amazement,
As he draws from his mat the carved fish-hook,
The jaw-bone well carved of his heroine ancestress.
Bright in the sunlight the *paua* that lined it,
The hair that adorned it waved bright in the wind.   150
'Ha, ha, ha!' laughs Maui the Fisher,
The Sun and the Sea also laugh, when they look on that hook!
But – where was the bait?
'Oh my Brothers', says Maui, 'Behold
To what catch I encouraged you hither!
Can we verily take it all home? See the gunwale, how low in the water!
Spare me, spare me one morsel of all these great fish of your fishing
For bait to my hook.'
But they jeered in delight: 'Aha! So art thou caught, little *Pipi*?
O friend! What is the use of fine fish-hooks, and ever so fine,   160
Without bait?' And they gave him no bait.

So then Maui bethought him.
He smote on his nostril. The blood of his head ran out, copious and
      living –
With his blood he baited his hook.
And, now laughing no longer, but grave, and firm of attention,
He casts the hook into the Sea.
'Prosper it, O Tangaroa!'
And Tangaroa,
Lord of the deep and the surface,
Lurer to enterprise, lover of daring adventure,   170
Heard!
    A bite! A bite!

Lift it! Pull! Pull!
Oh, the weight!
Hold, hook of noble extraction! Hold, trustworthy well-twisted line!
Tug! Pull, pull!
A rock! 'Tis a rock thou hast cleverly caught', cry the Brothers –
No! for in comes the line...in...in...
''Tis a whale. This great Maui! so mighty, no lesser fish suits him.
The water is troubled; I said if he came, so would grief.'   180
And truly the water was troubled, a wave struck the side,
The sun sank, it grew chilly and dark.
'The old ground was good. We were fools to have ventured beyond it –
Give up, Maui! Let us go home.'
His back is bent, his muscles are tautened,
Sweat pours in the Sea....Pull! Pull!
'A *taniwha*, surely! Some terrible monster has caught us!
Give over!' He would not. Pull! Pull!
Then, 'Over with *him*!' – urges one, but the rest were afraid.
'Cut his line!' But they could not: it held.   190

And now the waves bubble and gurgle indeed!
A storm he is raising, this fish!
Splash! Now the water foams into the boat – Now the Brothers must
      bale her,
Maui the Fisher would fish.

...Oh, the swirl and the tumult! Oh, waves, like great ridges and gullies!
Like a bladder of kelp, rooted firm there below, like a kite of the waves,
The canoe jerks and staggers. Bale! Bale!
Bale!....All the fish must go out!
Ah, sweet food! Ah, the horrible tricks of this mischievous Maui!
Ah, the huge billows bursting... Bale! Bale...   200
– Darkness, tumult and storm,
Thus all the night through, baled they and bellowed they,
All the night through, Maui fought with his fish.

Toward the Dawn,
Lo, a Sea of thick shining! Behold the thick waves of great fishes!
This way and that way darting and shooting in masses,
Anxious, in haste to escape.
What is lifting them? *Pull!*
What is under them? *Pull!*...
The first beam strikes on the water...   210
The Brothers rub at their eyes... *O pull!*
Pull! What is this that they see?

375

Thro' the waves, flashing!
To the light, flashing!
Bright, bright up-bursting, startling the light. –
Oh, the sharp spears and spikes! Oh, the sparkle of summits of crystal,
    Springing up, up!

'Tongariro! O Taranaki,
Your splendour! Your shooting of spear-points, keen, sea-wet, to the sun!
Ruapehu, Kaikoura, Aorangi, Tara-rua, long-armed Ruahine! –   220
Midsummer clouds, curling luminous up from the sky-line:
Far-fallen islands of light, summoned back to the sun:
Soaring *Kahawai-birds* –
How ye soared, shining pinions! straight into the heaven high above you:
How ye shot up, bright Surprises! seizing, possessing the sky:
How firm, great white Clouds, ye took seat!

Pull, Maui! Pull!
For what follows, beneath them?
A waving, a waving and weaving of light and of darkness –
A waving of hands and of hair in the dance!   230
Lo, is it a garden of kelp?
Is it Night, coming up from the deep, up through fold upon fold of the Sea?
Pull!
Behold, it approaches! it darkens, it pierces the water – Lo! Lo!
Tree-tops! Lo, waving of branches! Lo, mosses and fern of the forest!
– How sweet on the salt came the breath of the forest, that summer sea-
    morning!
Sweet on the spacious silence the ring of the Tui's rich throat!
Kauri and *Totara*, *Rimu*, and *Matai* and *Maire*,
Red-as-blood *Rata*, and bright-as-blood *Pohutu-kawa*,
Manuka dark-eyed, Convolvulus, Clematis star-eyed –   240
The glittering of you that morning! fresh, dripping with dews of the Ocean,
New rays to the young, early sun!
The host of your *taua*, addressed as to fight! Of your lances and *meres* of
    green-stone,
Bristling all suddenly upward, lustrously tossing in glory,
A green sea, high in the air!

Pull on! Pull away!
I see shining and shining below here.
Is there a Sun in the Sea? a young Sky in the water?
A Sea, deep in Sea?
Or is a great paua-shell, empty, vividly variegated,   250

Shadow playing with shine, blue and green in the arms of each other,
As they lie on the lap of the Sea?
Lo! it nears! it arrives! on the face of the water it floats –
Land – Ho! Land!
Yea, sparkling with freshness, audacious with newness, laughing with light,
Land! a young Land from the Sea!
A dark land, of forest; a bright land, of sky and of summits,
Of tussock sun-gilded, of headlands proclaiming the sun:
Tattooed with blue – behold Waikato! lo Wanganui!
Eyed with quick eyes –Wakatipu, and over there Taupo: 260
Plumed with sky-feathers, with clouds and with snow: begirt with the
    mat of the Ocean
Bordered with foam, with fine fringes of sand, with breast-jewels of
    clear-coloured pebbles:–
Up it sprang, out it burst from the folds of the foam, out it stood,
Bare-bright on the jewel-bright Sea:–
A new Land!

There it stood!
And the Sea, now at rest, laid her down with her arms round about it,
Thrusting the tongue and the touches of love 'gainst the limbs of the
    living,
Caressing her newly-born, laughing and singing for joy.
And, up-coiling his line, disentangling his fish-hook, now Maui laughed
    also –   270
'Ha, ha, ha!' laughed Maui the Fisher,
'Behold, I have caught me a Fish!'
Enough – Even so!
With a hook of the Dead, with a bait of the Living,
With the thought of his head, with the blood of his body, the sweat of
    his heart,
With pangs and with laughter, with labour and loss.
He truly had caught him a fish – the canoe was aground –
O Te Ika a Maui – The Fish!

But turn now your eyes on those worthy, wise Brothers of Maui, –
With grimaces nibbling their faces, with eyes and with mouths round
    as sea-eggs,   280
They squat on their haunches, stuck still:
Dumb as heads in the old days held fast in the mouth of the oven,
Dumb as fish, – who would ever have thought it?
But hear now their guile!

'O my Brothers', said Maui,
'Meet is it I go with thank-offerings to thank Tangaroa –
Tangaroa, who gave me this fish:
Rangi also, and Tawhiri-matea, who hid it below.
But abide till I come!' he besought them with earnest persuasions,
'Till these gods are bespoken, with hand or with foot,   290
O defile not my Fish!
When I come, I will portion it all'. So he went.
But what then said these Brothers?
Aha! As the *kotare*, perched and asleep, hears the fish-rippled water,
      and straightway awakes,
They awoke!
'Who is Maui?' said they 'who that babe, with his portion, and portion?
What wits he of division? What recks he of custom, time-honoured?
What does a young man know?
His fish! Was it not *our* canoe?
Come!' They trampled his words underfoot, and leapt out on the
      beaches.   300
'This my land!' shouted one, and he set up his paddle upon it,
'This to me!' 'This to me!' cried they all;
They wrangled and strove.
But the land, this *Te Ika a Maui*,
Beholding their impudence, seeing their greed and their quarrel,
Laughed – for they were not her master –
Laughed! Lo, she wrinkled her skin, shook her sides, laughed wide
      with her lips...
'Ha, ha!' and 'Ha, ha!'....
Till Maui, returning, instead of a smooth land, and Brothers in waiting,
Found this fellow, sprawled on the top of a sudden-reared mountain: 310
That, deep in a gully new-cloven: this other, head-first in a swamp;
And all abashed and ashamed.
Louder then laughed Maui the Fisher.
'Ha, ha! Well done, the land!'
Ha, Tangaroa, well done!
My Fish, my Fish, is alive!'

      This is the tale of the Fishing of Maui,
      Of the birth of New Zealand, *Te Ika a Maui*,
      Hear yet!
      I speak but one little word more.   320

   Still alive is that Fish!
Here, on the edge of the world, on the rim of the morning,

378

She stands, Tangaroa's dear daughter, a vigorous virgin,
Fresh from the foam.
Still the daylight is young in her eyelids, and on her full forehead;
Her brown limbs gleam from the bath,
Dew is yet in her wind-tossing hair.
The wild winds are her walls, and she stands here, untamed as sea-water,
Brave with the heart of the Ocean, sweet with the heart of the Sun.
Ay!   330
A sea-wind for freshness, a sea-wave for brightness,
A sea-sunrise for beauty, a strong sea for strength,
Here she stands, Maui's Fish, here she shines, a new Land from the Ocean,
Alive 'mid the ever-live Sea.

Alive! Yea, Te Ika –
Of the Bone of the Past, of the Blood of the Present,
Here, at the end of the earth, is the first of the Future,
Thou standest, courageous and youthful, a country to come!
Lo, thou art not defiled with the dust of the Dead, nor beclouded with
          thick clouds of Custom:
But, springs and quick sources of life all about thee, within thee,   340
Splendid with freshness, radiant with vigour, conspicuous with hope,
Like a beacon thou beckonest back o-er the waters, away o-er the world:
The while, looking ahead with clear eyes,
Like Maui, thou laugh'st, full of life!

And do not regard overmuch
Those tedious old Brothers, that still must be pribbling and prabbling
          about thee
(Paddlers inshore: when a Maui has fished, then they claim the canoe!)...
Laugh at them, Land!
They are old: are they therefore so wise?
Thou art young, Te Ika: be young!   350
Thou art new: be thou new!
With keen sight, with fresh forces, appraise those old grounds of their
          vaunting,
Dip in deep dew of thy seas what swims yet of their catch, and renew it, –
The rest, fish very long caught,
Toss it to them!
And address thee to catches to come.
Rich hauls to bold fishers, new sights to new sight, a new world to new eyes,
To discoverers, discoveries! Yea,
Offspring of Maui! recall the experience of Maui
A dead fish he did not receive it? No, No!   360

He endured, he adventured, he went forth, he experimented,
He found and he fetched it, alive!

Yea, alive! a Fish to give thanks for.
Ah, ah, Tangaroa, well done!
Thou livest, Te Ika a Maui!
Enough! My last word:–
Live! Dare! Be alive!

19 *paua:* the bright, iridescent shell of a sea mollusk found in New Zealand waters. 31
wharé: a Maori hut or traditional dwelling. 41 *tangi:* Maori funeral service. 66 *weka:*
woodhens. 101 *karakias:* prayers, invocations. 187 *taniwha:* water monster. 218-220
Tongariro...Taranaki...Ruapehu: Tongariro and Ruapehu are volcanoes of the Tongariro
volcanic centre; Taranaki is a huge volcano in the Taranaki region, not far from the coast.
220 *Kaikoura...Ruahine:* mountains and mountain ranges (Mount Aorangi, on South
Island, is the highest peak in New Zealand). 223 *Kahawai-birds:* white-fronted terns.
237 *Tui:* a blue, honey-eating bird with a white ball just below its neck and a sweet
song note. 238 *Kauri...Maire:* New Zealand trees (kauri is soft white pine, totara: soft
red pine, Rimu: hard red pine, matai: hard black pine, and maire is the second hardest
wood of all). 239 *Red...Pohutu-kawa:* rata and pohuhkawa, of the myrtle family, both
have hard, very heavy, dark red heartwood. 240 *Manuka:* tea tree; *convolvulus:* bindweed.
243 *taua:* war party; *meres:* war clubs. 259-60 *Waikato...Taupo:* rivers and lakes of New
Zealand. 278 *Te Ika a Maui:* the fish of Maui. 288 *Rangi...Tawhiri-matea:* Rangi or
Ranginui, the sky father, with Papatuanuku, gave birth to Tangaroa, god of the seas,
Tawhirimatea, god of the winds, and many other deities. 294 *kotare:* kingfisher.

INDEX OF AUTHORS

Consorting with Angels
Essays on Modern Women Poets
DERYN REES-JONES

In this pioneering critical study, Deryn Rees-Jones discusses the work of some of the major women poets of the last hundred years, showing how they have explored what it has meant to be a woman poet writing in a male-dominated poetic tradition. Beginning with Edith Sitwell, Stevie Smith, Sylvia Plath and Anne Sexton, she shows how an older generation resisted easy categorisation by forging highly individual aesthetics and self-presentation. But despite their brilliance, their perceived eccentricity – along with the suicides of Plath and Sexton – made these major figures difficult acts to follow.

She then considers the poetry written in their wake, with essays covering poets such as Moniza Alvi, Carol Ann Duffy, Vicki Feaver, Lavinia Greenlaw, Selima Hill, Kathleen Jamie, Jackie Kay, Gwyneth Lewis, Medbh McGuckian, Alice Oswald and Jo Shapcott. Taking account of the importance to these women of the work of their male contemporaries, her incisive essays open up new perspectives on the poetry of the 20th and 21st centuries.

Modern Women Poets
edited by DERYN REES-JONES

Modern Women Poets is the companion anthology to Deryn Rees-Jones's critical study, *Consorting with Angels*. While its selections illuminate and illustrate her essays, this wide-ranging and exciting anthology also works in its own right as the best possible introduction to a whole century of poetry by women.

Tracing an arc from Charlotte Mew to Stevie Smith, from Sylvia Plath and Anne Sexton to the writing emerging from the Women's Movement, and to the more recent work of poets such as Medbh McGuckian, Jo Shapcott and Carol Ann Duffy, the anthology draws together the work of women poets from Britain, Ireland and America as one version of a history of women's poetic writing. It draws important connections between the work of women poets and shows how – over the past century – they have developed strategies for engaging with a male-dominated tradition. *Modern Women Poets* allows the reader to trace women's negotiations with one another's work, as well as to reflect more generally on the politics of women's engagement with history, nature, politics, motherhood, science, religion, the body, sexuality, identity, death, love, and poetry itself.